Costs in Family Proceedings

Illustrations
by
John Edwards 'Jedd'

Costs in Family Proceedings

Second edition

Francis Wilkinson
Of the Middle Temple, Barrister

Dr Sara Hunton
Of the Inner Temple, Barrister

Bloomsbury Professional

LONDON • DUBLIN • EDINBURGH • NEW YORK • NEW DELHI • SYDNEY

BLOOMSBURY PROFESSIONAL
Bloomsbury Publishing Plc
41–43 Boltro Road, Haywards Heath, RH16 1BJ, UK

BLOOMSBURY and the Diana logo are trademarks of Bloomsbury Publishing Plc

First published in Great Britain 2020

British Library Cataloguing-in-Publication Data

A catalogue record for this book is available from the British Library.

ISBN:	PB:	978 1 52651 204 8
	ePDF:	978 1 52651 206 2
	ePub:	978 1 52651 205 5

Typeset by Evolution Design and Digital Ltd (Kent)

Foreword to the First Edition by Lord Wilson, Justice of the UK Supreme Court

There is only one feature which crops up, to a greater or lesser extent, in every type of family proceedings: costs. No order can be sought or opposed without incurring an element of costs. It is, so I belatedly realise, extraordinary that until now there has been no authoritative text on costs in the specific context of family proceedings.

Yet I confess that, on receipt this week of the proofs of Francis Wilkinson's and Sara Hunton's book, I was amazed by its size. 'But surely nowadays it's almost always just "no order" as to costs', I said to myself. My reaction betrayed a serious lack of imagination. The fact that one party in family proceedings is rarely ordered to pay the costs of another party in no way diminishes the importance of costs or the problems which they present to the courts as well as to the litigants.

This is a magisterial book. We can see what it contains in the list of chapters or, better still, by dipping into it, as I have done. The early chapters indeed address the limited scope for orders for costs between parties. I now believe that the abolition in 2006 of the right to refer to a *Calderbank* offer in relation to the costs of financial remedy proceedings was beneficial: a judge's previous duty to give effect, following judgment, to reasonable *Calderbank* offers often demolished his construction within the judgment of the parties' future economy; and it is insulting to our still excellent family judiciary to consider that they will assume uncritically an applicant's open offer to be too high or a respondent's to be too low.

But look also at the later chapters: costs allowances, security for costs, *Sears Tooth* deeds, other funding arrangements, wasted costs, legal aid, pro bono representation, court fees, indemnity costs, assessment of costs and enforcement of costs. These and other subjects explain the weight, the breadth and the value of the book.

Our library here will stock this book. Family practitioners should in my view expect that all family judges will want to work from it. There is nothing to suggest that the fast movement of the subject over the last 10 years will stall. The book will, I believe, proceed through a number of editions and I feel honoured to have been associated with the first.

Nicholas Wilson
Parliament Square, 9 October 2015

Introduction

A Cinderella subject is one that is 'undeservedly neglected or ignored' and one that 'unexpectedly achieves recognition or success after a period of obscurity and neglect'. Costs in family proceedings fit both these definitions. The question of how family cases are paid for has recently received statutory, judicial and professional attention so that the costs terrain has become varied and partly unexplored. Whether coping with the restrictions on legal aid, getting litigation loans, investigating cheaper alternatives to court proceedings, the limits of the court's powers on public funding, or just trying to get the other side to pay, recent changes have been substantial. The Law Commission is investigating the enforcement of family court orders and the Secretary of State is looking for further economies in the context of two-tier justice – those who can afford it and those who can't.

Even in areas where there have been no recent changes, ordinarily little time is spent in family proceedings on costs issues, and when the subject has come up we have found ourselves less familiar with the detail than we would have liked. It is all too easy to be uncertain about the costs regime for a trusts of land claim in financial remedy proceedings, not to be sure how to claim costs for a publicly funded client, and to be baffled by the assertion that 'costs in financial remedy proceedings are not the same as costs in proceedings for a financial remedy'.

So we have written this book with the intention of helping the reader to become, as the Court of Appeal described the King's Proctor a century ago, 'fearless as to costs'. Or, if you prefer, to give Cinders her carriage.

We are enormously grateful to Lord Wilson, the doyen of family costs, more of whose judgments are quoted in what follows than anyone else's, for his kindness in writing the foreword.

Gray's Inn
Hallowe'en 2015

Introduction to the second edition

The pursuit of clarity and certainty about costs continues to be our aim in this second edition. Since 2015 the most notable changes have been in the wider availability of legal aid exceptional funding and in the LAA's approach to the recoupment of sums paid in damages to legally-aided parties. The general unavailability of legal aid in private proceedings however continues to be a common cause of injustice. The increased pressures on the judiciary have not helped. The impact of Brexit will have to wait until the third edition.

Gray's Inn
Hallowe'en 2019

Contents

Table of Statutes

Table of Statutory Instruments

Table of European Legislation

Table of Cases

C

D

E

F

G

N

S

T

Abbreviations

CCR	County Court Rules
CPA 2004	Civil Partnership Act 2004
CPR	Civil Procedure Rules 1998
FDR	Financial dispute resolution hearing
FLA 1996	Family Law Act 1996
FPR	Family Procedure Rules 2010
HMCTS	Her Majesty's Courts and Tribunals Service
HMRC	Her Majesty's Revenue & Customs
I(PFD)A 1975	Inheritance (Provision for Family and Dependents) Act 1975
LASPO 2012	Legal Aid, Sentencing and Punishment of Offenders Act 2012
LSPO	Legal services payment order
MCA 1973	Matrimonial Causes Act 1973
MFPA 1984	Matrimonial and Family Proceedings Act 1984
PD	Practice Direction
SCA 1981	Senior Courts Act 1981
TLATA 1996	Trusts of Land and Appointment of Trustees Act 1996

CHAPTER 1

Family Proceedings – Definition and Powers

1.01 'Purveu est ensement que le deseysi recovre ses damages' ran the Statute of Gloucester in 1278: the successful claimant can also recover his costs. The Statute envisaged claims for property; its simplicity is enviable. In family proceedings the 'successful claimant' may have applied: for an adoption order, for arrangements so that he can see his child more often, to leave the country with his children, for an equal division of matrimonial assets on divorce, or for any one of a myriad of orders in which 'success' is not the appropriate description of an outcome where all parties have been reasonable, where the court's role is quasi-inquisitorial, and where the court's 'paramount' or 'first' consideration will be the welfare of any child.[1]

1.02 This variety of outcomes has led to comparative complexity in the rules for costs in family proceedings. In relation to public funding of family

1 'Paramount' in s 1 of the Children Act 1989 and s 1 of the Adoption and Children Act 2002, 'first' in s 25 of the Matrimonial Causes Act 1973 and s 18 of the Matrimonial and Family Proceedings Act 1984. For the quasi-inquisitorial jurisdiction see, for example, *Re S (A Child)* [2015] UKSC 20 at [20], Lady Hale DP in relation to children, and *Grey v Grey* [2009] EWCA Civ 1494, [2010] 1 FLR 1764 at [29], Thorpe LJ in relation to financial remedies.

proceedings there is the further complexity of the rules and regulations under the Legal Aid, Sentencing and Punishment of Offenders Act 2012. But first, what are family proceedings?

DEFINITION

1.03 The Family Procedure Rules 2010 (FPR) apply to proceedings in the Family Division of the High Court and in the Family Court. Upon the creation of the Family Court on 22 April 2014[2] the FPR were amended to remove their application to magistrates' courts.[3]

1.04 Family proceedings are defined as:

(a) proceedings in the family court; and

(b) proceedings in the Family Division of the High Court which are business assigned, by or under s 61 of (and Sch 1 to) the Senior Courts Act 1981, to that Division of the High Court and to no other.[4]

1.05 Dealing first with the second limb of that definition, Sch 1 to the Senior Courts Act provides a list of the proceedings which are assigned just to the Family Division of the High Court. That means that those proceedings may not be heard in any other division of the High Court, but it does not mean that they are proceedings which can only be heard in the High Court, as reference to the list in Sch 1 (see **1.07** below) readily makes clear.

1.06 This list of matters assigned to the Family Division of the High Court includes, as one would expect, matrimonial and civil partnership matters, and proceedings under the Children Act 1989, the Child Support Act 1991 and the Gender Recognition Act 2004, for example. It omits, however, some child maintenance provisions and it contains anomalies such as including s 42A of the Family Law Act 1996, which creates an offence triable in the criminal courts.

1.07 For the purpose of the FPR, therefore, the following matters are assigned to the Family Division and to no other Division and are family proceedings when in the High Court:

(a) all matrimonial and civil partnership causes and matters;

(b) all causes and matters relating to:
   (i) legitimacy;
   (ii) the exercise of the inherent jurisdiction of the High Court in relation to minors and the Children Act 1989 (except proceedings to appoint a guardian of a child's estate);

2 Crime and Courts Act 2013, s 17 inserting s 31A into the Matrimonial and Family Proceedings Act 1984.

3 FPR r 2.1.

4 Courts Act 2003, s 75(3) as amended. The same definition appears in the Matrimonial and Family Proceedings Act 1984, s 32.

   (iii) adoption;
   (iv) non-contentious probate business;

(c) applications for consent to the marriage or civil partnership of a minor;

(d) proceedings under the Children Act 1989;

(e) proceedings under s 79 of the Childcare Act 2006 (police entry warrants to educational establishments);

(f) all proceedings under:

   (i) Part 4 or 4A of the Family Law Act 1996 (injunctions and forced marriages);
   (ii) the Child Abduction and Custody Act 1985;
   (iii) the Family Law Act 1986;
   (iv) s 54 of the Human Fertilisation and Embryology Act 2008 (parental orders in donor cases);
   (v) Council Regulation (EC) No 2201/2003 (jurisdiction, recognition and enforcement of judgments in parental responsibility matters), known as Brussels IIA;
   (vi) the Hague Convention on the International Protection of Children 1996;

(g) all proceedings for enforcement of any of the above provisions;

(h) all proceedings under the Child Support Act 1991;

(i) all proceedings under ss 6 and 8 of the Gender Recognition Act 2004;

(j) female genital mutilation protection orders under Schedule 2 of the Female Genital Mutilation Act 2003;

(k) recognition of protection orders made in other jurisdictions in accordance with Reg (EU) No 606/2013.[5]

1.08 Before the Family Court came into being there was a further definition of family proceedings for the purpose of the FPR at s 65 of the Magistrates' Courts Act 1980. That definition filled in some of the gaps in the High Court list above, by including a number of child maintenance provisions, particularly the international recognition and enforcement provisions, which statutes do not appear in the list above. With the disappearance of that list from the definition of 'family proceedings' on the foundation of the Family Court, the Sch 1 list has gaps.

1.09 Because of the other limb of the definition of family proceedings, however, that does not matter, as a High Court Judge in the Family Division may equally well sit as a Judge of the Family Court. Thus the principal effect of the list in Sch 1 of the Senior Courts Act 1981 is to exclude other Divisions of the High Court from hearing cases brought under the statutes in that list.

5 Section 61 of and Sch 1 to the Senior Courts Act 1981.

1.10 The situation created by the first part of the definition of family proceedings as 'proceedings in the family court' was novel in 2014. Proceedings in the Family Court include:

(a) the matters listed under Sch 1 of the Senior Courts Act above, save for the exercise of the inherent jurisdiction of the High Court and applications reserved to the High Court (for example search orders).

(b) the family matters not mentioned in the High Court list, such as some maintenance statutes.

So far, so good, but they also include, for example:

(c) the Inheritance (Provision for Family and Dependants) Act 1975, the Protection from Harassment Act 1997 and the Trusts of Land and Appointment of Trustees Act 1996. These are matters which are not reserved to the Family Division of the High Court, and which may be dealt with in the County Court as well as the Family Court.

1.11 While the Family Court would not accept a freestanding application to start Trusts of Land proceedings, and would direct an applicant to the County Court, such proceedings are regularly heard in the Family Court in conjunction with financial remedy proceedings, for example.

INTERPRETING THE DEFINITION

1.12 As a Family Division High Court Judge may sit equally in the Family Division of the High Court and in the Family Court, both limbs of the definition in the Courts Act 2003, s 75(3) (**1.04** above) are available to such a judge. Thus any gaps there may be in the list of statutes at Sch 1 of the Senior Courts Act 1981 can be met by issuing the proceedings in the Family Court. That leaves the gatekeeping in the hands of the issuing staff at those courts, subject of course to the direction of the judges as to what is appropriate business to be commenced there.

1.13 This is an unusually flexible approach, but this flexibility has its advantages. The opposite extreme would be to exclude any proceedings not listed in Sch 1 to the Senior Courts Act from being family proceedings, but that would exclude proceedings which are indisputably family business. It is not just the approach to costs that is the issue here, but the application (or not) of the whole of the FPR.

1.14 The definition of family proceedings for the purposes of the FPR as including all 'proceedings in the family court' is effectively subject to the same gatekeeping process already. As pointed out above at **1.10**, some proceedings may be commenced either in the Family Court or in the County Court (or in the Chancery Division). An application for the court to, for example, make a declaration of a person's share in land would be made under the same Act in either court. Under the definition of family proceedings the procedure to be used would be the FPR in the Family Court and the Civil Procedure Rules 1998 (CPR) in the County Court.

1.15 The effect of these different jurisdictions on costs is considered below.

Family proceedings and others

1.16 Broadly, family proceedings may be said to consist of proceedings which relate to marriage and civil partnership, to children (both proceedings between parents and care proceedings), relevant financial proceedings, protective measures in relation to domestic violence and occupation of the family home. Within these main areas there is a body of (national and international) law relating to international family proceedings, as well as to child abduction, to egg and sperm donors and to gender recognition.

1.17 Other business which is not allocated to any particular division may be dealt with in the Family Division or in the Family Court, as we have discussed, for example: the Inheritance (Provision for Family and Dependants) Act 1975, the Protection from Harassment Act 1997 and the Trusts of Land and Appointment of Trustees Act 1996. However, the FPR do not apply to proceedings in the High Court under Acts not allocated solely to the Family Division. Where such proceedings are heard in the High Court they are subject to the costs rules in the CPR, Parts 44, 46 and 47.

1.18 It is an anomaly of the definition of family proceedings that the costs rules for such cases dealt with in the Family Court will be the FPR rules, while such cases dealt with in the High Court will be subject to the CPR costs rules. When appearing before the High Court in proceedings not reserved to the Family Division it will be necessary to know whether the Judge is sitting in the Family Division of the High Court or in the Family Court, in order to know which costs regime applies: costs will follow the event if it is the Family Division, but not if it is the Family Court.

1.19 The FPR adopt most of the CPR costs rules so that while the starting point differs, the principles thereafter in relation to costs are largely common between the two regimes, although the different subject matter of family proceedings from that of other civil proceedings creates differences which have generated distinctive case-law relating to costs in family proceedings, see **1.46–1.50** below.

1.20 The principal difference between the civil and family costs regimes is what is usually described as the starting point for considering costs orders:

(a) CPR r 44.3(2) provides that 'if the court decides to make an order about costs the general rule is that the unsuccessful party will be ordered to pay the costs of the successful party'. This civil proceedings starting point is commonly called 'costs follow the event';

(b) FPR r 28.2(1) disapplies r 44.3(2) in family proceedings and does not provide a replacement starting point, so leaving the general rule in family proceedings of a 'clean sheet' in relation to costs orders.

1.21 This means that there are two different costs regimes in the High Court, but on the basis set out above only one of those two – the FPR regime – in the Family Court. But as every reader of this book is likely to know, there is also a third regime which is intended to deal with costs in financial remedy proceedings on divorce.

(c) FPR r 28.3(5) applies only to proceedings for a financial remedy (and not to all of them – see **Chapter 3**) and provides that 'the general rule in financial remedy proceedings is that the court will not make an order requiring one party to pay the costs of another party'. This is known as the 'no order rule'.

1.22 Writers on the subject generally complain about the lack of clarity as to which proceedings are covered by the rules for financial remedies and which are not. The authors of the Family Court Practice have made the point that, for the purposes of costs, proceedings for a financial remedy are not the same thing as financial remedy proceedings. It is one of the intentions of this book to make rather impenetrable comments such as that luminously clear (see **3.01–3.24**).

1.23 There are therefore three costs regimes which may be encountered by practitioners in the Family Court and in the Family Division of the High Court:

(a) the clean sheet (the general FPR regime);

(b) costs follow the event (the CPR regime, in the High Court only);

(c) no order (the financial remedy regime).

1.24 We take the view that at any hearing at which costs may conceivably be mentioned (which is most hearings) the advocate should always be clear before the hearing which costs regime – or regimes, there may sometimes be more than one – applies to that hearing. While the answer to that will in many cases be straightforward, there are other hearings where identifying the applicable costs regime requires some consideration.

1.25 Because sometimes the court needs assistance in identifying the applicable regime and does not get it, three consequences tend to follow: costs orders are made without consideration of the starting point from which they are made (which can work!) or orders are made on the wrong basis (including in some reported cases), or courts are put off making such orders and they are not made at all. Our hope is that this work will help practitioners to be clear about when orders for costs are appropriate and when they are not, and to obtain or resist them effectively.

THE COURT'S POWERS

1.26 It is explicitly stated in primary legislation that costs are in the discretion of the court.[6] That discretion applies equally in the Family Court, in the High

6 Senior Courts Act 1981, s 51(1).

Court and in the Court of Appeal. In relation to family proceedings the FPR costs rules open with the provision that the court may at any time make such order as to costs as it thinks just.[7] This discretion is thus fundamental to the exercise of the court's jurisdiction to award costs in family proceedings, as elsewhere.

1.27 The discretion is, of course, subject to the relevant rules: principally Parts 44, 46 and 47 of the CPR and Part 28 of the FPR, though some rules about costs are to be found elsewhere.[8]

1.28 Courts also have 'full power to determine by whom and to what extent the costs are to be paid'.[9] This means that, subject always to the relevant rules and precedents, a court may order someone who is not a party to pay costs. Although not specified in the statute, this also means that courts can order that costs be paid to a non-party – for example under a conditional fee agreement or when they have incurred costs by attending court (see **Chapter 6**).

1.29 Specific power is given for the costs claimed by a legal or other representative to be disallowed, and for that representative to be ordered to pay the costs wasted by their improper, unreasonable or negligent act or omission.[10] We consider this 'wasted costs' jurisdiction at **6.70–6.126**.

THE OVERRIDING OBJECTIVE

1.30 In family proceedings all the other rules are to be interpreted in accordance with the overriding objective in the FPR.[11] It is:

> '1.1 The overriding objective
>
> (1) These rules are a new procedural code with the overriding objective of enabling the court to deal with cases justly, having regard to any welfare issues involved.'

This is not the same as the overriding objective in the CPR, which is:

> 'These Rules are a new procedural code with the overriding objective of enabling the court to deal with cases justly and at proportionate cost.'

The two differences are that in family proceedings welfare issues are 'overriding' and proportionate cost is not, at least not in the primary paragraph.

1.31 Proportionality does however appear in the next paragraph of the FPR (by way of contrast, welfare does not feature at all in Part 1 of the CPR).

7 FPR r 28.1.
8 For example, CPR r 45.8 deals with fixed enforcement costs and FPR r 20.6 with security for costs.
9 Senior Courts Act 1981, s 51(3).
10 Senior Courts Act 1981, s 51(6) and (7).
11 FPR r 1.2.

> '1.1(2) Dealing with a case justly includes, so far as is practicable –
>
> (a) ensuring that it is dealt with expeditiously and fairly;
>
> (b) dealing with the case in ways that are proportionate to the nature, importance and complexity of the issues;
>
> (c) ensuring that the parties are on an equal footing;
>
> (d) saving expense; and
>
> (e) allotting to it an appropriate share of the court's resources, while taking into account the need to allot resources to other cases.'

1.32 It is emphasised that, while the costs rules applicable in family proceedings are largely the CPR costs rules, those rules are applied in accordance with the overriding objective in the FPR rather than the overriding objective in the CPR. That is one reason why the case-law in civil proceedings on costs may not be directly applicable to family proceedings. Caution should always be exercised when quoting case-law decided without consideration of the welfare of the child as part of the overriding objective. For example, costs may not be ordered in children proceedings, as we shall discuss, if it would reduce the amount of money available for the children.[12] That is a reason relevant to the overriding objective in family proceedings, but not in civil proceedings.

1.33 Proportionality was considered by Holman J in an application for permission to appeal against an order that a father pay the costs of the mother in contact proceedings.[13] The costs at stake were too small to justify the expenditure that would have been required by the parties on the costs of pursuing the application. The judge concluded:

> 'My overall position is that the proposed appeal, although having a real prospect of success, is one that lacks any proportionality to the amount at stake. For that reason and that reason alone, I refuse this application for permission to appeal.'

1.34 Similarly, where there was a requirement under section 91(14) of the Children Act 1989 to make an application for permission, and permission had been given at first instance, Cobb J reversed that decision on appeal, one of his reasons being the 'escalating costs' that would otherwise arise and the need to save expense in accordance with FPR r 1.1(2)(d).[14]

1.35 Considerations of welfare and proportionality are themes found throughout the case-law where costs are being considered, sometimes being mentioned quite explicitly, and sometimes just understood.

12 See, for example *Re G (Children)* [2013] EWHC 1017 (Fam), [2014] 1 FLR 517 at [17].

13 *HH v BLW* [2012] EWHC 2199 (Fam), [2013] 1 FLR 420 at [36].

14 *Re P and N (Section 91(14): Application for permission to apply: Appeal)* [2019] EWHC 421 (Fam), [2019] 2 FLR 53 at [10(iv)] and [42(vi)].

THE CPR

1.36 As we have said, the great majority of the costs rules which apply in family proceedings are to be found in the CPR. While the FPR change the starting point for costs orders, which is of course a major difference, the only costs rules in Parts 44 to 47 of the CPR which do not apply in family proceedings[15] are:

(a) r 44.2(2) – the general rule that costs follow the event;

(b) r 44.2(3) – the rule disapplying the rule that costs follow the event to an appeal in the Court of Appeal from the Family Division or from family proceedings generally;

(c) r 44.10(2) – the rule that where either an order is made on an application without notice, or permission to appeal is granted, and there is no order for costs, then there is deemed to be an order for the applicant's costs in the case;

(d) r 44.10(3) – the rule allowing any party affected by a deemed order under r 44.10(2) to apply at any time to vary it;

(e) Part 45 (except for r 45.8) – Part 45 deals with fixed costs. This Part is disapplied as there are no fixed costs in family proceedings save in relation to enforcement costs which are set out in a table at CPR r 45.8, see **9.13** and **9.37**.

1.37 And the following further rules are disapplied in financial remedy proceedings:[16]

(a) r 44.2(1) – this rule gives the court discretion as to whether costs are payable by one party to another, their amount and when they are to be paid;

(b) r 44.2(4) – this rule lists the circumstances to which the court has to have regard when making a costs order (this list is replaced in relation to financial remedy proceedings by the one at FPR r 28.3(6) and (7));

(c) r 44.2(5) – this rule defines 'conduct' and is supplementary to r 44.2(4).

1.38 Thus CPR Part 46 (Costs – special cases) and Part 47 (Procedure for detailed assessment of costs) apply in family proceedings just as they apply in civil proceedings, in as far as they are relevant. CPR rr 46.11 to 46.13 apply only to small claims and fast-track claims, so have no relevance to family proceedings.

1.39 As the reader may have hesitated over the effect of disapplying CPR r 44.2(3), which itself disapplies a rule, it may be helpful to discuss that now in the interests of the luminous clarity set as our objective. If the composite effect of the two rules (CPR r 44.2(3) and FPR r 28.2(1)) is set out in a sentence it states:

> 'the disapplication in family appeals to the Court of Appeal of the general rule that the unsuccessful party will be ordered to pay the costs of the successful party, does not apply in family proceedings.'

15 FPR r 28.2(1).
16 By FPR r 28.3(1).

Well, you might observe, of course a rule about appeals to the Court of Appeal doesn't apply in family proceedings as proceedings in the Court of Appeal are not family proceedings. The rules about appeals to the Court of Appeal are in the CPR not the FPR. So disapplying the rule in relation to costs in family proceedings is redundant, a rule applying to the Court of Appeal doesn't apply in family proceedings anyway.

1.40 Removing, then, this redundancy, what are we left with? Simply r 44.2(3), which in combination with r 44.2(2) effectively says:

> 'the general rule, that the unsuccessful party will be ordered to pay the costs of the successful party, does not apply in family appeals to the Court of Appeal.'

In other words, the starting point for family appeals to the Court of Appeal is the clean sheet, according to this provision. This is the same starting point as for family proceedings (except for financial remedy proceedings), so that costs in family appeals to the Court of Appeal *including appeals in financial remedy proceedings* will be approached in the same way as costs in family proceedings generally. We shall deal later with costs in appeals.[17]

1.41 While CPR rr 44.10(2) and (3) are disapplied in family proceedings, that leaves r 44.10(1):

> 'Where the court makes an order which does not mention costs –
>
> (a) Subject to Paragraphs (2) and (3),the general rule is that no party is entitled –
>   (i) To costs; or
>   (ii) To seek an order under section 194(3) of the 2007 Act,
>
>   in relation to that order; but
>
> (b) This does not affect any entitlement of a party to recover costs out of a fund held by that party as trustee or personal representative, or under any lease, mortgage or other security.'

1.42 In *Timokhin v Timokhina*[18] the Court of Appeal considered, in the context of family proceedings, the rule in CPR r 44.10(1)(a)(i), namely the weight to be attached to this 'general rule' that if an order is made which does not mention costs then no party is entitled to costs in relation to that order. As neither counsel nor the court had identified any previous authority King LJ based her reasoning in part on the history of the statutory instruments leading to the rule. The Court of Appeal held that the general rule leaves the court with a residual discretion to make a costs order and found that the first instance judge was right to have done so on the facts of the case.

17 See **4.61-4.68**.
18 [2019] EWCA Civ 1284 at [45] to [52].

1.43 It follows from the above that the only significant differences between the CPR costs regime and the general FPR costs regime (as opposed to the costs regime for financial remedy proceedings) are:

(a) the general rule that costs follow the event does not apply in family proceedings;

(b) there are no fixed costs, except in relation to certain fixed enforcement costs.

This means that the detailed provisions in relation to issue-based costs orders at CPR rr 44.2(4)(b), 44.2(5) and 44.2(6) apply in family proceedings under the clean sheet rule. Although CPR r 44.2(4) and (5) are disapplied in financial remedy proceedings, r 44.2(6) remains applicable in those proceedings as in other family proceedings. Thus the CPR rules on issue-based costs orders apply to some extent in all family proceedings: they are discussed in **Chapter 3** at **3.45** onwards.

THE FACTORS RELEVANT TO MAKING AN ORDER

The clean sheet

1.44 There is no separate list of factors for the court to consider when making a costs order in family proceedings, except in relation to financial remedy proceedings. Thus, although most family proceedings approach the assessment of costs with a clean sheet, while civil proceedings start from the premise that costs follow the event, the factors subsequently considered in both jurisdictions will be the same, subject to relevance.[19]

1.45 The factors are set out at CPR r 44.2(4) and (5), which rules are not disapplied by FPR r 28.3:

> '(4) In deciding what order (if any) to make about costs, the court will have regard to all the circumstances, including –
>
> (a) the conduct of all the parties;
>
> (b) whether a party has succeeded on part of its case, even if that party has not been wholly successful; and
>
> (c) any admissible offer to settle made by a party which is drawn to the court's attention, and which is not an offer to which costs consequences under Part 36 apply.
>
> (5) The conduct of the parties includes –
>
> (a) conduct before, as well as during, the proceedings and in particular the extent to which the parties followed the Practice Direction – Pre-Action Conduct or any relevant pre-action protocol;

19 As to relevance see **1.46** and **1.47**.

(b) whether it was reasonable for a party to raise, pursue or contest a particular allegation or issue;

(c) the manner in which a party has pursued or defended its case or a particular allegation or issue; and

(d) whether a claimant who has succeeded in the claim, in whole or in part, exaggerated its claim.'

1.46 As the costs follows the event starting point has been disapplied, r 44.2(4)(b) loses its meaning. That paragraph relies on a primary position of there being a costs order in favour of a party which has succeeded on the whole of its case, and that primary position is removed from family proceedings. The Supreme Court has held, in a judgment by Lord Phillips P, that:[20]

> '(4)(b) is relevant in relation to a regime where the general rule in (2)(a) applies. For this reason we do not see that it has any direct relevance to family proceedings.'

That point was re-emphasised by the Supreme Court the following year.[21] Accordingly that paragraph does not apply in relation to Children Act proceedings and it is not considered further in this chapter.

1.47 'Nor', Lady Hale DP has pointed out, 'does rule 44.2(4)(c) readily fit the conduct of children's cases, save as an aspect of the general desirability of the parties co-operating and negotiating to reach an agreed solution which will best serve the paramount consideration of the welfare of the child. As such, it is part of the general conduct of the proceedings, some aspects of which are listed in rule 44.2(5).'[22] The phrase 'admissible offer to settle' is indeed out of place in children proceedings, but *Calderbank* offers are available in family proceedings other than financial remedy proceedings[23] and to that extent r 44.2(4)(c) has relevance to family proceedings.

1.48 As the opening words of r 44.2(4) make clear, it does not provide a closed list, so that for the purposes of family proceedings with a clean sheet starting point, and adopting the Supreme Court's decisions, these paragraphs may be re-stated as:[24]

> 'The court will have regard to all the circumstances, including
>
> (a) the conduct of all the parties, including
>
> (i) conduct before as well as during the proceedings including compliance with any relevant pre-action protocol

20 *Re T (Costs: Care Proceedings: Serious Allegation Not Proved)* [2012] UKSC 36, [2013] 1 FLR 133 at [11].
21 *Re S (A Child)* [2015] UKSC 20 at [17].
22 *Re S (A Child)* [2015] UKSC 20 at [17].
23 See discussion at **2.49–2.54**.
24 Lady Hale DP's formulation of r 44.2(4)(c) in *Re S* at [17].

(ii) whether it was reasonable for a party to raise, pursue or contest a particular issue
(iii) the manner in which a party has pursued or defended its case or a particular allegation or issue, and
(iv) whether a wholly or partly successful applicant has exaggerated his case

(b) the extent to which the parties have co-operated and negotiated, including any admissible offer to settle, which is part of the general conduct of the proceedings.'

1.49 Consideration of these factors requires the court to have regard to:

(a) the pre-action protocols that are relevant in family proceedings;

(b) offers to settle, including *Calderbank* offers;

(c) the case-law on reasonableness in proceedings and pre-proceedings conduct; and

(d) the interplay between the list of circumstances in the previous paragraph, the different starting point in family proceedings, and the different overriding objective, which requires civil proceedings precedents relating to these factors to be approached with considerable caution if it is proposed to apply them in family proceedings.

These subjects are each dealt with in later sections.

1.50 It will be apparent from this list that in clean sheet cases, the conduct of the proceedings (including pre-proceedings conduct) will be the major factor, indeed arguably the only factor, in deciding whether there will be any order for costs.

Financial remedy proceedings

1.51 CPR r 44.2(4) and (5), which provide the factors for the court's consideration in relation to costs orders in other family proceedings, do not apply to financial remedy proceedings.[25] Instead FPR r 28.3 provides both a different starting point at para (5) and a different set of considerations at paras (6), (7) and (8).

'(5) Subject to paragraph (6), the general rule in financial remedy proceedings is that the court will not make an order requiring one party to pay the costs of another party.

(6) The court may make an order requiring one party to pay the costs of another party at any stage of the proceedings where it considers it appropriate to do so because of the conduct of a party in relation to the proceedings (whether before or during them).

25 FPR r 28.3(2). As to the definition of financial remedy proceedings, see **3.05**ff.

(7) In deciding what order (if any) to make under paragraph (6), the court must have regard to –
   (a) any failure by a party to comply with these rules, any order of the court or any practice direction which the court considers relevant;
   (b) any open offer to settle made by a party;
   (c) whether it was reasonable for a party to raise, pursue or contest a particular allegation or issue;
   (d) the manner in which a party has pursued or responded to the application or a particular allegation or issue;
   (e) any other aspect of a party's conduct in relation to proceedings which the court considers relevant; and
   (f) the financial effect on the parties of any costs order.

(8) No offer to settle which is not an open offer to settle is admissible at any stage of the proceedings, except as provided by rule 9.17.'

1.52 FPR r 28.3(5) thus sets the starting point for costs in financial remedy proceedings, which is that (subject always to para (6)) there will be no order for costs.

1.53 Paragraph (6) includes a provision which differs from any provision in the CPR in that it explicitly refers to costs 'at any stage of the proceedings'. While costs may always be ordered in relation to some particular period during the proceedings or before proceedings commence (CPR r 44.2(6)), and that provision applies to financial remedy proceedings, this additional provision suggests an emphasis on the possibility of interim costs orders within a regime where a costs order at the end of the proceedings, because of the no order starting point at FPR r 28.3(5), is less likely.

1.54 Paragraph (7) provides a list of factors which are specifically applied by para (6) to costs 'at any stage of the proceedings'. However in the case of *Judge* the court distinguished between costs of proceedings *for* a financial remedy and costs of proceedings *in connection with* a financial remedy, when it was held that the clean sheet rule, not the no order rule, applied to proceedings of the latter description.[26] In **Chapter 3** we shall analyse the interplay of the case law and the rules in this area in more detail.

1.55 Paragraph (7) contains six factors for the court's consideration in relation to a costs order. Some of the factors are identical to those in the CPR which apply to family proceedings generally, and some differ:

(a) 'Any failure by a party to comply with these rules, any order of the court or any practice direction which the court considers relevant.'

   The CPR has no parallel to this factor, but refers to litigation conduct in general terms at r 44.2(5)(a). This factor is reinforced by the Practice

26 *Judge v Judge* [2008] EWCA Civ 1458, [2009] 1 FLR 1287 at [51], Wilson LJ. See also *Baker v Rowe* [2009] EWCA Civ 1162, [2010] 1 FLR 761 at [23], Wilson LJ.

Direction to FPR Part 9 ('Applications for a financial remedy') which states that any breach of that Practice Direction or of its Annex which sets out the pre-action protocol may lead to an adverse costs order.[27] There is a similar provision in the Practice Direction on court bundles.[28]

(b) 'Any open offer to settle made by a party.'

This factor is closely related to para (8) which excludes any offer to settle that is not open. FPR r 9.17 deals with the without prejudice offers to settle which are required for the purpose of Financial Dispute Resolution (FDR) hearings. Such offers may include costs offers: most commonly, but not necessarily, 'no order as to costs'. Any offer relating to costs at an FDR – say for example that a party is to pay the costs of an interim hearing because of some procedural failure – is eligible for consideration as part of the overall offer to settle the proceedings at the FDR, but being without prejudice such an offer will not be taken into account in relation to any decision at a final hearing that the court is asked to make about the division of assets or specifically about costs, unless the order has the consent of the parties.

This factor contrasts, therefore, with CPR r 44.2(4)(c) which allows any admissible offer to settle to be taken into account, whether open or without prejudice. Thus so-called *Calderbank* offers are admissible in relation to costs in family proceedings generally,[29] but not in financial remedy proceedings.

(c) 'Whether it was reasonable for a party to raise, pursue or contest a particular allegation or issue.'

This is identical to CPR r 44.2(5)(b).

(d) 'The manner in which a party has pursued or responded to the application or a particular allegation or issue.'

This is the same provision as CPR r 44.2(5)(c), save for the reference to 'respond' rather than 'defend', as is appropriate for family proceedings.

(e) 'Any other aspect of a party's conduct in relation to proceedings which the court considers relevant.'

There is no corresponding provision to this in the CPR. Unlike the list of factors at CPR r 44.2(4) which is prefaced by the word 'including', thus making the list an open one, that word does not appear in FPR r 28.3(6) or (7). Arguably, therefore, this list at FPR r 28.3(7) is a closed one and the court should not have regard to any other factors. That restriction is however mitigated by the inclusion of this factor which provides for 'any other aspect of a party's conduct' to be considered. Thus, while it is the major factor in clean sheet cases, conduct is the only factor to be taken into account in relation to costs in financial remedy proceedings, save for (f) below.

(f) 'The financial effect on the parties of any costs order.'

27 FPR PD9A [3.4].
28 FPR PD27A [12.1].
29 See **2.48–2.53**.

This provision is unique to financial remedy proceedings, and it is not surprising that a principal factor for the court to consider when making a financial remedy order is the needs of the parties.[30] Although the factors in FPR r 28.3(7) are expressed as being in relation to an order made under r 28.3(6), that paragraph refers only to making orders where appropriate because of 'the conduct of a party in relation to the proceedings'. The factor at r 28.3(7)(f) – the financial effect on the parties of any costs order – is not, though, related to the conduct of the parties in relation to the proceedings. This would appear to be no more than an inconsistency in drafting the rule.

1.56 In summary, the factors to be taken into account in relation to costs in financial remedy proceedings are significantly different from the factors relating to costs in other family proceedings. In particular it is entirely clear, being stated twice in the rule,[31] that it is the conduct 'in relation to the proceedings' that is to be considered in relation to any costs order. While a similar provision appears at CPR r 44.2(5)(a) it is less definite and arguably less clear than the requirement in financial remedy proceedings only to consider conduct in relation to the proceedings (conduct before or during the proceedings). From time to time that CPR provision has been interpreted to include conduct which gave rise to the proceedings, but the better view, supported by authority, is that it does not.[32]

THE FACTORS RELEVANT TO THE AMOUNT OF AN ORDER

1.57 CPR r 44.4 states:

> '44.4 Factors to be taken into account in deciding the amount of costs
>
> (1) The court will have regard to all the circumstances in deciding whether costs were –
> (a) if it is assessing costs on the standard basis –
> (i) proportionately and reasonably incurred; or
> (ii) proportionate and reasonable in amount, or
> (b) if it is assessing costs on the indemnity basis –
> (i) unreasonably incurred; or
> (ii) unreasonable in amount.
>
> (2) In particular, the court will give effect to any orders which have already been made.
>
> (3) The court will also have regard to –
> (a) the conduct of all the parties, including in particular –
> (i) conduct before, as well as during, the proceedings; and
> (ii) the efforts made, if any, before and during the proceedings in order to try to resolve the dispute;

30 Matrimonial Causes Act 1973, s 25(2)(b).
31 At r 28.3(6) and (7)(e).
32 Discussed further at **2.29–2.36**.

(b) the amount or value of any money or property involved;
(c) the importance of the matter to all the parties;
(d) the particular complexity of the matter or the difficulty or novelty of the questions raised;
(e) the skill, effort, specialised knowledge and responsibility involved;
(f) the time spent on the case;
(g) the place where and the circumstances in which work or any part of it was done; and
(h) the receiving party's last approved or agreed budget.'

1.58 Each of the paragraphs in CPR r 44.4 relates to a wide range of considerations. Paragraph (1) relates to the costs claimed, and in particular whether they were proportionate and reasonable, para (2) relates to any earlier costs orders in the case, para (3)(a) relates to conduct, para (3)(b) and (c) relate to the proportionality of the costs to the size of the claim and the importance of the claim to the parties, and paras (3)(d) to (g) to factors which are likely to have affected the level of costs. Paragraph (h) does not apply to costs in family proceedings, as there is no provision for approved or agreed budgets in such proceedings.

1.59 It has to be said, and so of course it has been said, by Brooke LJ in *R (on the application of Davies) v Birmingham Deputy Coroner*[33] at para. 45(7):

> 'There is nothing in the Costs Rules to suggest that the financial welfare of a party's lawyers is a legitimate consideration when a court makes an order as to costs.'

STANDARD AND INDEMNITY COSTS

1.60 The difference between the assessment of costs on the standard basis and on the indemnity basis, which is relevant to CPR r 44.4(1), is set out at CPR r 44.3. The central provision is at paras (2) and (3):

> '(2) Where the amount of costs is to be assessed on the standard basis, the court will –
> (a) only allow costs which are proportionate to the matters in issue. Costs which are disproportionate in amount may be disallowed or reduced even if they were reasonably or necessarily incurred; and
> (b) resolve any doubt which it may have as to whether costs were reasonably and proportionately incurred or were reasonable and proportionate in amount in favour of the paying party.
>
> (3) Where the amount of costs is to be assessed on the indemnity basis, the court will resolve any doubt which it may have as to whether costs

33 [2004] EWCA Civ 207, [2004] 1 WLR 2739.

were reasonably incurred or were reasonable in amount in favour of the receiving party.'

1.61 There is no definition of 'reasonable' or 'unreasonable' in the rules, but there is a definition of 'proportionate' at CPR r 44.3(5):

> 'Costs incurred are proportionate if they bear a reasonable relationship to –
>
> (a) the sums at issue in the proceedings;
>
> (b) the value of any non-monetary relief in issue in the proceedings;
>
> (c) the complexity of the litigation;
>
> (d) any additional work generated by the conduct of the paying party; and
>
> (e) any wider factors involved in the proceedings, such as reputation or public importance.'

This list is the basis for challenging or defending a challenge to a bill of costs awarded on the standard basis.

1.62 The courts' use of the standard and indemnity costs rules is dealt with in the discussion of assessment of costs in **Chapter 8**.

CHAPTER 2

The Clean Sheet

2.01 As we considered in the last chapter, there are three different starting points for costs orders that may be found in family proceedings: costs follow the event; a clean sheet; and no order for costs. In proceedings about children the starting point is a clean sheet – that is to say, there is no presumption as to whether there will be a costs order or not, nor does one find in the rules a general rule as to whether there will be a costs order or not. The clean sheet also applies in a variety of financial proceedings; we consider in **Chapter 3** exactly which ones.

2.02 Judges have nonetheless felt, from time to time, that you have to start somewhere, and 30 years ago the case of *Gojkovic*,[1] considered below, provided such a starting point. The case-law on costs in children cases has developed considerably since *Gojkovic*, particularly in *LB Sutton v Davis*,[2] and more

1 *Gojkovic v Gojkovic (No 2)* [1991] 2 FLR 233, CA at [236F].

2 *LB Sutton v Davis (Costs) (No 2)* [1994] 2 FLR 569, FD.

recently in two judgments of the Supreme Court,[3] so that the detail of the case-law now makes a starting point – save for the clean sheet – less relevant.

THE CLEAN SHEET APPROACH GENERALLY

2.03 In *Gojkovic*[4] Butler-Sloss P considered:

> 'What is the starting-point of entitlement to costs?
>
> The general principles as to entitlement to costs in civil litigation are to be found in RSC Ord 62. Order 62, r 3(3) states:
>
> "If the court in the exercise of its discretion sees fit to make any order as to the costs of any proceedings, the court shall order the costs to follow the event, except when it appears to the court that in the circumstances of the case some other order should be made as to the whole or any part of the costs."
>
> Rule 3(5) states:
>
> "Paragraph (3) does not apply to proceedings in the Family Division."
>
> However, in the Family Division there still remains the necessity for some starting-point. That starting-point, in my judgment, is that costs prima facie follow the event (see Cumming-Bruce LJ in *Singer (formerly Sharegin) v Sharegin* [1984] FLR 114 at 119), but may be displaced much more easily than, and in circumstances which would not apply, in other Divisions of the High Court. One important example is, as the judge pointed out, that it is unusual to order costs in children cases.'

2.04 In 1991 the general rule in civil proceedings that costs follow the event was as it is now, and the rule was disapplied in family proceedings, as it is now. The initially surprising conclusion reached by the then President of the Family Division was that the rule disapplying in family proceedings the ordinary civil costs follow the event regime has limited effect: 'The starting point is that costs prima facie follow the event … but may be displaced much more easily than, and in circumstances that would not apply, in other Divisions of the High Court.'

2.05 On the other hand Butler-Sloss P also concluded by saying that 'it is unusual to order costs in children cases'. That suggests a general rule that there will not be a costs order in such cases. So the judgment in *Gojkovic* can be taken to be saying that both rules – the costs follow the event rule and the no order rule – apply, but both apply in watered down forms.

3 *Re T (Costs: Care Proceedings: Serious Allegation Not Proved)* [2012] UKSC 36, [2013] 1 FLR 133 and *Re S (A Child)* [2015] UKSC 20.

4 *Gojkovic v Gojkovic (No 2)* [1991] 2 FLR 233 at [236F].

2.06 The developments in the case law on costs in clean sheet cases since 1991 mean that a search for a starting point when considering the appropriateness of a costs order in children proceedings is no longer appropriate. There is a list of factors to be taken into account when deciding whether a costs order should be made (CPR r 44.2(4) and (5)) and a further list of factors when deciding how much those costs should be (CPR r 44.4). We have considered them in Chapter 1. Those factors themselves, applied through the filter of the authorities, particularly *LB Sutton v Davis* and *Re S (A Child)*, see below, provide guidance for judicial decisions on costs in such proceedings. As we shall see, the more recent development of the law reflects that.

2.07 The question remains to what extent the approach in *Gojkovic* remains relevant. While, as we shall now discuss, it has been superseded by Supreme Court decisions in children cases, it has occasionally been applied in those financial remedy cases where the starting point is the clean sheet. An example is in the Court of Appeal judgment in *Solomon*, when in 2013 *Gojkovic* was applied where three judges refused an application for permission to appeal a costs order.[5]

THE CLEAN SHEET REGIME IN FINANCIAL REMEDIES

2.08 In **Chapter 3**, on financial remedy proceedings, we discuss the boundary between costs after a final order in financial remedy proceedings (the no order regime), and costs at other stages of the proceedings and in proceedings which are related to financial remedy proceedings (for example involving injunctions and interveners), where the clean sheet regime applies. The application of the no order regime is dealt with in that chapter.

2.09 In *Solomon*, on an appeal from a costs order made against a husband who had mistakenly started and pursued proceedings to set aside a transfer of property in financial remedy proceedings (a s 37 Matrimonial Causes Act application), and quoting the essential part of the passage from *Gojkovic* which has been set out above, Ryder LJ stated in bald terms that 'The starting point for what are described as "clean sheet" cases is that costs follow the event'.[6] That statement was not qualified by the further phrase in *Gojkovic* that that starting point 'may be displaced much more easily than, and in circumstances which would not apply, in other Divisions of the High Court'.

2.10 That unqualified statement was adopted in the High Court as providing the precedent to be followed.[7] In a case in which he did so, Blair J went on to consider the degree of success that each party had achieved and to order that the wife and intervener pay 25% of the husband's costs.[8] That order took into

5 *Solomon v Solomon and others* [2013] EWCA Civ 1095 at [25], Ryder LJ: 'I would refuse permission to appeal the costs order and would dismiss the appeal against same.'
6 *Solomon* at [22].
7 See *W v W and L* [2015] EWHC 1652 (Fam) at [14], Blair J.
8 At [18]–[26].

consideration the litigation conduct of both parties (principally an exaggerated claim by the husband and deceit by the wife and intervener). It may well be that had the court in that case explicitly considered that costs follow the event is a rule easily displaced in family proceedings, or indeed started from the 'no order' position, a similar result would have been reached.

2.11 Hoever, Sir Peter Singer has pointed out that Blair J was wrong to take Ryder LJ's judgment in *Solomon* as an authority, because 'Ryder LJ's judgment was given on the occasion of an unsuccessful application for permission to appeal, [so does not] establish a new principle or extend the present law'.[9] While in the light of Ryder LJ's decision that he would refuse permission to appeal 'and would dismiss the appeal' that may be arguable, there does not appear to be any further reported use of this authority. The usual approach is to start from the discretion as to costs provided in the primary statute[10] and then apply the test of whether the conduct of a party has been unreasonable or reprehensible.[11] That test is effectively a summary of the factors relevant to making a costs order, as discussed in **Chapter 1**, and is consistent with Supreme Court authority on costs in children cases.

2.12 Accordingly we conclude that *Gojkovic* has been superseded in both financial and children proceedings. Recent decisions of the Supreme Court in relation to children cases,[12] discussed in the next section, have replaced *Gojkovic* in children cases. The question arises whether *Gojkovic* has been so weakened as a result of those decisions that its application to financial cases may be doubted. As we shall see, the reasons for and against costs orders in children cases are not applicable in financial cases, so perhaps the rule in *Gojkovic* will survive in respect of those financial cases.

THE CLEAN SHEET REGIME IN CHILDREN CASES

2.13 Five years after *Gojkovic* in 1994 Wilson J expanded on the general rule that it is unusual to order costs in children cases, which he said had been applied every day for many years in the Family Division, by giving the justification for the 'proposition'.[13] He gave four reasons:

(a) the proceedings are partly inquisitorial;

(b) the child is the only winner;

(c) the 'spectre of an order for costs' should not be allowed to discourage those with a proper interest in a child from participating in the debate;

9 *Joy v Joy-Morancho and Others (No 3)* [2015] EWHC 2507 (Fam), [2016] 1 FLR 815 at [202].
10 Namely Senior Courts Act 1981, s 51.
11 A good example of an summary of the law since *Re S* and it being applied in this way is *Re M (Children) (Residence and contact: Costs)* [2016] EWHC 1998 (Fam), [2016] 4 WLR 139 at [39]–[44], Newton J.
12 *Re T (Costs: Care Proceedings: Serious Allegation Not Proved)* [2012] UKSC 36, [2013] 1 FLR 133 and *Re S (A Child)* [2015] UKSC 20.
13 *LB Sutton v Davis (Costs) (No 2)* [1994] 2 FLR 569.

(d) casting one party as successful and the other as unsuccessful might reduce the chance of future cooperation.[14]

Wilson J said that because of these reasons the proposition applied in its fullest form to disputes between parents, but also applied when the local authority was a party. That difference has been removed by the Supreme Court in *Re S*.[15]

2.14 Those reasons for there usually being no costs order in children cases were subsequently approved by the Court of Appeal in *R v R*.[16] In that case Hale J put the 'minimising conflict' argument at (d) above slightly differently: 'the possibility that in effect a costs order will add insult to the injury of having lost in the debate as to what is to happen to the child in the future; it is likely therefore to exacerbate rather than to calm down the existing tensions; and this will not be in the best interests of the child.' The justification in *LB Sutton v Davis* for costs orders in children cases being unusual has been followed in other cases since.

2.15 After a further decade the Court of Appeal was again called upon to consider costs in a children case, this time in relation to fact-finding hearings where there had been a 'split hearing'.[17] In that case the child's mother, with whom he lived, made allegations which were found to be, if not untrue, then unreasonably exaggerated, and which had been made in order to disrupt the child's contact with his father. It was said on the mother's behalf that her worries had made her believe the allegations, but the court's view was that objectively she was being unreasonable.[18] The court concluded:[19]

> 'We do not think that the orders for costs which we have upheld in the instant case are either likely to or should deter a resident parent from advancing a reasonable opposition to contact which is genuinely based on a proper perception of the child's interests. But those who unreasonably frustrate contact need to be aware that the court has the power to make costs orders in appropriate cases, and that the consequences of such unreasonable behaviour may well be an order for costs made against the resident parent who has behaved unreasonably.'

The mother's unreasonableness was found to have related 'both to the welfare of the child and to the conduct of the litigation'. The judge at first instance ordered the mother to pay the father's costs, and that decision was upheld on appeal.

2.16 The issue of costs in respect to allegations in a case concerning children came before the Court of Appeal in 2009.[20] The father had denied domestic violence, and it was proved against him. The Circuit Judge on the first appeal had refused an order that the father pay the mother's costs on the basis that the

14 *Ibid* at [571].
15 See **2.24** below.
16 *R v R (Costs: Child Case)* [1997] 2 FLR 95, Hale J at [96]–[97].
17 *Re T (Order for Costs)* [2005] EWCA Civ 311, [2005] 2 FLR 681.
18 *Re T* at [51], Wall LJ.
19 *Ibid* at [56].
20 *Re J (Costs of fact-finding hearing)* [2009] EWCA Civ 1350, [2010] 1 FLR 1893.

father had not acted unreasonably in giving evidence denying the allegations. Wilson LJ held to the contrary that 'I see no basis for [the] submission that it is unreasonable to expect the father to have admitted the allegations which he chose to deny'.[21] The Court of Appeal then held that:

(a) costs in fact-finding hearings raise different issues from costs relating to hearings at which the arrangements for the child are being determined, so that the factors in *LB Sutton v Davis* (see **2.08** above) do not apply in the same way; and

(b) the domestic violence by the father was misconduct, which provides the basis for an adverse costs order.

'The hearing was devoted exclusively to the court's consideration of serious and relevant allegations against the father of what can only be described as misconduct on his part.'[22] Over two-thirds of the allegations were found to be true and the father was ordered to pay two-thirds of the mother's costs. Wilson LJ observed that 'I would be concerned if our exercise of discretion in relation to mother's costs in this case today were to be taken as an indication that it was appropriate in the vast run of these cases to make an order for costs by reference to the court's determination of issues of historical fact'.[23] However, the reasoning would appear to be applicable to any fact-finding hearing where allegations are denied but largely proved, or on the other hand denied and found to have been largely spurious. The distinction between the approach to costs in fact-finding hearings and in other children hearings made in this case has since been removed by a decision of the Supreme Court.[24] This leaves unaffected, however, the costs consequences of acting unreasonably in this pair of cases, one relating to false allegations (unreasonably made), the other to the denial of allegations found to be true (unreasonably denied).

2.17 All the above cases were reviewed by the Supreme Court in 2012.[25] That case was one where there had been care proceedings brought, as usual, by a local authority. The child's grandparents were joined as parties and were not eligible for public funding so had to pay over £50,000 in legal costs in relation to allegations from which they were exonerated. They applied for the local authority to pay those costs, and the Court of Appeal had agreed, principally because of the injustice to the grandparents otherwise, that the local authority should be ordered to pay. The Supreme Court first held that, as the same case can be case-managed either by separating it into fact-finding part and 'disposal' part, or by keeping it in a single hearing, so it must follow that different costs principles should not arise just because of that case management decision.[26] That part of the decision in *Re J* in the last paragraph was thereby reversed. The court then decided that the

21 *Re J* at [18].
22 *Re J* at [19].
23 *Ibid.*
24 See **2.17**.
25 *Re T (Costs: Care Proceedings: Serious Allegation Not Proved)* [2012] UKSC 36, [2013] 1 FLR 133.
26 *Re T* at [28] and [43].

local authority should not be ordered to pay the grandparents' costs, and stated a conclusion with wide-ranging implications:

> '[44] For these reasons we have concluded that the general practice of not awarding costs against a party, including a local authority, in the absence of reprehensible behaviour or an unreasonable stance, is one that accords with the ends of justice and which should not be subject to an exception in the case of split hearings.'

2.18 The consequences of this decision would appear to be:

(a) costs in fact-finding hearings are to be dealt with in the same way as costs in cases where hearings have not been split (and for that matter in the same way as 'disposal' hearings following separate fact-finding);

(b) the approach of costs orders not being made against a public authority in Children Act proceedings (in the absence of reprehensible behaviour or an unreasonable stance) is recognised as 'the general practice';

(c) the question arises as to how far that general practice is to be applied in cases where there is no public authority, both in Children Act cases and in other family proceedings. Paragraph [44] of *Re T* is in the context of public law Children Act proceedings, but the judgment ranges over private law fact-finding judgments too, and it is clear that the point at (a) above is intended to apply to all family proceedings;

(d) that is made clear by the fact that para [44] applies to costs orders against 'a party, including a local authority'. This reference can only be intended to include other *private* parties;

(e) is there any reason to distinguish private parties in private law Children Act proceedings from those parties in public law Children Act proceedings? That question was answered in the next case before the Supreme Court to deal with the subject.

RE S (A CHILD)

2.19 Most recently the Supreme Court has again had the opportunity to clarify the position, this time in relation to a costs order made by the Court of Appeal against a local authority which opposed the parents' successful appeal.[27] The judgment of the court, handed down by Lady Hale DP, covers the issues highlighted in the previous cases on costs in children proceedings. The Court provides authority on:

(a) the general rule on costs in children proceedings;

(b) the reasons for that rule;

(c) the exceptions to the rule;

27 *Re S (A Child)* [2015] UKSC 20.

(d) what difference in approach there should be between private and public law children proceedings and, in particular, whether local authorities are to be treated differently from other parties;

(e) what difference there should be in relation to certain particular cases; and

(f) whether the fact that a party is publicly funded makes a difference.

2.20 As can be seen from the above list, this case draws together and indeed resolves a number of issues that have previously been dealt with separately, and gives the authority of the Supreme Court to the correct approach. It is a significant case justifying some detail of the court's conclusions in each of the above areas.

The general rule

2.21 The 'general practice of not awarding costs against a party in the absence of reprehensible behaviour or an unreasonable stance' stated in *Re T* (see **2.17**) is restated slightly differently. It is 'inappropriate as a general rule to make costs orders in children cases' and this leads 'to the conclusion that costs orders should only be made in unusual circumstances'.[28] Thus costs orders in children cases 'as a general practice are not awarded' are 'inappropriate as a general rule' and are 'unusual'.

The reasons for the general rule

2.22 The reasons given in *LB Sutton v Davis*, previously the most detailed authority, are quoted by the Supreme Court and then expanded and added to.[29] The reasons for costs not generally being awarded in children cases are:

(a) when the court determines any question in relation to the upbringing of a child the welfare of the child is the court's paramount consideration and thus:
   (i) the proceedings are adversarial with inquisitorial features;
   (ii) an application for a care or supervision order cannot be withdrawn without the court's consent;
   (iii) the court is not bound by the positions put forward by the parties, but can put forward its own solution;
   (iv) the court is not bound by the evidence put forward by the parties, but can decide for itself what evidence is to be heard;
   (v) the court is routinely assisted by independent experts;
   (vi) there are many possible outcomes available to the court;
   (vii) so 'it can readily be seen why in such proceedings there are no adult winners and losers – the only winner should be the child';[30]

28 *Re S* both at [26].
29 *Re S* at [19]–[24].
30 *Re S* at [20].

(b) each party 'has a role to play in helping the court to achieve the best outcome for the child'.[31] So, for example, parents are compellable witnesses in care proceedings: 'No-one should be deterred by the risk of having to pay the other side's costs from playing their part in helping the court achieve the right solution';[32]

(c) it 'can generally be assumed that the parties to the case are motivated by concern for the child's welfare';[33]

(d) 'It is important for the parties to be able to work together in the interests of the children both during and after the proceedings … Stigmatising one party as the loser and adding to that the burden of having to pay the other party's costs is likely to jeopardise the chances of their co-operating in the future';[34]

(e) paying costs may reduce what is available for the children.[35]

The exceptions to the rule

2.23 The exceptions as stated in *LB Sutton v Davis* and earlier authorities and in *Re T* are re-stated, namely 'where, for example, the conduct of a party has been reprehensible or the party's stance has been beyond the band of what is reasonable'.[36] It is then held that this is not a closed list (the 'for example' in the quotation reinforces that) and that 'there may be other such circumstances' in both private and public law proceedings where costs orders are appropriate.[37] No suggestions are made as to what the other exceptions might be.

Is there a different costs rule in public and in private proceedings?

2.24 The answer is 'no'. The approach that there should be costs orders only when there has been reprehensible behaviour or unreasonable conduct (and perhaps in other as yet undefined circumstances) should apply to local authorities as it applies to private parties. That is partly because local authorities have limited funds. While local authorities should be in no worse position than other parties, neither should they be in any better position, so that just as a richer parent might be ordered to pay the costs of a poorer primary carer in order not to jeopardise the child's welfare, so a local authority might also be ordered to make such a contribution to the same end.[38] We note that a rich parent will retain parental responsibility after the conclusion of private law proceedings, which includes

31 *Re S* at [21].
32 *Ibid.*
33 *Re S* at [22].
34 *Re S* at [23].
35 *Re S* at [24].
36 *Re S* at [26].
37 *Re S* at [30]–[33].
38 *Re S* at [32]–[33].

financial responsibility for the child,[39] but a local authority will not, save for the exceptional case where a care order is made. In public law proceedings the parents will usually be publicly funded so that the question will not arise for them, though it may arise in relation to an intervener, for example, a prospective special guardian or adopter or a person against whom allegations are made who has paid for legal representation. A distinction might be drawn between the payment of costs by an absent parent who has an ongoing responsibility for paying child maintenance and their payment by a local authority with no responsibility for the future financial support of the child (not something considered by the Supreme Court).

Are there particular cases where a different approach is required?

2.25 Some differences between cases are listed and dealt with:

(a) *Private and public law*. 'All the reasons which make it inappropriate as a general rule to make costs orders in children's cases apply with equal force in care proceedings between parents and local authorities as they do in private law proceedings between parents or other family members.'[40]

(b) *Interveners*. It makes no difference whether the person wishing to claim their costs is an intervener or a parent (a party), save that 'parents are always entitled to resist the claim of the state to remove their children from them' and will usually be taken to have acted reasonably in resisting the removal of their children from their care.[41]

(c) *Appeals*. The rule applies on appeal as much as at a first-instance hearing. Reasonableness at an appeal will be assessed having taken into account any factual findings made which are not being challenged, but the principle is the same.[42]

(d) *Pro bono costs*. There is no reason why pro bono costs should be dealt with differently (obiter).[43]

Public funding

2.26 There is no reason why publicly funded parties should be dealt with differently: 'the question of whether it is just to make an order for costs should as a matter of principle be determined irrespective of whether any of the parties are publicly funded'.[44] However, the procedure for dealing with costs where a

39 Child Support Act 1991, s 1(1).
40 *Re S* at [26].
41 *Re S* at [28].
42 *Re S* at [29].
43 *Re S* at [34].
44 *Re S* at [25].

publicly funded party is either receiving or paying them is subject to separate rules (see **7.87–7.112**).

2.27 Removing the detail, summarising the above authorities and giving greatest weight to the most recent Supreme Court judgment, we conclude that:

(a) the general rule is not to award costs in children cases;

(b) that general rule applies equally in public and private law proceedings;

(c) that general rule applies to all parties and interveners;

(d) but costs may be awarded when there has been 'reprehensible behaviour or an unreasonable stance'.

2.28 In a case where relatives with whom a child lived had been put to substantial legal expense, and requiring the father to pay £10,000 towards the costs of those relatives because he had behaved unreasonably in the litigation, Cobb J summarised the rules on awarding costs since *Re S* as—

(i) There is a wide discretion with the award of costs;

(ii) Costs do not ordinarily follow the event;

(iii) Orders to pay costs may reduce the chances of cooperation between the parties;

(iv) It can generally be assumed that all parties are motivated by concern for the child's welfare;

(v) A costs order may be justified if a party's behaviour has been reprehensible or unreasonable;

(vi) Orders for costs may reduce the money available for the family.[45]

2.29 Newton J, having found her conduct to have been unreasonable and reprehensible, in making an order for a grandmother who was a party to private law children proceedings to pay £70,000 costs, summarised the law in almost identical terms to those applied by Cobb J[46] – though without reference to *Re S*. In that case the grandmother transferred her property to her daughter in anticipation of an adverse costs order.[47] It was considered likely that the LAA would seek to set that transaction aside in order to recover their costs.

2.30 The judgment does not distinguish between reprehensible behaviour which gave rise to the proceedings and reprehensible behaviour in relation to the conduct of the proceedings. This issue is considered below.

45 *Re E-R (Child Arrangements)* [2016] EWHC 805 (Fam), [2017] 2 FLR 501 at [77].
46 *Re M (Children) (Residence and Contact: Costs)* [2016] EWHC 1998 (Fam).
47 *Re M* at [48].

2.31 In a costs case[48] the question arose as to whether an interim decision in children proceedings should be dealt with any differently from a final order, in relation to costs. Following a thorough review of the authorities the deputy High Court judge decided that they should be dealt with on the same principles. That issue did not arise in *Re S*, but it would be consistent with the thrust of the judgment in that case that interim orders should be dealt with in the same way.

2.32 The principles in *re S* apply equally to proceedings under the Children Act and to wardship proceedings. In a wide-ranging judgment considering the means by which a private party to wardship proceedings might meet their costs – in particular by legal aid or by a costs funding order – MacDonald J held:

> '**[1]** The question before me is whether the High Court has power, under its inherent jurisdiction, to make a costs funding order against a local authority requiring it to fund legal advice and representation for a parent in wardship proceedings brought by the local authority where that parent has lawfully been refused legal aid. I am satisfied that the answer to that question is "no".'[49]

There was no appeal from the very thorough judgment.

2.33 In an important extension to the application of the law as stated in *Re S* MacDonald J considered the position where an NHS Trust makes an application for an order as to the care of a child.[50] Having set out the detailed arguments relating to the making of a costs order in favour of the successful parents he observed:

> '[52] To make an order for costs against a public body simply to remedy the fact that Parliament has not provided for public funding in the circumstances in question would be impermissible unless such a costs order is justified on ordinary principles in the particular circumstances of the case. It is not for the court to fill a lacuna by making a costs order against an NHS Trust where there is otherwise no principled basis for such an order on ordinary principles.'
>
> '[53] … whether a costs order should be made in favour of the parents in the proceedings under the Children Act 1989 falls to be determined on the principles that ordinarily apply to the making of costs in proceedings concerning the welfare of children under the 1989 Act, and in particular proceedings concerning the welfare of children that are brought by public bodies that are under a duty to do so.'

Thus an NHS Trust is in the same position as a local authority in relation to costs in Children Act cases. No order was made for the NHS Trust to pay the parents' costs.

48 *C v FC (Children Proceedings: Costs)* [2004] 1 FLR 362.

49 *HB v A Local Authority and Another (Wardship: Costs Funding Order)* [2017] EWHC 524 (Fam), [2018] 1 FLR 538.

50 *Barts Health NHS Trust v Begum and others* [2019] EWHC 3320 (Admin).

THE FACTORS TO BE CONSIDERED

2.34 As previously discussed, the factors which the court has to apply when considering both whether or not to make a costs order and if so what proportion of a costs claim to allow, are those set out at CPR r 44.2(4) and (5) and r 44.4. The factors relevant to whether or not to make an order for costs were set out previously, and re-stated as they apply to children proceedings (the clean sheet regime) they are as follows:
The court will have regard to all the circumstances, including

(a) the conduct of all the parties, including
  (i) conduct before as well as during the proceedings including any relevant pre-action protocol
  (ii) whether it was reasonable for a party to raise, pursue or contest a particular issue
  (iii) the manner in which a party has pursued or defended its case or a particular allegation or issue, and
  (iv) whether a wholly or partly successful applicant has exaggerated its case.

(b) The extent to which the parties have co-operated and negotiated, including any admissible offer to settle, which is part of the general conduct of the proceedings.

These factors will be considered in turn.

2.35 In financial remedy proceedings, one of the factors to be considered is 'the financial effect on the parties of any costs order'.[51] There is no such factor in the rules relating to children proceedings. Nonetheless financial factors may be relevant to costs orders in children proceedings and will be very likely to be relevant in financial proceedings coming under the clean sheet regime. Financial effects may be taken into account as the rule requires the court to have regard to 'all the circumstances'. An example is where a father's failure to comply with a child arrangements order had been unreasonable and reprehensible and he was ordered to pay the mother £15,000 in costs, but the order would not be enforced without the court's permission so that it could not be used by the father to say that he could not afford to comply with the child arrangements order.[52]

Conduct before and during the proceedings

2.36

> '44.2(5) The conduct of the parties includes –
>
> (a) conduct before, as well as during, the proceedings and in particular the extent to which the parties followed the Practice Direction – Pre-Action Conduct or any relevant pre-action protocol.'

51 FPR r 28.3(7)(f).
52 *E-R (Child Arrangements Order No.2: Costs)* [2017] EWHC 2535 (Fam), Cobb J.

Under this rule the conduct which the court will 'have regard to' might be thought to include:

(a) conduct which gave rise to the proceedings (for example domestic violence, unjustifiably withholding contact with a child or making false allegations);

(b) conduct in relation to, but prior to the commencement of, proceedings – the court is specifically required to consider compliance with any pre-action protocol; and[53]

(c) conduct in the proceedings.

However, as we shall see, conduct which gave rise to the proceedings is not to be considered in relation to costs in children proceedings.

2.37 There is an obvious and important distinction between conduct on which the proceedings are based – for example allegations on the basis of which fact-finding takes place – and conduct in contemplation of possible proceedings. For example, in *Re J*,[54] there was the domestic violence that was found to have been perpetrated by the father, and there was the father's denial of that domestic violence which made the fact-finding hearing necessary. In earlier and subsequent cases[55] it has been stated repeatedly and unequivocally that 'the unreasonableness must relate to the conduct of the litigation rather than to the welfare of the child'.[56]

2.38 Peter Jackson J has held:[57]

> 'I do not accept the submission of LCC [the local authority] that the only conduct to which the court can have regard under 44.5(4)(a) is litigation conduct. If this were the case, a party to family proceedings who had behaved reprehensibly for years could escape a costs award by being sure to behave impeccably once the litigation for which they were responsible had begun.'

In that case the judge took into account, in ordering Lancashire County Council to pay the publicly funded costs of the other parties, 'LCC's conduct in relation to these boys over many years'.[58] In the light of the Court of Appeal authority cited in the previous paragraph, and indeed in the light of the wording of CPR r 44.5(4)(a), he was mistaken in doing so. On the basis that private individuals are to be in no better and no worse position in relation to costs than public authorities, as is required by *Re S*, abusive partners would be routinely liable to be ordered to pay costs on the basis proposed by Peter Jackson J. They are not, and 'conduct' for costs purposes means litigation conduct.[59] Peter Jackson J subsequently

53 CPR r 44.2(5)(a).

54 *Re J (Costs of Fact-finding Hearing)* [2009] EWCA Civ 1350, [2010] 1 FLR 1893.

55 *R v R (Costs: Child Case)* [1997] 2 FLR 95, CA; *Re T (Order for Costs)* [2005] EWCA Civ 311 (Fam), [2005] 2 FLR 681; *Re L (Costs of Children Proceedings)* [2014] EWCA Civ 1437.

56 *Re L (Costs of Children Proceedings)* [2014] EWCA Civ 1437 at [37], Gloster LJ.

57 *A and S (Children) v Lancashire County Council (No 2)* [2013] EWHC 851 (Fam), [2013] 2 FLR 1221 at [19].

58 *Ibid* at [22].

59 See, however, *Re Wyatt (A Child) (Medical Treatment: Continuation of Order) (Costs)* [2006] EWCA Civ 529 at [47]–[48], discussed in relation to cost protection at **7.96**.

considered the analysis of Cobb J in *Re E-R* – see **2.28** above – and justified a costs order because "I have found the father's behaviour to be reprehensible in certain respects in a way that has directly fed in to the way in which these proceedings arose, the way in which they have been pursued and the fact that they had to come to a final hearing."[60] This brings his approach into harmony with the other authorities.

2.39 The litigation conduct relevant to costs includes conduct before and during the proceedings, as the rule sets out. In children cases that leads in particular to Part 3 of the FPR: non-court dispute resolution.

2.40 Non-court dispute resolution (NCDR) applies to private law children applications and to financial remedy applications, including applications made under Sch 1 to the Children Act.[61] Under the rules in Part 3 the court can require parties, in those cases, to take part in a Family Mediation Information and Assessment Meeting (a MIAM) before the matter comes to court. The power to order parties to engage in NCDR derives from s 10 of the Children and Families Act 2014: 'Before making a relevant family application, a person must attend a family mediation information and assessment meeting.' There is a long list of excuses for not taking part in a MIAM[62] but if the court finds that an excuse is not a valid one it 'will direct the applicant, or direct the parties, to attend a MIAM'.[63]

2.41 The wording of the statute and of the rule is strong: a person 'must' attend a MIAM, unless they have a valid reason for not doing so, and if they have not attended and have no such reason the court 'will' direct the party to attend one unless in the circumstances of the case the application is exempted from a MIAM. These rules came into force in April 2014, and there has been no reported case of a MIAM being enforced or, more specifically, of consequences being imposed by the courts for failing to attend a MIAM. An obvious consequence would be a penalty in costs, as has typically been the case in civil proceedings, and we await an authority.

2.42 Conduct before the proceedings may include any refusal to negotiate which necessitated the issuing of proceedings and any rejection of an offer found by the court to be reasonable (see 'Offers' at **2.51**). Further examples of costs orders against local authorities for non-compliance are discussed at the end of this Chapter.

Reasonableness

2.43

> '44.2(5) The conduct of the parties includes –
>
> …

60 *S v S (Relocation)* [2017] EWHC 2345 (Fam), [2018] 1 FLR 825 at [40].
61 FPR PD3A [12]–[13].
62 FPR r 3.8.
63 FPR r 3.10(2).

(b) whether it was reasonable for a party to raise, pursue or contest a particular allegation or issue;

(c) the manner in which a party has pursued or defended its case or a particular allegation or issue.'

The test of reasonableness is an objective test. It is not possible to escape a finding of unreasonableness sufficient to found an order for costs by saying that the party took that position because of his or her beliefs as to the other party's conduct. It has been held that a party's unreasonable beliefs, however genuine, about contact, could not make the refusal of contact and opposing it in the proceedings reasonable. An adverse costs order was made in circumstances where there were wholly unwarranted allegations of sexual abuse used by the mother to try to stop contact.[64]

2.44 The Court of Appeal has held that it is not necessary for a party's conduct to have been 'irrational' in order for an order for costs to be made against that party,[65] and that it is not unreasonable to expect a person to admit true allegations (and not deny them). Reasonableness in this context requires perhaps more analysis than is available in that judgment. It might be said that it is reasonable to deny allegations you know to be true, on the basis that you believe they will not be proved against you. Wilson LJ seems to suggest that the reasonable man can be expected to admit what he has done. While that is a description of an honest man, we suggest that that is not the same thing.

2.45 The Court of Appeal distinguished in that case between 'legitimate litigation over reasonable disagreements' and 'irrational conduct which prolongs unnecessary litigation'.[66] The former carries no risk of a costs penalty whatever the outcome of the proceedings; the latter risks an adverse costs order.

2.46 The Court of Appeal considered costs in a case where 'The Judge took the view that the father's conduct was unreasonable' in that 'anyone who disagrees with him is incompetent, biased or wrong'.[67] Hale J held that 'Of course, the parties should not be deterred, by the prospect of having to pay costs, from putting before the court that which they genuinely think to be in the best interests of the child, but there have to be limits. Children should not be put through the strain of being subject to claims that have very little real prospect of success …'[68] That parental character and its effect on children is a sufficiently familiar scenario to mean that the decision to require the father to pay the mother's costs in that case remains relevant 20 years on. That was a case where the father, who was legally aided, was ordered to pay the mother's costs out of his share of the former matrimonial home.

64 *Re T (Order for Costs)* [2005] EWCA Civ 311 (Fam), [2005] 2 FLR 681.

65 *Re J (Costs of Fact-finding Hearing)* [2009] EWCA Civ 1350, [2010] 1 FLR 1893 at [18], Wilson LJ.

66 *Ibid* at [11].

67 *R v R (Costs: Child Case)* [1997] 2 FLR 95 at [97].

68 *Ibid* at [98].

2.47 Butler-Sloss LJ distinguished between hopelessness and unreasonableness when considering costs.[69] While a hopeless case could be pursued unreasonably, the fact that it was hopeless did not make it unreasonable to have pursued it. The point is put like this:

> 'If this judge in this case had found that this father had behaved unreasonably in the litigation and had gone beyond what many fathers do, seek orders which are hopeless, the point will come at which pursuing a hopeless application becomes unreasonable. But hopelessness and unreasonableness are not necessarily the same thing.'

It is left to the reader to consider whether this is a helpful distinction to pursue in defending an application for costs!

2.48 Munby J considered the relationship between finding that a litigant had behaved unreasonably and making an award of costs to the other side.[70] He held that:

> 'The fact that a parent has litigated in an unreasonable fashion may open the door to the making of an adverse costs order; but it does not of itself necessitate the making of such an order. There is, at the end of the day, a broad discretion to be exercised having regard to *all* the circumstances of the case. And a judge must be careful not to fall into the trap of simply assuming that because there has been unreasonable behaviour in the conduct of the litigation an order is therefore to be made without more ado. Careful attention must be paid to all the circumstances of the case *and* to the factors which, on the authorities I have referred to, indicate that normally it is inappropriate to make such an order – factors which do not simply disappear or cease to have weight merely because the litigation has been conducted unreasonably.'

2.49 Following that approach there is then a two-stage process when considering unreasonable behaviour in relation to costs in children cases: first, whether there has been unreasonable behaviour; second, if there has, considering whether in all the circumstances, and particularly those set out in *LB Sutton v Davis* as developed by the Supreme Court in *Re S*, a costs order is appropriate.

2.50 In the cases considered above some parties fund their representation themselves, some are publicly funded and others are unrepresented. As the Supreme Court has held,[71] there is no reason why a publicly funded party should not be the subject of an adverse costs order like any other party. Where a father had brought a case with 'absolutely no merit', it was 'not necessary to launch these proceedings' and 'he has abused the court process by using it as a vehicle to make the mother feel insecure and vulnerable' a costs order was made against

69 *Re G (Costs: Child Case)* [1999] 2 FLR 250 at [252G].
70 *Re N (A Child) v A and Others* [2009] EWHC 2096 (Fam), [2010] 1 FLR 454 at [47].
71 *Re S (A Child)* [2015] UKSC 20 at [25].

him even though he was on benefits; neither did the court consider that it was appropriate to say that the order was not to be enforced without leave of the court.[72]

Offers

2.51

> '44.2(4) In deciding what order (if any) to make about costs, the court will have regard to all the circumstances, including – …
>
> (c) any admissible offer to settle made by a party which is drawn to the court's attention, ….'[73]

A *Calderbank* letter[74] is an offer to settle an issue in the proceedings that is expressed in a letter and made without prejudice save as to costs. The court has a discretion[75] as to the weight that should be given to the offer, and the fact of the offer and its details will only be revealed to the court at the end of proceedings on addressing the issue of costs. Therefore, if there is a possibility of a costs order, it may be wise to make a reasonable offer to settle which, if refused, will be considered by the court and may provide some costs protection to the offeror.

2.52 Prior to a change in the rules in 2006 preventing their use in financial remedy proceedings, *Calderbank* letters were frequently used in such cases. The change came about in order to avoid situations where the court's careful determination of a fair financial remedy award could be undermined by the subsequent imposition of a costs order. Even if the difference between the *Calderbank* offer and the judgment was only slightly in one party's favour, that party could recover all their costs incurred from 28 days after the making of the offer.[76]

2.53 Nevertheless, this change has proved controversial. The argument for the re-introduction of *Calderbank* offers in financial remedy proceedings is that each side knows that if their *Calderbank* offer is 'beaten', they might end up paying the other side's costs (which could be assessed on the indemnity basis). It is claimed that these offers provided the parties with a powerful incentive to reach a settlement. Without the threat of a *Calderbank* offer, parties may be more inclined to 'fight' on to the final hearing in the knowledge that, provided there has been no litigation misconduct, they will only have to bear their own costs.[77]

72 *Re G (Contact Proceedings: Costs)* [2013] EWCA Civ 1017, [2014] 1 FLR 517 at [15] and [18], McFarlane LJ.

73 CPR r 44.2(4).

74 *Calderbank v Calderbank* (1975) FLR Rep 113, CA.

75 CPR r 44.2(4)(c) Admissible offers are akin to *Calderbank* letters: *John and others v Price Waterhouse (a firm) and another (Frere Cholmeley (a firm) and another, Part 20 defendants)* [2002] 1 WLR 953 at [65].

76 Family Proceedings (Amendment) Rules 2003, r 12.69(2)(b).

77 *ABX v SBX (DX intervening)* [2018] EWFC 81, [2019] 1 Costs LO 7 at [2].

2.54 To address this issue, the Family Procedure Rule Committee set up a Costs Working Group, with judicial leadership, in November 2018 to consider whether to recommend reform of the court's consideration of *Calderbank* offers in financial remedy cases. The objective of any change to the Rules would be to encourage parties to take settlement negotiations seriously and pragmatically. A consultation period ran from July to October 2019 to canvass views on whether *Calderbank* offers should be regarded as 'conduct' when the court considers whether a cost order should be made. However, the Working Group specified that any change would not affect the existing position that financial remedy proceedings were subject to the 'no order' rule. We await the results of the Working Group with interest.

2.55 However, *Calderbank* offers remain available in proceedings under: the Children Act 1989 (including Sch 1 cases); the Trusts of Land and Appointment of Trustees Act 1996; Part III of the Matrimonial and Family Proceedings Act 1984; and in relation to appeals, and the courts have encouraged their use.

2.56 Butler-Sloss LJ gave the leading judgment in *Gojkovic v Gojkovic (No 2)*[78] and stated that '*Calderbank* offers require to have teeth in order for them to be effective'.[79] She said that the offeree should appreciate the risk as to costs of declining a reasonable offer as 'the starting point in a case where there has been an offer is that, *prima facie*, if the applicant receives no more or less than the offer made, she/he is at risk not only of not being awarded costs, but also of paying the costs of the other party after communication of the offer and a reasonable time to consider it'.[80] As to the weight to be given to such an offer by the court in exercising its discretion as to costs, Ormrod LJ said, 'I see no advantage in the court surrendering its discretion in these matters as it has to all intents and purposes done where a payment into court has been made. A *Calderbank* offer should influence but not govern the exercise of the discretion'.[81]

When should a Calderbank *letter be written?*

2.57 In civil proceedings, a party may try to settle a claim by making a Part 36 offer which carries costs consequences. Such an offer cannot be made in family proceedings and therefore a *Calderbank* letter may be a useful device to settle the dispute and, if the matter does not settle, may assist the offeror if an order for costs is made. A *Calderbank* letter provides the flexibility for the offeror to make an original proposal which, if accepted, will bind the parties.

Family proceedings other than financial remedy proceedings

2.58 Wall LJ considered a father's application for permission to appeal an order for costs made in Children Act 1989 private law proceedings which had

78 [1992] Fam 40, [1990] 1 FLR 140, CA.
79 *Ibid* at [59B].
80 *Ibid* at [59F].
81 *McDonnell v McDonnell* [1977] 1 WLR 34, CA at [38].

been initiated by the father in respect to contact with his son.[82] Before Pauffley J, the mother had successfully appealed the order of the district judge and the father had been ordered to pay £20,000 towards the mother's costs. Wall LJ noted:[83]

> 'A party to a hearing at first instance who then faces an appeal has the opportunity to take stock, and to make *Calderbank* offers to compromise it. I appreciate, of course, that this places a burden on the shoulders of those advising the litigant who has succeeded at first instance: but if such a litigant – as here – opposes an appeal root and branch, and announces, as Mr Nicholls did to the judge, that he intends to seek his costs if successful, then in my judgment such a litigant cannot complain if, when allowing the appeal, the judge takes the view that he should contribute to, or pay, the appellant's costs.'

The approach that is advised is that in any appeal, but particularly in an appeal about costs, a *Calderbank* offer should be considered. The offer will not be disclosed to the appeal court until after its decision, as would be the case with any Part 36 offer in cases where such an offer is relevant.[84]

2.59 There is clearly a role for *Calderbank* letters in proceedings under Sch 1 to the Children Act 1989 where the no order as to costs principle does not apply. In *KS v ND (Schedule 1: Appeal: Costs)*,[85] the parties had made cross-applications to vary a consent order made under Sch 1. The district judge then adjusted the father's payments of general child support and school fees for a son (of sixth form age) and made no order as to costs. The mother appealed this decision before Mostyn J, and argued, in respect to costs, that an award in her favour should have been made. The judge dismissed the appeal on costs noting that he began his assessment of costs with a clean sheet[86] and observed that no *Calderbank* offers had been made. As to the costs of the appeal, both parties had written *Calderbank* letters. Finding the mother's offer 'did not in any way seek realistically to reflect the risks of her losing what to my mind was always a very weak appeal',[87] Mostyn J opined:[88]

> 'Even if the father had not made a *Calderbank* offer he would prima facie be entitled to his costs; the existence of his offer strengthens his case considerably. There are no good reasons why, subject to the questions of quantum and timing, he should not have his costs.'

2.60 This view underlines the value of writing a reasonable *Calderbank* letter at any stage in proceedings when costs may be a live issue.

82 *M (A Child)* [2009] EWCA Civ 311.
83 *Ibid* at [24].
84 See CPR r 52.22.
85 [2013] EWHC 464 (Fam), [2013] 2 FLR 698.
86 *Ibid* at [19].
87 *Ibid* at [30].
88 *Ibid* at [34].

Form of a Calderbank letter

2.61 It is important to express the terms of the offer clearly so that it is treated by the court as a *Calderbank* letter. In *Reed Executive plc v Reed Business Information Ltd*,[89] the Court of Appeal said the letter should be marked, 'without prejudice save as to costs' and these have been described by Cook as 'the magic words'.[90] It is also advised that this statement should be placed in a prominent position in order that the letter is not, inadvertently, provided to the court until the end of the proceedings. The risk of failing to follow the advice of the Court of Appeal is illustrated by the case of *WD v HD*. Presiding over an appeal, Moor J said he would admit any *Calderbank* offer but found the wife's purported offer to be no more than submissions on her position.[91]

2.62 To be effective an offer must be:

(a) sensible such that it warrants consideration;

(b) open for acceptance for a reasonable amount of time (to allow the other side time to consider their position fully);

(c) clearly accepted or rejected;

and counter-offers and further negotiations are advised.[92]

COSTS IN PUBLIC LAW CASES

2.63 As decided by the Supreme Court in *Re S* and described above, local authorities are to be in no better and no worse position than any other party in relation to costs. However, local authorities have statutory responsibilities which make their role in children proceedings a distinctive one. A body of case-law has grown up which remains of relevance.

2.64 Thus where a local authority has been guilty of 'inexcusable and deplorable' delay during the proceedings they were ordered to pay the publicly funded costs of the other parties.[93] Where the local authority had acted beyond its powers 'without any real authority whatsoever' the same order was made.[94]

2.65 More recently the courts, pursuant to imposing shorter timetables particularly for public law children proceedings, have become more strict in

89 [2004] EWCA Civ 887 at [27] per Jacob LJ.

90 Middleton and Rowley, *Cook on Costs 2019* (LexisNexis Butterworths, 2018) at [20.37].

91 *WD v HD* [2015] EWHJC 1547 (Fam), [2015] All ER (D) 81 (Nov) at [69]–[70].

92 *Gojkovic v Gojkovic (No 2)* [1992] Fam 40, [1990] 1 FLR 140, CA at [59B] per Butler-Sloss LJ.

93 *Bolton Metropolitan Borough Council v B and H* [1989] 2 FLR 349, [1990] FCR 57 at [58] per Ewbank J. A delay of 12 days in making an application for a care order, which led to a hearing not being fully effective, was penalised in costs by Keehan J – *Nottingham City Council v LM and Others* [2016] EWHC 11 (Fam), [2016] 2 FLR 1221 at [38]–[39].

94 *London Borough of Havering v S* [1986] 1 FLR 489.

relation to compliance with the court's orders. The Court of Appeal has put it in the following way:[95]

> 'The court is not dependent on a willing party. Indeed an unwilling party who flouts the court's orders may find itself in contempt, even if it is an agency of the State such as a local authority. It is necessary to point out for the discussion which follows that the court's orders are to be complied with. They are not preferences, requests or mere indications: they are orders and non-compliance with orders should be expected to and will usually have a consequence.'

2.66 Munby P has made the point on several occasions, for example: 'For present purposes that principle applies as much to orders by way of interlocutory case management directions as to any other species of order. The court is entitled to expect – and from now on family courts will demand – strict compliance with all such orders. Non-compliance with orders should be expected to have and will usually have a consequence.'[96] The consequence may be a costs order: Keehan J ordered a local authority to pay the costs of all the parties of a directions hearing made necessary by the 'contumelious failure' of the local authority to comply with directions (being late in filing final evidence and an amended schedule of facts) and he observed that 'the burden of other work is not an acceptable explanation'.[97]

2.67 In *London Borough of Bexley v V & Others*,[98] Keehan J had directed that a hearing should be listed following the 'contumelious failure'[99] by a local authority to comply with his earlier directions. Those directions had stated that if a party was unable to comply with the order then that party should apply to the judge, via his clerk and before the expiry of the time for compliance, for an extension of time. As a consequence of its failure to comply with that order and then a number of further failures to respond to communications from the court which resulted in an unnecessary hearing, the local authority was ordered to pay the costs of the directions hearing and the costs of obtaining a transcript of the judgment. The wasted costs procedure was not precisely followed by the judge, but his decision was subsequently quoted with approval by the President in *Re W (Children)*.[100] In that case, the President noted that parties to family proceedings were not permitted to agree to extend the time for compliance with a court order[101] but did not order wasted costs to be paid.

2.68 In his judgment, Sir James Munby P noted that Keehan J had directed publication of a transcript be anonymised *except* that the London Borough

95 *Re W (A Child) (Care Proceedings: Welfare Evaluation: Functions of Local Authority)* [2013] EWCA Civ 1227, [2014] 1 FCR 260 at [74] per Ryder LJ.
96 *Re W (A Child)* [2013] EWCA Civ 1177 at [52].
97 *London Borough of Bexley v W, W and D* [2014] EWHC 2187 (Fam).
98 [2014] EWHC 2187 (Fam).
99 *Ibid* at [1].
100 [2014] EWFC 22, [2015] 1 FLR 1092, at [5–6].
101 At [17–18]; FPR r 4.5(3).

concerned would be identified, so that its failings would be there for all to see. The 'naming and shaming' was made more pointed by a direction that the local authority pay the cost of the transcript.[102] The President thought that this 'ingenious and salutary requirement … might be thought an appropriate adaptation to the age of the internet of the penalty inflicted in 1596 by Lord Egerton LK in *Milward v Welden* Tothill 101'.[103] That report is accessible on Bailii[104] and, for entertainment rather than current guidance to judges, it is to be devoutly hoped, is quoted in full:

> 'FORASMUCH as it now appeared to this Court, by a report made by the now Lord Keeper, (being then Master of the Rolls,) upon consideration had of the plaintiff's replication, according to an order of the 7th of May anno 37th Reginæ, *that the said replication doth amount to six score sheets of paper*, and yet all the matter thereof which is pertinent might have been well contrived in sixteen sheets of paper, wherefore the plaintiff was appointed to be examined to find out who drew the same replication, and by whose advice it was done, to the end that the offender might, for example sake, not only be punished, but also be fined to Her Majesty for that offence; and that the defendant might have his charges sustained thereby; the execution of which order was, by a later order made by the late Lord Keeper the 26th of June, Anno 37th Reginæ, suspended, without any express cause shewed thereof in that order, and was never since called upon until the matter came to be heard, on Tuesday last, before the now Lord Keeper; at which time some mention was again made of the same replication; and for that it now appeared to his Lordship, by the confession of Richard Mylward, alias Alexander, the plaintiff's son, that he the said Richard himself, did both draw, devise, and engross the same replication; and because his Lordship is of opinion that such an abuse is not in any sort to be tolerated, proceeding of a malicious purpose to increase the defendant's charge, and being fraught with much impertinent matter not fit for this Court; it is therefore ordered, that the Warden of the Fleet shall take the said Richard Mylward, alias Alexander, into his custody, and shall bring him into Westminster Hall, on Saturday next, about ten of the clock in the forenoon, and then and there shall cut a hole in the *myddest* of the same engrossed replication (which is delivered unto him for that purpose), and put the said Richard's head through the same hole, and so let the same replication hang about his shoulders, with the written side outward; and then, the same so hanging, shall lead the same Richard, bare headed and bare faced, round about Westminster Hall, whilst the Courts are sitting, and shall shew him at the bar of every of the three Courts within the Hall, and shall then take him back again to the Fleet, and keep him prisoner, until he shall have paid 10*l.* to Her Majesty for a fine, and 20 nobles to the defendant, for his costs in respect of the aforesaid abuse, which fine and costs are now adjudged and imposed upon him by this Court, for the abuse aforesaid.'

102 *London Borough of Bexley v V and others* [2014] EWHC 2187 (Fam), at [9].
103 *Re W (Strict compliance with court orders)* [2014] EWFC 22, [2015] 1 FLR 1092, at [6].
104 *Mylward v Weldon* [1595] EWHC Ch 1.

2.69 *Re S* makes it clear that the same criteria apply when considering costs orders against a local authority as for a private individual, the same test for reprehensible behaviour or unreasonable conduct applies to both. But what is reprehensible for a local authority will be different from what will be so for an individual. Cobb J made a costs order against a local authority which he found had 'failed fundamentally to investigate, address, or analyse the serious issues in the case raised by the father's allegations when it prepared its s 37 report filed in July 2012 or at any time in the period which followed prior to the December 2012 hearing'.[105] That sort of responsibility can only fall on a public body, usually a local authority (and possibly Cafcass or NYAS), but that does not detract from the principle enunciated by Lady Hale DP in *Re S* that the same criteria are to be applied.

2.70 While the burden of other work is an excuse that may be made equally on behalf of a solicitor representing a parent in care proceedings, the tasks falling to local authorities are generally more numerous, so that there will be a risk that such costs orders may be made more often against local authorities. Generally, however, the reasons for costs orders to be made in children proceedings do not much differ whether the party is a local authority or a private individual.

105 *HB v PB and others* [2013] EWHC 1956 (Fam) at [52].

CHAPTER 3

Costs in Financial Remedy Proceedings

DEFINITIONS

'Financial remedy proceedings'

3.01 Proceedings for a financial remedy,[1] as we noted in opening, are not the same thing as 'financial remedy proceedings' as defined at FPR r 28.3 for the purpose of costs. The definition in that rule does not include a number of sorts of proceedings which are certainly for a financial remedy. The definition has been expanded and explained in case-law[2] so that certain stages in proceedings which are 'financial remedy proceedings' are not so treated for costs purposes. The process of definition is rather detailed, but the position when we come out at the other end of the definition process is relatively simple (see **3.24**).

1 'Financial remedy' is defined at FPR r 2.3.
2 In particular *Baker v Rowe* [2009] EWCA Civ 1162, [2010] 1 FLR 761 and *Judge v Judge* [2008] EWCA Civ 1458, [2009] 1 FLR 1287.

The Rules

3.02 As far as costs are concerned it is the definition at r 28.3 that is of importance since it lists the proceedings to which the costs provisions under that rule apply. Rule 28.3(5) provides the 'general rule' of no order for costs in such proceedings, the exceptions to that rule being set out at r 28.3(6) and (7). It will be helpful first to discuss just what is included in financial remedy proceedings for the purposes of this rule. To a certain extent that is just a matter of comparing lists of proceedings which are contained in the rules, but the boundary between the proceedings to be included within r 28.3 and those outside it requires consideration of case-law as well as the rules.

3.03 FPR r 28.3(4)(b) defines financial remedy proceedings in relation to costs.

> '(4) In this rule –
>
> (b) "financial remedy proceedings" means proceedings for –
> (i) a financial order except an order for maintenance pending suit, an order for maintenance pending outcome of proceedings, an interim periodical payments order, an order for payment in respect of legal services or any other form of interim order for the purposes of rule 9.7(1)(a), (b), (c) and (e);
> (ii) an order under Part 3 of the 1984 Act;
> (iii) an order under Schedule 7 to the 2004 Act;
> (iv) an order under section 10(2) of the 1973 Act;
> (v) an order under section 48(2) of the 2004 Act.'

3.04 This sub-paragraph depends for its meaning on definitions in other parts of the rules, as well as reference to the statutes mentioned. When that exercise is undertaken then 'financial remedy proceedings' as far as costs are concerned are:

(a) the financial orders as defined in FPR r 28.3, which exclude applications for interim orders[3] (except interim variation orders under r 9.7(1)(d)), namely:
  (i) an order for periodical payments or lump sum provision (excluding the failure to maintain provision at s 27 of the Matrimonial Causes Act 1973);
  (ii) a property adjustment order;
  (iii) an order for sale of property;
  (iv) a pension sharing order (and a pension compensation sharing order);
  (v) a variation order, including an interim variation order.

  Such orders are available on the dissolution both of marriages and of civil partnerships;

(b) an order under Part 3 of the Matrimonial and Family Proceedings Act 1984, that is to say financial relief following an overseas divorce. Part 3 includes final financial orders so that this parallels (a)(i) to (a)(v) above. Part 3 also

3 FPR r 28.3(4)(b)(i).

includes interim orders for maintenance under s 14 of that Act and avoidance of disposition orders but interim financial relief and freezing orders following an overseas divorce are excluded by r 28.3(4)(b)(i) from being 'financial remedy proceedings' for costs purposes, as those come under FPR r 9.7;

(c) an order under Sch 7 to the Civil Partnership Act 2004, that is to say financial relief following an overseas dissolution of a civil partnership. The same point applies about the exclusion of orders for interim maintenance under para 5 of Sch 7 and of avoidance of disposition orders under para 17 of Sch 7;

(d) an order under s 10(2) of the Matrimonial Causes Act 1973, that is to say following a respondent's application for financial relief after a divorce on the grounds of 2 or 5 years' separation;

(e) an order under s 48(2) of the Civil Partnership Act 2004, which parallels s 10(2) above but in relation to the dissolution of civil partnerships.

3.05 In terms of everyday use of the term 'financial remedy proceedings' in relation to costs, therefore, it includes final financial orders on divorce, nullity and judicial separation and on dissolution of civil partnerships, it includes variation orders, and it excludes all interim orders except interim variation orders. 'Financial remedy proceedings' specifically exclude applications to set aside a final order under FPR r 9.9A.[4]

3.06 Avoidance of disposition orders require separate consideration. They are interim orders in the sense that the purpose of s 37 of the Matrimonial Causes Act and the provisions to the same effect in the Civil Partnership Act and the Matrimonial and Family Proceedings Act is to preserve matrimonial assets until a final order can be made distributing them between the parties. They are not, however, separately mentioned in the list of interim orders which are excluded from FPR r 28.3. That is to say they are not mentioned in r 28.3(4)(b)(i), or in r 9.7(1) which list interim orders. Both lists, however, include the words 'any other form of interim order' and, as avoidance of disposition orders are undoubtedly interim orders, they should be caught by this provision. It is surprising, however, that they are not separately listed, being an important type of order. The same must apply to search orders. Thus the approach we take is that avoidance of disposition orders and search orders are interim orders for which the starting point for consideration for costs is the clean sheet, as such applications made within financial remedy proceedings are undoubtedly family proceedings. This comment is necessary as from time to time the courts have taken the approach that the starting point for costs in such applications is no order.[5]

3.07 So the no order as to costs starting point applies to:

(a) final financial orders in the Matrimonial Causes Act 1973 as defined in s 21 of the Act to include periodical and lump sum payments under s 23

4 FPR r 28.3(9).

5 See, for example, *Imerman v Tchenguiz (Costs)* [2010] EWHC 64 (Fam), [2010] 2 FLR 802 at [37], per Moylan J.

and property adjustment orders under s 24 (s 27 is included in s 21, but excluded by FPR r 28.3(4)(b)). Orders for sale of property (s 24A), pension sharing orders (s 24B) and pension compensation sharing orders (s 24E) are similarly final financial orders. No other Matrimonial Causes Act orders are final financial orders (but see 'variations' below);

(b) final financial orders in the Civil Partnership Act 2004 are described at Sch 5 to that Act at Part 1 (periodical and lump sum payments), Part 2 (property adjustment), Part 3 (sale of property), Part 4 (pension sharing) and Part 4A (pension compensation sharing). These are the only final financial orders which can be made on dissolution of a civil partnership;

(c) by s 17 Matrimonial and Family Proceedings Act 1984, final financial orders after an overseas divorce, annulment or judicial separation are identical to the orders that can be made under the Matrimonial Causes Act 1973 above;

(d) by para 9 of Sch 7 to the Civil Partnership Act 2004, final financial orders following an overseas dissolution, annulment or judicial separation of a civil partnership are the same as those that can be made following a domestic dissolution, etc;

(e) s 10(2) of the Matrimonial Causes Act and the parallel jurisdiction at s 48(2) of the Civil Partnership Act, provide a procedure for an application for divorce, dissolution etc on the basis of 2 or 5 years' separation not to be made final until adequate financial arrangements are made. These provisions are rarely used, but when financial orders are made under them they are the same financial orders as at (a) and (b) above and so are 'final financial orders';

(f) variation and interim variation orders under s 31 of the Matrimonial Causes Act 1973 and under Part 11 of Sch 5 to the Civil Partnership Act 2004.[6] The comment is particularly made in the Practice Direction to Part 28 that r 28.3 does apply to interim variation orders;[7]

(g) the Domestic Proceedings and Magistrates Courts Act 1978 provides for similar orders to be made by magistrates, but as such proceedings are now dealt with in the Family Court, there does not seem to be any continuing role for this Act.

3.08 There are very many sorts of family financial orders which are excluded from this definition of financial remedy proceedings. It will be obvious from what has been said about the definition above that almost all forms of interim maintenance are excluded. Several forms of final order are excluded too, for example: any order for the maintenance of a child under Sch 1 to the Children Act 1989; any order under the remaining jurisdiction of the court in relation to child maintenance, particularly s 8 of the Child Support Act 1991 and the international recognition and enforcement provisions for child maintenance; the Inheritance (Provision for Family and Dependants) Act 1975; and the Trusts

6 As defined in FPR r 9.3.
7 FPR PD 28A [4.2](a).

of Land and Appointment of Trustees Act 1996. All of these proceedings, if commenced in the Family Court or in the Family Division, have the clean sheet starting point for costs.

3.09 Variation orders[8] are available in relation to any order for income payments, or for the sale of property. What is the logic for interim variation orders to be included in the no order for costs regime when no other interim orders are? We take it to be that variation orders are made after the final order has been made, so that the final financial dispositions between the parties have been made, including in relation to costs. A variation to those final financial arrangements, whether by an interim or a final order, should not disturb the final order any more than is necessary, making no order for costs an appropriate general rule.

THE CASE LAW

3.10 Two Court of Appeal judgments in December 2008 and in November 2009, the principal judgment in each case being by Wilson LJ, have set the position in relation to costs at interim stages of financial remedy proceedings and in proceedings linked to financial remedy proceedings (as defined above).[9]

3.11 In *Judge*, the first of the pair of cases, one party contended that the 'no order for costs' regime applied because the proceedings were financial remedy proceedings and so came under the (now) FPR r 28.3(4), while the other party contended that the proceedings were not financial remedy proceedings and so came under the costs follow the event rule in the (now) CPR r 44.2(2). The court found that they were both wrong.

3.12 The facts of the case were that, because a large tax debt (about £14m) which had been shouldered by the husband had not materialised, the wife was applying to set aside orders made at an earlier financial remedy hearing, so that she could pursue a different outcome to the financial remedy proceedings. The court decided that this set aside application was proceedings 'in connection with' a financial remedy but not 'for' a financial remedy ('ancillary relief' as it then was).[10] The wording at FPR r 28.3(4)(b) applies that paragraph of the costs rules to proceedings 'for' a financial remedy as defined in that sub-paragraph.

3.13 Wilson LJ gave his reason for construing the rule narrowly:[11]

> 'I would have been willing to give the phrase "ancillary relief proceedings" in r 2.71(4) a wide, purposive construction so as to include proceedings *in*

8 Under s 31 of the Matrimonial Causes Act 1973 and Part 11 of Sch 5 to the Civil Partnership Act 2004.

9 *Judge v Judge* [2008] EWCA Civ 1458, [2009] 1 FLR 1287 and *Baker v Rowe* [2009] EWCA Civ 1162, [2010] 1 FLR 761.

10 At [51].

11 *Ibid*, emphasis in the original.

> *connection with* ancillary relief as well as *for* ancillary relief if my view had been that such would better reflect the rule-makers' purpose. But such is not my view. The general rule in r 2.71(4)(a) is only a concomitant of the modern approach in applications for ancillary relief that the sum owed by each party in respect of his own costs will be treated as his liability for the purposes of calculating the substantive award.'

Wilson LJ was applying the principle found in the rules since *Calderbank* offers were abolished in financial remedy proceedings. The rule now at r 28.3(4) is intended to prevent the validity of a final financial order being undermined by a costs order which the judge has to make but about which the judge would have no information until after the final order.

3.14 *Baker v Rowe* gave Wilson LJ, as he acknowledged, the opportunity to be more explicit about the reason for the rule and therefore its extent. He quoted from the relevant Government consultation paper[12] the reasons for the abolition of *Calderbank* offers and for the adoption of the rule in financial remedy proceedings that there be no order as to costs:

(a) 'the destabilising effect that costs can have on financial settlements that have been carefully constructed by the court ... the consequences of failing to exceed a *Calderbank* offer can undermine completely the substantive order for ancillary relief that the court has just made';

(b) 'to stress to the parties, and their legal advisers, that running up costs in litigation will serve only to reduce the resources that the parties will have left';

(c) 'to establish the principle that, in the absence of litigation misconduct, the normal approach of the court to costs in ancillary relief proceedings should be to treat them as part of the parties' reasonable financial needs and liabilities'.[13]

3.15 So, to return to Wilson LJ's judgment in *Judge*: the application to set aside the previous financial remedy order was not itself financial remedy proceedings, so the no order as to costs starting point did not apply. However, the proceedings were undoubtedly 'family proceedings' and so the CPR applied as varied by FPR r 28.2, so that the starting point was the clean sheet.[14] The first instance judge had awarded the husband half his costs because the wife's set aside application was unsuccessful, but the size of the 'windfall' to the husband was sufficiently large to make the costs of the proceedings appropriate. The Court of Appeal did not disturb that decision.[15]

12 'Costs in Ancillary Relief Proceedings and Appeals in Family Proceedings' No CP(L) 29/04, Department for Constitutional Affairs October 2004.

13 [2009] EWCA Civ 1162, [2010] 1 FLR 761 at [22].

14 *Ibid* at [53].

15 *Ibid* at [54].

3.16 *Baker v Rowe*[16] was a case in which the beneficial interests in a property of a husband and wife and their daughter and son-in-law were at issue. The daughter and son-in-law intervened in the financial remedy proceedings (then 'ancillary relief') to assert their beneficial interests. At first instance the judge had made a costs order against the son-in-law, who had been found to have no beneficial interest in the property, rejecting the starting point of no order as to costs on the basis that the proceedings relevant to the costs order were Trusts of Land and Appointment of Trustees Act 1996 (TLATA) rather than financial remedy proceedings. At first appeal the circuit judge agreed that the costs should follow the event, treating the TLATA application as governed by the CPR. Wilson LJ then had again to address which of the three starting points contended for in relation to costs was the right one.

3.17 He first dismissed the no order for costs principle: 'it makes no sense to apply the new general rule in ancillary relief proceedings. For in the present case it cannot, of course, be said that to make an order for costs against the son-in-law would destabilise financial arrangements made by the district judge … the proceedings before the district judge were *in connection with* ancillary relief but not *for* ancillary relief'.[17] He then continued: 'Equally, however, the general rule that the unsuccessful party will be ordered to pay the costs of the successful party … was also inapplicable: for the proceedings were family proceedings' and the circuit judge was wrong to have applied the rule to that effect in the CPR.[18] Ward LJ put it: 'Proceedings between interveners do not come within the ambit of the rule. In the result, costs do not follow the event.'[19]

3.18 The judge therefore started with a clean sheet – and in this case 'there was nothing for the judge to write on his sheet other than the potent reasons why the son-in-law should pay the daughter's costs'.[20]

3.19 The judgment continues that had the claim been brought under TLATA then the CPR general rule that costs follow the event would have applied.[21] The implication is that that would also have been the case in relation to a TLATA claim in family proceedings. As we have seen previously,[22] that is no longer the case, as all proceedings in the Family Court are family proceedings and therefore subject to the FPR. TLATA proceedings in the Family Division of the High Court are not, however, family proceedings, and so the CPR will apply to them and the starting point will be that costs follow the event.

3.20 These two Court of Appeal cases set the principle that FPR r 28.3 applies only to proceedings *for* a financial remedy, and in different circumstances other cases have applied that principle. Some examples are as follows:

16 [2009] EWCA Civ 1162, [2010] 1 FLR 761.
17 *Ibid* at [23] emphasis in the original.
18 *Ibid* at [24].
19 *Ibid* at [35].
20 *Ibid* at [25]–[26].
21 *Ibid* at [25].
22 See **1.10**.

(a) Where the wife had also taken proceedings against the parties' children and a company to which the husband had transferred family assets, although the husband was ordered to pay the wife's costs of the financial remedy proceedings, the wife's separate application against the children had been unsuccessful and she was ordered to pay the children's costs. In this case, however, it was a Pyrrhic victory for the husband, as he was also ordered to pay the costs to the wife that the wife was ordered to pay to the children, so that he took the whole costs burden.[23] The husband had forfeited the court's sympathy by his persistent flouting of court orders.[24]

(b) A similar result was reached in a case where a father-in-law was joined to proceedings by the wife's application – unnecessarily as the court found. The wife was ordered to pay the father-in-law's costs, and the husband to pay the wife one-half of the costs she was to pay to the father-in-law. The court considered that the matter would have been more appropriately and more economically dealt with by the father-in-law becoming a witness. Most of the matrimonial assets ended up being expended in costs, provoking the judge (Munby J) to append to his judgment the quotation from Dickens' *Bleak House* where counsel lets the solicitors know that the estate in the case of *Jarndyce v Jarndyce* has been entirely used up in legal costs.[25] We shall return to the issue of excessive costs.[26]

(c) The court found that the wife had failed to show cause, following the husband's application in response to her financial remedies application, why an agreement that had been negotiated between them through solicitors that had settled all financial matters prior to their divorce 20 years earlier should not be made an order of the court. These were not circumstances within the intention of the no order for costs rule: 'I take the view that these proceedings are not financial remedy proceedings of the normal nature to which the no order as to costs rule would apply. These are discrete proceedings. The rationale behind the principle that there is no order for costs usually in financial remedy proceedings is that each party has an interest in

23 *Ben Hashem v Ali Shayif and Radfan Ltd* [2009] EWHC 864 (Fam), [2009] 2 FLR 896, per Munby J.

24 *Ibid* at [18].

25 *KSO v MJO and JMO (PSO intervening)* [2008] EWHC 3031 (Fam), [2009] 1 FLR 1036 at [82]. In this case and in *Ben Hashem v Ali Shayif* costs orders were made, as the judge said 'analogous to what in other Divisions would be thought of as a "*Bullock*" order or in a form somewhat analogous to a "*Sanderson*" order'. He then described both types of order: 'A "*Bullock*" order (see *Bullock v London General Omnibus Company and Others* [1907] 1 KB 264) is an order that the successful defendant recovers his costs as against the claimant, the claimant being entitled to recover as against the unsuccessful defendant not merely his own costs of the action but also the costs he has been ordered to pay the successful defendant. A "*Sanderson*" order (see *Sanderson v Blyth Theatre Company* [1903] 2 KB 533) is an order that there be no order as to costs as between the successful defendant and the claimant but an order that the unsuccessful defendant should pay all the costs of both the claimant and the successful defendant.' *KSO v MJO and JMO* at [58]. Such orders are relevant where there are at least three parties, and were considered appropriate by Munby J in these two family cases. See also **5.108–5.112**.

26 See **3.34–3.37**.

determining how the matrimonial assets should be divided or allocated, and each is usually in a position to meet costs out of his/her allotted share. There are, of course, exceptions, particularly hardship.'[27] A costs order was made against the wife, despite her saying that she would suffer hardship.

(d) In a financial remedy claim based on a marriage in Nigeria which the court found not to have taken place, the claim was inevitably dismissed. It followed that no financial order was made and the costs were dealt with on the clean sheet basis (by reference to *Judge v Judge*). The wife, whose divorce petition was dismissed, was ordered to pay 80% of the husband's costs.[28]

(e) In a costs judgment following financial proceedings for declarations in relation to properties (not therefore financial remedy proceedings) Blair J set out the application of the no order and the clean sheet rules.[29] Having determined, in accordance with the rules and authority, that the clean sheet rule applied to the case before him, he then took the simple approach that Ryder LJ's decision was binding on him that 'The starting point for what are described as "clean sheet" cases is that costs follow the event'.[30] We discuss the disapproval of this approach in **Chapter 2**.

INTERIM HEARINGS

3.21 In a financial remedy case where there is no application for an interim order, no avoidance of disposition application, and no intervener there will still be interim hearings. There will usually be a first appointment and a financial dispute resolution hearing, as provided for in the rules.[31] The judge will not have to construct a final order at those hearings and indeed it is typical that at interim hearings there will be without prejudice offers and no possibility of a final order being made save by consent. It follows that there can be no justification for applying the no order for costs rule at interim hearings, and indeed it is not applied. Costs orders are routinely made at interim hearings, for example to penalise a failure to comply with the rules which has caused costs to be wasted, often because a party is not ready for a hearing or because of a lack of disclosure.

3.22 Just how routinely such interim costs orders can be made is well illustrated by the summary of interim costs orders made in one particular financial remedy case:[32]

> '… there are various other orders in relation to costs which have been made during the course of the litigation:

27 *T v T* [2013] Lexis Citation 25 at [67], per Parker J.
28 *M-T v T (Marriage: Strike-Out)* [2013] EWHC 2061 (Fam), [2014] 1 FLR 1352 at [117]–[141], per Charles J.
29 *W v W and L* [2015] EWHC 1652 (Fam) at [12].
30 *W v W and L* at [14], quoting *Solomon v Solomon* [2013] EWCA Civ 1095 at [22].
31 FPR rr 9.12(1)(a) and 9.15(4).
32 *A v A (No 2) (Costs)* [2007] EWHC 1810 (Fam), [2008] 1 FLR 1428 at [202].

(i) By her order dated 26 March 2004 District Judge Bowman ordered the husband to pay one half of the costs of and occasioned by that application. That half is estimated by the wife's solicitor to amount to some £3,000.

(ii) By her order dated 6 September 2004 District Judge Bowman ordered the husband to pay costs assessed in the sum of £2,552.18 and, in addition, costs (to be assessed if not agreed) claimed in the further sum of £2,065.19.

(iii) By an order dated 22 September 2004 District Judge Bradley ordered the husband to pay costs in the agreed sum of £1,992.87.

(iv) By an order dated 18 February 2005 Singer J ordered the wife to pay £3,000 towards the husband's costs.

(v) By an order dated 10 November 2006 I ordered the husband to pay £3,000 towards the wife's costs.'

Those interim costs orders were undisturbed by the eventual final costs orders in the case.[33]

3.23 Many of the rules in Part 9 of the FPR dealing with financial remedy proceedings include the word 'must' in relation to the parties' duties. Indeed, the rules emphasise that a party who does not comply with the rules can be penalised in costs,[34] and that is usually done at the interim hearing. Also 'Failure to comply with any part of this Practice Direction [27A – Family Proceedings: Court Bundles] may result in … a "wasted costs" order or some other adverse costs order'.[35] Such procedural defaults at interim hearings are also relevant to orders for costs at final hearings, as will be considered shortly.

SUMMARY

3.24 Our intention is to make the position as clear as possible, while providing the background detail to support a simply expressed conclusion. We particularly want to achieve that in relation to this area where the definition of financial remedy proceedings requires reference to several rules and where both the Court of Appeal authorities cited have dealt with the three competing starting points. In summary, the position can be expressed as:

The starting point of no order for costs applies to the substantive final hearing of an application for an order in financial remedy proceedings and (with the exception of interim variation orders) does not apply to any other sort of order in those proceedings, such as interim orders, interim hearings, or final orders setting

33 *Ibid* at [263].
34 FPR PD 9A [3.4].
35 FPR PD 27A [12.1].

aside an application, determining a beneficial share in property or disposing of the application in some other way than by making a final financial order.

THE APPLICATION OF THE RULE

3.25 As discussed at **1.51–1.56**, the factors to be considered when a court is deciding whether or not to make a costs order from the starting position that there will be no order as to costs are set out at FPR r 28.3(6) and (7), that is to say:[36]

> 'where it considers it appropriate to do so because of the conduct of a party in relation to the proceedings (whether before or during them).'

3.26 Thus, by r 28.3(6), conduct in relation to the proceedings is the only factor allowing a departure from the no order for costs rule, although, as we have previously noted, one reason for departure from the no order for costs rule at FPR r 28.3(7)(f) (the financial effects on the parties of any costs order) is not related to conduct. The rule at 28.3(7) is set out at **1.51**, and in summary it states that the factors for the court's consideration in departing from the no order rule are:

(a) lack of compliance with any rule, order or practice direction;

(b) any open offer to settle;

(c) whether a party raised or responded to a particular issue reasonably or not;

(d) 'any other aspect of a party's conduct in relation to proceedings which the court considers relevant; and

(e) the financial effect on the parties of any costs order'.[37]

This is a closed list, but the inclusion of 'any other aspect of a party's conduct' means that there is no restriction on aspects of conduct in relation to the proceedings which can be considered.

Lack of compliance with a rule

3.27 The relevance to the need for an order for costs where there has been a failure to comply with orders or rules is repeated in Part 9 of the FPR: 'In considering whether to make a costs order under rule 28.3(5), the court must have particular regard to the extent to which each party has complied with the requirement to send documents with the financial statement and the explanation given for any failure to comply.'[38] As we have seen in the example from *A v A* above, failures to comply with practice directions, rules and orders at interim stages may result in adverse final costs orders.[39] The Practice Direction to Part 9

36 FPR r 28.3(6).
37 FPR r 28.3(7)(e)–(f).
38 FPR r 9.15(6).
39 *A v A (No 2) (Costs)* [2007] EWHC 1810 (Fam), [2008] 1 FLR 1428 at [202] and [263].

of the FPR specifies that any breach of that Practice Direction may also result in an adverse costs order.[40] Common defaults which have been penalised in costs are: lack of disclosure, whether by failing to file Form E as directed, or by omitting information from it; failing to attend court when so directed; failing to negotiate, perhaps by failing to make an offer in accordance with the practice directions; and failing to file bundles as required with the necessary documents (for which there is the specific warning as to costs consequences at PD 27A [12.1]).

Any open offer to settle

3.28 FPR r 28.3(8) applies to financial remedy proceedings and specifies: 'No offer to settle which is not an open offer to settle is admissible at any stage of the proceedings, except as provided by rule 9.17.' Other than at the FDR, this prohibits the consideration of a *Calderbank* offer (or any without prejudice offer) when determining costs at the final hearing in financial remedy proceedings.[41]

3.29 Rule 9.17 relates to the FDR appointment and requires offers to be filed seven days prior to that appointment. While it is obligatory to make such an offer, it can be either open or without prejudice. If agreement is not reached at the FDR, then details of any without prejudice offers (and indeed their existence) are not admissible[42] and a party who has made such an offer should request that the offer letter held in the court file be returned at the end of the FDR.[43]

3.30 An offer letter written for these purposes should be marked simply 'without prejudice' since it cannot have the effect of a *Calderbank* letter.

3.31 Although no without prejudice offer made at any stage of the proceedings will be considered in relation to costs at a final hearing in financial remedy proceedings,[44] open offers are required to be made not less than 14 days before a final hearing.[45] It follows that the judge at a final hearing will, assuming this requirement has been complied with, know the position of each party. The judge will be able to take into account that position, and any resulting costs order, when determining the final order. This is of course different from the previous position when parties could rely on without prejudice offers which, when revealed, might sabotage a carefully constructed final order.[46]

40 FPR PD 9A [3.4] 'Any breach of the Practice Direction or the pre-application protocol annexed to it will be taken into account by the court when deciding whether to depart from the general rule as to costs.' The general rule being no order as to costs, this paragraph is saying in a roundabout way that a breach may be penalised in costs.

41 PD 28A para 4.3.

42 *Re D (Minors) (Conciliation: Disclosure of Information)* [1993] Fam 231, [1993] 1 FLR 932, CA at [236] per Sir Thomas Bingham MR.

43 FPR r 9.17(5).

44 FPR r 28.3(8).

45 FPR r 9.28.

46 See the comments of Wilson LJ previously quoted in *Baker v Rowe* [2009] EWCA Civ 1162, [2010] 1 FLR 761 at [22].

3.32 There has been some recent debate about the merits of re-introducing *Calderbank* letters to financial remedy proceedings.[47] In *J v J*, Mostyn J acknowledged this debate and made his own views crystal clear, saying: 'For my part I will fight its reintroduction to the last ditch. In my opinion it would be retrograde and unconscionable to allow a carefully crafted disposition to be turned upside down by virtue of a without prejudice letter produced after judgment has been given.'[48] His concern was that the court's decision, 'which will usually be strongly influenced by considerations of need, is not undone and subverted by a costs order'.

3.33 The comparative lack of reported cases dealing with costs orders made to reflect the fact that a party has achieved or bettered their open offer leaves it unclear whether or not parties are generally inclined to make realistic open offers so that such offers are rarely bettered, or whether courts are not being asked to take open offers into account in relation to costs orders.

Costs control

3.34

> 'Plus ça change …'

In a financial remedy case as long ago as 1990 when deploring the waste of joint assets through unnecessary expenditure on litigation, and setting out a list of ways by which such waste could be reduced in future cases, the judge concluded:[49]

> 'I am aware that many issues have been raised and much evidence adduced with which I have not considered it necessary to deal in this judgment. This is and was at all times an essentially straightforward case and if they are united in nothing else this husband and wife must be united in bitterly regretting the dissipation of their assets which has so unfortunately occurred.'

3.35 Whether matters have improved since must be doubtful. The language of judges in such cases has, though, become stronger:

(a) In 2007 Munby J dealt with a case where 'Directly or indirectly this family has incurred costs amounting in all to £1,113,207.29 in fighting over matrimonial assets which at the end of the day I have found to amount to only £2,669,715 and which even if the wife's case on sham had succeeded would still have been worth only £4,290,315. So some 41.5% of the matrimonial assets have gone in costs.'[50] He went on to say: 'That is a heavy price for

47 Wilson T *Something must be done – will a partial return to Calderbank fit the Bill (or at least reduce it)?* Family Law Week, 12 February 2015.

48 *Ibid* at [55].

49 *Evans v Evans* [1990] 1 FLR 319 at [329], per Booth J.

50 *A v A (No 2) (Costs)* [2007] EWHC 1810 (Fam), [2008] 1 FLR 1428 at [269].

the wife to have to pay, but it is the consequence of the misplaced zeal with which she chose to conduct a case built on exiguous foundations. I only hope that others will pay heed and that similar cases will in future be pursued with more circumspection.'[51]

(b) The following year the same judge heard another case with excessive costs and expressed himself more strongly: 'The present case is a sobering, and for me deeply saddening, example. If, instead of spending – squandering – over £430,000 in costs, the wife and the husband had been able to resolve their differences at a more modest and, dare I say it, more seemly level of costs, there might very well have been enough left in the matrimonial "pot" to house the wife and children and to enable the children to remain at their school, whilst still leaving something more than a mere consolation prize over for the husband. As it is, it is hard to see much being left from the wreck, not least after the trustee in bankruptcy has had his costs, expenses and remuneration … Something must be done about the problems highlighted by this and by too many similar cases. We simply cannot go on as we are. The expenditure of costs on the scale exemplified by this and by too many other such cases is a scandal which must somehow be brought under control.'[52]

(c) But still in 2014 the same problems are seen. Mostyn J found at the end of a final hearing that 'The upshot will be that from the pre-costs starting point of £2,885,000 the wife will receive £1,123,500 (38.9% of the assets); the lawyers and experts will receive £920,000 (31.9%); and the husband £841,500 (29.2%). These figures speak for themselves. Such a result should not be allowed to happen again.'[53]

3.36 Solicitors wish to make a profit from their business. Counsel too. Both are happy to be able to charge high fees. In divorce cases feelings may run sufficiently high for clients to be determined on victory at all costs, and lawyers can service those wishes. To a considerable extent costs can be controlled by detailed judicial examination of the evidence available at an interim stage when an application is being made for an expert, or an avoidance of disposition order, or for a further 'schedule of deficiencies' (not a document found in the FPR), or for witness statements, and so on. After all 'Active case management includes … considering whether the likely benefits of taking a particular step justify the costs of taking it'.[54] But in practice courts do not usually take the time at interim hearings to examine cases in sufficient detail to exercise such cost control. Judges at FDRs are often under time pressures. It would not be difficult to tighten up procedures to prevent such enormously wasteful litigation, by adopting some of the Jackson reforms introduced in civil proceedings such as a fixed costs regime, or by applying the tighter control of experts that applies in children proceedings to financial remedy proceedings, and other proposals are not far to seek. Mostyn J in *J v J* quoted above suggests fixed pricing for each of the three stages of a

51 *Ibid* at [271].
52 *KSO v MJO and JMO* [2008] EWHC 3031 (Fam), [2009] 1 FLR 1036 at [80]–[81].
53 *J v J* [2014] EWHC 3654 (Fam), [2015] 1 Costs LO 31 at [58].
54 FPR r 1.4(2)(i).

financial remedy case – up to first appointment, up to FDR hearing and up to final hearing – and a costs cap set by the court.[55]

3.37 There are instances of judges taking initiatives to control costs, or being encouraged to do so –

(a) Peter Jackson J, when giving permission to appeal a final financial order, to limit the costs that could be claimed by the appellant wife on appeal to £5,000. He was aware that her appeal costs were already £12,500 'a sum that is completely disproportionate to the issues in the case'.[56] His intention was 'to prevent what the district judge described as a haemorrhaging of money'.[57] That is one way of attempting to constrain unnecessary expenditure on costs, where the judge had decided that permission to appeal was merited in the case before him.

(b) Holman J had before him an application where the issue between the parties was maintenance of £4,000 pa and the wife's costs were £30,000 plus VAT before trial.[58] He described his approach to the management of disproportionate costs: 'I have repeatedly today encouraged, urged, cajoled and ultimately hectored these parties to try to resolve their differences.' He was not able to say that it had worked.

(c) In *Wyatt v Vince*, after the case had been to the Supreme Court and was before Cobb J for the final order to be made, Mr Vince wanted the published judgment to show that the whole of the lump sum to be paid to W would be swallowed up by her costs. The judge declined to do so because the sum due to the wife's solicitors was not yet certain.[59]

Nonetheless, in cases like that where the husband said he had to sell his Ferrari to meet his costs, where the judge described the costs as 'horrific' at well over £1 million,[60] it may be felt that if wealthy people choose to spend their money on lawyers rather than Ferraris then it will be hard to stop them.

3.38 Nonetheless, in response no doubt at least in part to Munby P's statement that 'something must be done' there is since 27 May 2019, the following addition to paragraph 4.4 of FPR PD27A:

> 'The court will take a broad view of conduct for the purposes of this rule [28.3] and will generally conclude that to refuse openly to negotiate reasonably and responsibly will amount to conduct in respect of which the court will consider making an order for costs. This includes in a "needs" case where the applicant litigates unreasonably resulting in the costs incurred by each party becoming disproportionate to the award made by the court. Where an order for costs is made at an interim stage the court

55 *J v J* [2014] EWHC 3654 (Fam), [2015] 1 Costs LO 31 at [13]–[18].
56 *TF v FF* [2013] EWHC 390 (Fam) at [16].
57 *Ibid* at [17].
58 *EDG v RR* [2015] EWHC 3097 (Fam).
59 [2016] EWHC 1368 at [15].
60 *AF v MF, OF and AB* [2016] EWFC 65, Moor J at [42].

will not usually allow any resulting liability to be reckoned as a debt in the computation of the assets.'

This addition does two things:

— While entirely consistent with rule 28.3(7) it specifies a broader scope than might otherwise have been thought to be the case by introducing a requirement to negotiate 'reasonably and responsibly', and

— It excludes any award of interim costs from a party's schedule of liabilities at a final hearing.

Pursuing or defending a case unreasonably

3.39 The point though, as far as the individual case is concerned, is that when a party has unreasonably pursued or contested a particular issue they will suffer a costs penalty (unless, of course, the other side has been equally unreasonable). In many cases one party's misconduct is cancelled out by the other's so that there is no order as to costs. Moylan J concluded lengthy and complex proceedings with a decision that 'Both failed to abide by their obligations under the overriding objective. They both pursued and contested issues which should not have been pursued or contested and both made open offers to settle which are significantly different from the terms of my judgment … In my judgment they are both to blame and there is no sufficient discriminating feature to justify one paying the other's costs.'[61] This is an example of a not uncommon outcome by which there is no order for costs.

3.40 We discuss later in connection with standard and indemnity costs the effect of conduct in relation to the proceedings on the costs orders made.[62] Included there are details of cases in which costs were awarded because of unreasonableness in pursuing or defending them. Unreasonableness is shown through those cases to include:

(a) pursuing a case which lacks any adequate evidence;

(b) pursuing a case on the off-chance that evidence might turn up;

(c) defending or pursuing a case dishonestly (where the party is found to have been dishonest); and

(d) defending a case when the evidence against is so strong that it should have been accepted.

Any other aspect of conduct

3.41 We are not able to identify a case in which it has been found necessary to refer to this provision. Failing to comply with rules, orders and practice

61 *Evans v Evans* [2013] EWHC 506 (Fam), [2013] 2 FLR 999 at [204].

62 See **8.79–8.114**.

directions, and pursuing or defending a case, or an aspect of it, unreasonably, seem to be broad enough provisions to cover the cases.

The financial effects on the parties

3.42 This consideration is regularly referred to in judgments as it is integral to the final financial order. Mostyn J put it this way: 'Subparagraph (f) is highly important. This requires the court to ensure that its primary disposition, which will usually be strongly influenced by considerations of need, is not undone and subverted by a costs order.'[63] In the case before him where the judge would otherwise have made a costs order against the husband of £276,750 because of his litigation misconduct, consideration of the financial effect on him meant that the husband was ordered instead to pay the wife's costs in the smaller sum of £50,000.

3.43 Charles J, in a typically careful consideration of the effect on a wife of making a costs order against her when she had been unsuccessful on appeal, decided that he could make such an order without upsetting the original final order by increasing the husband's charge against the property in which the wife was to continue living.[64]

3.44 In a case where the wife had failed in her attempt to set aside a previous agreement, having regard to r 28.3(7)(f) Parker J expressed concern about ordering the wife to pay all the husband's costs. But as the wife had capital of £1m, albeit tied up in property, the judge concluded 'I understand the wife has no liquid capital but she is capital rich, and she chose to bring this application so I am afraid she must pay the costs on the standard basis'.[65] This case was not one, however, where the court was making a final order, so there was no requirement to consider the overall effect of making the costs order on the division of the assets.

ISSUE-BASED COSTS ORDERS

3.45 At the conclusion of a case, costs in relation to interim issues may need to be to be considered as well as costs in relation to the final outcome. Indeed in financial remedy proceedings as the regime is for no costs at final order but a clean sheet in relation to interim matters, it may be more likely that costs of interim matters will fall to be dealt with at the conclusion of the proceedings. Equally it may be the position that there was merit in part of a case, but that another part of the case was unreasonably pursued. In such cases an order may be

63 *J v J* [2014] EWHC 3654 (Fam), [2015] 1 Costs LO 31 at [55].

64 *V v V (Ancillary relief: pre-nuptial agreement)* [2011] EWHC 3230 (Fam), [2012] 1 FLR 1315 at [110]–[116].

65 *T v T* [2013] Lexis Citation 25 at [72].

made for a party to pay some part of the costs of another party. This is an issue-based costs order.

3.46 CPR r 44.2(6) and (7), which apply to family proceedings including financial remedy proceedings, provide as follows:

(6) The orders which a court may make under this rule include an order that a party must pay –
  (a) a proportion of another party's costs;
  (b) a stated amount in respect of another party's costs;
  (c) costs from or until a certain date only;
  (d) costs incurred before proceedings have begun;
  (e) costs relating to particular steps taken in the proceedings;
  (f) costs relating only to a distinct part of the proceedings; and
  (g) interest on costs from or until a certain date, including a date before judgment.

(7) Before the court considers making an order under paragraph (6)(f), it will consider whether it is practicable to make an order under paragraph (6)(a) or (c) instead.

3.47 Where a party has made an application within the proceedings, for example for a set aside order, for enforcement, for an injunction or committal, and the court has found that the application had no merit, then the issue of costs can be dealt with for that discrete issue on the clean sheet basis, separately from the overall outcome of the proceedings. When, however, the question is whether part of a party's case was unreasonably put forward, and as a result costs were increased by that party, even though the party may have been successful overall, the court may consider an issue-based costs order.

3.48 Eleanor King J has reviewed[66] the precedents in non-family civil proceedings for making issue-based costs orders: having first reviewed cases in which judges had exercised caution as to how much of the costs might be allocated to particular issues, she then followed the authority of the Court of Appeal:[67]

> 'Separate assessments of the costs relating to individual issues are likely to be complex and expensive: difficult to carry out in circumstances in which there are common factors which spread over a number of issues … A more convenient method, while keeping in mind the issue-based approach, is to assess all the costs together and then apply a proportion which reflects the fact that one party has won on some issues and lost on the other issues.'

The Court of Appeal then held that such an approach is not only convenient but required:[68]

66 *M v M (Costs)* [2009] EWHC 1941 (Fam), [2010] 1 FLR 256.
67 *National Westminster Bank v Kotonou* [2007] EWCA Civ 223 at [22], per Chadwick LJ.
68 *Ibid* at [23], per Chadwick LJ.

'... if practicable, the court must make an order under paragraph 6(a).[69] The judge indicated ... that he had decided to make ... an issue-based order ... but, to translate that split into simple percentages of the overall costs. That would obviate the need for a detailed assessment of the separate costs of each issue. That, as it seems to me, is not only a proper approach, it is the approach which is positively required by the Rules.'

3.49 Eleanor King J first decided that the financial remedy case before her was suitable for an issue-based costs order in relation to one matter (the wife's application for a transfer of shares in the husband's company to her should never have been made) but also bore in mind 'the backdrop of W's approach to the litigation as a whole'.[70] Thus a schedule of costs broken down by issues was not required, and an issue-based costs order was made requiring the wife to pay 20% of the husband's total costs. The judge then went further than the Court of Appeal in minimising the costs of assessment by stating the percentage as a fixed sum (£175,000) with the intention that detailed assessment would then not be necessary.[71]

3.50 In a subsequent financial remedies case Eleanor King J again reviewed the law governing the making of issue-based costs orders.[72] Her judgment in that case draws together comprehensively yet concisely the relevant rules and case-law.[73] At the conclusion the husband was ordered to pay one-third of the wife's costs, again expressed as a sum of money (£55,000) to avoid the necessity for detailed assessment.[74]

3.51 The conclusion of her analysis was that 'The court, following the approach of Chadwick LJ in *National Westminster Bank plc v Kotonou*, suggests the following approach:

(i) decide whether or not this is a case calling for an issue-based costs order and if so:

(ii) make the order for costs, if practical under CPR 44.2(6)(a) or (c) by expressing the order by way of a percentage or that the costs are to run to or from a particular date.'[75]

Although both these judgments are first instance decisions they are based on a thorough review of the law and have not been the subject of appeal. They continue to represent the best authority on issue-based costs orders. The Court of Appeal endorsed the making of issue-based costs orders in financial remedy proceedings without doubting the principle in *Lemmens v Brouwers*[76]. In that

69 Now CPR r 44.2(6)(a) – an order that a party must pay 'a proportion of another party's costs'.
70 *M v M (Costs)* at [46].
71 *Ibid* at [65].
72 *GS v L (No 2) (Financial Remedies: Costs)* [2011] EWHC 2116 (Fam), [2013] 1 FLR 407.
73 *Ibid* at [24]–[33].
74 *Ibid* at [46].
75 *Ibid* at [33].
76 [2018] EWCA Civ 2963.

case the issue-based consideration of the effect on the wife's costs of the husband filing a 'deliberately misleading' Form E had led to an order for the husband to pay £30,000 of the wife's costs of £127,000, which was unsuccessfully appealed.

3.52 In some cases the issues are simply too numerous and interwoven to allow such an approach. In a monolithic judgment in which 52 paragraphs were devoted to costs,[77] Sir Peter Singer contemplated the complexities caused by some of the costs being subject to the no order rule and some being subject to the clean sheet rule and decided that 'it would be impractical to attempt an application-by-application or issue-by-issue analysis and assessment of the costs of this hydra-headed litigation' and a broad brush approach was appropriate.[78] He also made the point that the practical difference of the two regimes would make little difference to the exercise of his discretion, since the case he was considering was one in which 'one party hatches a wholly deceptive presentation, pursues it persistently to the conclusion and … should expect no quarter from the court when it comes to costs'.[79]

PRACTICALITIES OF COSTS ORDERS

3.53 In order to take costs into account the court has to know what they are. Estimates of costs are required at interim hearings[80] on Form H, and at the final hearing on the rather more detailed (and time-consuming) Form H1, which requires costs to be divided into five sections: before Form A, between Form A and FDR, between FDR and final hearing, estimated costs of final hearing and costs of implementation.[81] Both forms require the amount paid and the amount still owed by the client to be shown, so that the party's outstanding liability for costs is clear to the court. 'The purpose of this rule is to enable the court to take account of the impact of each party's costs liability on their financial situations.'[82]

3.54 The court may decide to make a costs order, in accordance with the regime discussed in this chapter. But if no costs order is made, what should the court's approach be to costs liabilities in relation to the assets and other liabilities the parties have which are to be divided between them at the conclusion of a financial remedies case? There are several possibilities:

(a) The assets are divided excluding the costs liabilities and the costs left to lie where they fall for each side.

(b) The costs still owed are included in the parties' liabilities before division.

77 *Joy v Joy-Morancho and Others (No 3)* [2015] EWHC 2507 (Fam), [2016] 1 FLR 815 at [190]–[242].
78 *Ibid* at [196].
79 *Ibid* at [225].
80 FPR r 9.27.
81 See statutory materials for copies of the forms at **Appendix 1**.
82 FPR PD 9A [3.2].

(c) The costs paid are added back in to the parties' assets, and the amount of costs still owed that would be recoverable on a costs order being made in each parties' favour are excluded (the amount of costs owed that would not be recoverable still being included as a liability) – the *Leadbeater* approach.[83]

3.55 In *Leadbeater* the argument for the wife, accepted by the judge, was that if costs liabilities that might be recoverable through a costs order were not added back (in relation to costs paid) or were deducted (in relation to liabilities) then it would pre-empt any decision the court might make about a costs order: 'If, in estimating the wife's present capital position, and in particular what money she has available to buy a house, I left out of account the money she has already spent on account of costs and deducted her future liability to her solicitors for her costs then, whatever order I might then make by way of an order for costs – and of course as yet I have heard no argument on costs – I would be anticipating that order.'[84] The judge proceeded to:

– add back into her assets the wife's costs paid of £10,000;

– deduct the amount of the future liability for costs which would not be recoverable under a costs order (estimated as £5,000 out of her £22,000 costs debt);

– include in the wife's schedule of assets the remainder of that liability (£17,000).

Ironically, perhaps, the judge then did not make an order for costs, as far as the reported judgment records.

3.56 There are several problems with the *Leadbeater* approach, and it has been increasingly disapproved to the extent that it may probably be regarded as dead. The problems include:

(a) What is the appropriate amount to deduct from the costs debt as irrecoverable costs? £17,000 is 77% of £22,000, rather higher than the conventional 70% if costs were to be awarded on the standard basis, but lower than the 90% that has been said to be the recovery level on the indemnity basis.[85] However, we emphasise that to take a percentage approach in this way is not in accordance with the rules for summary assessment.

(b) The general rule now is that there should be no order for costs. Is there any reason why that general rule should not be applied to the calculation of assets and liabilities which would mean that costs paid are not added back and costs owed are included as a liability?

(c) If, following FPR r 28.3(6) and (7), some conduct reason is found for a costs order, then that order can be made and considered at the same time that the

83 *Leadbeater v Leadbeater* [1985] FLR 789 at [794], per Balcombe J.

84 *Ibid.*

85 See, for example, *W v W and L* [2015] EWHC 1652 (Fam) at [7], per Blair J.

proper division of the assets is being made. Since the risk of sabotage to a final order by a *Calderbank* offer has been removed, the court will have full costs information at that time.

(d) In a case where no costs order is made the result of a *Leadbeater* approach is to calculate assets on a false basis: the costs will actually have to be paid by the party. As Thorpe LJ put it: 'There is therefore an artificiality in the practice and judges must be careful not to lose sight of the reality.'[86]

3.57 Thorpe LJ concluded the paragraph in which he referred to the artificiality of the *Leadbeater* approach by commenting that 'the adoption of the *Leadbeater* mechanism should never be automatic. It is probably more useful in cases where one party has paid money out and the other has obtained credit by offering security or where the court suspects some element of contrivance or artificiality in the arrangements which one party has set up'. In other words, such an approach should be restricted to a small group of cases.

3.58 In *GW v RW* Mostyn J was more blunt: 'It seems to me that if the starting point is no order as to costs then the *Leadbeater* technique should be abandoned. Costs paid should not be added back, and costs outstanding should be included as a debt in the schedule of assets.'[87] We suggest that in an era when the general rule is no order for costs, where the costs are available and known to the court and when the only offers relevant to costs are open offers, the approach in *Leadbeater* is outmoded and unlikely to be relevant.

3.59 The question remains as to whether the costs still owed at the time of the final hearing should be treated as liabilities for the purpose of dividing the assets. If the liabilities are roughly equal then there is no inequity in including them in the overall assets, and indeed it is an efficient way of identifying the actual capital that the parties will be left with. But, if one party has a costs liability two or three times as much as the other, then the effect of including the liabilities in the assets will be to give the party with the higher costs what has been described as a 'back door costs order' in their favour.[88] Thus, if one party spends £40,000 on costs and the other party spends £120,000, on a 50% asset split the one who has spent less will be paying £40,000 towards the costs of the one who has spent more.

3.60 A separate inequity arises if only the costs owed are excluded, and one party has paid their costs and the other one has not. The effect would be that the one who has paid their costs would receive a backdoor costs order of half their costs. The solution would seem to be that while it is more convenient (only one sum is needed) to include costs paid and costs owed in the assets (and liabilities) for division where the parties' costs are similar, where the costs are significantly

86 *Wells v Wells* [2002] EWCA Civ 476, [2002] 2 FLR 97 at [31].

87 *GW v RW (Financial Provision: Departure from Equality)* [2003] 2 FLR 108, [2003] 2 FCR 289 at [101].

88 HHJ Martin Cardinal in his *Matrimonial Costs* (Jordans Family Law, 2nd edn, 2007) inveighs against this at p 84.

different the costs paid and owed should be excluded before the division is made, and the result reviewed taking the parties' costs liabilities into account.

3.61 The difficulties with this area in producing a fair final order have surfaced in several recent cases. What is to be done when a court wishes to provide a party with a home but can only do so by making a lump sum order to that party which includes their costs: otherwise there will not be enough left for the purpose? Holman J has held that 'If I were to order her to pay to him a lump sum with which to pay off those debts that would be tantamount to making an order for costs in his favour, which could not be justifiable.'[89] In that case the judge simply decided that the husband had no need to own his own home so that the fact that the lump sum would be too small for him to do so was not relevant.

3.62 However that will not usually be the case. Francis J considered two cases where the same problem arose.[90] He identified the issue before him:

> 'People cannot litigate on the basis that they are bound to be reimbursed for their costs. The wife has chosen to instruct one of the highest regarded and consequently one of the most expensive firms of solicitors in the country. Whilst I have no doubt that the representation has, at all times, been of the highest quality, no one enters litigation simply expecting a blank cheque. A judge, in a position as I am now in, is facing the invidious position of seeing his or her order undermined by the extent of litigation loan or costs liability. If, here, I make no provision for the wife's costs or litigation loan, then half of the Duxbury fund will be wiped out and she will be left with insufficient money to manage, according to my assessment. Doing the best that I can to recognise that her costs are excessive, to recognise that she has presented an unreasonable case in financial remedy proceedings but to recognise that her Duxbury fund cannot be completely undermined and that the husband's offer was too low, I am going to add to the lump sum, already referred to above, an additional £400,000 which is a little bit less than half of the total sum due.'[91]

The judge entered into no consideration of the costs rules applying to financial remedy cases. He took a pragmatic approach which was, if not the opposite, at least on markedly different principles from the reasoning in the judgment of Holman J above.

3.63 In the other case, Francis J prefaced his judgment with the only too common diatribe against the excessive costs incurred by the parties in disputing the case,[92] which were almost £1.1 million in what was by no means a 'big money' case. The subject of costs was not however referred to in the division of assets

89 *Daga v Bangur* [2018] EWFC 91 at [67].
90 *WG v HG* [2018] EWFC 84, [2019] 4 WLR 16 and *ABX v SBX* [2018] EWFC 81.
91 *WG v HG* [2018] EWFC 84, [2019] 4 WLR 16 at [91].
92 *ABX v SBX* [2018] EWFC 81 at [2].

and liabilities: indeed the table of assets did not separately list the costs.[93] Francis J commented on the fact that the wife would have needed to be more cautious in running up her costs if the rule in *Calderbank* still applied:'I recognise all of the pitfalls that were associated with the *Calderbank* principles, but I fear that there are cases where litigants now feel able to continue without the sanction of costs, save in cases of serious litigation misconduct.'

3.64 There is a clear tension between the FPR rule at final hearings in financial remedy proceedings that there will be no order for costs, and the ability for a court to make an order providing for capital needs without effectively ordering one party to pay the other's costs. Some seek the return of the *Calderbank* rule, or something like it.[94] This is an area where the rules can be expected to develop before long.

93 *Ibid* at [52].
94 See discussion of the rule in **Chapter 2**.

CHAPTER 4

Costs in Other Types of Proceedings

ALTERNATIVE DISPUTE RESOLUTION (ADR)

4.01 Part 3 of the FPR is headed 'Non-court dispute resolution' (NCDR). It applies to private law children applications and to financial remedy applications, including applications made under Sch 1 to the Children Act.[1] Under the rules in Part 3 parties are required, in those cases, to take part in a Family Mediation Information and Assessment Meeting (MIAM) before issuing an application. The requirement for parties to engage in NCDR originates in s 10 of the Children and Families Act 2014: 'Before making a relevant family application, a person must attend a family mediation information and assessment meeting'. There is a long list of excuses for not taking part in a MIAM[2] but if the court finds that an excuse is not a valid one it 'will direct the applicant, or direct the parties, to attend a MIAM'.[3]

1 FPR PD3A [12].
2 FPR r 3.8.
3 FPR r 3.10(2).

4.02 The wording of the statute and of the rule is strong: a person 'must' attend a MIAM, unless they have a valid reason for not doing so, and if they have not attended and have no such reason the court 'will' direct the party to attend one unless in the circumstances of the case the application is exempted from a MIAM. These rules came into force in April 2014, and there has been no reported case of a MIAM being enforced or, more specifically, of consequences being imposed by the courts for failing to attend a MIAM. An obvious consequence would be a penalty in costs, as has typically been the case in civil proceedings, and indeed in family proceedings outside the MIAM procedure, and we await an authority.

4.03 Part 9 of the FPR provides for judge-led mediation in financial remedy proceedings in the form of the Financial Dispute Resolution (FDR) hearing.[4] The FPR however provide no general power to order parties to engage in NCDR. Thus, if the court considers that NCDR is appropriate at a later stage in the proceedings, or in proceedings outside the scope of Part 3 and Part 9, there is no power to order it.

4.04 The power in Part 3 to order parties to engage in non-court mediation is a new one which has no parallel in the CPR. In the absence of any rules of court a body of case-law has grown up in civil proceedings which acknowledges both the fact that the court has no power to order such mediation and, on the other hand, the court's role in encouraging parties to engage in NCDR. A principal means of encouragement is the threat of a penalty in costs if a party unreasonably refuses to engage in NCDR.

4.05 In *Halsey v Milton Keynes General NHS Trust; Steel v Joy*[5] Dyson LJ said at [19]: 'It seems to us that to oblige truly unwilling parties to refer their disputes to mediation would be to impose an unacceptable obstruction on their right of access to the court.' It is presumably considered that the requirement to participate in a MIAM has enough exceptions to provide a balance between allowing access to justice and ensuring that the access is reasonably required.

4.06 In *Halsey* the question of a penalty in costs was raised, though not imposed. In considering in relation to costs the conduct of a party who refuses mediation the court held:

> '[16] … factors which may be relevant to the question whether a party has unreasonably refused ADR will include (but are not limited to) the following: (a) the nature of the dispute; (b) the merits of the case; (c) the extent to which other settlement methods have been attempted; (d) whether the costs of the ADR would be disproportionately high; (e) whether any delay in setting up and attending the ADR would have been prejudicial; and (f) whether the ADR had a reasonable prospect of success … We wish to emphasise that in many cases no single factor will be decisive, and that these factors should not be regarded as an exhaustive checklist.'

4 See r 9.17.
5 [2004] EWCA Civ 576, [2004] 1 WLR 3002.

In 2013 the Court of Appeal said that these factors had 'stood the test of time'.[6]

4.07 In *Halsey* the court went on to consider the effect of a party ignoring the court's 'encouragement' to engage in mediation. Where a successful party refuses to agree to ADR despite the court's encouragement: 'that is a factor which the court will take into account when deciding whether his refusal was unreasonable. The court's encouragement may take different forms. The stronger the encouragement, the easier it will be for the unsuccessful party to discharge the burden of showing that the successful party's refusal was unreasonable.'[7]

4.08 In fact, in *PGF II SA v OMFS Co 1 Ltd* a costs order was made against the party who had failed to respond to a proposal for mediation. Briggs LJ said at [34]: 'silence in the face of an invitation to participate in ADR is, as a general rule, of itself unreasonable, regardless whether an outright refusal, or a refusal to engage in the type of ADR requested, or to do so at the time requested, might have been justified by the identification of reasonable grounds.'

4.09 It follows that the inducement, or 'coercion' as Mostyn J calls it in *Mann v Mann*,[8] that is available to the court is to penalise in costs an unreasonable refusal to engage in NCDR. The court's power to do this has been recently re-emphasised by an addition to FPR PD28A paragraph 4.4.[9]

4.10 In *Mann v Mann* the court was confronted with the position where, in an application to enforce an order for periodical payments, neither Part 3 nor Part 9 of the FPR applied so that there was no power to order mediation. Mostyn J, however, commented at [24] that there ought to be such a power in other cases too, including enforcement proceedings. This was a case where the parties had agreed in principle to mediate, but then had failed to do so, with fault on both sides. The judge ordered at [36]:

> '(i) If either party considers that the case is unsuitable for resolution by ADR, that party shall be prepared to justify that decision at the conclusion of the enforcement proceedings, should the judge consider that such means of resolution were appropriate, when he is considering the appropriate costs order to make.
>
> (ii) The party considering the case unsuitable for ADR shall, not less than 7 days before the commencement of the adjourned enforcement hearing, file with the court a witness statement without prejudice save as to costs, giving reasons upon which they rely for saying the case was unsuitable.'

4.11 In a financial remedies case Eleanor King J heard an appeal in relation to the amount of the husband's bonus payments that a wife should receive.[10] Mostyn

6 *PGF II SA v OMFS Co 1 Ltd* [2013] EWCA Civ 1288 at [1], per Briggs LJ.
7 *Halsey* at [29].
8 [2014] EWHC 537 (Fam), [2014] 2 FLR 928.
9 See **3.37** above.
10 *H v W (Cap on Wife's Share of Bonus Payments)* [2013] EWHC 4105 (Fam), [2015] 1 FLR 75.

J had, at a previous hearing, encouraged the parties to negotiate an agreement. The husband was successful at the appeal hearing and Eleanor King J found that the wife had been unreasonable in her approach to negotiation. At the subsequent costs hearing the judge took account both of the husband's success at appeal and of the wife's unreasonableness in relation to mediation in ordering the wife to pay the husband's costs of the appeal.[11] In the High Court at least, the fact that the MIAM procedure does not apply does not prevent those who unreasonably refuse to take part in mediation from being penalised in costs.

4.12 The Court of Appeal has operated an ADR scheme for many years prior to the introduction of MIAMs. While that scheme itself is free of charge to the parties, they may well incur legal costs in relation to it. In deciding to make no order for costs in a case in which a husband caused the wife some limited additional costs by vacillating in relation to the mediation, the court has commented that 'if the parties arrive at a compromise, a clear compromise, within the mediation process, then that compromise will be robustly upheld by this court'.[12]

4.13 One would expect that if a party considered NCDR unsuitable for their case, the statement justifying their position would either consider the factors listed in *Halsey*,[13] or would have recourse to one or more of the MIAM exceptions at FPR r 3.8 (domestic violence, child protection, urgency, residence abroad, one party is a child, etc). This is a developing area of law. It might be suggested that there is an anomaly between the FPR and the CPR: the former Rules contain a procedure for non-binding mediation at Part 3, and no procedure for binding arbitration; the latter have a procedure for binding arbitration (Part 62) and none for mediation. We are not able to see the basis for this difference.

Arbitration

4.14 The primary legislation on arbitration is the Arbitration Act 1996 which applies to civil proceedings including family proceedings.[14] Arbitration receives a Part of the CPR to itself (Part 62), but there is currently no reference to arbitration in the FPR. That has not prevented arbitration in family financial disputes from becoming established; and indeed there are good reasons in many cases why arbitration will be the most appropriate form of dispute resolution. It has the advantages of being final, private and probably cheaper than taking a case to a final court hearing.

11 *H v W (Cap on Wife's Share of Bonus Payments) (No 2)* [2014] EWHC 3411 (Fam), [2015] 2 FLR 153.
12 *Rothwell v Rothwell* [2008] EWCA Civ 1600, [2009] 2 FLR 96 at [8], per Thorpe LJ.
13 At **4.06**.
14 See *BC v BG* [2019] EWFC 7, [2019] 2 FLR 337 and *H v W* [2019] EWHC 1897 (Fam), Clare Ambrose sitting as a Deputy High Court Judge.

4.15 There are now two sets of Practice Guidance issued by the President of the Family Division, one for arbitration in financial remedy proceedings[15] and one (principally) for Children Act proceedings.[16] There is however no reference to costs in either Guidance.

4.16 The Institute of Family Law Arbitrators (IFLA) has devised the Family Law Arbitration Scheme (FLAS) to enable parties to bind themselves to the outcome of arbitration in the same way as in the scheme in Part 62 of the CPR. In *S v S* an arbitration decision settling finances on divorce was submitted to the court to be made into a consent order. In that case the parties simply wished the order to be made in accordance with the arbitrated decision, but the President considered cases in which a party might oppose an arbitration decision being made into an order and said that: 'In the absence of some very compelling countervailing factor(s), the arbitral award should be determinative of the order the court makes.'[17]

4.17 The statutory scheme has given rise to cases in civil proceedings where arbitration awards have been set aside for a variety of shortcomings, but the value of arbitration is that it is binding, as long as the process has been fairly conducted and the outcome is not obviously unfair.

4.18 By FPR rr 28.2 and 28.3, with important exceptions, CPR Part 44 applies to all family proceedings including financial remedy proceedings. In particular CPR r 44.1(2) applies, which provides that:

> '(2) The costs to which Parts 44 to 47 apply include –
>
> (a) The following costs where those costs may be assessed by the court –
>   (i) Costs of proceedings before an arbitrator or umpire …'

Thus *to the extent that* the costs of arbitration in family proceedings may be assessed by the court, the CPR costs rules, as modified by the FPR, apply. The costs of the arbitration itself, which are likely to be governed at least initially by arrangements made between the parties, are not the same as the costs of any court proceedings following an arbitration. The position in relation to those two types of costs are discussed below.

4.19 The significance of this is that the Arbitration Act provides some distinctive features for costs in arbitration, as we go on to consider. The following costs provisions apply only to arbitration under the FLAS and (in theory at least) parties could submit to arbitration under some other scheme, including one of their own devising, and could make their own agreement as to costs under such an arrangement.

15 President's *Practice Guidance (Family Court: Interface with Arbitration)* [2016] 1 WLR 59.
16 *Practice Guidance: Children Arbitration in the Family Court* [2018] 2 FLR 1398.
17 *S v S (Financial Remedies: Arbitral Award)* [2014] EWHC 7 (Fam), [2014] 1 FLR 1257 at [19].

4.20 Article 14 of the FLAS provides:[18]

'14.1 In this article any reference to costs is a reference to the costs of the arbitration as defined in section 59 [of the Arbitration Act 1996] (costs of the arbitration) including the fees and expenses of IFLA, unless otherwise indicated.

14.2 The arbitrator may require the parties to pay his or her fees and expenses accrued during the course of the arbitration at such interim stages as may be agreed with the parties, and in the absence of agreement, at reasonable intervals.

14.3 The arbitrator may order either party to provide security for the arbitrator's fees and expenses and the fees and expenses of IFLA.

14.4 Unless otherwise agreed by the parties, the arbitrator will make an award allocating costs as between the parties in accordance with the following general principle:
(a) the parties will bear the arbitrator's fees and expenses and the fees and expenses of IFLA in equal shares;
(b) there will be no order or award requiring one party to pay the legal or other costs of another party.

This principle is subject to the arbitrator's overriding discretion set out in Art. 14.5 and 14.6.

14.5 Where it is appropriate to do so because of the conduct of a party in relation to the arbitration (whether before or during it), the arbitrator may at any stage order that party:
(a) to bear a larger than equal share, and up to the full amount, of the arbitrator's fees and expenses and the fees and expenses of IFLA;
(b) to pay the legal or other costs of another party;

and may make an award accordingly.

14.6 In deciding whether, and if so how, to exercise the discretion set out in Art 14.5, the arbitrator will have regard to the following:
(a) any failure by a party to comply with these Rules or any order or directions which the arbitrator considers relevant;
(b) any open offer to settle made by a party;
(c) whether it was reasonable for a party to raise, pursue or contest a particular allegation or issue;
(d) the manner in which a party has pursued or responded to a claim or a particular allegation or issue;
(e) any other aspect of a party's conduct in relation to the arbitration which the arbitrator considers relevant; and
(f) the financial effects on the parties of any costs order or award.

18 Family Law Arbitration Scheme, *Arbitration Rules 2018* (for financial remedies on divorce 6th edn, 1 January 2018, for Children Act cases 3rd edn 1 July 2018) at ifla.org.uk.

14.7 Unless the parties agree otherwise, no offer to settle which is not an open offer to settle shall be admissible at any stage of the arbitration.

14.8 These rules as to costs shall not apply to applications made to the court where costs fall to be determined by the court.'

The only difference between Article 14 in the IFLA financial scheme and in the IFLA children scheme is the addition of a further matter to which the arbitrator will have regard in the children scheme as follows: 'the principles applied by the courts in relation to cases concerning child welfare'. The effect of that is not clear, though it is readily seen why it would have been added.

4.21 Article 14 has some noteworthy features:

(a) The costs of the arbitration are the arbitrator's fees and expenses, the fees and expenses of IFLA and the legal and other costs of the parties to the arbitration.

(b) The general principle is that the parties share the costs equally – the starting point thus being no order as to costs as in financial remedy proceedings.

(c) But the arbitrator may make some other order.

(d) The factors to which the arbitrator will have regard when considering a costs order are lifted from FPR rr 28.3 and 28.4, which are the factors to which a court has to have regard when considering a costs order in financial remedy proceedings, with the addition of the need to have regard to welfare in children arbitrations.

(e) These rules will not apply when costs are determined by the court, which implies (it is not mentioned explicitly in the rules) that costs may be dealt with not by the arbitrator but by the court, or if dealt with by the arbitrator may be challenged, and then determined by the court. No distinction is made in the Article between: (a) costs of a court challenge to costs issues within the arbitration, for example the quantum of the costs or the arbitrator's decision on the payment of the costs of the arbitration, and (b) the court costs of a challenge to the arbitration decision.

4.22 The question then arises which rules will apply when the costs are to be determined by a court. In the previous edition of this work we commented on the lack of authority in this area and proposed that the clean sheet starting point would be the appropriate one. There have since been two judgments by Clare Ambrose, an experienced arbitrator, sitting as a deputy High Court Judge[19] in two challenges to arbitration decisions. In the first of those cases she concluded, by analogy with the decision of the Court of Appeal in a set aside application in *Judge v Judge*,[20] that a challenge to the implementation of an arbitrator's decision is not financial remedy proceedings, so that the 'no order' rule does not apply

19 *BC v BG* [2019] EWFC 7, [2019] 2 FLR 337 and *H v W* [2019] EWHC 1897 (Fam).
20 [2008] EWCA Civ 1458, [2009] 1 FLR 1287.

and the starting point is the clean sheet. In the circumstances of both cases it was decided that costs should follow the event[21].

4.23 We come back to the question of whether, in the event that there is disagreement over the parties' arbitration costs or over the payment of the arbitrator's fees or expenses, a family court would have the power to order a party to pay those costs. The costs rules in the CPR apply to family proceedings except as excluded by FPR r 28.2 and r 28.3, and permit the court to make an order for payment of the costs of arbitration proceedings. The question is whether it makes a difference that arbitration in family proceedings lacks any FPR rules. In other words is 'arbitrator' in CPR r 44.1(2)(a)(i) limited to an arbitrator appointed in accordance with Part 62 of the CPR? There is no definition of the word in Part 44, and in the absence of authority we hesitantly suggest that as a family court would wish to be in the best position to make a fair order, for that purpose it would wish to be able to make an order for the payment of the arbitration costs. We suggest that a family court, in the absence of any rule to the contrary, would do so in an appropriate case.

4.24 The IFLA Arbitration Rules permit variation from their standard rules in any particular case (Art 1, r 1.3(c)). So if the parties wish to make some other arrangement about costs than the one provided in the Rules then they can do so in their arbitration agreement at the outset of the arbitration. For example they might wish to include that:

(a) one party pays the whole of the arbitration costs; or

(b) the parties will each pay their own legal and other costs and the arbitrator is not asked to make any determination in relation to the parties' costs; or

(c) where one party has little money, the other party will pay both parties' legal costs in the first instance, half to be deducted from the receiving party's share of the assets at the conclusion of the proceedings (like a legal services payment order).

4.25 While each of those alternatives might be considered attractive in particular cases, the parties will not wish to fall foul of s 60 of the Arbitration Act 1996 which states that 'An agreement which has the effect that a party is to pay the whole or part of the costs of the arbitration in any event is only valid if made after the dispute in question has arisen'. This section is intended to exclude from contracts those clauses that might be seen to provide one party with control over the arbitration. It follows that clauses should not be included in pre-nuptial or cohabitation agreements which provide for one party to pay the costs of arbitration in the event that the relationship breaks down.

21 At [90] of *BC v BG* and at [78] of *H v W.*

DIVORCE AND DISSOLUTION

Decree nisi and conditional orders

4.26 On an uncontested application for a matrimonial or civil partnership order (or more specifically, an application for a decree of divorce[22], of judicial separation[23] or of nullity[24] and the civil partnership equivalents[25]), an applicant may apply for costs. Applicants routinely do so.

4.27 The respondent, upon receiving that application, may not wish to defend the main application but may object to the costs application. That objection can be registered without the need to file a formal answer,[26] but the respondent may wish to note briefly his position on costs (such as an agreement to pay a proportion of the costs or to pay a specified sum towards the costs) in the acknowledgement of service.

4.28 The respondent requires permission to file an answer out of time.[27] It is noted in The Family Court Practice that a respondent attending the permission hearing cannot be awarded the costs of his attendance.[28]

Legal services payment orders

4.29 The court's power to award legal services payment orders in matrimonial and civil partnership proceedings falls under the MCA 1973, ss 22ZA and 22ZB and the CPA 2004, Sch 5, Pt 8, paras 38A and 38B.[29] Such an order may cover the cost of legal advice, assistance and representation, and of mediation and alternative dispute resolution including arbitration.[30] Legal services payment orders are considered more fully at **5.02–5.45**.

Undefended applications for decree nisi and conditional orders

4.30 In an undefended divorce or dissolution, if satisfied that the applicant is entitled to the decree nisi of divorce or the conditional order ending a civil partnership, the court must issue a certificate under FPR r 7.20(2)(a) to verify that fact and must direct the application to be listed before a judge in open court at a block hearing on the next available date. The court may also, if so satisfied,

22 Under the MCA 1973, s 1.
23 Under the MCA 1973, s 17.
24 Under the MCA 1973, s 11 or s 12.
25 Under the CPA 2004, para 37 in respect to: dissolution, nullity, presumption of death, and separation orders.
26 FPR r 7.12(9).
27 FPR r 7.12(8).
28 *The Family Court Practice* (LexisNexis, June 2019), para [3.199[4]].
29 Inserted by the Legal Aid, Sentencing and Punishment of Offenders Act 2012, s 49(2).
30 MCA 1973, s 22ZA(10).

certify that the applicant is entitled to a costs order (and though this does not mean that a costs order must be granted at a later date, the award is likely to be made). If not satisfied that the applicant is entitled to his costs, the court will make no direction as to costs.[31]

4.31 In cases where the court is not satisfied that the applicant is entitled to the decree nisi or the conditional order, the court may either direct that the matter be listed for a case management hearing or direct a party to provide further information or to take such steps as the court may specify.[32]

4.32 The hearing to finalise an unopposed decree nisi or conditional order will usually be unattended and in such circumstances, when it has been certified that the applicant is entitled to costs and the respondent has not objected, an order that the respondent shall pay the applicant's costs will be made.

4.33 A court may hear any party to matrimonial or civil partnership proceedings on the matter of costs at a hearing of the proceedings (and this rule applies whether or not the application is defended).[33] In particular, when a party wishes either to apply for or to oppose a costs order, after a direction has been made under FPR r 7.20(2)(a), then at least 14 days before the hearing that party must file at court and serve on all the other parties a written notice of that party's intention to attend the hearing and to make such an application.[34]

4.34 On receipt of such a notice, the court will make such directions in relation to the hearing as it sees fit.[35]

Defended applications for decree nisi and conditional orders

4.35 On receiving an application for a decree nisi or a conditional order in a defended case, the court must direct that the case be listed for a case management hearing.[36] At that hearing, the court will investigate whether alternative dispute resolution may be suitable and, if that is not the case, will give directions in readiness for the final hearing.

4.36 Should a party allege that there are matrimonial or civil partnership proceedings underway in another jurisdiction which are concerned with the marriage or partnership that is before the court in England and Wales, then that party may seek a discretionary stay by making a Part 18 application.[37] Such an

31 FPR r 7.20(3).
32 FPR r 7.20(2)(b).
33 FPR r 7.21(1).
34 FPR r 7.21(2).
35 FPR r 7.21(3).
36 FPR r 7.20(4).
37 Under the Domicile and Matrimonial Proceedings Act 1973, Sch 1, para 9 and the Family Procedure (Civil Partnership: Staying of Proceedings) Rules 2010, SI 2010/2986, r 4.

application should be made at the earliest opportunity to minimise the costs incurred by the parties.

4.37 Where there is a contested hearing in such proceedings, costs orders are made on the clean sheet basis having regard to the usual factors and this is discussed at **4.39**.

Applications for a decree absolute or a final order

4.38 When a decree nisi has been granted but the applicant has failed to apply for a decree absolute within three months of the earliest date for such an application, a respondent may make an application to the court,[38] and upon that application the court may:

(a) make the decree absolute;

(b) rescind the decree nisi;

(c) require further inquiry; or

(d) deal with the case as the court thinks fit.[39]

The respondent should also make any application for costs at this time. The same applies:

(a) when a civil partner applies under the CPA 2004,[40] because a conditional order has been made against him and the applicant has failed to apply for a final order within three months of being entitled to do so; and

(b) in an application under FPR r 7.33 to make a decree nisi absolute or to make a conditional order final where the Queen's Proctor has intervened or there are circumstances that should be brought to the court's attention before the application is granted.[41]

The costs award

4.39 The costs of matrimonial or civil partnership proceedings are determined on the clean sheet basis.[42] In as much as it is possible to give guidance as to the court's position on costs in such proceedings, the following propositions are made:

(a) In cases where the petition is based on a period of separation,[43] costs are not usually awarded.

38 MCA 1973, s 9(2).
39 MCA 1973, s 9(1).
40 CPA 2004, s 40(2).
41 FPR r 7.33(2).
42 FPR r 28.2.
43 Under the MCA 1973, s 1(2)(d)–(e) and under CPA 2004, s 44(5)(b)–(c) in relation to the parties living apart for two years where the divorce is consensual or in a separation of at least five years.

In *Grenfell v Grenfell*,[44] Ormrod LJ said: 'All that *Chapman v Chapman*[45] decides, as I see it, is that if the court dissolves a marriage on the ground of five years' separation, it should not, in the ordinary way, grant costs to either side, the object being to prevent parties insisting on the court conducting an inquiry as to why they have been living apart for five years; in other words, having a contested suit simply for the purpose of deciding who should pay the costs.'

However, Sir George Baker P in *Hymns v Hymns*[46] stated the parties, though both publicly funded, should share the 'small' costs of a consent divorce on grounds of two years' separation.

(b) In 'fault divorces or dissolutions',[47] costs are usually awarded to the party who is found to have been aggrieved.

In *Waller v Waller and another*,[48] the decree was granted by the lower court on the grounds of the respondent's behaviour and the husband was ordered to pay the costs. The husband obtained permission to appeal, but the Court of Appeal upheld the decision of the lower court.

(c) *Beales v Beales*[49] is authority for the rule that a respondent may consent to the decree on the condition that the applicant pays all the costs. (In this case both parties were publicly funded).

(d) Costs followed the event in the controversial case of *Owens v Owens*, in which the wife unsuccessfully petitioned for divorce, alleging the husband had behaved in such a way that she could not reasonably be expected to live with him. HHJ Tolson QC ordered the wife to pay the costs of the husband.[50]

4.40 Costs orders in matrimonial and civil partnership proceedings cover the costs up to and including the grant of the decree absolute or the final order. They do not include the costs of any associated financial remedy proceedings or matters related to children, to which different rules and considerations apply.

Co-respondents

4.41 A co-respondent may be cited in an application as a person who committed adultery with the respondent (or in a cross-application, the third party adulterer would be described as the 'party cited').[51] That third party either

44 [1978] 1 All ER 561, [1977] 3 WLR 738, CA at [143].
45 [1972] 3 All ER 1089, [1972] 1 WLR 1544, CA.
46 [1971] 3 All ER 596n, [1971] 1 WLR 1474 at [596].
47 Under the MCA 1973, s 1(2)(a)–(c) in relation to adultery, unreasonable behaviour and desertion, and under the CPA 2004, s 44(5)(a) and (d) in relation to unreasonable behaviour and desertion.
48 [2000] Lexis Citation 3274, All England Official Transcripts (1997–2008), CA.
49 [1972] 2 All ER 667, [1972] 2 WLR 972.
50 *Owens v Owens* [2017] EWCA Civ 182 at [50], [2017] 2 FCR 569.
51 FPR r 7.10(2)–(5) and FPR r 7.4(2).

may be the beneficiary of a costs order or may have such an order made against them.[52] Most of the reported cases in respect to such situations are at least 60 years' old and our view is that the facts and circumstances of those cases bear little relevance to today's applications.

Cases involving the Queen's Proctor

4.42 A court may decide to involve the Queen's Proctor (who will, under the directions of the Attorney-General, instruct counsel) when it is necessary or expedient to argue fully a matter related to the matrimonial or civil partnership proceedings. This is where some deceit or collusion is suspected which the court requires to be investigated. The Queen's Proctor may show cause why a decree nisi should not be made absolute.[53] If this should occur, there is a statutory provision for the court to award costs for or against the Queen's Proctor.[54]

4.43 The court will determine, on a basis that is just, whether the other parties to the proceedings should pay some or all of the costs incurred by the Queen's Proctor, or if the Queen's Proctor should pay to the other parties a sum in respect to the costs they have incurred as a result of his intervention. As these are family proceedings, costs will be considered on the clean sheet basis. In practice, if the Queen's Proctor does show cause as to why the decree should not be granted then he is likely to be awarded his costs, and if he fails to do so then he may be ordered to pay the costs of the parties.[55]

4.44 Where the Queen's Proctor intervenes to assist the court rather than to show cause why a decree should not be made, no costs order can be made either in favour of or against the Queen's Proctor.[56] The statutes specifically provide for the Queen's Proctor to charge 'the expenses of his office' including any costs that he may be ordered to pay[57] which means that 'being assured of the loyal support of the Treasury', the Queen's Proctor can discharge the duties of his office 'fearless as to costs'.[58]

4.45 In the interesting case of *Rapisarda v Colladon*,[59] the Queen's Proctor alleged that 180 divorce petitions had been founded upon a lie (that the applicant or respondent was habitually resident at a specific address in England and

52 *Rogers v Rogers* [1974] 2 All ER 361, [1974] 1 WLR 709 at [364] per Davies LJ.
53 MCA 1973, s 9(1) and FPR r 7.31.
54 MCA 1973, s 8(2) and CPA 2004, s 39(4).
55 *Westcott v Westcott (The King's Proctor Shewing Cause)* [1908] P 250 at [255], per Sir Gorell Barnes P; *Kennard v Kennard (The King's Proctor Showing Cause), Morris v. Morris (The King's Proctor Showing Cause)* [1915] P 194 at [197]–[198] per Bargrave Deane J.
56 *Thompson (otherwise Hulton) v Thompson* [1939] P 1, [1938] 4 All ER 1, CA.
57 MCA 1973, s 8(3) and CPA 2004, s 39(5).
58 *King's Proctor v Carter* [1910] P 151, [1908–1910] All ER Rep 104 at [110], CA, per Buckley LJ.
59 [2014] EWFC 35, [2015] 1 FLR 597.

Wales).[60] Sir James Munby P heard the case and found for the Queen's Proctor. Although the Queen's Proctor had claimed his costs,[61] the judgment makes no mention as to any costs award. On the particular facts of that case, it seems unlikely that such an award would have resulted in payment of the costs due.

4.46 A few years later, in 2017, Sir James Munby P presided over a similar case to *Rapisarda*. On this occasion the Queen's Proctor succeeded in an application to dismiss 21 petitions applied for by a disbarred barrister, Mr Bhatoo, and to set aside the decrees. Mr Bhatoo was ordered to pay the costs of the Queen's Proctor on an indemnity basis after summary assessment.[62]

HAGUE CONVENTION (INTERNATIONAL ABDUCTION) CASES

4.47 The Hague Convention on the Civil Aspects of Child Abduction has the force of law in the United Kingdom.[63] Article 26 of that Convention commences with the words 'Each Central Authority shall bear its own costs in applying this Convention' and goes on to provide: 'In particular, they may not require any payment from the applicant towards the costs and expenses of the proceedings or, where applicable, those arising from the participation of legal counsel or advisers.'

4.48 Article 26 continues:

> 'However, a Contracting State may, by making a reservation in accordance with Article 42, declare that it shall not be bound to assume any costs referred to in the preceding paragraph resulting from the participation of legal counsel or advisers or from court proceedings, except in so far as those costs may be covered by its system of legal aid and advice.'

The effect of that provision (as the UK has made an Art 42 reservation) is that the free provision of legal aid is under the relevant statutory provision (namely Part 1 of the Legal Aid, Sentencing and Punishment of Offenders Act 2012).

4.49 As a result of its obligations under the Hague Convention to meet the legal costs of applicants in international child abduction cases, such applications are placed in the category of cases which are eligible for non-means and non-merits tested legal aid.[64] Respondents, however, are not in that position and any application they may make for legal aid is subject to a means and merits test. It

60 [2014] EWFC 35, [2015] 1 FLR 597 at [35].
61 [2014] EWFC 35, [2015] 1 FLR 597 at [64].
62 *Grasso v Naik and Bhatoo (Twenty One Irregular Divorces)* [2017] EWHC 2789 (Fam), [2018] 1 FLR 753.
63 By s 1(2) of the Child Abduction and Custody Act 1985, to which the Hague Convention is the first Schedule.
64 Section 9 of and Part 1 of Sch 1 to the Legal Aid, Sentencing and Punishment of Offenders Act 2012, and Chapter 6 of the Civil Legal Aid (Merits Criteria) Regulations 2013, SI 2013/104.

is therefore commonly the case that applicants in these cases have public funding and respondents are either unrepresented or fund their own representation.

4.50 Thorpe LJ and Munby LJ separately inveighed against the injustice of this position[65] in a case where the applicant had specialist leading counsel, junior counsel and solicitor and the respondent had only an interpreter. As a result the court spent longer on the case than would have been necessary if the respondent had been represented and 'what is intended to be an economy turns out to be an extravagance.'[66] Not only that, but it results in a state of affairs 'very far from the equality of arms that is supposed, consistently with Article 6 of the European Convention for the Protection of Human Rights and Fundamental Freedoms 1950, to underlie proceedings of this sort.'[67] The availability of public funding more generally is dealt with in **Chapter 7**.

4.51 In Hague Convention cases where there is a question of international abduction it is commonly the case that there may be proceedings in two jurisdictions. The Court of Appeal considered a case where, perhaps by a failure to distinguish adequately between the two sets of proceedings, the first instance judge had awarded costs against a party which were incurred in relation to proceedings in Germany.[68] The Court found that Article 26 of the Convention is not broad enough to allow payments to be made in relation to proceedings in another jurisdiction: the application for costs could have been made in Germany.

4.52 Ryder J was confronted with an application that the legally aided applicant in a Hague Convention case be ordered to pay the costs of the privately funded respondent.[69] The court found that the applicant had indeed conducted her case unreasonably, including 'the deliberate and persistent falsification of a case in an attempt to deprive the child of his or her habitual residence'[70] and that she (or the Legal Services Commission) should pay the respondent's costs. Ryder J held that there is no reason why the principles to be applied to costs orders in Hague Convention cases should be any different from those in other children cases.[71] Making a costs order and noting that the court's costs jurisdiction did not permit summary assessment on making a costs order against the LSC, Ryder J ordered detailed assessment.[72]

4.53 Since that case the Legal Services Commission has been replaced by the Legal Aid Agency (LAA), the Access to Justice Act 1999 by the Legal Aid, Sentencing and Punishment of Offenders Act 2012 (LASPO) and there are new rules and regulations. Hayden J was faced with a costs application in a Hague

65 *Re K (Abduction: Case Management)* [2010] EWCA Civ 1546, [2011] 1 FLR 1268 at [33]–[36] and [44]–[46].
66 At [36] Thorpe LJ.
67 At [45] Munby LJ.
68 *B v B* [2015] EWCA Civ 1166.
69 *EC-L v DM (Child Abduction: Costs)* [2005] EWHC 588 (Fam), [2005] 2 FLR 772.
70 *Ibid* at [66].
71 *Ibid* at [67].
72 *Ibid* at [75]–[76].

Convention case under the current public funding legislation.[73] He found that the detailed analysis by Ryder J of the principles in relation to costs orders was unchanged by the introduction of LASPO and 'the principles identified in the case continue to hold, by parity of analysis, with the framework of the Family Procedure Rules 2010'.[74] Hayden J found that the necessity for the hearing had largely been caused by the father's deliberate camouflage of the facts and his general dissimulation to the court. 'In his terms it was "war" and he wanted to win'.[75] Because some of the costs had been generated by the mother's 'opportunistic pleading'[76] he ordered that half her costs be paid by the father.

COMMITTALS

4.54 Proceedings for committal in family proceedings are less frequent since s 42A of the Family Law Act 1996 provided for breaches of non-molestation orders to be dealt with criminally. Breaches of occupation orders may still be the subject of committal applications, as may breaches of other injunctions in family proceedings such as freezing orders or a prohibition on the removal of a child. Committals may also be made for contempt of court.

4.55 Public funding for committals in family proceedings is dealt with not under the rules for public funding in civil cases, but those for public funding in criminal proceedings.[77] The routes to obtaining public funding for a person to defend himself in a committal application differ in the High Court and in the Family Court, and the relevant legislation has been described as 'disgracefully complex' by the Court of Appeal in *Brown*.[78] Fortunately the Court of Appeal has summarised what they are: in High Court cases the court has the power to make a 'representation order' (an order that the contemnor be represented at public expense) while in the Family Court that power lies with the LAA.[79] In *Brown* as a result of administrative failures the alleged contemnor was unrepresented and the Court of Appeal allowed the appeal.

4.56 The rules for criminal legal aid are generally beyond the scope of this book, but the complexity of the grant of legal aid in committal proceedings featured again in Baker J's consideration of the LAA's disagreement with the

73 *SB v MB* [2014] EWHC 3721 (Fam).
74 *Ibid* at [4].
75 *Ibid* at [7].
76 *Ibid* at [8].
77 Section 14(g) and (h) of LASPO and reg 9(v) of the Criminal Legal Aid (General) Regulations 2013, see *Kings Lynn and West Norfolk Council v Bunning* [2013] EWHC 3390 (QB), [2014] 2 All ER 1095, [2015] 1 WLR 531, per Blake J.
78 *Brown v London Borough of Haringey* [2015] EWCA Civ 483 at [3], per McCombe LJ.
79 Regulations 6, 7 and 8 of the Criminal Legal Aid (Determinations by a court and choice of representative) Regulations 2013, SI 2013/614 and s 18 of the Legal Aid, Sentencing and Punishment of Offenders Act 2012.

application of *Brown* by Blake J in *Bunning*.[80] Having referred to *Bunning* and *Brown* he was assisted by the LAA who expressed the view that where the application is for a committal other than for contempt in the face of the court – that is to say it is under s 14(h) rather than s 14(g) of LASPO – then the decision as to the grant or refusal of legal aid is to be made by the LAA rather than by the High Court. And while anyone facing committal is entitled to representation in accordance with Article 6(3)(c) of the European Convention on Human Rights, the LAA takes into account the person's ability to pay for his or her own legal representation. The LAA's 'Guidance for Providers' sets out how to apply for legal aid in these circumstances.[81] Baker J declined to rule on the disagreement between the courts and the LAA, confining himself to advising an approach to the LAA for funding first, before asking the court to make a representation order.

4.57 In the past it has been held that successful applicants for committal will be paid their costs on the indemnity basis,[82] while the respondent may receive his costs but on the standard basis if the committal application is unsuccessful.[83] Those (non-family) cases have been superseded by more recent decisions in which the payment of costs and the question of whether they should be on the standard or indemnity basis have depended more on the facts of the individual cases.

4.58 In an application to commit for a failure to disclose assets, where the respondent was found not to have been at fault save for one failure to disclose which he had admitted before most of the costs were incurred, the applicant was ordered to pay 80% of the respondent's costs, subject to assessment.[84] Those costs were to be on the standard basis. In another case where the defendant's conduct was 'unmeritorious' but not so contemptuous that a committal order was appropriate, no order for costs was made: no order for costs reflected the fact that no party was found to be in contempt of court but neither was the defendant without blame.[85]

4.59 There is a paucity of authority on the award of costs in relation to committals in family proceedings. It seems to us that where committal proceedings do result in a committal or other penalty it will almost inevitably be the case, subject to the application to commit having been proportionate, that the person committed will have been found to have acted unreasonably in relation to the proceedings (namely by flouting a court order) so that their conduct will justify an order that the committed party pay the applicant's costs – on the clean

80 *CH v CT (Committal: Appeal)* [2018] EWHC 1310 (Fam), [2019] 1 FLR 700 at [37]–[47] considering *Kings Lynn and West Norfolk District Council v Bunning* [2013] EWHC 3390 (QB), [2014] 2 All ER 1095.

81 LAA, *Apply for legal Aid in Civil Contempt – Committal Proceedings* (2015).

82 *GCT Management Ltd v Laurie Marsh Group Ltd* [1973] RPC 432; *Stancombe v Trowbridge UDC* [1910] 2 Ch 190.

83 *Plating Co v Farquharson* (1881) 17 Ch D 49, CA.

84 *Public Joint Stock Company Vseukrainskyi Aktsionernyi Bank v Maksimov and others* [2014] EWHC 4370 (Comm) at [28].

85 *Knight v Clifton* [1971] Ch 700, [1971] 2 All ER 378, CA.

sheet approach. Where an application to commit is unsuccessful it seems to us that the question of costs will be dealt with on the same principles as in other family proceedings.

HUMAN FERTILISATION AND EMBRYOLOGY ACT 2008

4.60 There is a specific procedure for the courts to make declarations of parentage under s 55A of the Family Law Act 1986 in cases where ss 43 and 44 of the Human Fertilisation and Embryology Act apply. There have been several cases where the original documentation was not adequate for that purpose and applications have had to be made to the court. The fault usually lies with the clinic which performed the procedure so that a costs order against the clinic is made. Following a series of cases in which costs awards were made against clinics, Sir James Munby P provided a standard costs order for the purpose.[86]

APPEALS

Costs of appeals

4.61 Appeals in family proceedings from district judges and from magistrates are to circuit judges, or to the Family Division of the High Court in the case of appeals from district judges in the Central Family Court in financial remedy proceedings,[87] and in Inheritance Act and Trusts of Land Act cases. The destination table for appeals in family proceedings is at FPR PD30A [2.1] and [2.2]. Such appeals heard by circuit judges are family proceedings and so the FPR costs rules apply. Thus, if such an appeal is in a children case the clean sheet rule will apply, and if the appeal is in financial remedy proceedings then the no order rule will apply.

4.62 In general appeals from circuit judges are to the Court of Appeal in public law children cases and otherwise to the High Court.[88] Appeals from High Court judges are to the Court of Appeal.[89] As was discussed when dealing with the three costs regimes, the combined effect of the relevant FPR and CPR rules[90] is that all appeals in family proceedings to the Court of Appeal are under the clean sheet costs regime, which means that in financial remedy proceedings the costs regime changes from no order for costs at first instance to clean sheet on appeal to the Court of Appeal. In cases heard by a High Court judge of the Family

86 *Re Human Fertilisation and Embryology Act 2008 (Cases AD, AE, AF, AG and AH) (No 2)* [2017] EWHC 1782 (Fam).

87 FPR PD30A [2.1].

88 The detail is at FPR PD30A [2.1] and [2.2].

89 There is no appeal to the Court of Appeal from decrees absolute of divorce or from final orders of dissolution of civil partnerships by a party who has failed to appeal the decree nisi/ conditional order: s 18(d) and (fa) of the Senior Courts Act 1981.

90 FPR r 28.2(1) and CPR r 44.2(2) and (3).

Division at first instance which are not family proceedings (such as Inheritance Act and Trusts of Land Act cases), the rule in the Court of Appeal will be the same as at first instance – that costs follow the event.

4.63 Part 52 of the CPR applies to appeals to the Court of Appeal. It does not apply to appeals in family proceedings to circuit or High Court judges,[91] except in relation to appeals against a decision of an authorised court officer in detailed assessment proceedings.[92] Instead Part 30 of the FPR applies. The CPR has five Practice Directions associated with Part 52, and the FPR has PD30A. Some of the provisions of these rules and practice directions are the same, for example: any appeal court has (with no relevant exceptions) the power to make any order which the lower court could have made and, in case there could be any doubt about it, both sets of rules specifically provide that an appeal court can make a costs order.[93] Other provisions differ.

4.64 Wall LJ in a permission hearing for a second appeal, the first appeal having been before a High Court judge, set out how the rules on costs in appeals in a children case correctly led to the High Court judge applying the clean sheet rule on appeal.[94] He also set out why there is a difference between a hearing at first instance and an appeal hearing in relation to costs. The two reasons are linked: 'at first instance, nobody knows what a judge is going to find' and 'a party to a hearing at first instance who then faces an appeal has an opportunity to take stock, and to make *Calderbank* offers to compromise it'.[95] It will be a more straightforward exercise to assess reasonableness in a party's approach to an appeal because the issues before the appeal court are clearly defined.

4.65 What are the distinctive features of the rules as to costs on appeal?

(a) *Security for costs* is more likely to be ordered in relation to appeals, as we have considered elsewhere.[96] That is because in most family cases at first instance there will be no order for costs, and so security for costs would not be appropriate. Not only are costs orders more frequent in family cases on appeal; there is also specific provision under the FPR for orders to be made for security for the costs of an appeal.[97] Such security for costs orders must only be made where they would be justifiable, non-discriminatory and 'a

91 CPR PD52A [2.2].

92 FPR r 30.1(2) and CPR rr 47.21–47.24.

93 CPR r 52.10(2)(e) and FPR r 30.11(2)(e).

94 *EM v SW* [2009] EWCA Civ 311 at [16]–[17].

95 *Ibid* at [23]–[24].

96 At **5.51–5.69**.

97 FPR r 20.8, and FPR r 30.3(8)(b) provides, more generally, for appeals to be made subject to conditions. The 'compelling reasons' for attaching such conditions, which concerned the court in *Radmacher v Granatino* [2008] EWCA Civ 1304, [2009] 1 FLR 1566 at [11]–[12] per Wall LJ, are not found in the FPR, although they survive at CPR r 52.9(1)(c) in relation to appeals to the Court of Appeal.

justifiable and proportionate exercise of discretion'[98] and the terms must not be such as to effectively 'stifle a meritorious appeal'.[99]

These rules apply to family appeals to circuit and High Court judges. For appeals to the Court of Appeal the provisions of the CPR on security for costs apply, which are similar in effect.[100]

Long before the introduction of legal services payment orders an impecunious wife could provide her solicitors with some security of funding in responding to an appeal by applying for a security for costs order.[101] Now, where a respondent to an appeal lacks the funds to pay for legal representation there are a number of other alternatives available, and in many cases a LSPO may be the most attractive of those.

(b) *Attaching conditions.* In financial remedy proceedings an order for security for costs can be combined with the court's powers to impose conditions on appeal more generally.[102] In the 'big money' case of *Radmacher v Granatino* when granting permission to appeal to the Court of Appeal the court required the wife to provide security for the full amount of the lump sum which she had been ordered to pay in the financial remedy proceedings, with interest, the sum required to buy a property in Germany, the costs of the five previous hearings and for her to pay the spousal and child periodical payments which had been ordered. The permission to appeal was to lapse if the periodical payments were more than 14 days' late.[103]

(c) *A transcript* of the judgment below, and less commonly of part of the evidence, is likely to be needed for an appeal. The CPR provides that such transcripts may be provided at public expense if the cost of doing so would be 'an excessive burden' on the appellant.[104] The FPR provides more specifically that such transcripts will be provided at public expense where the cost of doing so would be an excessive burden on an appellant who is unrepresented or whose legal representation is provided free of charge (but where a party is publicly funded the LAA will be expected to pay for the transcript); the court must also be satisfied that there are reasonable grounds for appeal.[105]

(d) *Respondents* are not usually required to file a skeleton argument in reply to an application for permission to appeal, neither are they usually directed to attend an oral permission hearing[106]. In the Court of Appeal they are however 'encouraged' to file a brief statement of any reasons why an appeal should

98 *Nasser v United Bank of Kuwait* [2001] EWCA Civ 556, [2002] 1 All ER 401 at [49], per Mance LJ.
99 *Blue Sky One Ltd v Mahan Air* [2011] EWCA Civ 544 at [38]–[39], per Stanley Burnton LJ.
100 The conditions for security for costs are the same at FPR r 20.7 and CPR r 25.13.
101 See, for example, *Norris v Norris* [1969] 1 WLR 1264, CA, per Denning LJ.
102 At FPR r 30.3(8)(b) and CPR r 52.3(7)(b).
103 [2008] EWCA Civ 1304, [2009] 1 FLR 1566 at [26]–[32], per Wilson LJ.
104 CPR r 52.5A – an indicator would be if the appellant was entitled to fee remission.
105 FPR PD30A [5.33] and [5.34].
106 FPR PD30A [4.22].

be refused, the costs of which are not recoverable from the other side.[107] If a respondent nonetheless either volunteers a skeleton argument or similar document, or attends the permission hearing, then he will not usually be entitled to his costs of doing so.[108] If, on the other hand, a respondent is directed to respond to an application for permission or to attend a permission hearing and the application is unsuccessful, then he will normally be allowed his costs.[109] We observe that this is the sole provision in family proceedings for costs to follow the event.

(e) *Summary assessments* of costs may be made at an application hearing for permission to appeal, at any hearing for directions on appeal or at a full appeal lasting up to one day.[110] The rules contain a reminder that those who wish to claim their costs should ensure that their schedules of costs are before the court for that purpose.[111] Where neither side provided schedules of costs and as a result there had to be a separate assessment hearing, the costs of that further hearing were deducted from the costs payable to the successful party.[112] While courts have generally taken the approach that a failure to file a schedule of costs as required must have caused prejudice to the other party in order to deny the claimant the costs to which they are otherwise entitled,[113] the generally stricter approach to procedure suggests that more generous approach should not be relied upon.

4.66 Appeals to the High Court against orders made in family proceedings are not included in Sch 1 to the Senior Courts Act 1981, and so are not family proceedings if they are heard in the Family Division of the High Court (as opposed to being heard by a High Court Judge in the Family Court, when they will be family proceedings). Does it follow that costs follow the event in such Family Division appeals? In our view it does not, for the following reason. Appeals to the Court of Appeal from a decision in family proceedings are not subject to the costs follow the event rule as there is a specific provision that costs in such cases will be dealt with on the clean sheet basis.[114] In family proceedings where there are two appeals – the first to the High Court and the second to the Court of Appeal – it would be anomalous to the point of being nonsensical to have one regime (the clean sheet) apply at first instance and at the Court of Appeal, and a different regime (costs follow the event) in the High Court, all in the same case. The omission from the rules relating to costs of any separate reference to appeals heard in the High Court also suggests that there should not be a different costs regime for such hearings. It is just that: an omission. It can be rectified by the

107 CPR PD52C [19(1)]. In public law cases local authority respondents should take advantage of this – *Re B (A child)* [2015] EWCA Civ 1053.
108 CPR PD52C [20(1)], FPR PD30A [4.23].
109 CPR PD52C [20(2)], FPR PD30A [4.24]. *Mickovski v Liddell* [2017] EWCA Civ 251 is an example of such a costs order.
110 FPR PD30A [17.1].
111 FPR PD30A [17.2].
112 *Wheeler v Chief Constable of Gloucestershire Constabulary* [2013] EWCA Civ 1791.
113 See, for example, *Kingsley v Orban* [2014] EWHC 2991 (Ch) at [19], per Nugee J.
114 CPR r 44.2(3), and see **1.39–1.40** above.

same costs regime being adopted throughout. Where the appeal is from financial remedy proceedings where at first instance the starting point is no order, while on appeal to the Court of Appeal it is the clean sheet, we suggest that the clean sheet approach will be appropriate in the High Court, as being an appeal it is more like the Court of Appeal.

4.67 Moor J took this view[115] when considering whether *Calderbank* offers (see **2.51-2.62**) are eligible in appeals to a High Court Judge in financial remedy proceedings. He decided that they are eligible: 'I have come to the clear conclusion that when it states, in r 28.3(8), "No offer to settle which is not an open offer to settle is admissible at any stage in the proceedings" it is referring to first instance proceedings. I take the view that an appeal brings it out of that regime'.[116]

4.68 Although, with the occasional exceptions discussed, we conclude that it is the clean sheet rule that applies in family appeals to the High Court and Court of Appeal, it is quite usual for a successful respondent to be awarded their costs when an appeal is dismissed. It has become common enough to be done without consideration of conduct or any other of the reasons at CPR r 44.2.[117] The Court of Appeal, having noted that on appeals the clean sheet rule applies, in 2018 adopted Wilson LJ's rule in *Baker v Rowe*: 'the fact that one party has been unsuccessful, and must therefore usually be regarded as responsible for the generation of the successful party's costs, will often count as the decisive factor in the exercise of the judge's discretion'[118]. In that case the husband was successful in the appeal and the wife partly successful in the cross-appeal, and the husband was awarded two-thirds of his costs, to be assessed on the standard basis.[119]

Costs appeals

Appealing costs decisions

4.69 Appeals of costs assessments are dealt with below. Appeals of costs orders generally are referred to throughout the book, and provide the authority for much of what is said.

Appealing costs assessments

4.70 Appeals from costs assessment decisions are infrequent in family proceedings, and will be dealt with only in outline. Appeals from costs decisions

115 In *WD v HD* [2015] EWHC 1547 (Fam), [2017] 1 FLR 160 at [65]–[69].
116 [2017] 1 FLR 160 at [68].
117 See, for example the financial remedy case of *S v S* [2018] EWHC 627 (Fam), MacDonald J.
118 [2009] EWCA Civ 1162, [2010] 1 FLR 761 at [25].
119 *Martin v Martin* [2018] EWCA Civ 2866, [2019] 2 FLR 291, ancillary paragraphs appended to main judgment.

by judges are subject to Part 30 of the FPR (Part 52 of the CPR if the appeal is to the Court of Appeal). Appeals from authorised court officers are provided for by rules at CPR rr 47.21–47.24 and PD47 paras 20.1–20.6. As a result permission is required to appeal a costs assessment by a judge, while no permission is required to appeal an assessment by an authorised court officer. The usual rules on appeals are applicable to appeals from a costs order by a judge.[120]

4.71 Part 30 of the FPR explicitly includes costs judges.[121] The filter to be applied when considering granting permission for the appeal is set out in the rules: permission to appeal will be given only where the court considers that the appeal would have a real prospect of success, or there is some other compelling reason why the appeal should be heard.[122] Applications for permission to appeal may be (and should be[123]) made to the first instance judge at the hearing where the decision to be appealed is made (if possible), and if unsuccessful they may be renewed before the appeal judge.[124] If permission is refused by the appellate judge there is no further appeal.[125] Appeals will be allowed where the decision of the lower court was wrong, or unjust because of some serious procedural or other irregularity in proceedings in the lower court.[126]

4.72 Detailed assessment in family proceedings may be undertaken by a district judge or by a costs judge. The routes of appeal differ. An appeal against a detailed assessment by a district judge (other than at the Central Family Court) is to a circuit judge (though it may be taken by a High Court judge)[127] while an appeal against the decision of a costs judge or of a district judge at the Central Family Court is heard by a Family Division High Court judge.[128] Appeals from the decisions of authorised court officers are to a district judge of the High Court or a costs judge.[129]

4.73 Success in relation to applications for a hearing by a party who wishes to contest a provisional assessment is defined: 'Any party which has requested an oral hearing will pay the costs of and incidental to that hearing unless it achieves an adjustment in its own favour by 20% or more of the sum provisionally assessed, or the court otherwise orders.'[130] The conduct of the parties and any offers will be taken into account in making such a decision.[131] Provisional assessment is

120 As set out at FPR r 30 and PD30A, dealt with only cursorily here.
121 FPR r 30.3(1). 'Costs judge' is defined at FPR r 30.1(3).
122 FPR r 30.3(7).
123 FPR PD30A [4.2].
124 FPR r 30.3(3).
125 Access to Justice Act 1999, s 54(4).
126 FPR r 30.12(3).
127 FPR PD30A [2.1].
128 FPR PD30A [2.2].
129 CPR r 47.22.
130 CPR r 47.15(10). Provisional assessments are considered in more detail in **Chapter 8**.
131 CPR PD47 [14.5].

routine when the amount of costs does not exceed £75,000,[132] so any appeal after an oral hearing in such a case will effectively be a second appeal.

4.74 Something similar is true of appeals against public funding assessments: a solicitor dissatisfied with the LAA's assessment of his costs has an initial contractual route of appeal to an independent assessor. Only if still dissatisfied following that assessor's decision does an application to court for detailed assessment arise.[133] Again, there will first be a provisional assessment.[134] Thus in a publicly funded case at the point where a solicitor challenges a provisional assessment there will already have been two reviews of the LAA's assessment: by an independent assessor and by a judge – the challenge to the provisional assessment is in effect a request for a third review of the assessment. This suggests that there will be very few appeals against such assessments, because of the costs involved, not to mention the stamina required by any appellant! The LAA contract emphasises that the costs of any such application to court, which can only be made by a solicitor not by a client, and which in most cases will be of no interest to the client but only to the solicitor, are not claimable on the public funding certificate. There are cases, for example where the publicly funded costs are to be charged on property recovered in the proceedings, where a client may have an interest in the amount of the costs, but the procedure does not allow such a client to initiate a challenge, either with the independent assessor or in court, to the size of the debt he owes to the LAA.

132 CPR PD47 [14.1].

133 In accordance with CPR r 47.18.

134 CPR r 47.18(5). The relevant rule does not refer to an upper limit of £75,000 for provisional assessments, but it is considered that the combined effect of the rules means that limit would be applied. CPR r 47.15 is expressed to apply to 'any detailed assessment proceedings commenced in the High Court or the county court' – although not amended to do so this is taken to include proceedings in the Family Court.

CHAPTER 5

Other Forms of Costs Orders

INTRODUCTION

5.01 This chapter covers:

(a) Orders for one party to pay in advance towards another party's legal services;

(b) Orders to provide security for costs;

(c) The costs of litigants in person;

(d) Costs where a party is represented pro bono;

(e) *Beddoe* orders providing protection in costs for a fiduciary party; and

(f) *Sanderson* and *Bullock* orders to resolve costs issues where there is more than one respondent and not all have been successful.

LEGAL SERVICES ORDERS

5.02 Provision for one party to pay another party's costs in advance has been available for many years in financial remedy cases as an element of maintenance pending suit under the common law. Since 1 April 2013,[1] that provision has had a statutory basis under MCA 1973, ss 22ZA and 22ZB and CPA 2004, Sch 5, Pt 8, paras 38A and 38B.[2] The previous law remains relevant in situations where the specific statutory provisions do not apply. We deal below firstly with the specific statutory provisions and then with the approach where it is not available.

5.03 The FPR defines an order for the payment of legal services as a financial order.[3] The application procedure is set out at FPR Pt 9 (and **5.27–5.28**). Awards of costs in applications for legal services orders (LSOs) (also known as legal services payment orders or costs allowance orders) are dealt with under the clean sheet rule.[4] Under the Financial Orders Project, the President of the Family Division has issued guidance regarding the use of standard family orders which include a LSO.[5] This precedent can be found at **Appendix 4**.

Divorce and civil partnership dissolution proceedings

5.04 The jurisdiction under MCA 1973, s 22ZA applies only to certain proceedings:

(a) divorce (MCA 1973, s 1(1));

(b) nullity (MCA 1973, ss 11 and 12);

(c) judicial separation (MCA 1973, s 17(1)); and

(d) proceedings under Pt II of the MCA 1973 for financial relief connected with proceedings for divorce, nullity or judicial separation.[6]

5.05 Schedule 5, Pt 8, para 38A of the CPA 2004 applies to:

(a) dissolution (CPA 2004, s 44(1));

(b) nullity (CPA 2004, ss 49–50);

(c) separation (CPA 2004, s 56(1)); and

1 Legal Aid, Sentencing and Punishment of Offenders Act 2012 (Commencement No 7) Order 2013, SI 2013/773.
2 Inserted by LASPO 2012, s 49(2).
3 FPR r 2.3(1).
4 FPR r 28.3(4)(b)(i) and PD28A para 4.1(a)(iii).
5 *Practice Guidance: Standard Financial and Enforcement Orders* [2018] Fam Law 89.
6 Ie proceedings for maintenance pending suit (s 22), financial provision for periodical or lump sums (s 23), property adjustment orders (s 24), orders for sale of property (s 24A), pension sharing (s 24B) and pension sharing compensation (s 24E) orders.

(d) proceedings under Sch 5 to CPA 2004 for financial relief connected with proceedings for dissolution, nullity or separation.[7]

5.06 As the provisions for financial relief under MCA 1973 and CPA 2004 correspond and provide the same financial remedies to married couples as to civil partners, in order to avoid repetition the rest of this section will refer only to orders under MCA 1973.

5.07 An LSO granted under the provisions of s 22ZA may cover the cost of legal advice, assistance and representation, and specifically it may include the costs of mediation and alternative dispute resolution including arbitration.[8]

> '22ZA Orders for payment in respect of legal services
>
> (1) In proceedings for divorce, nullity of marriage or judicial separation, the court may make an order or orders requiring one party to the marriage to pay to the other ("the applicant") an amount for the purpose of enabling the applicant to obtain legal services for the purposes of the proceedings.
>
> (2) The court may also make such an order or orders in proceedings under this Part for financial relief in connection with proceedings for divorce, nullity of marriage or judicial separation.
>
> (3) The court must not make an order under this section unless it is satisfied that, without the amount, the applicant would not reasonably be able to obtain appropriate legal services for the purposes of the proceedings or any part of the proceedings.
>
> (4) For the purposes of subsection (3), the court must be satisfied, in particular, that—
> (a) the applicant is not reasonably able to secure a loan to pay for the services, and
> (b) the applicant is unlikely to be able to obtain the services by granting a charge over any assets recovered in the proceedings.
>
> (5) An order under this section may be made for the purpose of enabling the applicant to obtain legal services of a specified description, including legal services provided in a specified period or for the purposes of a specified part of the proceedings.
>
> (6) An order under this section may—
> (a) provide for the payment of all or part of the amount by instalments of specified amounts, and
> (b) require the instalments to be secured to the satisfaction of the court.

7 Ie proceedings for maintenance pending outcome (Pt 8), financial provision for periodical or lump sums (Pt 1), property adjustment orders (Pt 2), orders for sale of property (Pt 3), pension sharing (Pt 4) and pension sharing compensation (Pt 4A) orders.

8 MCA 1973, s 22ZA(10).

(7) An order under this section may direct that payment of all or part of the amount is to be deferred.

(8) The court may at any time in the proceedings vary an order made under this section if it considers that there has been a material change of circumstances since the order was made.

(9) For the purposes of the assessment of costs in the proceedings, the applicant's costs are to be treated as reduced by any amount paid to the applicant pursuant to an order under this section for the purposes of those proceedings.

(10) In this section "legal services", in relation to proceedings, means the following types of services—
- (a) providing advice as to how the law applies in the particular circumstances,
- (b) providing advice and assistance in relation to the proceedings,
- (c) providing other advice and assistance in relation to the settlement or other resolution of the dispute that is the subject of the proceedings, and
- (d) providing advice and assistance in relation to the enforcement of decisions in the proceedings or as part of the settlement or resolution of the dispute,

and they include, in particular, advice and assistance in the form of representation and any form of dispute resolution, including mediation.

(11) In subsections (5) and (6) "specified" means specified in the order concerned.

22ZB Matters to which court is to have regard in deciding how to exercise power under section 22ZA

(1) When considering whether to make or vary an order under section 22ZA, the court must have regard to—
- (a) the income, earning capacity, property and other financial resources which each of the applicant and the paying party has or is likely to have in the foreseeable future,
- (b) the financial needs, obligations and responsibilities which each of the applicant and the paying party has or is likely to have in the foreseeable future,
- (c) the subject matter of the proceedings, including the matters in issue in them,
- (d) whether the paying party is legally represented in the proceedings,
- (e) any steps taken by the applicant to avoid all or part of the proceedings, whether by proposing or considering mediation or otherwise,
- (f) the applicant's conduct in relation to the proceedings,
- (g) any amount owed by the applicant to the paying party in respect of costs in the proceedings or other proceedings to which both the applicant and the paying party are or were party, and
- (h) the effect of the order or variation on the paying party.

(2) In subsection (1)(a) "earning capacity", in relation to the applicant or the paying party, includes any increase in earning capacity which, in the opinion of the court, it would be reasonable to expect the applicant or the paying party to take steps to acquire.

(3) For the purposes of subsection (1)(h), the court must have regard, in particular, to whether the making or variation of the order is likely to—
(a) cause undue hardship to the paying party, or
(b) prevent the paying party from obtaining legal services for the purposes of the proceedings.

(4) The Lord Chancellor may by order amend this section by adding to, omitting or varying the matters mentioned in subsections (1) to (3).

(5) An order under subsection (4) must be made by statutory instrument.

(6) A statutory instrument containing an order under subsection (4) may not be made unless a draft of the instrument has been laid before, and approved by a resolution of, each House of Parliament.

(7) In this section "legal services" has the same meaning as in section 22ZA.'[9]

5.08 The court has dealt with a number of applications for such orders under the statute.

5.09 The case of *Makarskaya v Korchagin*[10] was heard by Moylan J and concerned parties in a short, childless marriage with assets of around £3.1 million in issue. The court refused to re-open the wife's application for extensive backdated legal services costs (which had been dismissed under the provisions of s 22ZA(3) by King J at an earlier hearing). At that previous hearing, King J had awarded the wife an LSO of £40,200 to cover her costs of the proposed three day fact finding hearing. In fact, that hearing was subsequently vacated upon the husband's acceptance of those facts. Moylan J determined that the wife's earlier award of £40,200 would provide her with sufficient funds both to finance her legal costs up to and including the FDR, and to pay a judgment debt of £21,000 in favour of her former solicitors.

5.10 In a subsequent case, Moylan J decided that a wife would be unable to obtain legal representation and would be placed on an unequal footing without the benefit of an LSO.[11] However, the judge decided not to exercise the power available under s 22ZA despite noting that: the litigation was complex;[12] both parties would benefit from representation; and the wife would be unable to cover the costs of legal services by other means.[13] The ownership of various properties was in dispute, but the judge stated that 'the only asset which I can safely conclude

9 And in similar terms in Sch 5, Part 8, paras 38A and 38B to CPA 2004.
10 [2013] EWHC 4393 (Fam).
11 *AM V SS* [2013] EWHC 4380 (Fam) at [34], [2015] 1 FLR 1237.
12 At [31].
13 At [34].

is or might be available is the equity (of at least £200,000)[14] in the Maida Vale Property'.[15] Moylan J was concerned that the wife's solicitors were already owed £104,000 and that her estimated future costs were £122,000. The husband was ordered to provide the wife a charge over the Maida Vale Property in the amount of £150,000. £100,000 of that sum was to be used to cover the wife's future costs to the conclusion of the final hearing,[16] and £50,000 was in respect of the costs she had already incurred.[17]

5.11 The cases of *MET v HAT*,[18] *BN v MA*[19] and *Rubin v Rubin*[20] then came before Mostyn J in quick succession. In *MET v HAT*, the judge decided that the subject matter of the proceedings appeared to lack any merit and, in consideration of s 22ZB(1)(c) on this point, the wife's application was dismissed.[21]

5.12 The wife in *BN v MA* had received two offers of litigation loans of £400,000 and £250,000 respectively. Mostyn J noted that although the interest to be charged on each loan was 'fairly steep', it could be rolled up.[22] On that basis, the wife's application fell foul of s 22ZA(4)(a). The judge went on to look at the issue more generally by considering s 22ZB. He found the wife's claim to be highly speculative and with doubtful prospects of success and stated he would not have made a costs award under this section either. Practitioners will also wish to note that Mostyn J remarked that the wife had failed to provide a detailed costs schedule and the information she had provided was entirely inadequate for an LSO to be made.[23] As the wife's application was dismissed the judge allowed the husband his costs.

5.13 The award of an LSO was considered by the Supreme Court in *Wyatt v Vince*,[24] a case in which the husband had applied to strike out the wife's financial remedy application on the basis that the marriage had ended almost 20 years earlier. The LSO had been made in the lower court, before s 22ZA came into force, under the provisions of *Currey*[25] and *A v A*.[26] The wife submitted to the deputy judge of the High Court that her solicitors had agreed to recover their costs from any lump sum ordered as a consequence of her application for interim maintenance and legal costs. That arrangement was to be reviewed after the application for interim maintenance had been decided.[27]

14 At [25].
15 At [36].
16 Contrast with Mostyn J's view on funding beyond the FDR set out at **5.17**.
17 At [39].
18 [2013] EWHC 4247 (Fam), [2014] 2 FLR 692.
19 [2013] EWHC 4250 (Fam).
20 [2014] EWHC 611 (Fam), [2014] 2 FLR 1018.
21 [2013] EWHC 4247 (Fam), [2014] 2 FLR 692 at [22].
22 [2013] EWHC 4250 (Fam) at [37].
23 At [38].
24 [2015] UKSC 14.
25 Discussed at **5.30**.
26 *A v A (Maintenance pending suit: provision for legal costs)* [2000] All ER (D) 1627.
27 *Vince v Wyatt* [2013] EWCA Civ 495, [2014] 1 FLR 246 at [38].

5.14 The matter came before the Court of Appeal where the primary appeal to strike out succeeded and therefore the court did not have to consider the husband's appeal of the costs order. Nevertheless, the court said that the costs appeal would have been allowed. The court decided the case was unconventional and difficult, with the consequence that the husband might defeat the wife's application for a financial remedy, be unable to recover his own costs and have to pay those of his wife.[28]

5.15 The Supreme Court, reversing the Court of Appeal's decision on the primary matter, restored the LSO. The court noted the wife had owed her solicitors £88,000 and was likely to recover, at best, only a small sum. In addition, the husband was described as litigious and having instigated an acceleration in the interim costs.[29]

5.16 In reinstating the LSO on appeal,[30] Lord Wilson considered the position in respect to the money that had already been paid and spent under that order. He noted that the court had the power to order all the sums be repaid, but in this case the Court of Appeal had exercised its discretion properly in ordering only a partial repayment. Lord Wilson held that where money has been provided under an LSO and has been used accordingly, and there has been a successful appeal against that LSO, the court should decide how much of the money spent should be returned, having considered all the circumstances including: whether a stay might have been applied for by the payer (and such an application had not been made in this case); whether the recipient has the ability to repay; and whether the payer should be permitted to enforce the repayment without the leave of the court.[31]

Rubin v Rubin

5.17 The leading case on LSOs under ss 22ZA and 22ZB is *Rubin v Rubin*.[32] Here, Mostyn J set out fairly detailed directions which have since been used to assist the court in determining such applications:

> 'Therefore it may be helpful and convenient if I were to set out my attempt to summarise the applicable principles both substantive and procedural:
>
> i) When considering the overall merits of the application for a LSPO the court is required to have regard to all the matters mentioned in s 22ZB(1) – (3).
>
> ii) Without derogating from that requirement, the ability of the Respondent to pay should be judged by reference to the principles summarised

28 At [42] per Thorpe LJ.
29 At [40].
30 At [41].
31 At [42].
32 At [13].

in *TL v ML* [2005] EWHC 2860 (Fam) [2006] 1 FCR 465 [2006] 1 FLR 1263 at para 124 (iv) and (v), where it was stated:

> "iv) court should not hesitate to make robust assumptions about his ability to pay. The court is not confined to the mere say-so of the payer as to the extent of his income or resources. In such a situation the court should err in favour of the payee.
>
> v) Where the paying party has historically been supported through the bounty of an outsider, and where the payer is asserting that the bounty had been curtailed but where the position of the outsider is ambiguous or unclear, then the court is justified in assuming that the third party will continue to supply the bounty, at least until final trial."

iii) Where the claim for substantive relief appears doubtful, whether by virtue of a challenge to the jurisdiction, or otherwise having regard to its subject matter, the court should judge the application with caution. The more doubtful it is, the more cautious it should be.

iv) The court cannot make an order unless it is satisfied that without the payment the Applicant would not reasonably be able to obtain appropriate legal services for the proceedings. Therefore, the exercise essentially looks to the future. It is important that the jurisdiction is not used to outflank or supplant the powers and principles governing an award of costs in CPR Pt 44. It is not a surrogate inter partes costs jurisdiction. Thus a LSPO should only be awarded to cover historic unpaid costs where the court is satisfied that without such a payment the Applicant will not reasonably be able to obtain in the future appropriate legal services for the proceedings.

v) In determining whether the Applicant can reasonably obtain funding from another source the court would be unlikely to expect her to sell or charge her home or to deplete a modest fund of savings. This aspect is however highly fact-specific. If the home is of such a value that it appears likely that it will be sold at the conclusion of the proceedings then it may well be reasonable to expect the Applicant to charge her interest in it.

vi) Evidence of refusals by two commercial lenders of repute will normally dispose of any issue under s 22ZA(4)(a) whether a litigation loan is or is not available.

vii) In determining under s 22ZA(4)(b) whether a Sears Tooth arrangement[33] can be entered into a statement of refusal by the Applicant's solicitors should normally answer the question.

viii) If a litigation loan is offered at a very high rate of interest it would be unlikely to be reasonable to expect the Applicant to take it unless the

33 An arrangement by which a party to the proceedings assigns to their solicitors part of a future interest to cover their legal costs; see **6.04–6.08**.

Respondent offered an undertaking to meet that interest, if the court later considered it just so to order.

ix) The order should normally contain an undertaking by the Applicant that she will repay to the Respondent such part of the amount ordered if, and to the extent that, the court is of the opinion, when considering costs at the conclusion of the proceedings, that she ought to do so. If such an undertaking is refused the court will want to think twice before making the order.

x) The court should make clear in its ruling or judgment which of the legal services mentioned in s 22ZA(10) the payment is for; it is not however necessary to spell this out in the order. A LSPO may be made for the purposes, in particular, of advice and assistance in the form of representation and any form of dispute resolution, including mediation. Thus the power may be exercised before any financial remedy proceedings have been commenced in order to finance any form of alternative dispute resolution, which plainly would include arbitration proceedings.

xi) Generally speaking, the court should not fund the Applicant beyond the FDR, but the court should readily grant a hearing date for further funding to be fixed shortly after the FDR. This is a better course than ordering a sum for the whole proceedings of which part is deferred under s 22ZA(7). The court will be better placed to assess accurately the true costs of taking the matter to trial after a failed FDR when the final hearing is relatively imminent, and the issues to be tried are more clearly defined.

xii) When ordering costs funding for a specified period, monthly instalments are to be preferred to a single lump sum payment. It is true that a single payment avoids anxiety on the part of the Applicant as to whether the monthly sums will actually be paid as well as the annoyance inflicted on the Respondent in having to make monthly payments. However, monthly payments more accurately reflects [sic] what would happen if the Applicant were paying her lawyers from her own resources, and very likely will mirror the position of the Respondent. If both sets of lawyers are having their fees met monthly this puts them on an equal footing both in the conduct of the case and in any dialogue about settlement. Further, monthly payments are more readily susceptible to variation under s 22ZA(8) should circumstances change.

xiii) If the application for a LSPO seeks an award including the costs of that very application the court should bear in mind s 22ZA(9) whereby a party's bill of costs in assessment proceedings is treated as reduced by the amount of any LSPO made in his or her favour. Thus, if an LSPO is made in an amount which includes the anticipated costs of that very application for the LSPO, then an order for the costs of that application will not bite save to the extent that the actual costs of the application may exceed such part of the LSPO as is referable thereto.

xiv) A LSPO is designated as an interim order and is to be made under the Pt 18 procedure (see FPR r 9.7(1)(da) and (2)). 14 days' notice must be given (see FPR r 18.8(b)(i) and PD9A para 12.1). The application must be supported by written evidence (see FPR r 18.8(2) and PD9A para 12.2). That evidence must not only address the matters in s 22ZB(1)-(3) but must include a detailed estimate of the costs both incurred and to be incurred. If the application seeks a hearing sooner than 14 days from the date of issue of the application pursuant to FPR r 18.8(4) then the written evidence in support must explain why it is fair and just that the time should be abridged.'

5.18 Of particular note is the principle that an LSO should not make provision for historic costs that are due, unless failure to do so will affect the applicant's reasonable ability to procure future legal services in the proceedings. It is worth mentioning that this rule restricting the payment of historic costs also applies in applications for security for costs (see also **5.37**).

5.19 Furthermore, whilst the court may order a single sum to be paid, monthly instalments are favoured. Moreover, an LSO should not cover funding beyond the FDR, and if the matter progresses a further application will be required.

5.20 We also note that, at para 13x of *Rubin*, Mostyn J makes the obiter comment that the power to order a legal services payment may be exercised before financial remedy proceedings have begun. It appears to us that this premise remains to be considered further, as there is no specific legislative power enabling the court to make such an order in advance of proceedings. Therefore, whilst there is an absence of case law on this point, practitioners are advised to treat the proposition with caution.

Cases since Rubin

5.21 The case of *Baldwin v Baldwin*[34] was heard by Mrs Justice Parker, a few days after *Rubin* had been determined and without reference to that case. The judge found that the husband had deliberately sought to starve the wife of her litigation funds.[35] The wife had applied for interim maintenance plus an LSO of £4,000 monthly.[36] The judge found the wife's application fell within s 22ZA and that she had exhausted the litigation loan provided by her family and would be unable to obtain alternative funding.[37] An LSO was ordered in the terms applied for. The judge further ordered that the wife should be granted all her costs of the application on the standard basis.

5.22 Mrs Justice Roberts applied the *Rubin* principles in the case of *US v SR*.[38] Both parties had applied to the court for LSOs in regard to their ongoing

34 [2014] EWHC 4857 (Fam).
35 [2], [61] and [67].
36 At [25].
37 At [60].
38 [2014] EWHC 2864 (Fam).

costs. It was suggested the orders should be funded from an offshore account in Jersey which had been frozen earlier in the proceedings. The wife had outstanding historic costs of £75,000.[39] The judge found: the wife lacked the means to make any substantive payment towards her costs; she had provided adequate evidence that she was unable to raise funds from external commercial sources; she owed Novitas, the litigation funder, around £200,000 plus interest at 18%. An LSO in her favour was granted to pay £127,577 (less any set-off due to money raised from the sale of a car) directly to the wife's solicitors. This sum covered costs incurred but unpaid and an estimate of her costs going forward to a five-day hearing.

5.23 The husband sought the release of a sum of £60,000 from the frozen account to enable him to cover his costs to the end of the five-day hearing. The judge dismissed his application having found the husband had access to liquid funds of around £275,000 to finance his ongoing legal costs

5.24 The judge noted that applying the *Rubin* principles in this case was difficult as it was not 'a standard free-standing application'.[40] Further, the husband's earlier litigation misconduct (particularly in respect to some significantly misleading disclosure he had made) affected her decision. She made an award to cover the wife's historic costs since, due to time constraints at the earlier fact-finding hearing, the husband had not been penalised in costs.

5.25 The case of *LKH v TQA AL Z (Interim Maintenance and pound for pound costs funding)*[41] was a 'big money' financial remedy case in which the wife had been awarded a monthly costs allowance of £40,000 for six months to cover her litigation costs in financial and children proceedings. The matter came back before Mr Justice Holman, as the LSO had been ignored by the husband and £120,000 was owed to the wife. During the period of default, the husband had paid £95,000 to his own solicitors. The wife asked for £100 for every £1 paid by the husband to his own legal representatives. The judge noted that the objective of a pound for pound order was to create equality of arms and that therefore it was right that the wife receive £1 for every £1 spent by the husband. An injunction was granted to prevent the husband from paying further money to any legal representative he had instructed unless he paid an equal amount to the wife's solicitors to discharge the arrears and ongoing instalments of the LSO.

5.26 In *De Gafforj (Appeal – Hadkinson Order)*[42], the court granted the wife's application for a *Hadkinson* order[43] by dismissing the husband's appeal on a jurisdiction point unless he paid sums due under a maintenance and LSO order. The wife had been awarded a LSO of £80,099 to cover a debt to her former

39 At [22].
40 At [18] and [30].
41 [2018] EWHC 2436 (Fam).
42 [2018] EWCA Civ 2070.
43 *Hadkinson v Hadkinson* [1952] P 285. An order preventing a party stubbornly in breach of court orders from making further applications or for arguing their case.

solicitors plus £12,000 monthly to fund her ongoing litigation costs. In his leading judgment, Lord Justice Peter Jackson set out the necessary conditions for the making of a *Hadkinson* order,[44] and found them all made out. In particular, the husband's failure to pay the LSO was impacting 'in the most direct way possible upon the course of justice'.[45]

Application procedure

5.27 A free-standing s 22ZA application may be made under FPR Pt 18[46] with an application notice in Form D11, a statement in support and a draft order. Clearly, the statement should address all the principles set out at ss 22ZA(3) and (4) and 22ZB(1), (2) and (3) and by Mostyn J in *Rubin*.[47] In particular, evidence of the applicant's financial position and their inability to raise a loan or to grant a charge over assets in order to finance legal services will be required. In addition, full statements of the costs already incurred and the predicted future costs should be provided.

5.28 The judge at the FDR appointment must not deal with an LSO application.[48]

Proceedings other than those related to divorce and civil partnership dissolution

5.29 As the statutory provisions under the MCA 1973 and the CPA 2004 only apply to proceedings related to divorce and civil partnership dissolution, in all other family proceedings it is still necessary to apply for an interim order for costs funding under the common law principles set out in *Currey v Currey*.[49] This disparity was addressed in *Rubin* by Mostyn J,[50] who stated that the principles he had outlined[51] should also apply (with any amendments required) to applications for LSOs in proceedings under: the CA 1989, Sch 1 in respect to financial relief for children; IP(FD)A 1975; and the MFPA 1984, Pt III for financial relief following an overseas divorce.

5.30 In *Currey*, Wilson LJ said the primary question in determining an application for a costs allowance was whether there are any other means by which the applicant is able to obtain legal advice and representation.[52] Such other means might include raising a loan, offering a charge upon the final capital

44 [2018] EWCA Civ 2070 at [11].
45 *Ibid* at [17].
46 FPR r 9.7(2).
47 At **5.17**.
48 FPR r 9.17(2).
49 [2006] EWCA Civ 1338, [2007] 1 FLR 946.
50 At [14]-[15].
51 See **5.17**.
52 [2006] EWCA Civ 1338, [2007] 1 FLR 946 at [20].

recovery, or obtaining public funding. If the applicant shows an inability to raise the necessary funds by other means, the court should then assess the subject matter of the proceedings and the reasonableness of the applicant's position in respect to those proceedings. Other features of the case may also be relevant; for example, in *Currey* the court noted, 'the arresting fact that the husband already owes £46,000 to the wife in respect of costs'.[53]

Children Act 1989, Sch 1 and s 8

5.31 Sch 1 to the CA 1989 concerns financial provision for children and allows a parent to apply for an interim costs order to fund litigation, that will be for the benefit of the child concerned, by allowing the parties to litigate with equal arms.[54] The court has a discretion in making such an award but should consider the statutory checklist,[55] and take care that an award is not 'spent to satisfy the applicant's taste for litigation'.[56] Any payments ordered can later be considered in the substantive order to reduce any possible unfairness between the parties.[57]

5.32 Charles J in *CF v KM*[58] determined that the court's jurisdiction to order such a lump sum is not barred by the Child Support Act 1991, s 8 (which limits the court's power to grant periodical payments where a child maintenance calculation below the maximum assessment is in place) and that the order may be made using statutory powers in relation to proceedings under both the CA 1989, Sch 1 and s 8. At the time, this seemed to be a radical decision which offered a considerable attraction to an impecunious parent who could have the child's other parent pay for their legal costs.

5.33 Subsequently, in *Dickson v Rennie*[59] Holman J noted that a lump sum order under CA 1989, Sch 1 may be made 'in order to enable a parent to fund proportionate and justifiable litigation designed to achieve a higher level of underlying maintenance for the child concerned'. The judge made a lump sum order of £10,000 to cover the mother's costs of lawyers' fees in her appeal to the First-tier Tribunal. The mother was ordered to pay that sum directly to her solicitors and, at the conclusion of the appeal, she was to provide the father with an itemised bill of the legal costs of her appeal and to refund the father appropriately if that bill totalled less than £10,000. It is of note that Holman J's order circumvented the position that neither First-tier Tribunals nor Upper Tribunals are empowered to award costs in child maintenance cases.

53 At [21].
54 *M-T v T* [2006] EWHC 2494 (Fam), [2007] 2 FLR 925 at [22].
55 CA 1989, Sch 1, para 4.
56 *MT v OT* [2007] EWHC 838 (Fam), [2008] 2 FLR 1311 at [154] per Charles J.
57 *MT v OT* [2007] EWHC 838 (Fam), [2008] 2 FLR 1311 at [155] per Charles J.
58 [2010] EWHC 1754 (Fam), [2011] 1 FLR 208.
59 [2015] 2 FLR 978, [2014] EWHC 4306 (Fam) at [40].

5.34 In early 2015, Mostyn J had the opportunity to address the matter of a costs allowance application made under CA 1989, Sch 1 in *MG and another v JF and another*.[60] The application was made by the two mothers of a child who had been born by donor sperm of the father. The father had been named on the birth certificate and had contact with the child until the parties' relationship broke down. Consequently, the father brought proceedings seeking to spend time with the child and then made further applications pursuing specific issue orders concerning education and vaccination and requesting assessment and therapeutic intervention from a child psychiatrist. The mothers and the father had instructed counsel under the direct access scheme; whilst the child had been granted public funding and was represented by a guardian and a solicitor. The father had reasonable resources at his disposal. However, although the mothers had increased the mortgage on their property by £20,000, they owed fees to their counsel. There had been eight hearings and there was the prospect of an issues resolution hearing and a five day final hearing if the matter could not be concluded by consent.

5.35 Having assessed the means of the three parties, Mostyn J ordered the father, 'should pay 80% of each of the claims of MG and JG [the mothers]. Therefore he will pay MG £12,202 and JG £8,394. In addition he will pay 80% of all future professional costs in respect of therapeutic work and MG and JG will each pay 10% of such costs.'[61] The payment to the mothers was to cover the fees they owed to counsel and the ongoing costs of their legal representatives. The judge further ordered that the costs of the outstanding expert evidence should be paid by the child and gave reasons why those charges were a reasonable disbursement on his legal aid certificate.[62] The judge noted, 'MG and JG have not applied for exceptional funding under s 10(3)(b) of LASPO 2012, no doubt taking the realistic view that any such application would be rejected summarily.'[63]

5.36 Mostyn J also stated:[64]

> 'In this case it is my firm view that it is impossible for MG and JG to be expected to represent themselves having regard to the factual and legal issues at large. There would be a gross inequality of arms, and arguably a violation of their rights under Articles 6 and 8 of the European Convention on Human Rights and Article 47 of the European Charter of Fundamental Rights. So even though it cannot be said that JF has behaved reprehensibly or unreasonably he is the only realistic source of costs funding, subject to whatever contribution MG and JG should make from their own very limited resources. Some may say (and have said) that this is grossly unjust; I myself refrain from comment.'

60 [2015] EWHC 564 (Fam), [2016] 1 FLR 424.
61 At [34].
62 At [38]-[40].
63 At [14]. Exceptional case funding is now more widely granted: see **7.08**.
64 At [10].

5.37 It is noteworthy that this costs order was partly prospective and partly retrospective. As we have seen, the provisions of s 22ZA leave the way open for the court to make LSOs for costs already incurred if by paying off those legal debts future representation can be obtained. Mostyn J made it clear in his judgment that the payments towards the costs arrears were to enable representation to continue.[65]

5.38 In July 2016, Cobb J considered two applications in CA 1989 proceedings, for legal services funding orders. The judge noted his power to make such orders under the jurisdiction of the common law[66] and accepted Mostyn J's view that (with some alterations) the principles under the statute and under the common law are the same and are as set out in the *Rubin* principles.

5.39 In the first case, *BC v DE*,[67] an impecunious mother had claimed legal costs orders related to proceedings under CA 1989, Sch 1 and s 8. She sought lump sums in respect to her unpaid and future legal costs of around £140,000 and £150,000 respectively. The judge described the father as 'extraordinarily wealthy'.[68] The mother had succeeded in her earlier applications for legal costs funding awards for 'certain past' costs and prospective costs.[69] The key decision for the judge was whether or not an award covering the historic unpaid costs should be made. Cobb J reasoned that a large outstanding debt owed by a party to their solicitor may impact upon their professional relationship such that the child's interests might be adversely affected. The judge also noted that, 'It is neither fair nor reasonable to expect solicitors and the bar to offer unsecured interest-free credit in order to undertake their work; there is indeed a solid reason for lawyers not to have a financial interest in the outcome of family law litigation.'[70] Cobb J considered that, when describing 'historic costs' in *Rubin*, Mostyn J had been referring to costs incurred in separate, concluded proceedings. *BC v DC* was distinguished, as the historic costs related to the current proceedings. Curiously, the judge allowed the costs of the CA 1989, s 8 proceedings which he said could be argued to have concluded. He justified this approach as the dispute regarding the child had, 'been proceeding in parallel on these two related fronts over the last nine months.'[71] Cobb J assumed that the instructing solicitors' s 8 files remained open. A 15% discount from all the costs claimed was made to reflect a notional standard basis of assessment[72] and the award was to be paid in instalments.

5.40 In the second case, *MG v FG*,[73] Cobb J dismissed a mother's application for a legal services funding order in CA 1989, Sch 1 proceedings. The judge applied the *Rubin* guidelines and found: the parties' resources were limited; the

65 At [22].
66 [2016] EWHC 1806 (Fam) at [11]–[12].
67 [2016] EWHC 1806 (Fam).
68 At [3].
69 At [5].
70 At [22].
71 At [31].
72 At [28].
73 [2016] EWHC 1964 (Fam).

mother had already made numerous, unsuccessful applications in both Australia and this jurisdiction; the mother was subject to an unpaid costs order in the father's favour; the mother's claim appeared doubtful and so was judged with caution; and it was unlikely that the father would recover sums paid to the mother under a legal costs funding award by way of a final costs order.[74]

MCA 1973 and CPA 2004 (save proceedings related to divorce and dissolution)

5.41 An applicant may obtain an award for legal costs within an application for an interim order under MCA 1973, s 27[75] by applying the case law that exists for applications under CA 1989, Sch 1.[76]

Matrimonial and Family Proceedings Act 1984, Part III

5.42 The MFPA 1984, Pt III concerns financial relief after an overseas divorce. Under this statute, a party may apply for funding in respect to legal costs within an application for interim maintenance.[77] As at **5.32** to **5.40**, such applications are considered under the case law prior to the introduction of ss 22ZA and 22ZB.

5.43 In *Rubin*, Mostyn J noted that, under MFPA 1984, Pt III, an interim order only permits periodical payments.[78]

Inheritance (Provision for Family and Dependants) Act 1975

5.44 The Inheritance (Provision for Family and Dependants) Act 1975 (I(PFD)A 1975), s 5 provides for claims for interim relief if the 'Applicant is in immediate need of financial assistance but it is not yet possible to determine what order (if any) shall be made under that section'. *Smith v Smith* was heard in the Chancery Division and Mann J held that a requirement to pay lawyers to conduct litigation would meet the criteria under this section.[79] In determining the application, the court will consider the matters set out at I(PFD)A 1975, s 3.

Proceedings under the Inherent Jurisdiction

5.45 In *HB v A Local Authority (Local Government Association intervening)*[80], Mr Justice MacDonald was clear that the court could not make a costs funding

74 At [31].
75 Or under CPA 2004, Sch 5, Pt 9 'Failure to Maintain: Financial Provision (and Interim Orders)'.
76 See **5.29–5.40**.
77 Matrimonial and Family Proceedings Act 1984, s 14.
78 At [15].
79 [2011] EWHC 2133 (Ch), [2012] 2 FLR 230 at [41].
80 [2017] EWHC 524 (Fam).

order to a mother in wardship proceedings, relating to alleged radicalisation, brought by a local authority under the inherent jurisdiction of the High Court.[81] The mother was ineligible for legal aid due to the level of her monthly disposable income. The judge noted that the statutory scheme for legal funding was clear and that the mother had lawfully been refused legal aid under that scheme. A general power of the court was not to be used to circumvent the statute and could not be used to compel a local authority to incur expenditure for which there was no clear statutory authority. The judge was of the view that it was appropriate that the proceedings should be dealt under CA 1989, Pt IV and this approach would enable the mother to obtain representation with public funding.

Fighting funds or war chests

5.46 The courts have found an alternative method of assisting litigants with litigation costs in financial remedy cases. Under MCA 1973, s 23(1)(c) one party may be ordered to pay a lump sum to the other, provided the paying party has the appropriate financial resources[82] and the court has considered all the circumstances of the case.[83] Using this approach, the court has on occasions ordered sums to be paid, which have been referred to as 'war chests' or 'fighting funds', in anticipation of further litigation by the paying party.

5.47 Munby J made an order granting a wife a £2.5 million war chest in the big money case of *Al-Khatib v Masry*.[84] That capital sum (along with accrued interest) was to be made available to the wife so that she could fund any further litigation required to enforce the return of her five children from Saudi Arabia. The unused portion of the fund was to be returned to the husband once he had returned the children either to the court's jurisdiction or to the wife. In making this order, Munby J relied upon MCA 1973, s 25(1) and (2)(b) which required the court to consider the welfare of the children and the wife's financial needs, obligations and responsibilities in the foreseeable future.

5.48 The husband was granted permission to appeal on various points, including the grant of the war chest of £2.5 million. After the parties had mediated under the Court of Appeal ADR scheme, the Court of Appeal approved an agreed order which concluded proceedings and removed the obligation upon the husband to provide the war chest.[85]

5.49 In the financial remedy case of *Minwalla v Minwalla*.[86] Singer J followed Munby J's approach in *Al-Khatib*. A separate and additional lump sum instalment of £500,000 was to be paid by the husband to the wife to enable her to respond

81 At [94].
82 MCA 1973, s 25(2)(a).
83 MCA 1973, s 25(1).
84 [2002] EWHC 108 (Fam) at [133–134], [2002] 1 FLR 1053.
85 [2004] EWCA Civ 1353.
86 [2004] EWHC 2823 (Fam) at [92–93], [2005] 1 FLR 771.

to his threatened, future litigation. That sum was to be paid after payment of the balance of the lump sum and costs. Singer J suggested the husband might apply to vary that payment[87] if it proved to be excessive or if he chose to bind himself such that his wife would not need the fund in future.

5.50 In the subsequent case of *Thiry v Thiry*[88] (again concerned with a financial remedy), Sir Peter Singer made a similar order in a similar sum. In relation to the husband, the judge stated: 'I take seriously what I regard not only as the risk but also his threat that by seeking to engage her or her companies in attritional litigation in this country or elsewhere he will attempt to delay the day of reckoning, in effect counterclaiming in respect of damages said to flow from her alleged denunciation of him to state authorities in Belgium.'[89]

ORDERS FOR SECURITY FOR COSTS

5.51 *Civil Procedure 2019* states:[90]

> 'The purpose of an order for security for costs is to protect a party in whose favour it is made against the risk of being unable to enforce any costs order they may later obtain. The order, if complied with, will provide the party in whose favour it is made with a fund normally held by the court against which he can enforce any award of costs they may later obtain.'

Application procedure

5.52 Applications for security for costs in family proceedings are seldom made. This is no doubt because in family proceedings the rule that costs follow the event does not apply and accordingly costs orders are not routine. The procedural rule relating to security for costs originated under the CPR pertaining to civil proceedings where costs orders are the norm. However, the FPR 2010[91] came into force on 6 April 2011 and Pt 20, Chap 2 sets out the applicable family procedural rules; there is no Practice Direction in this respect.

5.53 The application for security must be made by the respondent to an application using the FPR Pt 18 procedure and with the support of written evidence.[92] If the order is made, the court will specify the sum of the security and will direct how and when that security must be provided.[93] This procedure mirrors the practice under CPR r 25.12. Although the evidence required is not

87 Under MCA 1973, s 31(2)(d).
88 [2014] EWHC 4046 (Fam), [2015] 2 FLR 743.
89 At [43].
90 *Civil Procedure 2019, Volume 1* (Thomson Reuters, 2019), 25.12.2.
91 SI 2010/2955.
92 FPR r 20.6(2).
93 FPR r 20.6(3).

specified under the procedural rules, it has been suggested that details of costs incurred and estimated future costs should be attached to the application or a schedule in the form of Precedent H[94] (the costs budget prescribed under the CPR).[95]

Conditions on which the security will be granted

5.54 The court may make the order having considered all the circumstances of the case and decided that it is just to do so,[96] and either:

'(i) one or more of the conditions in paragraph (2) applies; or
(ii) an enactment permits the court to require security for costs.[97]

(2) The conditions are—
(a) the applicant is—
(i) resident out of the jurisdiction; but
(ii) not resident in a Brussels Contracting State, a State bound by the Lugano Convention, a State bound by the 2007 Hague Convention which is an EEA State, a Regulation State or a Maintenance Regulation State, as defined in Section 1(3) of the Civil Jurisdiction and Judgments Act 1982, or a Member State bound by the Council Regulation;[98]
(b) the applicant has changed address since the application was started with a view to evading the consequences of the litigation;
(c) the applicant failed to give an address in the application form, or gave an incorrect address in that form;
(d) the applicant has taken steps in relation to the applicant's assets that would make it difficult to enforce an order for costs against the applicant.'[99]

5.55 Following the judgment of David Donaldson QC, sitting as a deputy High Court Judge, in *Dass v Beggs and another* it is clear that generally the

94 Rowley and Middleton, *Cook on Costs 2019* (LexisNexis Butterworths, 2018), 19.23.
95 See https://www.gov.uk/government/publications/form-precedent-h-and-r-costs-budget-precedent-h-and-budget-discussion-report-precedent-r.
96 FPR r 20.7(1)(a).
97 FPR r 20.7(1) replicates CPR r 25.13(1) and under the CPR certain enactments (such as the Life Assurance Companies (Payment into Court) Act 1896 and the Trustee Act 1925) allow for payments into court.
98 https://eur-lex.europa.eu/legal-content/EN/ALL/?uri=CELEX%3A22007A1221%2803%29
https://www.hcch.net/en/instruments/conventions/status-table/?cid=131
Civil Jurisdiction and Judgments Act 1982, s 1(3) where 'Regulation State' and 'Maintenance Regulation State' mean a Member State. https://europa.eu/european-union/about-eu/countries_en
Austria, Belgium, Bulgaria, Croatia, Republic of Cyprus, Czech Republic, Denmark, Estonia, Finland, France, Germany, Greece, Hungary, Iceland, Ireland, Italy, Latvia, Lithuania, Luxembourg, Malta, Netherlands, Norway, Poland, Portugal, Romania, Slovakia, Slovenia, Spain, Sweden, Switzerland and the United Kingdom (at the time of writing).
99 FPR r 20.7.

court will consider the test under FPR r 20.7(2) as the 'gateway condition' before considering, under FPR r 20.7(1), whether it is just to make the order.[100]

5.56 The Court of Appeal has found CPR r 25.13(2)(a) (and by analogy FPR r 20.7 (2)(a)) to be discriminatory against applicants or potential applicants who are not resident in the UK or another Convention state.[101] However the provision is justified provided the court exercises its powers by considering the difficulties in enforcing a costs order. In *Chernukhin and others v Danilina*,[102] Hamblen LJ set out the test to be adopted by the court to ensure its discretion is exercised without discrimination:

> '...
>
> (4) This requires "objectively justified grounds relating to obstacles to or the burden of enforcement in the context of the particular foreign claimant or country concerned" ...
>
> (5) Such grounds exist where there is a real risk of "substantial obstacles to enforcement" or of an additional burden in terms of cost or delay ...
>
> (6) The order for security should generally be tailored to cater for the relevant risk ...
>
> (7) Where the risk is of non-enforcement, security should usually be ordered by reference to the costs of the proceedings ...
>
> (8) Where the risk is limited to additional costs or delay, security should usually be ordered by reference to that extra burden of enforcement ...'

5.57 Hamblen LJ also concluded that the starting point for determining the quantum of security should be that the entirety of the costs be secured. Then matters of discretion based upon delay or stifling should be considered to determine any adjustment to quantum.[103]

5.58 A further restriction is that the court may not order security for costs under the FPR r 20.6 in respect to the costs of proceedings under the Hague Convention 1980.[104]

5.59 Since 2001, the Children and Family Court Advisory and Support Service (CAFCASS) has held responsibility for representing a child in family proceedings where the welfare of that child is in issue.[105] Otherwise the child will need a litigation friend. If no one else suitable is available, the Official Solicitor

100 [2014] EWHC 164 (Ch) at [12].
101 *Bestfort Developments LLP v Ras Al Khaimah Investment Authority* [2016] EWCA Civ 1099 at [53] per Gloster LJ.
102 [2018] EWCA Civ 1802 at [51].
103 At [64]–[65].
104 FPR r 20.7(3).
105 Criminal Justice and Court Services Act 2000, s 12.

may act as the child's litigation friend of last resort provided there is satisfactory security for their costs.[106]

5.60 As to appeals dealt with in the Family Court or in the Family Division of the High Court, the court may order an appellant or a respondent (who is also appealing) to give security for costs. The grounds for making such an order are those stated at FPR r 20.7.[107] Indeed, it is in respect to appeals that most applications for security for costs are made as in most family cases at first instance there will be no costs order.

5.61 However, as the FPR do not apply to the Court of Appeal, when an application for security for costs is made to that court, it will be considered under CPR Pt 25, s II. Two additional conditions which may enable the security to be granted are prescribed under the CPR:[108]

> '(c) the claimant is a company or other body (whether incorporated inside or outside Great Britain) and there is reason to believe that it will be unable to pay the defendant's costs if ordered to do so;[109] …
>
> (f) the claimant is acting as a nominal claimant, other than as a representative claimant under Part 19, and there is reason to believe that he will be unable to pay the defendant's costs if ordered to do so; …'[110]

Legal aid and security for costs

5.62 Under the Civil Legal Aid (Costs) Regulations 2013,[111] a legally-aided party must not be directed to provide a sum for security for costs which is greater than is reasonable considering all the circumstances. The circumstances to be taken into account include the party's resources and the party's conduct in the dispute associated with the proceedings. The resources belonging to the legally-aided party's partner must not be treated as a resource of that party.

Case law

5.63 *Penny v Penny*[112] concerned a wife's application for security for her costs of the new proceedings after her husband had applied to vary a periodical payments order. Earlier proceedings had concluded with the husband having

106 FPR PD16A [4.5]; Practice Note January 2017: Appointment in Family Proceedings and Proceedings Under the Inherent Jurisdiction in Relation to Adults [17(b)] and [23(c)].
107 FPR r 20.8.
108 CPR r 25.13(2).
109 The interpretation of this test is considered in *Sarpd Oil International Ltd v Addax Energy SA and another* [2016] EWCA Civ 120 at [12–13] per Sales LJ, confirming that the test 'reason to believe' should not be elevated to 'balance of probabilities'.
110 The litigation friend of a child or a protected party is not a nominal claimant. In *Chuku v Chuku* [2017] EWHC 541 (Ch) at [26], Newey J reviews the definition of a nominal claimant.
111 SI 2013/611, reg 12.
112 [1996] 2 All ER 329, [1996] 1 FLR 646, CA.

been ordered to pay periodical payments to the wife plus costs of £11,500. Those costs had neither been assessed nor paid by the husband at the time the wife sought security for that sum. Butler-Sloss LJ gave the leading judgment and held that it was not just to attempt to enforce the earlier costs order in this way, at a time when costs had not been assessed and it was not evident that the husband had either refused or failed to pay the costs due. Rather, the court determined that the wife might have applied for her costs of the new proceedings, without which those proceedings could be stayed.[113] It was noted that an order for security for costs was intended to cover future costs rather than those already incurred in proceedings that had been decided.[114]

5.64 The Court of Appeal considered the wife's application for permission to appeal a financial remedies order in *Radmacher v Granatino*.[115] In his leading judgment, Wilson LJ noted that the wife had an arguable case for appeal but that she had made several 'gross and subsisting breaches' of Baron J's earlier order that had required various financial remedies to be provided to the husband.[116] Therefore, Wilson LJ made it a condition to the grant of permission that a sum must be paid into an account in England and Wales in the names of the parties' solicitors. That sum comprised: the lump sum previously ordered and the interest that had accrued thereon; the sum ordered to enable the husband to purchase a property in Germany; the sum estimated by the husband's solicitors to represent his legal costs of five earlier hearings in the Family Division; and a sum representing security for the husband's costs of the proposed appeal. The wife was granted 28 days to pay that sum. It was also a condition of the grant of permission to appeal that the wife must comply with the previous order in respect to interim periodical payments, and that her failure to do so within 14 days of the due date would cause the grant of permission to lapse.[117] As to the payment of security for the costs of the appeal, Wilson LJ found that CPR r 25.13(1)(a) and (2)(g) were satisfied and therefore it was just to make such an order as the wife had taken steps in relation to her assets that would make it difficult to enforce a costs order against her.[118]

5.65 The Court of Appeal considered an application for security for costs in the 'big money case' of *Charman v Charman (No 3)*[119] under the provisions of CPR r 25.13(2)(a). The husband lived outside the jurisdiction and outside the Brussels and Lugano Contracting States. It had been put, but not decided, that the husband 'has taken steps in relation to his assets that would make it difficult to enforce an order for costs against him'. The wife's estimated costs of appeal were £227,000, and her itemised costing was not challenged by opposing counsel.[120] Although observing the costs were high, the court ordered security

113 At [333].
114 At [332].
115 [2008] EWCA Civ 1304, [2009] 1 FLR 1566.
116 At [24].
117 At [26]–[32].
118 At [35].
119 [2006] EWCA Civ 1791, [2007] 1 FLR 1237.
120 At [40].

for costs of £225,000 and in his leading judgment Sir Mark Potter P noted: 'The order providing for such payment should allow, in my view, for some alternative means of security provided that it is acceptable to the respondent's solicitors.'[121]

5.66 *M v M*[122] concerned a wife's application for security for costs and was considered by Thorpe LJ and Holman J; the former gave the leading judgment. The husband, resident in Nigeria, sought permission to appeal an order made in the Family Division. The court noted that the husband had failed to pay around £290,000 in respect to previous costs orders. In addition, the wife's assets were secured in a property which was being sold under the auspices of the Chancery Master. Therefore, the court found it was just to make an order for the payment of £15,000 in cleared funds to the court within seven days. The order was made in the Court of Appeal under CPR Pt 25.

5.67 The matter came back before Holman J and Wall LJ a few weeks later when the husband applied to vary the order for security for costs.[123] The court refused to interfere either with the decision that security for costs should be provided or with the sum to be secured. However, as the permission hearing was unlikely to be listed for several months, the time for payment of funds into court was extended by five and a half weeks.

5.68 In *Wilmot (now Maughan) v Wilmot*,[124] the parties had been involved in litigation for over a decade following the making of a final order in proceedings for ancillary relief. The husband was found to have pursued the litigation regarding the maintenance of his three children 'with quite extraordinary vigour.'[125] He was granted permission to appeal on the ground of defective service by email under the Hague Service Convention.[126] As the husband had chosen to argue a test case on a point of law, the judge determined the wife must be protected in costs in the event the husband did not succeed. The husband was ordered to pay security for costs in the sum of £40,000 to enable the wife to instruct leading counsel to argue complex points on jurisdiction and jurisprudence.[127]

5.69 In *Re K (Minor: Temporary Removal from Jurisdiction)*, HHJ Moradifar permitted a mother to remove her child temporarily to China for a period of up to eight months. To protect the father's position should he need to issue proceedings for the child's return, £5,000 was to be held by the mother's solicitors as security for costs and a charge was placed upon a property owned jointly and outright by the mother and the maternal grandmother and with a value of around £250,000.[128]

121 At [42].
122 [2009] EWCA Civ 737.
123 *Moore v Moore* [2009] EWCA Civ 433, [2009] 2 FLR 957.
124 [2016] EWCA Civ 925.
125 At [18].
126 Convention of 15 November 1965 on the Service Abroad of Judicial and Extrajudicial Documents in Civil or Commercial Matters.
127 At [19]–[20].
128 [2017] Lexis Citation 8, 48 and 51.

Is it just to order security for costs?

5.70 There is little case law in the family jurisdiction on the court's discretion, under FPR r 20.7(1)(a), as to whether it is just to order security for costs. However, this discretion has been exercised in numerous civil matters where a similar test, under CPR r 25.13(1)(a), applies and these authorities may be of some use to family practitioners. In *Olatawura v Abiloye,* Simon Brown LJ warned, 'the court should be alert and sensitive to the risk that by making such an order it may be denying the party concerned the right to access to the court. Whether or not the person concerned has (or can raise) the money will always be a prime consideration, not least since the incorporation of art 6 of the European Convention for the Protection of Human Rights and Fundamental Freedoms 1950'.[129] In *Sir Lindsay Parkinson & Co Ltd v Triplan Ltd*, Lord Denning MR set out some particular circumstances, relating to a company's application for security for costs, which should be considered:[130]

> 'The court has a discretion which it will exercise considering all the circumstances of the particular case. So I turn to consider the circumstances. Mr Levy helpfully suggests some of the matters which the court might take into account, such as whether the company's claim is bona fide and not a sham and whether the company has a reasonably good prospect of success. Again it will consider whether there is an admission by the defendants on the pleadings or elsewhere that money is due. If there was a payment into court of a substantial sum of money (not merely a payment into court to get rid of a nuisance claim), that, too, would count. The court might also consider whether the application for security was being used oppressively – so as to try to stifle a genuine claim. It would also consider whether the company's want of means has been brought about by any conduct by the defendants, such as delay in payment or delay in doing their part of the work.'

5.71 For further details on civil authorities it may be helpful to refer to *Cook on Costs 2019.*[131]

Arbitration

5.72 Under the Arbitration Act 1996, when parties are in arbitration the arbitrator (or the court should it become involved) may require security for the costs of the arbitration.[132] This order may not be made solely because the party

129 Under ECHR, Art 6; [2002] EWCA Civ 998 at [22]; and also considered in *Goldtrail Travel Ltd (in liquidation) v Onur Air Taşimacilik AŞ* [2017] UKSC 57 at [12] and [14] per Lord Wilson.
130 [1973] QB 609 at [626], [1973] 2 All ER 273, CA.
131 Rowley and Middleton, *Cook on Costs 2019* (LexisNexis Butterworths, 2018), 19.4–19.13.
132 [2017] Lexis Citation 8 at [48] and [51].

resides outside the UK.[133] Further discussion of costs in arbitration can be found at **4.14–4.25**.

Securing costs under FPR rule 4.1(4)(a) and CPR rule 3.1

5.73 The court also has a narrow discretion through its case and cost management powers under FPR r 4.1(4)(a) to make an order subject to a condition that there is a payment into court. This is identical to the power at CPR r 3.1(3)(a). Whilst case law on this point in family proceedings is lacking, it is useful to consider the precedents in civil proceedings.

5.74 Further, CPR r 3.1(5) provides a power to order a payment into court by a party who has unreasonably failed to follow a rule, practice direction or pre-action protocol. Under CPR r 3.1(6A), payments made under CPR rr 3.1(3)(a) and 3.1(5) shall stand as security for any amount payable by that party to other parties in the proceedings. According to CPR r 3.1(6), in employing its power under CPR r 3.1(5) the court must consider both the value of the disputed sum and the costs the parties have incurred or may incur. It should be noted that this provision is only relevant to family practitioners appearing in front of the Court of Appeal, as the rule is not replicated in the FPR.

5.75 Both these powers were compared to the provision to order security for costs under CPR r 25.12 by Moore-Bick LJ in *Huscroft v P&O Ferries Ltd*:[134]

> 'It would be wrong, in my view, to encourage litigants to regard r 3.1(3) as providing a convenient means of circumventing the requirements of Pt 25 and thereby of providing a less demanding route to obtaining security for costs. In my view, when the court is asked to consider making an order under r 3.1(3) or 3.1(5) which is, or amounts to, an order for security for costs, or when it considers doing so of its own motion, it should bear in mind the principles underlying rr 25.12 and 25.13. These include the principle that a personal Claimant who is resident within the jurisdiction or in one of the other member states of the European Union cannot be required to provide security for costs just because he is impecunious, even though his conduct of the proceedings may be open to criticism. Although it might be argued that the Defendant in such a case should be entitled to obtain protection against the risk of being unable to enforce a judgment for costs, a policy decision has been taken to the contrary. This suggests that an order of that kind should not be made in the exercise of the power under r 3.1(3) unless one or more additional factors are present which make it appropriate to impose a burden of that kind on one party and a corresponding benefit on the other.'[135]

133 Arbitration Act 1996, ss 38(3)(a) and 70(6)(a).
134 [2010] EWCA Civ 1483, [2011] 1 WLR 939.
135 At [14].

5.76 Moore-Bick LJ went on to quote the dicta of Clarke LJ in *Ali v Hudson*:[136]

> 'a party only becomes amenable to an adverse order for security under rule 3.1(5) (or perhaps 3.1(2)(m)) once he can be seen either to be regularly flouting proper court procedures (which must inevitably inflate the costs of the proceedings) or otherwise to be demonstrating a want of good faith – good faith for this purpose consisting of a will to litigate a genuine claim or defence as economically and expeditiously as reasonably possible in according with the overriding objective.'[137]

5.77 On considering the power under CPR r 3.1(3) in *IPCO (Nigeria) Ltd v Nigeria National Petroleum Corporation*,[138] the Supreme Court approved the position of the Court of Appeal (set out above at paras **5.75–5.76** in *Huscroft*.

5.78 Thus, the powers under CPR r 3.1 should not be used to avoid the more rigorous tests involved in ordering security for costs and, by analogy, this also applies to the powers under FPR r 4.1(4).

Costs before permission to appeal granted

5.79 Evidently then, the courts will be hesitant to employ the FPR r 4.1(4) and CPR r 3.1 powers to sidestep the greater constraints to their powers under FPR r 20.6 and CPR r 25.12. One instance, though, in which practitioners may wish to consider an application under FPR r 4.1(4) is in respect to costs in the period before permission to appeal has been granted. During this period, the court cannot entertain an application under the security for costs provisions, as the appeal has not begun, and yet the prospective respondent may sustain a considerable liability for costs.

5.80 The Court of Appeal addressed this lacuna in the course of an application for permission to appeal in *Shlaimoun & Anr v Mining Technologies International Inc* [139] when Lord Neuberger MR remarked:[140]

> 'the court nonetheless has power, by combination of CPR Rule 3.1(2)(f) and 3.1(3)(a), in practice to grant security for costs in a case such as this. … Assuming, as I do, that the court's power is not under CPR 25.15 but under Rules 3.1(3) and 3.1(2), it nonetheless seems plain to me that I should apply the same tests as if I was exercising a security for costs jurisdiction under CPR 25.15.'

136 [2003] EWCA Civ 1793 at [25].
137 At [12].
138 [2017] UKSC 16 at [44].
139 [2012] EWCA Civ 772.
140 At [13]–[14].

5.81 Employing the CPR r 3.1 powers, the court made an order that the applicants must provide security for the respondent company's costs within one month and all further proceedings should be stayed until that security was given. Further, the court directed that in the event the security was not provided according to the terms of the order, then the respondent company was at liberty to have the application for permission to appeal struck out and judgment entered for their costs.[141]

5.82 Whilst this type of application for security by way of a payment into court has been made in the civil courts, there seems to be no relevant case law in respect to family proceedings. Nevertheless, in circumstances when the security for costs jurisdiction is unavailable, FPR r 4.1(4) may provide an opportunity to protect a party's position as to the costs of proceedings.

COSTS OF LITIGANTS IN PERSON

5.83 A litigant may himself pay for legal representation, may apply to be publicly funded, may try to raise the money in some other way, or may attempt to obtain pro bono representation. Family practitioners will be only too aware that the drastic reduction in the availability of family legal aid has resulted in a substantial rise in the number of litigants in person appearing in family proceedings.

5.84 The term 'litigant in person' is 'used to describe individuals who exercise their right to conduct legal proceedings on their own behalf'.[142] Litigants remain litigants in person when they instruct counsel by direct access or McKenzie Friends. The fees of such counsel can be claimed in the usual way. Apart from direct access counsel's costs, the costs recoverable by such litigants in family proceedings are governed by the Litigants in Person (Costs and Expenses) Act 1975 and by CPR r 46.5. Section 1 of that Act states:

> '(1) Where, in any proceedings to which this subsection applies, any costs of a litigant in person are ordered to be paid by any other party to the proceedings or in any other way, there may, subject to rules of court, be allowed on the taxation or other determination of those costs sums in respect of any work done, and any expenses and losses incurred, by the litigant in or in connection with the proceedings to which the order relates.
>
> This subsection applies to civil proceedings—
>
> (a) in England and Wales in the county court or in Northern Ireland in a county court, in the family court, in the Senior Courts, in the Court of Judicature or in the Supreme Court on appeal from the High Court or the Court of Appeal, …'

141 At [19].
142 Lord Dyson MR, Terminology for Litigants in Person, Practice Guidance March 2013, 5.

5.85 Therefore, under the Litigants in Person (Costs and Expenses) Act 1975, s 1(1), if a party to the proceedings is ordered to pay the costs of a litigant in person then those costs may comprise sums related to work done and expenses and losses met by the litigant in relation to the proceedings. The sum due in respect to costs will be decided by either summary or detailed assessment under CPR r 46.5(1).

5.86 Costs permitted under the CPR must be no more than two-thirds of the sum ordered had the litigant been represented by a legal representative, but actual (and reasonable) disbursements[143] may be reimbursed in full.[144] Even though a litigant may have been represented for some of the proceedings, they are still entitled to recover their costs for those periods when they acted in person.[145]

5.87 Costs may be claimed by the litigant for: the type of work and disbursements which a legal representative would have been allowed to claim had they been working for the litigant; the litigant's reasonable payments for legal services in respect of the conduct of proceedings;[146] and the costs of expert assistance in assessing the costs claim.[147] In *The Law Society v Persaud,*[148] a litigant in person was permitted his travel expenses from South Africa to London in order to represent himself, since by making the journey he had avoided the need to employ both a solicitor and counsel. A litigant in person may not, however, claim the costs for any assistance they have received from a non-legally qualified person such as a tax adviser[149] or the director of a debt collection company.[150] The costs claimed by a litigant in person must be proportionate to the issues before the court.[151]

5.88 Where a litigant in person claims costs for carrying out work himself, these costs should be calculated according to their financial loss in respect to the time they reasonably spent doing that work. The litigant bears the burden of proving, on the balance of probabilities, that they have suffered such a financial loss.[152] The litigant must adduce evidence of how much they would have earned during the time they carried out work in respect to the proceedings.[153] If there is no such loss, then they will be allowed a sum for the time they reasonably spent on the work and this is charged (since 6 April 2015) at the rate of £19 an hour.[154] A litigant in person may be entitled to claim more time to carry out work than a

143 Such as court fees and payments for legal services pertaining to the conduct of proceedings.
144 CPR r 46.5(2).
145 *Agassi v Robinson (HM Inspector of Taxes)* [2005] EWCA Civ 1507 at [25].
146 *Campbell v Campbell* [2018] EWCA Civ 80, 11, as long as those services are provided by or under the supervision of a lawyer who is entitled to practice in this jurisdiction.
147 CPR r 46.5(3).
148 *The Times*, May 10, 1990.
149 *Agassi v Robinson (HM Inspector of Taxes)* [2005] EWCA Civ 1507 at [75].
150 *Uhbi (t/a United Building & Plumbing Contractors) v Kajla* [2002] EWCA Civ 628.
151 CPR r 44.3(2)(a) and *Grand v Gill* [2011] EWCA Civ 902.
152 *Mealing-McLeod v The Common Professional Examination Board* [2000] All ER (D) 436 at [23] and [25].
153 *Boyd & Hutchinson (a firm) v Joseph* [2003] EWHC 413 (Ch) at [23].
154 CPR r 46.5(4)(b) and PD46 [3.4].

solicitor may take, but their maximum claim will be based upon two-thirds of a solicitor's likely costs rather than two-thirds of a solicitor's hourly rate.[155]

5.89 There are, however, inconsistent authorities as to how a litigant in person's time should be assessed. In *Mealing-McLeod v The Common Professional Examination Board*,[156] Buckley J noted that:

> 'A solicitor's charging rate includes or takes account of the fact that he has support staff, secretaries, messengers and so forth. A Litigant in Person, for example, must himself post letters, take files to court and photocopy documents.'

The judge went on to make an allowance for the litigant's time in carrying out such administrative tasks and allowed a sum for the costs of postage and faxes.[157] In *Grand v Gill*,[158] the court only allowed the litigant's claim for time spent on relevant legal research (and reduced that claim from 730 hours to ten hours), whilst in *Ex p Wulfsohn*[159] the judge refused to award the litigant's claim for costs of more than 1,200 hours of research.

5.90 Perhaps not surprisingly, a litigant in person who is awarded costs under the provisions of the Litigants in Person (Costs and Expenses) Act 1975 may not also claim their costs of attending court as a witness.[160]

5.91 CPR r 46.5(6) provides a list of those that may be classed as a litigant in person under Pt 46, which includes amongst others: a company or corporation acting without a legal representative, a barrister, a solicitor, or an employee of a solicitor who acts for themselves (unless that person is represented by a firm in which that person is a partner).

5.92 Litigants in person have the right, in most circumstances, to be assisted by a person without legal training, known as a 'McKenzie Friend' (MF). In some circumstances, the court may grant MFs a right of audience and/or a right to conduct litigation.[161] On occasions, litigants in person may pay fees to MFs for the services provided. The Practice Guidance on McKenzie Friends sets out the rules for remuneration of MFs:

(a) Litigants may agree to pay MFs fees for providing assistance in or out of court. Those fees are not recoverable from opposing parties.

(b) If the court has granted a MF a right to conduct litigation, then the associated fees incurred by a MF are in principle recoverable from the litigant for whom the work was carried out but not from the opposing party.

155 *R v Legal Services Commission Ex p Wulfsohn* [2002] EWCA Civ 250 at [21].
156 [2000] All ER (D) 436 at [13].
157 [2000] All ER (D) 436 at [33].
158 [2011] EWCA Civ 902 at [11].
159 *R v Legal Services Commission Ex p Wulfsohn* [2002] EWCA Civ 250 at [21].
160 CPR r 46.5(5).
161 Practice Guidance: McKenzie Friends (Civil and Family Courts) [2010] 4 All ER 272 at [18–26].

(c) Without the court granting a right to conduct litigation, a MF's fees cannot lawfully be recovered from either party.

(d) Where MFs have (with the permission of the court) exercised a right of audience, then the fees incurred by MFs are in principle recoverable from the instructing litigant. Further, 'such fees are recoverable, in principle, from the opposing party as a recoverable disbursement'.[162]

The basis for this distinction between being unable to recover fees from an opponent for the conduct of litigation but being able to do so for exercising a right of audience is not clear to us.

5.93 Since the Litigants in Person (Costs and Expenses) Act 1975 and the CPR came into force, there have been few recorded family proceedings cases that deal with the assessment of the costs of litigants in person. Munby J, in *G v A*[163] decided an order for costs following claims under CA 1989, s 8 and Sch 1. The father had claimed costs of £2,500 as a litigant in person and had asked for a summary assessment. However, if the judge was not minded to deal with the matter summarily, then the father claimed he had spent over 300 hours working on the case and had also incurred costs of £8,084 in respect of counsel's legal advice. The father therefore submitted that, at a detailed assessment, his claim for costs would be no less than £38,000, based on an hourly rate of £150 (which he said was two-thirds of the hourly rate of a solicitor) for his own work. (Clearly, following *Ex p Wulfsohn*, the father's calculation of the cost of his own time was misconstrued). Nevertheless, Munby J found that there had been no overall winner in the case and agreed with the father that it would be inappropriate to determine the costs based upon all the issues that the court had dealt with. After summary assessment, the judge made no order as to costs.

PRO BONO COSTS

5.94 At the time of writing there is a surge in the number of applicants for pro bono representation in family proceedings. Some of them are cases where allegations are maliciously made and a costs order may be appropriate. The various pro bono legal organisations receive some of their funds from a registered charity, the Access to Justice Foundation, and it is always looking for financial support for its work. Advocates (whether solicitors or counsel) instructed through national pro bono organisations are encouraged to claim costs for the Foundation if possible.

5.95 There is a second principle involved in the availability of pro bono costs orders. If the court would make a costs order in favour of a party whose representation is paid for, why should the 'losing' party avoid paying the costs of the other side because the 'winning' party is represented pro bono? Adverse costs orders have a number of purposes, and one of them is to deter malicious, wasteful

162 *Practice Guidance: McKenzie Friends (Civil and Family Courts)* [2010] 2 FLR 962 at [27–30].
163 [2009] EWHC 484 (Fam), [2009] 2 FLR 687.

and meritless applications. If parties who represent themselves know they are at risk of an adverse costs order if they lose it will help to deter such applications. The Access to Justice Foundation encourages parties who are represented pro bono to let the other side know in advance of their liability for a costs order, in suitable cases.

5.96 The court may order 'any person' to pay to a prescribed charity the costs that would have been incurred by a legal representative acting pro bono if they had been paid a fee for the work.[164] The only prescribed charity is the Access to Justice Foundation.[165] There is no requirement for a representative to have been instructed through a national pro bono organisation, and any advocate appearing pro bono may apply for a costs order when merited, but the only possible destination for the payment, the only permitted recipient of the costs ordered, is the Access to Justice Foundation.

5.97 When the relevant s 194 of the Legal Services Act 2007 came into force there was no separate family court and the power to make a pro bono costs order was exercisable in a civil court, defined as the civil division of the Court of Appeal, the High Court, or any county court.[166] The Supreme Court has since been added to this list,[167] as has the Family Court.

5.98 The considerations when making a pro bono costs order are the same as those in respect to costs orders in general, save that a pro bono costs order cannot be made against a party who is publicly funded or who is also represented pro bono.[168] The Supreme Court has reinforced the position that parties in children proceedings should receive their costs on the same basis whether represented pro bono or otherwise.[169]

5.99 In some cases a legal representative may have done part of the work pro bono and part for payment. For example, a person's public funding may have been withdrawn during the proceedings and the representative has continued to represent the client pro bono or the client may have run out of money. In those circumstances two costs orders will be needed, one for the part of the costs paid by the client or by the LAA, the other for the costs payable to the Access to Justice Foundation for the pro bono part of the representation. Similarly, if the solicitor is paid and counsel is pro bono, or the other way round, two costs orders are likely to be needed.

5.100 In order to claim pro bono costs there is a requirement for a written statement of the costs that would have been incurred had the representation not

164 Legal Services Act 2007, s 194(3).
165 Legal Services Act 2007 (Prescribed Charity) Order 2008, SI 2008/2680.
166 Legal Services Act 2007, s 194(10).
167 Legal Aid, Sentencing and Punishment of Offenders Act 2012, s 61.
168 Legal Services Act 2007, s 194(4) and (5).
169 *Re S (A Child)* [2015] UKSC 20 at [34].

been pro bono to be filed at the time the application for costs is made.[170] It is suggested that Form H1 would serve that purpose rather than the (less familiar to family practitioners) Form N260 that would be used in other civil proceedings. It will be necessary, where part of the costs are pro bono and part not, to divide the bill into two parts[171] or to provide two bills. VAT is not to be included in a bill for pro bono costs.[172]

5.101 The recommended form of order is:[173]

> 'The [party] must pay costs for pro bono representation on or before [date] to The Access to Justice Foundation (PO Box 64162, London WC1A 9AN), [summarily assessed at £____] [or] [to be assessed on the standard / indemnity basis if not agreed].'

5.102 The pro bono costs order must be sent to the Access to Justice Foundation within 7 days.[174] This is necessary so that the Foundation can, if necessary, take action to enforce the order. If there is also a costs order in favour of the client for a part of the proceedings where the representation was not pro bono, or if there is a money judgment which the client applies to enforce, then the Access to Justice Foundation suggests that the costs order in its favour could be enforced at the same time.[175]

BEDDOE ORDERS

5.103 A party acting in a fiduciary role may seek the protection of a *Beddoe* order[176] which can make provisions for prospective costs. The order permits a trustee to spend funds from a trust or other fund in order to bring or defend proceedings and it safeguards a trustee from any allegation by a trust's or fund's beneficiaries that the proceeds of the fund have wrongly been used to finance and conduct the proceedings. A *Beddoe* order enables the costs of proceedings (including the initial application for directions) to be recouped from the trust or the fund. Without the protection of such an order, the trustee risks being held personally liable for any costs or losses sustained by the trust or fund.

5.104 The order may be relevant in proceedings under the I(FPD)A 1975 and in financial remedy proceedings in matters relating to pension funds, mortgages and bankruptcy.

170 CPR PD46 [4.1].
171 CPR PD47 [5.8].
172 CPR PD44 [2.14].
173 *Unlock Funds for Justice* The Access to Justice Foundation at www.atjf.org.uk.
174 CPR r 46.7(3).
175 See n 178.
176 *Re Beddoe (Downes v Cottam)* [1893] 1 Ch 547, CA.

5.105 The court's power to award a *Beddoe* order is dealt with under the provisions of CPR r 46.3 and the Practice Direction at 46PD.1.[177] This rule applies where a party to proceedings has acted or acts in the role of trustee or personal representative, and where costs are not payable under a contract (such as would occur under the terms of a mortgage deed which allows the mortgagee to recover their costs from the mortgagor).[178]

5.106 When a *Beddoe* order is granted, the trustee's costs will be assessed on the indemnity basis.[179]

Application and procedure

5.107 An application for a *Beddoe* order in family proceedings requires a Part 18 application.[180] CPR Pt 64, s I deals with procedure applying to claims relating to the administration of estates and trusts; this rule has not been adopted in the FPR. Nevertheless, PD64B provides some assistance to trustees who wish to apply to the court for directions in relation to the administration of a trust. The main guidelines are outlined below:

(a) If it is imperative to maintain the confidentiality of the directions required, then the remedy sought may be described on the claim form in broad terms, with full details provided in the supporting evidence.[181]

(b) Evidence in support of the application should be in the form of a witness statement with full disclosure of all relevant matters. In particular, CPR 64BPD.7 advises the applicant to provide evidence of:

> '(1) the advice of an appropriately qualified lawyer as to the prospects of success;
> (2) an estimate in summary form of–
>   (a) the value or other significance to the trust estate of the issues in the proceedings;
>   (b) the costs likely to be incurred by the trustees in the proceedings, by reference to the principal stages in the proceedings; and
>   (c) the costs of other parties to the proceedings for which, if unsuccessful, the trustees may be exposed to liability;
> (3) any known facts concerning the means of other parties to the proceedings; and
> (4) any other factors relevant to the court's decision whether to give the directions sought.'

177 Applicable in family proceedings under FPR Pt 28.

178 CPR r 46.3(1)(b) and CPR r 44.5.

179 CPR r 46.3(3).

180 An application under the Inheritance (Provision for Family and Dependants) Act 1975 would be made by a claim under CPR Pt 8, to a Master in the Chancery Division, with the trustee as the claimant. The matter may be decided on the papers: CPR Pt 64.

181 CPR 64BPD.2.

The witness statement should include information about any discussions which have been held with the beneficiaries and the outcome of those consultations.[182]

(c) The initial proceedings will be listed in private.[183]

(d) Consideration of which beneficiaries, if any, to join as defendants will be required.[184]

(e) If case management directions are required then they may be provided without a hearing.[185] Indeed, if the matter is straightforward, the application itself may be dealt with on the papers.[186]

SANDERSON AND *BULLOCK* ORDERS

5.108 *Bullock* orders are named after the case of *Bullock v London General Omnibus Co*.[187] Such orders may be appropriate when the court finds it has been reasonable for an applicant to bring proceedings against two respondents and yet the court has found against only one of those respondents. The court may then order the applicant to pay the costs of the successful respondent but will allow the applicant to receive from the unsuccessful respondent both their own costs and the costs they are to pay to the successful respondent.

5.109 By contrast, under a *Sanderson* order[188] the unsuccessful respondent must pay the costs of the successful respondent directly.

5.110 Clearly, under both types of order the costs of the applicant and the successful respondent are paid. However, a *Bullock* order can be appropriate when the applicant lacks the funds to pay the successful respondent directly.

5.111 In financial remedy proceedings, Munby J made a form of *Bullock* order requiring the wife to pay the father-in-law's costs and the husband to pay to the wife half of the costs she was to pay to the father-in-law.[189] The judge held that the father-in-law was entitled to his costs from the wife as she had joined the father-in-law in the proceedings after he had disclosed documents to her and she had then continued to maintain her case against him although it was clear her position was flawed. Nevertheless, the judge found that the husband's inadequate responses to the questionnaire, which were described as 'so contemptuous, so brazen, as to be calculated to arouse the deepest suspicions' should be penalised in costs.

182 CPR 64BPD.8.
183 CPR 64BPD.3.
184 See n 173.
185 CPR 64BPD.5.
186 CPR 64BPD.6.
187 [1907] 1 KB 264, CA.
188 *Sanderson v Blyth Theatre Co* [1903] 2 KB 533, CA.
189 *KSO v MJO and JMO* [2008] EWHC 3031 (Fam) at [70–71].

5.112 Munby J had reason to consider *Bullock* orders again in the case of *Ben Hashem v Al Shayif* which was concerned with financial remedy and chancery proceedings.[190] In the chancery matter, the husband was ordered to pay to the wife the sum that she had been ordered to pay to the company and the children. The judge found that the wife had been compelled to litigate with the company and the children as a result of the husband's defiance of court orders and his attempts to avoid the court's jurisdiction. In addition, the wife's stance had been justified by representations made to her by the husband about the ownership of properties and the company.

190 [2009] EWHC 864 (Fam), [2009] 2 FLR 896.

CHAPTER 6

Non-Party Funding and the Liabilities of Non-Parties

NON-PARTY FUNDING

6.01 With the shrinkage of public funding by legal aid, other sources of funding for litigants have become more common. They include:

(a) conditional fee agreements (an arrangement with a solicitor and/or barrister that all or most of the legal costs are taken from the 'winnings');

(b) litigation loans from commercial funders;

(c) *Sears Tooth* agreements (where the solicitor takes their fees out of the client's share of the matrimonial assets at the end of a financial remedy case);

(d) litigation funding agreements (where an organisation other than the legal representative provides funding on the basis that they will share in the winnings);

(e) legal expenses insurance (where a party insures themselves against an adverse costs order);

(f) liquidators and receivers (where the company or individual may be bankrupt but the litigators provide or continue to provide funding);

(g) courts (increasingly, but exceptionally, orders have been made for the Courts and Tribunals Service itself to fund aspects of litigation) and courts services (on the basis of the contracting companies having a duty to provide services to the courts);

(h) 'pure funders' (loans and gifts from relatives and friends with no personal interest in the proceedings);

(i) trades unions, insurance companies and other bodies who have an interest in the proceedings and may, for instance, wish to fund a test case;

(j) pro bono (professional representation without funding);

(k) costs allowance orders including legal services payment orders, see **5.02–5.28**.

6.02 Nearly all of these may be found in family proceedings, some more commonly than others. Three of them (conditional fee agreements, legal expenses insurance and public funding) are statutorily controlled (see **6.13–6.30**, **6.48–6.52** and **Chapter 7**). The arrangements for the others for which there is no statutory regime are available to litigants by whatever personal or business arrangements they may wish to, and be able to, make.

6.03 Where there are statutory rules about third party funding, as there are in relation to conditional fees, insurance for legal expenses and legal aid, there are also rules about the liabilities of those third parties for the costs of the other party/ies in the event that the case they are supporting is unsuccessful. Third party funders of other types have no statutory protection against being made liable to pay an adverse costs order, and a body of case-law has grown up as a result.

Sears Tooth agreements

6.04 In the days before the wider range of funding arrangements now available in financial remedy proceedings, the problems of litigation funding were hardly different from what they are now. In the original *Sears Tooth* case Wilson J identified:[1]

> 'a point of principle which impacts upon a grave and widespread problem encountered increasingly in the Family Division: namely, how can a spouse, usually a wife, who is ineligible for legal aid but who has negligible capital, secure legal advice and representation in order to pursue her rights against the husband, particularly one who is rich, litigious or obstructive or whose

1 *Sears Tooth v Payne Hicks Beach and Others* [1997] 2 FLR 116 at [118]–[119].

financial circumstances are complex or unclear?'

6.05 While a variety of other arrangements are now available for such funding, the main one being litigation loans, the *Sears Tooth* arrangement remains available. It consists of an agreement whereby clients assign to their own solicitors from the lump sum they receive at the conclusion of the financial remedy proceedings a sum equal to the legal costs due to their solicitor. Wilson J found that such an arrangement was lawful, and it has been adopted widely since. The legality of such a 'mortgage on the fruits',[2] as established before Wilson J, has never been appealed further:[3]

> 'the deed between Sears Tooth and the wife is not champertous[4] or otherwise contrary to public policy and is valid. Far from striking at public justice, the main tendency of such a deed is to promote it by securing proper advice and representation for a significant constituency of wives.'

6.06 In *Sears Tooth* itself and subsequently in *Sandler*[5] the question has been raised of the priority of a debt to a solicitor under such an agreement over other payments to be made out of the lump sum received by the party who has entered into the agreement. In *Sears Tooth* the other debt was a garnishee order obtained against her by the wife's previous solicitors. Wilson J decided that the garnishee order had priority over any costs debt to Sears Tooth incurred after it was made, and that meant that there was enough, once the earlier debts were paid, to satisfy the garnishee order. Wilson J did not need to decide on the priorities of the costs incurred prior to the garnishee order.

6.07 In *Sandler*, however, the issue was more pointed, as the costs order made in the husband's favour was in competition for the same money as would otherwise be paid to the wife's solicitors. Macur J held that the husband had a right of 'set off' of the costs due to him from his wife against the lump sum he was due to pay her, so that he did not have to pay the proportion of the lump sum that he was due in costs, which was in fact the whole lump sum, and the wife's solicitors would have to pursue their claim against her for their costs against property in the wife's name.[6] Thus those entering into *Sears Tooth* agreements will need to be confident not only of sufficient funds being available to satisfy their bill, but that sufficient funds will remain after satisfying any adverse order for costs.

6.08 In *ABC v PM*[7] the husband endeavoured to secure the payment of his solicitors' costs by a charge on the former matrimonial home. The outcome of

2 *Glegg v Bromley* [1912] 3 KB 474, CA at [490], Parker J.
3 *Sears Tooth* at [133].
4 For champerty see discussion at **6.35**ff.
5 *Sandler v Sandler and Lloyd Platt and Co* [2010] EWHC 1415 (Fam); [2011] 1 FLR 607, Macur J.
6 *Sandler* at [31].
7 *ABC v PM and Another* [2015] EWFC 32, Moor J.

the proceedings was that that home was transferred in its entirety to the wife who had, prior to the charge in favour of the husband's solicitors, registered at the Land Registry her rights to the property under the Matrimonial Homes Act. The court decided that the husband's solicitors were aware that the equity in that property was an asset at issue in the case, but that they had failed to inform the wife of the intention to register the charge in their favour. Had they done so the wife would have objected and could have applied to the court for an injunction to defeat the charge. In the circumstances the wife's restriction on the property was sufficient to defeat the charge in favour of the solicitors. The court's view was that the husband had enough other assets to meet his solicitors' costs.

CFAs and LFAs

6.09 More inventive ways of providing funding for legal services have been developed over recent decades. They are usually seen as being available only in civil proceedings and having no application to family proceedings. While to some extent that is true, it is not so much the case as it was, so to the extent that such costs arrangements may, in practice or in theory, be found in family proceedings they are considered here.

6.10 The difficulty of a person with ordinary means being able to afford to have access to the courts has a history going back to the earliest reported cases, and before. Of twentieth-century cases a typical example of judicial comments is the decision of the Court of Appeal in *Hill v Archbold*.[8] In that case an issue arose as to whether a trade union, which had funded an unsuccessful libel action by two claimants had done anything wrong by funding the claimant to make the claim (the old legal term for such funding being 'maintenance'). Giving the leading judgment Lord Denning MR held that it had not. He said:[9]

> 'Much maintenance is considered justifiable today which would in 1914 have been considered obnoxious. Most of the actions in our courts are supported by some association or other, or by the state itself. Comparatively few litigants bring suits, or defend them, at their own expense. Most claims by workmen against their employers are paid for by a trade union. Most defences of motorists are paid for by insurance companies. This is perfectly justifiable and is accepted by everyone as lawful, provided always that the one who supports the litigation, if it fails, pays the costs of the other side.'

6.11 Since the 1960s when 'maintenance' ceased to be a crime the arrangements for litigants to be funded by others have continued to develop both in statute and in case-law, so that it is no longer impermissible for lawyers and others who fund litigation to profit from these arrangements.

8 [1968] 1 QB 686.
9 At [494–5].

6.12 The last part of Lord Denning's judgment deals with an area of particular difficulty. If someone supports the litigation financially and they lose, are they responsible for paying the other side's costs if an adverse costs order is made against the party they have funded in the proceedings? The answer, we shall see, is 'it depends'. It depends both on who they are and on the nature of their involvement in the case.

Conditional fee agreements

6.13 'A conditional fee agreement is an agreement with a person providing advocacy or litigation services which provides for his fees and expenses, or any part of them, to be payable only in specified circumstances; and a conditional fee agreement provides for a success fee if it provides for the amount of any fees to which it applies to be increased, in specified circumstances, above the amount which would be payable if it were not payable only in specified circumstances.'[10]

6.14 So in a conditional fee agreement (CFA) 'specified circumstances' and 'success' have to be defined. While who has won and who has lost may be easy to define in many civil cases, that is usually not so in family proceedings. While one could perhaps define 'success' in a particular set of Children Act proceedings as 'an order placing the children in the client's care at the end of the proceedings', and in the Matrimonial Causes Act as 'receiving no less than 60% of the assets as determined by the court', CFAs in such proceedings would, the reader may consider, be unappealing for several reasons.

6.15 In fact whether such CFAs would be attractive or not does not need to be considered as CFAs are not permissible in family proceedings[11] as defined in the Courts and Legal Services Act 1990, which has its own definition of 'family proceedings' for the purpose.[12] That definition is:

(a) the Matrimonial Causes Act 1973;

(b) the Adoption and Children Act 2002;

(c) the Domestic Proceedings and Magistrates' Courts Act 1978;

(d) Part III of the Matrimonial and Family Proceedings Act 1984;

(e) Parts I, II and IV of the Children Act 1989;

(f) Parts 4 and 4A of the Family Law Act 1996;

(g) Chapter 2 of Part 2 of the Civil Partnership Act 2004 (proceedings for dissolution etc of civil partnership);

(h) Schs 5 and 6 to the 2004 Act (financial relief after dissolution of a civil partnership);

10 Courts and Legal Services Act 1990, s 58(2).
11 Courts and Legal Services Act 1990, s 58A(1)(b).
12 At s 58A(2).

(i) Sch 7 to the 2004 Act (financial relief in England and Wales after overseas dissolution etc of a civil partnership); and

(j) the inherent jurisdiction of the High Court in relation to children.

6.16 This definition does not include the Inheritance (Provision for Family and Dependants) Act 1975 or the Trusts of Land and Appointment of Trustees Act 1996. It does not refer to Sch 1 to the Children Act 1989. Schedule 1 is referred to in s 15 of the Children Act, which is covered by the exclusion clause for CFAs as it is in Part II of that Act. But s 15 itself contains no powers, neither does it give any powers to Sch 1. The question arises whether proceedings under Sch 1 are 'family proceedings' by the Courts and Legal Services Act definition.

6.17 The powers in Sch 1 are a consolidation of the powers in five statutes which were repealed on the commencement of the Children Act.[13] They are long-established powers for the court to order the financial support of children. It must be assumed that the drafters of the Courts and Legal Services Act were alert to them, especially in the light of the exclusion of proceedings in specified Parts of that Act from CFAs, see **6.15**(e). In other statutes, where similar lists are provided and parts of statutes are referred to, schedules are separately specified. That suggests that a CFA could be used in a Children Act, Sch 1 application. Although financial proceedings on divorce are excluded from CFAs, Sch 1 has no connection with divorce and could be seen as more similar to the Inheritance Act and Trusts of Land Act provisions. We are inclined to think that a CFA could be used in Sch 1 proceedings, and await an authority on the subject.

6.18 Several pieces of legislation which are family proceedings under other definitions also do not appear in this list.

(a) Part III of the Children Act is not in the list, which is understandable as in that Part of the Act only s 25 (secure accommodation orders) relates to proceedings before a court. A CFA could hardly have any relevance to an application for a secure accommodation order;

(b) the Adoption Act 1976 and the Adoption (Intercountry Aspects) Act 1999;

(c) the Child Abduction and Custody Act 1985;

(d) the Senior Courts Act 1981 and the County Courts Act 1984;

(e) the Domicile and Matrimonial Proceedings Act 1973;

(f) the Family Law Act 1986;

(g) the Gender Recognition Act 2004;

(h) the Human Fertilisation and Embryology Acts;

(i) the Maintenance Enforcement Act 1991 (and other maintenance acts);

(j) the Married Women's Property Act 1882.

13 See Children Act 1989, s 15(1).

6.19 It is possible to find in each of these statutes applications where CFAs *could* be used. For example, a person might apply for a gender recognition certificate under s 1 of the Gender Recognition Act, and success would be the granting of such a certificate. A declaration of interest in property prior to divorce under the Married Women's Property Act 1882 might be associated with a CFA. A freezing order application under s 37 of the Senior Courts Act might be funded by a CFA (whereas a similar application under s 37 of the Matrimonial Causes Act could not).

6.20 However, such use of CFAs might well not meet with the court's approval because these proceedings will be heard in the Family Court (or in the Family Division of the High Court) where the view is likely to be taken that while the use of CFAs in these (family) proceedings is not explicitly excluded by s 58 of the Courts and Legal Services Act 1990, it would be against the spirit of that Act to order their enforcement. There does not appear to be any case-law that deals with such an application for enforcement.

6.21 But setting to one side these technically legitimate but perhaps rather unlikely uses of CFAs in the Family Court, CFAs are certainly available in relation to Trusts of Land Act and Inheritance Act applications – financial proceedings which often relate to families. Accordingly their use and effect is discussed below.

6.22 The Bar Council issued comprehensive guidance on the use of CFAs by counsel,[14] containing invaluable advice particularly to those family practitioners unfamiliar with CFAs. Paragraphs 54-65 and the flowcharts are particularly useful when considering whether to enter into a CFA, and what sort of CFA to select. However this document is no longer maintained online, though there is limited advice on the Bar Council website about Direct Access CFAs. The Law Society fortunately maintains a full model CFA.

The enforceability of a CFA

6.23 The statutory existence of CFAs enables them to be enforced. A CFA which satisfies all of the conditions required is enforceable; but other CFAs are unenforceable (save for solicitors' non-contentious business agreements).[15]

6.24 The conditions that a CFA has to satisfy in order to be enforceable are:

(a) it must be in writing;

(b) it must not relate to proceedings which cannot be the subject of an enforceable conditional fee agreement; and

(c) it must comply with any requirements prescribed by the Lord Chancellor.[16]

14 Guidance to Barristers and Clerks relating to Privately Funded Civil Litigation 18.12.13.

15 Courts and Legal Services Act 1990, s 58(1).

16 *Ibid* s 58(3).

6.25 If the CFA includes a success fee there are three further relevant conditions:

(a) the CFA must relate to proceedings of a description specified by order made by the Lord Chancellor (the Lord Chancellor's only exclusion is not relevant here[17]);

(b) it must specify in the agreement the amount of the success fee as a percentage of the fee otherwise to be paid in the proceedings; and

(c) that percentage must not exceed the percentage specified by the Lord Chancellor,[18] which is 100%.[19]

6.26 A CFA in writing in a Trusts of Land claim heard in the Family Division or the Family Court with a success fee of up to 100% would therefore appear to be an enforceable CFA.

6.27 What percentage should a success fee be? The first step is to assess the risk by listing the risks and assessing the percentage likelihood of each risk. This is an open-ended exercise depending very much on the individual's past experience and, we suggest, the individual's attitude to risk. If you are considering offering, or you are being offered, a success fee then as well as doing a written exercise of listing the risks and how big they are we suggest that you ask someone else to spend a few minutes doing the same thing. If you are rather risk averse, choose someone less risk averse to give a second view, and vice versa.

6.28 Having listed the risks you may like to use Law Society's approach to decide on the percentage success fee. They have produced a graduated table in which if the chance of winning is 50% then the success fee is 100%, while if the chance of winning is 99% then the success fee is 1%. For each level x (prospects of failure) is divided by y (prospects of success) and the result multiplied by 100 to give a percentage. So if you decide the prospects of success are 71% then x divided by y times 100 = a success fee of 41%.

6.29 Under this formula if success is estimated at below 50% you will not take the case on as you are not allowed to charge (or at least you cannot enforce) a success fee of more than 100%. To put it another way, you can't charge enough to make it worthwhile taking the case on. Solicitors and counsel may make different judgments about this so that a solicitor could charge one percentage uplift for success and counsel another.

6.30 Success fees cannot be claimed in costs at the conclusion of a case.[20] The amount of the CFA excluding any success fee can be claimed in costs from the losing side in the usual way, but the client will be liable for the success fee if he

17 Conditional Fee Agreements Order 2013, SI 2013/689.
18 Courts and Legal Services Act 1990, s 58(4), (4A) and (4B).
19 Conditional Fee Agreements Order, para 3.
20 Courts and Legal Services Act 1990, s 58(6) as amended by Legal Aid, Sentencing and Punishment of Offenders Act 2012 (LASPO 2012), s 44.

wins. Thus if the success fee is 100% and if the case successfully concludes with an order that the other side pay the whole of the client's costs (which will exclude the success fee) then the client would still be liable to his solicitor for the success fee, which will be equal in value to the costs paid by the other side. If, on the other hand, the client loses, then under the usual arrangement where the whole risk as to their costs is taken by the legal representatives, the client will have no fee to pay to his representatives. That does not of course alter the fact that the client will still be liable to pay any costs order in favour of the other side.

Litigation funding agreements

6.31 CFAs may be entered into between legal representatives and clients without the involvement of any third party, in which case the legal representative bears the risk of being paid less than usual where the claim is unsuccessful, and of sharing in the winnings where it is successful.

6.32 But an assessment of the risk of proceedings, and funding them based on that assessment, is an obvious area for insurance, for a third party to offer funding in return for taking the risk and sharing in the success. Litigation funding agreements (LFAs) are agreements between a third party funder and the client which provide for the litigation funder to take the risk and to share the proceeds.

6.33 In 1999 the Access to Justice Act introduced prospectively statutory regulation of litigation funding.[21] That statutory provision has not however been brought into force and litigation funding has developed through voluntary self-regulation. There is an Association of Litigation Funders (ALF) which represents 16 providers of such funding and provides a Code of Conduct for its members, the Code being supported by the Civil Justice Council. But any other business can provide litigation funding, and a quick search under 'litigation funding' on the internet will show many providers in addition to the members of ALF.

6.34 Litigation funding has become common in divorce cases, where the litigation funder can be fairly sure of there being a sufficient financial award at the end of the proceedings to make it worthwhile. Indeed litigation funding in financial remedy proceedings ought to have a considerably lower premium than in civil proceedings, since there is the conventional equal division of assets between the divorcing parties after a long or even after a medium-length marriage, making the proceedings much lower risk for the funder. Anyone thinking of litigation funding for divorce should shop around for the best deal.

6.35 This is particularly important in a sector without statutory regulation and where many funders are not members of the ALF and do not sign up to its Code of Practice. Concerns have been expressed about litigation funders withdrawing

21 Through s 58B of the Courts and Legal Services Act 1990.

their funding part way through a case (with possible dire effects for the client) or interfering too much with the proceedings. However, this is a book on costs and we are not advising clients on how to negotiate litigation loans. We only observe that the business of litigation loans has a long and disreputable history involving the crimes of maintenance and champerty – funding someone else to take proceedings and, in the case of champerty, taking a share of the profits – which remain as torts, to a limited extent. As Oliver LJ said in *Trendtex*[22] 'one must today look at the facts of the particular case and consider whether those facts suggest that the agreement in question might tempt the allegedly champertous maintainer for his personal gain, to inflame the damages, to suppress evidence, to suborn witnesses or otherwise to undermine the ends of justice'.

6.36 The fact that those torts do remain (and they were criminal offences until 50 years ago) may make some readers wary of involvement with litigation loans. The fact that such funding has been strongly supported by Lord Neuberger as President of the Supreme Court[23] and by Sir Rupert Jackson[24] in connection with his review of civil costs should, on the other hand, allay that concern.

Liability for adverse costs orders under CFAs and LFAs

6.37 The issue of whether it was champertous for a solicitor to enter into an agreement with a client to pay the costs of the other side if the claim was unsuccessful was considered in *Sibthorpe v LB Southwark*.[25] The point made on behalf of LB Southwark was that CFAs, as defined by s 58 of the Courts and Legal Services Act 1990, do not include the payment of the other parties' costs by a client's solicitor, and where there is a statutory definition (of CFAs) the court should be slow to permit an agreement that steps outside it.

6.38 Lord Neuberger MR in *Sibthorpe* held that there was nothing champertous about a solicitor agreeing to meet the costs of the other side if the application was unsuccessful, as champerty, at least as far as the case-law is concerned, relates to profiting from a victory not to suffering a financial loss if a case is unsuccessful.[26] As Lord Neuberger acknowledged in his judgment, that is perhaps a fine distinction since in both cases there is a financial consequence for the solicitor. The effect of the judgment is that an element of the CFA which steps outside s 58 does not render the whole CFA unenforceable, but that element of it that is outside s 58 will be unenforceable. Thus, in this case, the solicitor could not be ordered to pay the costs of the other side, although in the CFA he had said that he would do so.

22 *Trendtex Trading Corporation v Credit Suisse* [1980] 1 QB 629 at [632]; [1980] 3 All ER 721.

23 'From Barretry, Maintenance and Champerty to Litigation Funding' Harbour Litigation Funding First Annual Lecture Lord Neuberger, President of The Supreme Court, 8 May 2013 on Supreme Court website.

24 'Third Party Funding or Litigation Funding' Sixth Lecture in the Civil Litigation Costs Review Implementation Programme, 23 November 2011 on MoJ website.

25 [2011] EWCA Civ 25, [2011] 1 WLR 2111.

26 At [43].

6.39 Lord Neuberger went on to express views about public policy for litigation funding:

> '[49] Access to justice is an essential ingredient of a modern civilised society, but it is difficult to achieve for the great majority of citizens, especially with the ever reducing availability of legal aid. This has been accompanied by a shift in legislative policy towards favouring the relaxation of previously tight professional ethical constraints, in order to enable a variety of more flexible funding arrangements (which some applaud and others believe give too much weight to consumerism and involve expensive regulation). In these circumstances, I find it hard to accept that, by shouldering the risk of an adverse order for costs against his client, a solicitor is acting contrary to public policy, which is, of course, the basis for the law of champerty. It is one thing to say, in relation to contracts with those who conduct litigation, that the reach of champerty should not be curtailed by the courts. It is quite another to say that, in relation to such contracts, the law of champerty should be expanded.'

6.40 Attention is drawn also to *Dix v Townend*[27] in which case Master Victoria Williams came to the opposite conclusion on the facts before her. As the judgment is long, erudite and practical in its approach, although it is not an authority it is an admirable source when considering the enforceability of a CFA.

6.41 Ironically the liability for the opposing party's costs for professional litigation funders is currently rather different. That liability was considered in *Arkin v Borchard Lines Ltd.*[28] In refusing, at first instance, to hold the litigation funders liable for the opposing parties' costs (which were some £6 million) Colman J held:[29]

> '71. It is indeed highly desirable that impecunious claimants who have reasonably sustainable claims should be enabled to bring them to trial by means of non-party funding. It is further highly desirable in the interests of providing access for such claimants to the courts that non-party funders … should be encouraged to provide funding, subject always to their being unable to interfere in the due administration of justice, particularly in order to forward their own interest in their stake in the amount recovered. If all professional funders were by definition to be subject to non-party costs orders, there would be no such funders to provide access to the courts to those who could not otherwise afford it.'

6.42 The Court of Appeal took a different view of the case, endeavouring to strike a balance between a claimant being able to afford to pursue his claim in court and a successful defendant getting at least some of his costs back.

27 [2008] EWHC 90117 (Costs).
28 [2005] EWCA Civ 655, [2005] 1 WLR 3055.
29 [2005] EWCA Civ 655, [2005] 1 WLR 3055.

The balance that they struck, which the court expressly intended to be used in subsequent cases, they put as follows (with the court's own italics):

> '[42] We consider that a professional funder, who finances part of a claimant's costs of litigation, should be potentially liable for the costs of the opposing party *to the extent of the funding provided.* The effect of this will, of course, be that, if the funding is provided on a contingency basis of recovery, the funder will require, as the price of the funding, a greater share of the recovery should the claim succeed. In the individual case, the net recovery of a successful claimant will be diminished. While this is unfortunate, it seems to us that it is a cost that the impecunious claimant can reasonably be expected to bear. Overall justice will be better served than leaving defendants in a position where they have no right to recover any costs from a professional funder whose intervention has permitted the continuation of a claim which has ultimately proved to be without merit.'

The effect in that case was that instead of paying £6 million in defence costs, the funders had to pay £1.3 million.

6.43 Thus, while a solicitor who enters into a CFA, including a CFA which has elements which are unenforceable because they are outside of s 58 of the Courts and Legal Services Act, is not liable for the other side's costs if his client loses, a professional funder will be held liable for those costs to the extent that he has funded the claim or application.

6.44 The case law is quoted because, while *Arkin v Borchard Lines* provides a compromise between the principles that

(a) an impecunious claimant should be able to pursue his claim, and that

(b) a successful defendant should be able to claim his costs back,

it does not reconcile those principles. Sir Rupert Jackson's report on civil costs[30] proposed the more principled approach that a litigation funder should be liable for the whole of the other party's costs in the circumstances of *Arkin*, so there may be further developments.

Litigation funding agreements in family proceedings

6.45 None of these reported cases is a family case. Litigation loans for financial remedy proceedings are, however, increasingly common, and it is worth considering how the case-law in civil proceedings might be applied to a litigation funding agreement in a financial remedy case.

6.46 There are some inherent protections for the professional funder in financial remedy proceedings:

30 *Review of Civil Litigation Costs: Final Report* Norwich: The Stationery Office. ISBN 978-0-11-706404-1, 2010.

(a) The fact that the parties will share the matrimonial assets should mean that the client will receive sufficient for the professional funder to be paid. A professional funder who provided funds approaching half the matrimonial assets would be running a financial risk or, seen another way, committing a disproportionate amount of the couple's assets to the payment of litigation costs.

(b) The no order for costs starting point in financial remedy proceedings means that the risk that there will be an adverse costs order is reduced.

(c) If an order for costs against the side with litigation funding is made, at the time of a final order the client should have sufficient funds to pay those costs, if a reasonable assessment of risk has been made by the professional funder, without the funder having to be asked to contribute.

(d) In the event that there is an interim costs order made against the client with litigation funding, at a stage where the client does not have the funds to meet such an order, then the professional funder may have to contribute to that costs order at the time that it is made, but should expect to recoup that contribution at the time of the final order.

6.47 It follows that it would be a rare case where it will become necessary for a party to financial remedy proceedings in whose favour a costs order has been made to take proceedings against a litigation funder. This does not, of course, mean that it will not happen, as has been shown in relation to *Sears Tooth* agreements.[31] If and when it does happen the liability of the professional funder to pay the other side's costs should be restricted to the same amount as the costs they have funded for their own client, in accordance with the rule in *Arkin v Borchard Lines Ltd* – unless an argument is successfully run on the basis of Sir Rupert Jackson's more recent proposal that a litigation funder should in those circumstances be liable for the whole of the defence costs.

Legal expenses insurance

6.48 When a party is starting proceedings he or she may wish to be protected against an adverse costs order in the event of losing the case. There are many providers of legal expenses insurance who offer what is known as after the event insurance (ATE) to cover this eventuality. The way it works is that the claimant enters into an agreement to pay a premium usually payable at the end of the proceedings, subject to the outcome. The agreement may provide that the premium goes up in stages as the case progresses, so is lower if the case settles before trial.

6.49 The party taking out the ATE insurance then knows that on winning the case the premium will be taken out of the sum she or he receives, while on losing

31 *Sandler v Sandler* [2010] EWHC 1415 (Fam), [2011] 1 FLR 607, Macur J.

the case the insurers will pay any adverse costs order, and the premium itself will not need to be paid (that adverse event being covered by the ATE insurer).

6.50 We do not see a role for such insurance in either children or financial remedy cases, but it can certainly be used in Trusts of Land cases which may be heard in family proceedings in conjunction with financial remedy proceedings and other financial proceedings, as we shall see.

6.51 Under the 1999 Access to Justice Act there was specific provision for ATE premiums to be claimed in costs if the person with the ATE insurance won. However, the person taking out the insurance was not concerned as to the amount of the premium since if they lost they would not need to pay it and if they won then they would expect (in civil proceedings where costs follow the event) the other side to pay it. Perhaps unsurprisingly the result was inflated premiums and energetic 'costs wars' arose from the resistance of losing parties to paying the over-large premiums. In order to deal with this problem this position was reversed in 2013 (except in certain specified proceedings not relevant to family proceedings) so that 'A costs order made in favour of a party to proceedings who has taken out a costs insurance policy may not include provision requiring the payment of an amount in respect of all or part of the premium of the policy'.[32]

6.52 LASPO 2012 applies in England and Wales, but the Supreme Court, in a first instance judgment on costs in a Scottish case, had the opportunity to consider the general point about ATE premiums being claimable in costs in a case between a father and a son that would in England and Wales have been a Trusts of Land Act case.[33] The father claimed beneficial ownership of a property legally in the name of his son. The father took out ATE insurance with a premium of £40,000, covering him for an adverse costs order of up to a maximum of £100,000 in the event that he lost. The father won and included in his claim for costs the ATE insurance premium. Lord Neuberger giving the judgment of the Supreme Court held that an ATE premium 'is simply not part of the costs of the appeal, in ordinary language'.[34] He went on to say:[35]

> 'In the absence of an agreement or a specific statutory sanction (either expressly or through valid delegated legislation) to the contrary, a successful party to litigation cannot recover an ATE premium, however reasonable it was to have incurred it, as part of his costs or expenses of legal proceedings.'

Lord Neuberger will have had in mind that there had been 'specific statutory sanction' in England and Wales under the Access to Justice Act, which had been revoked, and he perhaps also had in mind that if the Supreme Court allowed a different position in Scotland then cases might be commenced there in order to get round the prohibition on claiming ATE premiums as costs in proceedings south of the border.

32 Courts and Legal Services Act 1990, s 58C as inserted by LASPO 2012, s 46.
33 *McGraddie v McGraddie* [2015] UKSC 1.
34 At [13].
35 At [19].

The liability of non-party funders in general

6.53 The House of Lords held in 1985 that the broad scope of s 51 of the Senior Courts Act 1981 (then the Supreme Court Act) was sufficient to allow the making of an adverse costs order against a third party.[36]

6.54 The CPR provides the procedure for making costs orders for or against non-parties:[37]

> '(1) Where the court is considering whether to exercise its power under section 51 of the Senior Courts Act 1981 (costs are in the discretion of the court) to make a costs order in favour of or against a person who is not a party to proceedings, that person must –
>
> (a) be added as a party to the proceedings for the purposes of costs only; and
>
> (b) be given a reasonable opportunity to attend a hearing at which the court will consider the matter further.'

Subsection (2) of the rule goes on to disapply these requirements in relation to people against whom disclosure orders are made (where the general rule is that that person is entitled to their costs[38]), against the Lord Chancellor in a publicly funded case,[39] and in relation to a wasted costs application,[40] all of which have separate rules.

6.55 Thus there should be no question of an adverse costs order being made against a non-party without the non-party having a fair chance to be heard by the court as to why such an order should not be made. It follows that a non-party can become a third party in relation to a costs application. In doing so, he or she is likely to incur costs – whether by attending court or otherwise. If the costs application is unsuccessful, the third party can, in the usual way, claim their costs in the costs hearing from the party who has made the unsuccessful application.

6.56 The general rules about the liability of third parties to pay costs were established by the Court of Appeal[41] in 1993. The categories of third party that were considered separately in that case were:

(1) where a person has some management of the action;

(2) where a person has maintained or financed the action;

36 *Aiden Shipping Co Ltd v Interbulk Ltd* [1986] AC 965, [1985] 2 WLR 1051.
37 CPR r 46.2.
38 CPR r 46.1(2).
39 Governed by Part 3 of the Civil Legal Aid (Costs) Regulations 2013, SI 2013/611 which relates to cost protection and the recovery of the statutory charge, see **7.60–7.65** and **7.87–7.110**. A costs order may be made against the LAA where the LAA's own actions are at fault, as with any other third party, see **6.110**.
40 The rule in relation to wasted costs is CPR r 46.8.
41 *Symphony Group Plc v Hodgson* [1994] QB 179 at [191F–194D] per Balcombe LJ.

(3) where a person has caused the action (the example being a costs award in a divorce case against the person whose negligence had caused the brain damage which had led to the divorce);

(4) where a person is a party to a closely-related action;

(5) a test case for group litigation.

As relevant to family proceedings, this list implies that the closer the involvement of the third party in the action the more likely it is that a costs order will be considered.

6.57 In *Symphony v Hodgson* the court listed 'material considerations to be taken into account' when considering making an adverse costs order against a third party. As far as relevant those considerations were:

(1) such an order is always exceptional;

(2) it would be more exceptional to make such an order where the third party, if he had had notice of the proceedings, and therefore an opportunity to defend, might have affected the outcome, so facts found when the third party was not present should not be relied upon unless it would not be unjust to do so;

(3) the application should normally be determined by the judge who tried the case (which cannot be said to introduce bias);

(4) the judge must be alert to the possibility that an application against a non-party may be motivated by resentment at not being able to get costs from the other party.[42]

6.58 In 2004 the Privy Council 'summarised the position' as follows:[43]

(1) 'Exceptional' just means 'out of the ordinary run of cases where parties pursue or defend cases for their own benefit and at their own expense'.

(2) Costs orders will not generally be made against 'pure funders'.[44]

(3) Where a non-party funds and substantially controls the proceedings it will be just for that party to pay the costs. There is no need for the non-party to be the only real party so long as they are 'the only real party in … very important and critical respects'.[45]

(4) In relation to liquidators and receivers, as also to a non-party financially linked to a bankrupt company or person: 'Generally speaking, where a non-party promotes and funds proceedings by an insolvent company solely or substantially for his own financial benefit, he should be liable for the costs if his claim or defence or appeal fails. As explained in the cases, however, that

42 *Symphony v Hodgson* at [192G–194D].

43 *Dymocks v Todd* [2004] UKPC 39, Lord Brown at [25].

44 On the authority of *Al Fayed v Hamilton & Others* [2002] EWCA 665; [2002] 3 Costs LR 389 at [40] per Simon Brown LJ, where the term is defined, see next section of this chapter.

45 Quoting *Arundel Chiropractic Centre Pty Ltd v Deputy Commissioner of Taxation* (2001) 179 ALR 406.

is not to say that orders will invariably be made in such cases, particularly, say, where the non-party is himself a director or liquidator who can realistically be regarded as acting rather in the interests of the company (and more especially its shareholders and creditors) than in his own interests.'[46]

6.59 In 2016 the Court of Appeal reviewed the authorities[47] and concluded that–

- orders against third parties have become more common;
- the authoritative statement of the law in such cases is that of the Privy Council in *Dymocks v Todd*, see above at **6.58**;
- each case turns on its own facts.

6.60 It appears from these authorities that the key to whether a non-party may be made liable to an adverse costs order lies in what their status was in the proceedings. If they have a central role or central interest in the proceedings, and particularly if they stand to gain personally from them, then they will be vulnerable to a costs order against them. The question is then how these general principles are applied in cases involving different sorts of third parties. We shall deal first with 'pure funders' – a category not infrequently occurring in family proceedings.

'Pure funders'

6.61 It is not unusual for relatives to provide the funds for family proceedings. A divorcing wife may have insufficient ready cash and her father will pay her legal costs; parents who seek contact with their children may have their costs funded by their new partners. Such funding is more common since the sharp reduction in public funding for such litigants. Such providers of funding for litigation are sometimes called 'pure funders'. Having reviewed what he described as a 'substantial body of Court of Appeal authority' Simon Brown LJ described 'pure funders' as 'being those with no personal interest in the litigation, who do not stand to benefit from it, are not funding it as a matter of business, and in no way seek to control its course'.[48]

6.62 Family members may not be quite as disinterested as that, and may indeed have a financial interest in the extent to which their son or daughter is financially independent following divorce, and will in any case have some sort of emotional stake in the outcome. However, the courts have held that funding by a family member who is not otherwise involved in the proceedings and does not stand to profit personally from them, is the paradigm case of the 'pure funder'.[49]

46 *Dymocks v Todd* at [29].

47 *Deutche Bank v Sebastian Holdings and Vik* [2016] EWCA Civ 23.

48 *Al Fayed v Hamilton & Others* [2002] EWCA 665, [2002] 3 Costs LR 389 at [40] per Simon Brown LJ.

49 See *Murphy v Youngs Brewery* [1997] 1 WLR 1591 at [1603], CA, per Phillips LJ; *Condliffe v Hislop* [1996] 1 WLR 753, CA at 762 per Kennedy LJ.

6.63 In each case where the question arises as to whether a private third party funder should be ordered to pay costs the courts have weighed the competing interests of the claimant's freedom of access to the courts and of a successful defendant suffering the injustice of irrecoverable costs. In relation to 'pure funders' the balance between those two interests has always been answered in the same way, in favour of the ability to have access to the courts.[50] *Al Fayed v Hamilton* laid down the general rule, also described as a presumption at [57], with which all three Lords Justice concurred 'that pure funders generally are exempt from s 51 [Senior Courts Act 1981] liability' (at [51]).

6.64 Neil Hamilton MP raised his legal fees for *Al Fayed v Hamilton* from friends and supporters. Some gave large sums, many gave small. The twenty-first century version of that is crowd-funding, and Charles Keidan and Rebecca Steinfeld successfully used crowd-funding to raise the money for their judicial review of the denial of civil partnerships to heterosexual couples.[51] Those crowd-funders are protected from adverse costs orders by the general rule set out in *Al Fayed v Hamilton*, though perhaps an aggrieved and victorious defendant facing a crowd-funded claim may yet challenge that rule.

6.65 Access to the courts does not just mean being able to make an application. However scrupulous judges may be to ensure that a litigant in person is assisted to put a case effectively 'It would be idle to pretend that an unrepresented claimant in complex proceedings will not be at some disadvantage against a skilled and experienced advocate'.[52] It will often be the case that a reasonable chance of success requires 'ensuring that the parties are on an equal footing', as stated in the overriding objective.[53] Access to the courts therefore includes professional representation, which means in the case of an impecunious litigant that some way has to be found of footing the legal bill. In family cases an obvious place to turn is within the family.

6.66 The reported cases where the question of whether family members who have helped with funding proceedings should be liable for the costs of the successful opponent have not been family proceedings. In family financial proceedings in the comparatively unusual cases where there is a costs order at a final hearing the issue is unlikely to arise as the person who has received the funding from a relative or friend will at that stage usually have enough capital to pay an adverse costs order without asking the relative to help. In the at least equally rare case where there is such a costs order at the end of private law children proceedings there will probably be no information as to who provided the funds for the litigation and, without making enquiries and establishing that, any enforcement could only be against the party.

50 See, for example *Abraham v Thompson* [1997] 4 All ER 362 per Millett LJ; *Al Fayed v Hamilton* at [86] per Hale LJ.

51 *Steinfeld v Secretary of State for Education* [2016] EWHC 128 (Admin), [2016] 1 FLR 1034, ultimately successful in [2018] UKSC 32, [2018] 2 FLR 906.

52 *Al Fayed v Hamilton* at [65] per Chadwick LJ.

53 FPR r 1.1(2)(c).

6.67 Not all relatives are pure funders. In a civil action where a husband had funded his former wife's case and it was found that:

(a) he knew his former wife would not be able to satisfy a costs order if she lost;

(b) he identified 'intensely' in his evidence with his former wife's position (he gave evidence himself);

(c) he was indifferent to the legal and factual issues; and

(d) the judge rejected the factual basis of his former wife's case,

he was ordered to pay the costs for which his former wife was otherwise liable.[54] His wealth made such a payment unproblematic for him.

6.68 But short of such close involvement in the case, where a friend or relative has funded family proceedings, the person in whose favour a costs order is made will be advised that the case-law strongly suggests that an application for the family member who has funded the litigation to pay the costs would be unsuccessful. In situations where malice has led to a person funding someone to take proceedings which were from the start unreasonable, or which were unreasonably pursued, an application for a third party costs order might stand a chance of success under the general rules on costs liability – but no such case is so far known in family proceedings.

Non-party non-funders

6.69 There are several other sorts of individuals and businesses who can become involved in proceedings and, although not parties and providing no funding, might be made the subject of adverse costs orders. There is immunity against any such order against some, but not all, of the following: barristers, experts, witnesses, judges and solicitors. Of this list judges and lay witnesses alone retain their immunity against costs orders. Solicitors and barristers are liable under the wasted costs regime, as we now consider. We shall go on to consider the position in relation to third party costs orders against other particular non-parties.

COSTS AGAINST LEGAL REPRESENTATIVES

Introduction

6.70 Rose LJ defined three instances in which a solicitor may be ordered to pay costs:[55]

> '(i) if it is within the wasted costs jurisdiction of section 51(6) and (7);

54 *Locabail (UK) Ltd v Bayfield Properties Ltd (No 3)* [2000] 2 Costs LR 169, Ch D, Lawrence Collins QC.

55 *Tolstoy-Miloslavsky v Aldington* [1996] 2 All ER 556 at [565].

(ii) if it is otherwise a breach of duty to the court, such as, even before the Judicature Acts, could found an order, eg if he acts, even unwittingly, without authority or in breach of an undertaking;

(iii) if he acts outside the role of solicitor, eg in a private capacity or as a true third party funder for someone else.'

6.71 This section deals with costs against all legal and other representatives and focuses on the wasted costs jurisdiction. Point (ii) above, concerns the inherent jurisdiction of the court and is discussed at **6.124**, whilst point (iii) is dealt with in relation to third party funding at **6.61–6.68** and at **6.125–6.126**. The court's additional power to impose a costs sanction for misconduct, under CPR r 44.11, is also discussed at **6.115–6.123**.

Wasted costs orders

6.72 The case of *Ridehalgh v Horsefield*[56] is essential reading for any practitioner considering wasted costs orders. In the Court of Appeal, Sir Thomas Bingham MR gave the unanimous and comprehensive judgment (beginning at 224B) which, among other things, addresses the relevant jurisdiction,[57] procedure[58] and interpretation.[59] The case has been endorsed by the House of Lords[60] and has been referred to in all subsequent published judgments on the issue.

The applicant

6.73 A party to proceedings may ask the court to make an order for wasted costs in their favour provided a legal or other representative has caused them to incur legal costs which have been wasted and which consequently they should not reasonably pay. The term 'legal or other representative' is defined as 'any person exercising a right of audience or right to conduct litigation on his behalf'.[61] The court may also order wasted costs of its own volition.[62] Indeed, the Court of Appeal has noted, 'In straightforward cases (such as failure to appear, lateness, negligence leading to an otherwise avoidable adjournment, gross repetition or extreme slowness) there is no reason why it should not do so. But save in the most obvious case, courts should in our view, be slow to initiate the inquiry'.[63]

56 [1994] Ch 205, CA.
57 At [226D]–[232B].
58 At [238]–[239].
59 At [232C]–[233E].
60 *Medcalf v Mardell* [2002] UKHL 27, at [13] and [50], save for a strengthening on the position in respect to legal professional privilege, [23].
61 Senior Courts Act 1981, s 51(13).
62 CPR PD46 [5.3].
63 *Ridehalgh v Horsefield* [1994] Ch 205 at [238D].

Legislation and rules

6.74 The Senior Courts Act 1981 gives the Court of Appeal's Civil Division, the High Court and the Family Court the discretion to make an order for wasted costs against a legal or other representative.[64] The Act defines 'wasted costs' as costs incurred by a party:[65]

> '(a) as a result of any improper, unreasonable or negligent act or omission on the part of any legal or other representative or any employee of such a representative; or
>
> (b) which, in the light of any such act or omission occurring after they were incurred, the court considers it is unreasonable to expect that party to pay.'

6.75 In this respect, CPR r 46.8 (Personal liability of legal representative for costs – wasted costs orders) applies to family proceedings:[66]

> '(1) This rule applies where the court is considering whether to make an order under section 51(6) of the Senior Courts Act 1981 (court's power to disallow or (as the case may be) order a legal representative to meet, "wasted costs").
>
> (2) The court will give the legal representative a reasonable opportunity to make written submissions or, if the legal representative prefers, to attend a hearing before it makes such an order.
>
> (3) When the court makes a wasted costs order, it will—
> (a) specify the amount to be disallowed or paid; or
> (b) direct a costs judge or a District Judge to decide the amount of costs to be disallowed or paid.
>
> (4) The court may direct that notice must be given to the legal representative's client, in such manner as the court may direct—
> (a) of any proceedings under this rule; or
> (b) of any order made under it against his legal representative.'

Application procedure

6.76 Normally, a wasted costs application should be made at the end of the trial when the behaviour of the legal representative can be properly assessed.[67] The application should generally be heard by the trial judge.[68] However, if the conduct complained of relates to a discrete issue which would not be better

64 Section 51(6).

65 Section 51(7).

66 FPR r 28.2(1).

67 *Film Lab Systems International Ltd v Pennington* [1994] 4 All ER 673 at [678-679] and CPR 46 PD.5 [5.2].

68 *Gray v Going Places Leisure Travel Ltd* [2005] EWCA Civ 189 at [11].

assessed after the trial or where the legal representatives complained of are no longer acting, then it may be appropriate to apply promptly.[69]

6.77 An application should be made according to FPR Pt 18 by filing an application notice with evidence in support, or by oral application during a hearing.[70]

6.78 The evidence should indicate:[71]

'(a) what the legal representative is alleged to have done or failed to do; and

(b) the costs that the legal representative may be ordered to pay or which are sought against the legal representative.'

6.79 The court will give directions about the procedure to be followed to ensure that the issues are handled in a manner which is as fair, simple and summary as the circumstances permit. The legal representative must be added as a party to the proceedings for the purposes of costs only and then be given a reasonable opportunity to attend the further hearing of the matter.[72]

6.80 Where an application is settled without the need for a hearing, the Court of Appeal has stated a short statement may be provided to the court by the respondent setting out succinctly, 'the position where there is a compromise'.[73] The applicant may also provide a short statement in response if the parties do not agree on the statement. These statements may be circulated to all members of the judiciary who have been involved with the wasted costs application. This approach enables the legal representative to answer the accusations of the applicant, to protect their professional reputation and to do so without incurring the costs of a further hearing.

Burden of proof

6.81 Under CPR r 46.8(2) the court must allow the legal representative an opportunity to show cause why a wasted costs order should not be made.[74] Regardless of this, the burden of proof is on the applicant for the order. It is remarked that the burden of proof only shifts to the representative when the court is of the view that, 'an apparently strong prima facie case had been made against him or her and the language of the rule recognised a shift in the evidential burden'.[75] The standard of proof to be applied is the balance of probability.[76]

69 *B v B (wasted costs order)* [2001] 1 FLR 843, [2001] 3 FCR 724 at [27–30].
70 CPR PD46 [5.4].
71 CPR PD46 [5.9].
72 CPR r 46.2(1).
73 *Manzanilla Ltd v Corton Property & Investments Ltd (No.2)* [1997] 3 FCR 389, CA.
74 *London Borough of Redbridge v A and others* [2016] EWHC 2627 at [28–29], (Fam).
75 *Ridehalgh v Horsefield* [1994] Ch 205 at [239] endorsed in *Medcalf v Mardell* [2002] UKHL 27 at [13].
76 At [249].

The court's discretion

6.82 CPR PD46 para 5.7 states the court will usually exercise its discretion in deciding whether to make a wasted costs order by adopting a two-stage approach:[77]

> '(a) at the first stage the court must be satisfied—
> (i) that it has before it evidence or other material which, if unanswered, would be likely to lead to a wasted costs order being made; and
> (ii) the wasted costs proceedings are justified notwithstanding the likely costs involved;
>
> (b) at the second stage, the court will consider, after giving the legal representative an opportunity to make representations in writing or at a hearing, whether it is appropriate to make a wasted costs order [in accordance with the test outlined at **6.83**].'

The test for making a wasted costs order

6.83 Under CPR PD46 para 5.7(b), the court must consider the three-part test set out at para 5.5 of the Practice Direction and may only order costs against a legal representative if:

> '(a) the legal representative has acted improperly, unreasonably or negligently;
>
> (b) the legal representative's conduct has caused a party to incur unnecessary costs, or has meant that costs incurred by a party prior to the improper, unreasonable or negligent act or omission have been wasted;
>
> (c) it is just in all the circumstances to order the legal representative to compensate that party for the whole or part of those costs.'[78]

6.84 The tests at **6.82** and **6.83** above are not unconnected. There is a clear overlap between CPR PD46 para 5.7(b) and para 5.5. The paragraphs below break down the elements of both tests.

The first stage of the court's discretion (para 5.7(a)(ii)): proportionality

6.85 The court should not offer the representative an opportunity to show cause automatically. Rather, as Sir Thomas Bingham noted in *Ridehalgh v Horsefield*,[79] the court should use its discretion:

77 CPR PD46 [5.7].
78 CPR PD46 [5.5].
79 At [239D]–[239F].

> 'This is not something to be done automatically or without careful appraisal of the relevant circumstances. The costs of the inquiry as compared with the costs claimed will always be one relevant consideration. This is a discretion, like any other, to be exercised judicially, but judges may not infrequently decide that further proceedings are not likely to be justified.'

This step has frequently been referred to as the first stage of the court's discretion, at which the proportionality of the costs of the wasted costs investigation compared to the value of the alleged wasted costs will be considered before a decision to continue proceedings is made.

The first limb of the test at para 5.5(a): improper, unreasonable or negligent

6.86 First, we shall look at what is meant by improper, unreasonable or negligent behaviour by a legal representative.[80] These terms were considered in detail by the Court of Appeal in *Ridehalgh*.[81]

6.87 In a unanimous judgment, the court defined improper conduct as that which violates the letter of a professional code. Unreasonable conduct was described as behaviour that does not permit a reasonable explanation. Negligence 'should be understood in an untechnical way to denote failure to act with the competence reasonably to be expected of ordinary members of the profession'.[82] However, the court stated the 'wish firmly to discountenance any suggestion that an applicant for a wasted costs order under this head need prove anything less than he would have to prove in an action for negligence.'[83] The court in *Ridehalgh* concluded: 'Conduct which is unreasonable may also be improper, and conduct which is negligent will very frequently be (if it is not by definition) unreasonable. We do not think any sharp differentiation between these expressions is useful or necessary or intended.'[84] Legal representatives will only be liable for a wasted costs order if they have breached their duty to the court.[85]

6.88 Reviewing the dicta in *Ridehalgh* and *Medcalf*, in his leading judgment in *Persaud v Persaud*, Peter Gibson LJ concluded: 'there must be something more than negligence for the wasted costs jurisdiction to arise: there must be something akin to an abuse of process if the conduct of the legal representative is to make him liable to a wasted costs order.'[86] In a unanimous decision, the Court of Appeal in *Patel v Air India Ltd and another* followed *Ridehalgh* and *Persaud*

80 Negligence discussed in *Dempsey v Johnstone* [2003] EWCA Civ 1134 at [24–25] and [32].

81 [1994] Ch 205, 232C–233E with guidance subsequently endorsed in *Medcalf v Mardell* [2002] UKHL 27 and discussed by Mostyn J in *Fisher Meredith v JH and PH (Financial Remedy: Appeal: Wasted Costs)* [2012] EWHC 408 (Fam).

82 At [233B].

83 At [233C].

84 At [233E].

85 *Ridehalgh v Horsefield* [1994] Ch 205 at [232H–233A]; *Medcalf v Mardell* [2002] UKHL 27 at [60].

86 [2003] EWCA Civ 394 at [27].

and noted there were no findings to support the allegation that a solicitors' firm had breached their duty to the court or that the proceedings were an abuse of the court's process. Although the case advanced by the claimant's solicitor had a less than 50 per cent chance of success, it was 'a long way from the case being hopeless' and did not satisfy the s 51(7) test.[87]

The second limb of the test at para 5.5(b): causation

6.89 Under the second limb of the test, it is necessary to show a causal link between the legal representative's conduct and the costs incurred by the applicant. In *Ridehalgh*, the court noted that 'Where the conduct is proved but no waste of costs is shown to have resulted, the case may be one to be referred to the appropriate disciplinary body or the legal aid authorities, but it is not one for exercise of the wasted costs jurisdiction'.[88]

The third limb of the test (para 5.5(c)) and the second stage of the court's discretion (para 5.7(b))

6.90 The court then considers the third limb of the test whilst exercising the second stage of discretion. This step of the proceedings was described by Sir Thomas Bingham MR in *Ridehalgh*:[89]

> 'Even if the court is satisfied that a legal representative has acted improperly, unreasonably or negligently and that such conduct has caused the other side to incur an identifiable sum of wasted costs, it is not bound to make an order, but in that situation it would of course have to give sustainable reasons for exercising its discretion against making an order.'

6.91 The court will therefore consider all the circumstances before deciding whether a wasted costs order is justified. Sumner J looked at this point in *Dean v Hashemi*[90] where a husband obtained a costs order against his wife and applied for a wasted costs order against her solicitors in respect of the same costs. Afterwards, in a consent order, the husband waived his costs claim against his wife. Considering all the circumstances and mindful of his discretionary powers, the judge found that the husband's failure to ring-fence his claim for wasted costs against the solicitors, when he waived his right to costs from his wife in the consent order, had removed the causal link between the conduct and the loss.[91] Sumner J also noted that in this situation there was a risk of double recovery.[92] The order for wasted costs was set aside.

87 [2010] EWCA Civ 443 at [18].
88 At [237E]–[237F].
89 At [239E]–[239F].
90 [2008] EWHC 559 (Fam), [2008] 2 FLR 824.
91 At [34].
92 At [31]; see also *Harrison v Harrison* [2009] EWHC 428 (QB) at [27].

6.92 The second stage of discretion may directly follow stage one if the legal representative has been provided with a reasonable opportunity to make submissions.[93]

Privilege

6.93 An applicant for a wasted costs order against their own legal representative waives their legal professional privilege in respect to their relevant confidential communications.[94] Yet, if a wasted costs order is sought against the other side's legal representative then the opposite party may refuse to waive their privilege. Clearly, this position may handicap the respondent legal representative and limit the evidence they can offer in their defence.

6.94 In *Metcalfe v Mardell*, the House of Lords sought to safeguard a representative caught in this position. Firstly, the court said had the defendant practitioner not received his client's waiver to disclose his full account, then,

> 'the court should not make an order unless, proceeding with extreme care, it is (a) satisfied that there is nothing the practitioner could say, if unconstrained, to resist the order and (b) that it is in all the circumstances fair to make the order.'[95]

6.95 The court went on to say it would be rare that an application against lawyers acting for the opposition could be fairly dealt with on a summary basis and the litigation was likely to be costly in time and money.[96] The position is summed up in *Halsbury's Laws*, 'An application for a wasted costs order against another party's legal representative is therefore unlikely to succeed unless his conduct can be shown to have been improper without recourse to privileged material.'[97]

Hopeless cases

6.96 The court in *Metcalf* noted the practitioner's duty to present their client's case even though the practitioner may be of the opinion it is hopeless and may have advised their client of that view. To do so is not a breach of duty to the court. Rather, in such cases the court's other powers may be deployed to resolve matters by, for example, striking out or giving summary judgment.[98] Lord Pearce observed in *Rondel v Worsley*:

93 CPR PD46 [5.8].
94 *Medcalf v Mardell* [2002] UKHL 27 at [31].
95 At [23].
96 At [24].
97 *Halsbury's Laws of England, Civil Procedure* (Volume 12A (2015)), 1746.
98 At [56].

'It is easier, pleasanter and more advantageous professionally for barristers to advise, represent or defend those who are decent and reasonable and likely to succeed in their action or their defence than those who are unpleasant, unreasonable, disreputable, and have an apparently hopeless case. Yet it would be tragic if our legal system came to provide no reputable defenders, representatives or advisers for the latter.'[99]

Case law

6.97 A solicitor successfully appealed a wasted costs order made against him in respect to an abortive two day contact hearing. The Court of Appeal had the benefit of additional information which had not been before the lower court and which demonstrated that the solicitor had faced difficulties in ascertaining that the Legal Aid Board would continue to fund his client. Both Nourse LJ and Butler-Sloss LJ determined that the solicitor had made an error of judgment in failing to inform the court and the other party that it may be necessary to adjourn the hearing. However, neither the threshold for improper, unreasonable or negligent behaviour nor dereliction of duty to the court was satisfied.[100] This case was heard in 1993 and, considering changes to family court procedure as exemplified in *HU v SU*,[101] it is unlikely that today's court would be so accommodating of a representative's failure to inform the court of their difficulties in complying with directions and the consequent loss of a two day hearing.

6.98 In public law children proceedings, counsel for the local authority was subjected to a wasted costs order having failed to keep an expert up to date with relevant events.[102] Wall J stated that counsel for the local authority had been responsible for the presentation of the local authority's case, and declined to order wasted costs against the authority's solicitors. The judge stated an expert should see all relevant material (and in particular updating documents created since the expert's report had been written) before giving oral evidence.[103] Wall J noted his belief that a judge in the Family Division had not previously given judgment in open court to order wasted costs against a member of the Bar in non-adversarial proceedings relating to children. Nevertheless, he stated that the intervention was necessary to ensure the costs were not met by public funds.[104]

6.99 Several applications for wasted costs have failed due to the proportionality test. In *Regent Leisuretime Ltd v Skerrett*,[105] Lloyd LJ found the first limb of stage one of the test under the Practice Direction (ie para 5.7(a)(i)) was made out, but stated, 'it is plain from the rule and from the Practice Direction and from authorities in relation to wasted costs that it is necessary to preserve a sense and

99 [1969] 1 AC 191 at [275].
100 *Re A Solicitor (Wasted Costs Order)* [1993] 2 FLR 959.
101 See **6.106**.
102 *Re G, S and M (Wasted Costs)* [2000] 1 FLR 52 at [64A].
103 At [53E]–[53F].
104 At [59].
105 [2006] EWCA Civ 1032.

a degree of proportion between the costs likely to be at risk and the costs that will be incurred in relation to the application for wasted costs'.[106] On that basis (and at the second limb of stage one of the test (para 5.7(a)(ii)), he determined the value of wasted costs was insufficient for it to be just and proportionate for the application to proceed. The judge in the lower court had wrongly allowed an oral application to be considered without evidence or an indication of the wasted costs sought. Instead, the judge should have directed a Part 23 application notice with supporting evidence.[107]

6.100 The proportionality of applying for a wasted costs order was again considered by the Court of Appeal in *Equity Solicitors v Javid*.[108] A solicitor had acted *pro bono* for the wife in divorce proceedings. He then consulted with the senior partner of another firm ('the firm') and they agreed the firm would take over, act for the wife and attend the next hearing. The firm failed to serve a notice of change of solicitor and the wife was unrepresented at the subsequent hearing. The judge at the lower court made a wasted costs order against the first solicitor. At appeal, the court found it was reasonable for the original solicitor to rely upon his conversation with the senior solicitor of the firm and the wasted costs order for £981.13 was set aside. Holman J stated the application had been disproportionate and that once the respondent's statement was received the applicant should have reconsidered the application.[109]

6.101 *Harrison v Harrison*[110] concerned a husband's application for wasted costs against a barrister who had acted for his wife by applying for a without notice freezing order in the course of their acrimonious matrimonial finance proceedings. Mackay J noted that the claim was for wasted costs in the sum of £59,000. The costs of the application were £57,784 and £85,000 for the applicant and the respondent respectively. The judge stated, 'the proceedings are therefore disproportionate to any benefit they could possibly bring' and refused to use his discretion to grant the order.[111]

6.102 Mostyn J considered an appeal against a wasted costs order in *Fisher Meredith LLP v JH*.[112] In the lower court the judge had ordered costs of £15,000 to be paid by the wife's solicitors in respect to costs thrown away due to the adjournment of the final hearing plus the costs of the wasted costs hearing.[113] On appeal, the finding of negligence against the solicitors was overturned.[114] Further, as there was nothing 'to suggest that the District Judge performed the discretionary second stage of the decision making process as he was required to do',[115] his decision was found to be plainly wrong.

106 At [44].
107 At [36]–[37].
108 [2009] EWCA Civ 535.
109 At [26].
110 [2009] EWHC 428 (QB).
111 At [28].
112 [2012] EWHC 408 (Fam), [2012] 2 FLR 536.
113 At [29].
114 At [58].
115 At [59]–[60].

6.103 In *B v A*,[116] Charles J awarded the applicant mother wasted costs of £18,000. The award was based upon the legal representative's negligence in failing to comply properly with the appropriate principles and procedures in applying for a without notice order. The judge noted the failures to conform to the prescribed rules could not 'be justified or excused by endemic failures to apply them by practitioners and judges in the Family Division'.[117] However, acknowledging this situation, the judge reduced the award on the basis that such abuse of procedure in the Family Division was relatively commonplace and had not been questioned by a number of judges.[118]

6.104 In *Re A (a child) (child proceedings: wasted costs order)*, McFarlane LJ considered an application for wasted costs by a local authority against the solicitors of parents in public law child proceedings in which there had been a finding of non-accidental injury to a baby by one or other of the parents.[119] A number of allegations were made as to the conduct of the parents' solicitors (such as failures to provide full and frank disclosure at a without-notice hearing and to provide an expert with essential reading). However, whilst the court found some of these claims to be made out, it was determined that the conduct had not caused the other parties to incur costs. It was also alleged that the parents' solicitors should have abandoned their application for permission to appeal on receiving the expert's negative opinion on the matter. McFarlane LJ found that the solicitors had been right to take counsel's advice on this matter and that it was the over-optimistic approach of counsel that had led to the matter being pursued further, saying:[120]

> 'These various factors, high intellect, a lack of understanding of the justification for the approach taken in family proceedings and the brave championing of a cause, are, in my view, the unhelpful cocktail of elements which have come together in counsel's presentation of the parents' case in these proceedings.'

Counsel for the local authority then applied to include the parents' counsel in the wasted costs application, but the judge held that the matter had by then been heard and it would therefore be oppressive to include the barrister.

Financial penalties for failure to comply with court orders

6.105 Cobb J had before him a private law case (*Re OB (Private law proceedings: Costs)*[121] in which a direction was made for a local authority to complete a report under s 37 of the CA 1989; a report which requires the local authority to decide whether or not to apply for a care or supervision order. The

116 [2012] EWHC 3127 (Fam), [2013] 2 FLR 958.
117 At [106].
118 At [114].
119 [2013] EWCA Civ 43.
120 At [39].
121 [2013] EWHC 1956 (Fam), [2016] 1 FLR 92.

local authority did an inadequate report and a hearing took place which was a waste of time as a result. The local authority was not a party but had to pay the father's costs of the hearing, and the judgment considers the relevant case law in detail. The local authority's legal duty put it in a position different from that of any private litigant. The FLR headnote uses the not uncommon practice of calling this a 'wasted costs order' – and although the order was made because costs were wasted, we consider that it helps to avoid confusion for that label to be reserved to costs orders against legal representatives.

6.106 In *HU v SU*, Keehan J made a wasted costs order against a mother's solicitors having described their conduct as, 'so serious and so inexcusable that I find that they acted improperly and unreasonably'.[122] The mother's solicitors had sought a further extension to their client's public funding certificate, and this was not granted for almost a month. As a result, the mother's solicitors did not request police disclosure or file the mother's statement as had been directed. Further, the solicitors did not seek from the court an extension of time before the expiry of the time for compliance. The matter was brought back to court by the father's solicitors who requested an urgent directions hearing to deal with the timetabling issues. The judge stated:

> 'The failure to seek the leave of the court to extend the time for compliance with the directions order of 15.12.14 is to be characterised as incompetence, the result of which could have been the adjournment of this fact finding hearing. Their actions, as set out above, are redolent of past poor practices which should no longer feature in private or public law family proceedings.'

Keehan J found this behaviour had caused the father (who was privately funded) unnecessarily to incur the costs of a directions hearing, which the mother's solicitors were ordered to pay in full. In support of his decision, Keehan J quoted from *Re W (a child) (adoption order: leave to oppose); Re H (children) (adoption order: application for permission for leave to oppose)*,[123] in which the President had railed against Bristol City Council's non-compliance with orders made by the Family Court, although without making an order for wasted costs. Keehan J also referred to the President's judgment in *Local Authority v DG and others*,[124] where, despite finding the failure to comply with case management directions lamentable, again he had not ordered wasted costs to be paid.

6.107 The type of conduct that led to Keehan J's decision has also met with the strong displeasure of Theis J who quoted the President with approval[125] when he said, 'Non-compliance with orders should be expected to have and will usually have a consequence'.[126] Although neither the President nor Theis J ordered wasted costs in the cases referred to, it is evident that the Family Court places the

122 [2015] EWFC 18 at [60].
123 [2013] EWCA Civ 1177, [2014] 1 FLR 1266 at [51–53] per Sir James Munby P.
124 [2014] EWHC 63 (Fam), [2014] 2 FLR 713 at [43–44].
125 *Kent County Council v C & Ors* [2014] EWHC 604 (Fam), [2015] 1 FLR 115 at [6–7].
126 *Re W (a child) (adoption order: leave to oppose)* [2013] EWCA Civ 1177 at [52].

utmost importance upon compliance with its orders and that failure to observe those orders runs the real risk of an adverse costs order.

6.108 In wardship proceedings in the Family Division, *F v M*,[127] Cobb J found a father's solicitors had failed to act 'with the competence reasonably expected of ordinary members of the profession' such that a wasted costs order was justified. The solicitors' misconduct included failure to comply with various court orders along with failure to inform the court listing office promptly of a change in circumstances. Finding that the mother's solicitors were not without some blame for the poor preparation of the matter, Cobb J ordered payment of the lower of £1,250 or 25 per cent of the assessed costs of the mother by the father's solicitors.

6.109 HHJ Bellamy made an order under the wasted costs regime penalising the solicitors representing all four parties.[128] The three legally aided parties argued, under s 51(6), part of a standard fee payable to a legally-aided solicitor could not be disallowed; the standard fee was payable regardless of the amount of work carried out. The only exception to this position being when, 'calculated on an hourly rate basis, the fees for the work undertaken are more than two times the standard fee, a solicitor is entitled to be paid on an hourly rate basis for the work actually undertaken.'[129] The Legal Aid Agency (LAA) wrote to the court supporting the legally aided parties' view. If the LAA was correct, HHJ Bellamy noted a legally aided solicitor could be ordered to pay the wasted costs of another party but could not have their own costs disallowed. The judge's initial view was that the s 51(6) power could not be so restricted but that the question needed 'to be authoritatively addressed.'[130] He ordered wasted costs, without resolving the jurisdiction point, with the local authority paying 50 per cent of the costs wasted by the legally-aided parties and the legally-aided parties sharing equally the payment of 50 per cent of the costs wasted by the local authority.

6.110 Where the Legal Aid Agency was remiss in failing to state its position on the recovery, through the statutory charge, of damages from a litigant who was making a claim against a local authority, and as a result the costs to the litigant had been unreasonably increased, the Legal Aid Agency was ordered to pay those additional costs.[131]

The order

6.111 The order may require payment of a sum by the legal representative in respect to the applicant's costs or may disallow the representative's costs in

127 [2015] EWHC 3259 (Fam).

128 *Re L (Case Management: Wasted Costs)* [2016] Lexis Citation 24.

129 At [73].

130 At [82].

131 *PW, MT, SW & TW v Luton Borough Council* [2017] EWHC 3028 (Fam), [2018] 1 FLR 1593, per Cobb J.

respect to a particular sum or a piece of work.[132] The objective of a wasted costs order is to provide compensation to the offended party.

6.112 In *Ezair v Ezair*,[133] the Court of Appeal considered the decision by the lower court to make a lump sum order under MCA 1973, s 23. The sum awarded had been increased by the judge at first instance on account of the husband's litigation misconduct, as a litigant in person. The order was not made under the 'wasted costs' jurisdiction at s 51 of the Senior Courts Act 1981 which does not apply to a litigant in person. The appeal court held that the two sums could not be combined in this way and that the 'safe and orthodox approach' is to determine the lump sum in accordance with MCA 1973, s 25 criteria and then consider the costs wasted by the husband's conduct.[134] The lump sum was reduced accordingly and the matter was returned to the trial judge for separate consideration of the amount of the wife's costs to be paid by the husband.

McKenzie friends

6.113 There are circumstances where McKenzie friends may be granted rights of audience by the court and may conduct litigation,[135] and in doing so they may recover fees from their clients.[136] Not surprisingly, perhaps, it seems the majority of McKenzie friends are not insured. Indeed, they can find it difficult to procure professional indemnity insurance.[137] It is also clear that, acting as a representative, a McKenzie friend may be subject to a wasted costs order.[138] The Senior Courts Act 1981, s 51(6) refers to the court's power to allow or disallow wasted costs against 'legal or other representatives';[139] McKenzie friends are 'other representatives' for the purpose of wasted costs orders.

6.114 Simler J considered a case in which 'the McKenzie friends appear on the face of the documents to have considerably aggravated the position by unnecessarily adding to the costs. I am persuaded that there is a basis for making a provisional partial order of costs against them as non-parties'.[140] The judge said there was a strong inference that numerous unmeritorious applications had unnecessarily prolonged the proceedings.[141] However, as the judge did not rule

132 CPR PD46 [5.1].
133 [2012] EWCA Civ 893, [2013] 1 FLR 281.
134 At [20].
135 Legal Services Act 2007, ss 12–19 and Sch 3; Practice Guidance *McKenzie Friends (Civil and Family Courts)* [2010] 2 FLR 962 at [18–26].
136 Practice Guidance *McKenzie Friends (Civil and Family Courts)* [2010] 2 FLR 962 at [27–30].
137 *Fee-charging McKenzie Friends* Legal Services Consumer Panel, April 2014, para 3.9.
138 *R (on the application of Laird) v Secretary of State for the Home Department* [2014] EWHC 2200 (Admin); *R (on the application of Laird) v Secretary of State for the Home Department* [2014] EWHC 3371 (Admin).
139 Defined at s 51(13) as any person exercising a right of audience or right to conduct litigation on behalf of a party.
140 *R (on the application of Laird) v Secretary of State for the Home Department* [2014] EWHC 2200 (Admin) at [115].
141 At [108].

that the McKenzie friends had acted in the capacity of representatives, the order was made under the power at CPR r 46.2 in respect to non-parties.[142]

Misconduct under CPR r 44.11

6.115

CPR r 44.11 (Court's powers in relation to misconduct) applies to costs in family proceedings:[143]

'(1) The court may make an order under this rule where—
 (a) a party or that party's legal representative, in connection with a summary or detailed assessment, fails to comply with a rule, practice direction or court order; or
 (b) it appears to the court that the conduct of a party or that party's legal representative, before or during the proceedings or in the assessment proceedings, was unreasonable or improper.

(2) Where paragraph (1) applies, the court may—
 (a) disallow all or part of the costs which are being assessed; or
 (b) order the party at fault or that party's legal representative to pay costs which that party or legal representative has caused any other party to incur.

(3) Where—
 (a) the court makes an order under paragraph (2) against a legally represented party; and
 (b) the party is not present when the order is made,

the party's legal representative must notify that party in writing of the order no later than 7 days after the legal representative receives notice of the order.'

6.116 It is noted that, unlike the wasted costs regime, CPR r 44.11 relates to costs for misconduct which apply to legal representatives and also to parties but not to McKenzie friends.

6.117 At first sight, CPR r 44.11 appears to apply to misconduct in respect to assessment proceedings. However, under r 44.11(1)(b) the conduct of a party's legal representative in the substantive proceedings may also be scrutinised. The Practice Direction to r 44.11 states: the court must allow the legal representative to make written submissions or to attend the hearing before an order under r 44.11 is made;[144] that conduct intended to prevent or constrain the court from furthering

142 At [111].
143 FPR r 28.2.
144 FPR PD44 [11.1].

the overriding objective is unreasonable or improper;[145] and that the court may call for evidence to be adduced to show that the legal representative took reasonable steps to comply with their duty under r 44.11(3).[146]

6.118 In some respects this rule duplicates the wasted costs rule at CPR r 46.8. Indeed, it is hard to think of an occasion when it would be more suitable to address the misconduct of a legal representative by an order that he should personally pay costs under the provisions of r 44.11 rather than under the wasted costs regime of r 46.8. However, r 44.11 is appropriate if the court is considering disallowing costs which are being assessed as a result of misconduct of the legal representative or the party and where the party is to pay wasted costs personally. Interestingly, the editorial note to r 44.11 in *Civil Procedure 2019*[147] refers to various cases where legal representatives have been ordered to pay costs under the wasted costs regime of r 46.8, such as *C v C (Wasted Costs Order)*,[148] and does not mention any recent cases under r 44.11 which concern legal representatives.

6.119 Some years after hearing *Re G, S and M (Wasted Costs)*,[149] Wall J was again called upon to consider a wasted costs order following a party's failure to provide the court with bundles, which resulted in the hearing taking about four times longer than it should have done.[150] Referring *to Re G, S and M (Wasted Costs)*, the judge noted:[151]

> 'that the preparation of evidence for a child case is the collective responsibility of the advocates involved. I said ([1999] 3 FCR 303 at 327, [1999] 4 All ER 371 at 391):
>
> > "I emphasise that I regard all these points as the *collective* responsibility of the solicitors and counsel in the case. Counsel and solicitors, as has been said many times, must talk to each other freely about case preparation, which is a non-adversarial collective responsibility."'

6.120 Contemplating the overhead of time and costs involved in making an order for wasted costs, Wall J decided a better approach would be to reduce the fees under the r 44.11 provision:[152]

> 'The difficulty about making orders for wasted costs, as I found in *Re G, S and H* is the real risk of satellite litigation which takes up a disproportionate amount of the court's time. In the instant case, in my judgment, the obvious course is to disallow fees … the particular point which caused time and costs to be wasted was the failure of the solicitors and counsel for the

145 FPR PD44 [11.2].
146 FPR PD44 [11.3].
147 *Civil Procedure 2019, Volume 1* (Thomson Reuters, 2019) para 44.11.3.
148 [1994] 2 FCR 1012, 1014, [1994] 2 FLR 34.
149 See **6.98**.
150 *Re CH (a minor) (Court Bundles: Wasted Costs)* [2000] 2 FCR 193.
151 At [199].
152 At [199].

> paternal grandparent to prepare a bundle in accordance with the Practice Direction. I therefore propose to direct that one-half of the fees for this hearing to which the solicitor and counsel for the paternal grandparents would otherwise be entitled on a detailed assessment be disallowed.'

He referred to CPR r 44.11 and stated:[153]

> 'This is, however, so far as I am aware, the first case under the Practice Direction in which an order disallowing fees has been made.'

Obviously, a provision for disallowing costs is also available under r 46.8(1).

6.121 The issue of misconduct in respect to bundles was subsequently addressed by Sir James Munby P in *Re L (A Child).*[154] The President referred to judgments by Mostyn J in *J v J*[155] and Holman J in *Seagrove v Sullivan,*[156] in which he stated they,

> 'have been driven to express themselves in justifiably strong terms. Having complained that "routinely the profession pays no attention to" PD27A, Mostyn J suggested (para 52) that the remedy might be:
>
> > "to set up a special court before which delinquents will be summoned to explain themselves in open court, just as delinquent practitioners in the Administrative Court are summoned before the President of the Queen's Bench Division pursuant to the decision in *R (on the application of Hamid) v Secretary of State for the Home Department* [2012] EWHC 3070 (Admin). Perhaps such a court would regularly consider whether to disallow fees pursuant to CPR 44.11(1)(b) and/or section 51(6) Senior Courts Act 1981."'

6.122 In 2018, the President had cause to refer again to misconduct in relation to bundles. He expressed,

> 'It is depressing that *eighteen* years after the Practice Direction was first issued, almost ten years after I gave judgment in *Re X and Y*, and three years since, as President, I gave judgment in *Re L*, it is still necessary to repeat these elementary points.'[157]

The misconduct was not penalised in costs on this occasion.

6.123 Whether the courts decide in future to penalise legal representatives under the CPR or under the statute, it is evident that their tolerance in dealing

153 At [200].
154 [2015] EWFC 15 at [11].
155 [2014] EWHC 3654 (Fam).
156 [2014] EWHC 4110 (Fam).
157 *Re the person previously known as Jon Venables* [2018] EWHC 1037 at [12].

with non-compliant bundles will be low and brings the risk of a wasted costs (or other adverse costs) order as stated in FPR PD27A.[158]

Inherent jurisdiction

6.124 Where legal representatives fail in their duty to the court, perhaps by acting without authority, then the court may use its inherent jurisdiction to order those representatives to pay costs unnecessarily incurred.[159] Lord Bingham of Cornhill noted this power in *Medcalf*, but went on to consider that matter under the s 51 wasted costs jurisdiction.

Costs under s 51(3)

6.125 In *Count Tolstoy-Miloslavsky v Lord Aldington*,[160] Rose LJ set out six reasons why the court does not have the jurisdiction to order costs against a legal representative under s 51(1) and (3) of the Senior Courts Act 1981. Further, the judge recorded that acting without a fee does not, by itself, provide the jurisdiction to order costs against a legal representative.[161] Also in *Tolstoy*, Roch LJ clarified that, 'a legal representative who goes beyond conducting proceedings as a legal representative and behaves as a quasi-party will not be immune from a costs order under s 51(1) and (3) merely because he is a barrister or a solicitor.'[162] An example of a quasi-party was given as, 'being a party to separate proceedings which have been heard together with the proceedings in which the costs order is sought, or by funding the proceedings or by initiating them for some purpose of his own and it is reasonable and just to make the order.'

6.126 In *Flatman v Germany*[163] the Court of Appeal considered a case in which the claimant's solicitors in a personal injury case had funded disbursements themselves in the hope of recovering them in the event of a successful claim: the claim failed and the question was whether the defendant's costs should be paid by the claimant or by his solicitors. In accordance with the principles of liability of non-party funders generally the court considered whether the 'real party' was the solicitor or the claimant. It was found that while funding disbursements was an insufficient ground to found a claim for costs against the claimant's solicitors,[164] it was arguable that the solicitors had been 'taking a lead in the litigation and effectively seeking "to control its course"', which could justify a costs order against them.[165]

158 At [12.1].
159 *Medcalf v Mardell* [2002] UKHL 27 at [24], referring to *Harley v McDonald* [2001] UKPC 18.
160 [1996] 2 All ER 556 at [563–565].
161 At [565].
162 At [570].
163 *Flatman v Germany* [2013] EWCA Civ 278, [2013] 4 All ER 349, [2013] 1 WLR 2676.
164 At [50].
165 At [52].

EXPERT WITNESSES

6.127 Witnesses benefit from immunity from civil proceedings. In 1873 it was stated that 'The authorities are clear, uniform and conclusive, that no action for libel or slander lies, whether against judges, counsel, witnesses or parties for words written or spoken, although falsely and maliciously and without any reasonable and probable cause, in the ordinary course of any proceeding in any court or tribunal recognised by law'.[166] That statement of the law was still approved by the House of Lords in 2001[167] and cited by the Supreme Court in 2011, but no longer with approval in relation to expert witnesses.[168]

6.128 This immunity used to be held to extend to an expert's report, for example one prepared in circumstances where, if there were to be proceedings for child abuse, the report would be relied upon.[169] The immunity has only ever been from civil proceedings and does not protect a witness from criminal prosecution for perjury or contempt.[170]

6.129 The purpose of the immunity is stated to be:

(a) so that witnesses can give their evidence in the knowledge that no one (for example a disappointed client) can sue them for what they say; and

(b) to stop the same facts and opinions being tried more than once.[171]

6.130 The rule however does not really fit with the obligations placed on an expert by Part 35 and PD35 of the CPR and the similar provisions at Part 25 and PD25B of the FPR. Experts have 'an overriding duty to the court'[172] with which their reports have to certify compliance[173] and a set of more specific duties.[174] This was considered by Peter Smith J in the context of whether an expert witness might be ordered to pay the costs of a party.[175] Peter Smith J observed, in a typically forward-looking judgment, that, while experts can

(a) be prosecuted for contempt or perjury;

(b) have their costs disallowed, including from their client; and

(c) be referred for disciplinary action (as in *GMC v Meadow*),

166 Kelly CB in *Dawkins v Lord Rokeby* (1873) LR 8 QB 255 at [264], approved.

167 Lord Hutton in *Darker v Chief Constable of West Midlands* [2001] 1 AC 435 at [464B].

168 Lord Phillips in *Jones v Kaney* [2011] UKSC 13.

169 *X (Minors) v Bedfordshire County Council* [1995] 2 AC 633 per Lord Browne-Wilkinson at [755G].

170 *Roy v Prior* [1971] AC 470 at [477F] per Lord Morris.

171 *General Medical Council v Meadow* [2006] EWCA Civ 1390 at [14] per Sir Anthony Clarke MR.

172 FPR r 25.3.

173 FPR r 25.10.

174 Practice Direction 25B, para 4.1.

175 *Phillips v Symes* [2004] EWHC 2330 (Ch).

none of these provides compensation for a party who suffers loss as a result of the expert's failings.

6.131 He concluded that 'The idea that the witness should be immune to the most significant sanction that the court could apply for that witness breaching his duties owed to the court seems to me to be an affront to the sense of justice' and 'the proper sanction is the ability to compensate a person who has suffered loss by reason of that evidence … in flagrant reckless disregard of his duties to the court'.[176] Peter Smith J emphasised repeatedly that this sort of costs order will not be made where there is mere negligence:[177] it would have to be aggravated and serious in its consequences. A costs order would therefore be considered.

6.132 The immunity of a witness from civil suit is tightly restricted and will not be extended unless absolutely necessary.[178] 'Immunity conferred by the law in respect of legal proceedings needs always to be checked against a broad view of the public interest.'[179] In *GMC v Meadow* the court specifically declined to extend the immunity to cover fitness to practise proceedings where the expert's evidence might, if it was so negligent as to amount to serious professional misconduct, lead to the expert no longer being able to practise.

6.133 In *Jones v Kaney*,[180] seven years after the judgment of Peter Smith J, the Supreme Court addressed the question of whether an expert has immunity from suit in relation to his witness statement. It was decided by a seven-justice Supreme Court, Lady Hale dissenting, that 'the immunity from suit for breach of duty that expert witnesses have enjoyed in relation to their participation in legal proceedings should be abolished'.[181] Lord Dyson specifically stated that this abolition applies as much to family proceedings as to civil proceedings which were the subject of that case.[182]

6.134 Cobb J, in a costs judgment in the Family Division that we have had cause to consider elsewhere,[183] cited both *Jones v Kaney* and *Phillips v Symes* in support of the making of a costs order against a third party in Children Act proceedings. In that case the third party ordered to pay the costs was not the expert in person (who was a social worker who had filed a report under s 37 of the Children Act and who had given evidence based on her report) but the local authority to whom the direction for a s 37 report had been made, the failings in the case being systemic as much as personal. The judge held that the local authority's connection with proceedings generated by a direction for a report under s 37, which requires the local authority to consider instituting proceedings,

176 *Ibid* at [95]–[98].
177 *Ibid* at [20].
178 See *General Medical Council v Meadow* at [17].
179 *Roy v Prior* at [480].
180 [2011] UKSC 13, [2011] 2 All ER 671.
181 *Ibid* at [62].
182 *Ibid* at [125].
183 *HB v PB and others* [2013] EWHC 1956 (Fam) reported as *Re OB (Private Law Proceedings: Costs)* [2016] 1 FLR 92 at [59] and see **2.69**.

is close enough to justify a costs order.[184] Although the judge did not refer to s 7 Children Act reports, we suggest that it follows from the judge's reasoning in this case that a direction for a s 7 report would not establish the same required close connection.

6.135 In all those cases where an expert witness has been held liable in costs it has been because of persistent or 'flagrant' error, the sort that might amount to professional negligence. In a criminal appeal dealing with the failure to provide an interpreter to court it was held (under a statute applying in criminal proceedings) that the necessary serious misconduct did not arise when 'there was no evidence that the failure was anything other than an isolated failure'.[185] The court then remarked (obiter) that 'where there was evidence that there had been similar failure in the past [it] might constitute serious misconduct'.[186]

6.136 However the court applied a different threshold for ordering costs to be paid by an expert in relation to a 'clerical error' in blood analysis results by a firm when there was no suggestion of any persistent or flagrant error.[187] On the other hand the consequence of the error would have been very serious – the child would have been likely to be permanently cared for by someone other than the mother, whereas when the error was corrected the child was able to be returned to its mother. This sort of error is of course rather different from errors by court experts who provide narrative reports. While the case does not provide a formal precedent, it is a case where a single error, later corrected, provided grounds for an expert witness (or rather, the company) to be ordered to pay costs.

6.137 We conclude on the basis of the recent case-law that where an expert has egregiously breached their duties under Part 25 of the FPR and PD25B, and costs have been wasted as a result, the court has the power to make an order that the expert pay the costs of the parties. In other cases, particularly those where a costs order would be borne by a business rather than an individual, such an order may be made following a single error.

COURTS SERVICES

6.138 Her Majesty's Courts and Tribunals Service (HMCTS) enters into contracts with companies which provide services, for example building maintenance, interpreting, intermediaries and for the production of prisoners

184 The judge drew the 'close connection' test from *Northampton Health Authority v The Official Solicitor and the Governors of St Andrews Hospital* [1994] 1 FLR 162, CA at [170] 'the jurisdiction should only be exercised where the non-party payer, although not a party to the proceedings, is so closely connected with, or responsible for, the proceedings as to make it just to saddle him with liability for the costs.'

185 *In re Applied Language Solutions Ltd* [2013] EWCA Crim 326, [2013] 1 WLR 3820 at [39] per Sir John Thomas P.

186 *Ibid* at [40].

187 *X Local Authority v Trimega Laboratories* [2013] EWCC 6 (Fam), [2014] 2 FLR 232, HHJ Williams.

from custody. If the companies breach the terms of their contracts they can be sued in the usual way. But because the fulfilment of the contracts has a direct bearing on court proceedings the contractors face an additional hazard: the court may hold them liable for any costs caused by their shortcomings.

6.139 Unlike the position with some other categories of people involved in providing services to the court, there is no question of the contractors having any immunity from proceedings.

6.140 In the Criminal Division of the Court of Appeal it has been held that serious misconduct sufficient to justify a costs order might arise if Capita (the contractor with HMCTS for interpreter services) persistently failed to supply an interpreter: 'A court is entitled to view successive non-attendance of an individual interpreter or successive failures in systems as amounting to serious misconduct, thus rendering the company liable for costs thereby incurred to the CPS and the defence.'[188]

6.141 In an adoption case before Munby P, the parents required interpreters. HMCTS made the necessary request of Capita Translation and Interpreting Limited but on the date of the hearing no interpreters attended court. The hearing could not go ahead as a result.[189] Capita consider that 'in suitable cases, interpreters can be joined in proceedings as third parties and required to answer for their actions in their own right'.[190] However, in the circumstances of the Capita contract with its interpreters, which left the interpreters apparent freedom to choose which commitment they met, it is difficult to see how, in most cases, that would be possible.[191] In practice it is the contractor who is liable to the court.

6.142 Capita's shortcomings in that case involved the failure to provide interpreters on time or at all on six occasions, the weakness of their system in simply not having enough Slovak interpreters and, as it was put by Sir John Thomas in the criminal jurisdiction in *Applied Language Solutions* 'a failure to remedy a defect in the company's administrative systems which had caused non-attendance in the past'.[192] Accordingly Munby P made an order for Capita to pay the costs of the hearing that had not been able to go ahead because of the lack of interpreters.

6.143 That order was made without the court having been shown the contract between Capita and HMCTS, which in fact emphasises the free-standing nature of the jurisdiction under s 51 of the Senior Courts Act. Perhaps surprisingly then, Munby P suggested that the detail of the contracts with 'other private-sector contractors whose failures can impact adversely on the court sitting day' would be determinative of whether those other contractors would be held liable for

188 *In re Applied Language Solutions* [2013] EWCA Crim 326, [2013] 1 WLR 3820 at [41].
189 *In the Matter of Capita Translation and Interpreting Limited* [2015] EWFC 5.
190 *Ibid* at [13].
191 *Ibid* at [16].
192 At [40].

costs.[193] It would seem, on the basis of the reasoning in relation to Capita, that a company responsible for providing intermediaries, a company responsible for providing heating and lighting, one responsible for maintaining technical equipment (for example video and recording equipment), or one responsible for producing people from custody, if they repeatedly and systematically fail to provide an adequate service so that court proceedings are unable to go ahead, would find themselves similarly liable to an adverse costs order. The nature of their contract might then be pleaded in their defence, and perhaps the contract would be undemanding enough for them to avoid liability.

6.144 At the time of writing no service save that of interpreters has been the focus of judicial attention.

HMCTS (and the LAA)

6.145 The Courts Service meets a number of costs relating to litigation. It provides the courtrooms, the judges and the court staff; it contracts for interpreters and the delivery of people in custody. But what more should it do? What are the limits of what HMCTS should pay for and how are they defined?

6.146 In relation to family proceedings the restrictions on legal aid under LASPO have brought this question into sharp focus and there have been a number of cases where judges have had to face down opposition from both the Legal Aid Agency and the Lord Chancellor in the interest of ensuring that the courts themselves are not in breach of their Human Rights Act obligations to litigants.

6.147 *Q v Q*[194] considered the position in three private law cases where fathers accused of sexual offences sought contact with their children. The questions arose of how to pay for experts to attend court at a final hearing, how to pay or otherwise arrange for representation of a party who engaged in the proceedings through an interpreter, and how to pay for or otherwise obtain assistance to be able to draft documents. In each case the other party (the mother) was in receipt of public funding and the father, at some stage, was not, so that the question of the parties being on an unequal footing[195] also arose.

6.148 Of the three conjoined cases in *Q v Q*, one – *Re B* – was granted exceptional Legal Aid following an application for judicial review on behalf of the father made by the Public Law Project. A threat of judicial review had not been enough, and the claim had to be issued before the Legal Aid Agency agreed to fund the case.[196] A second case – *Re C* – was later granted exceptional public funding by the LAA.[197] *Q v Q* itself has not been subsequently reported,

193 At [42].
194 *Q v Q; Re B; Re C (Private Law: Public Funding)* [2014] EWFC 31, [2015] 1 FLR 324.
195 Contrary to an element of the overriding objective, FPR r 1.1(2)(c).
196 *Q v Q* [2014] EWFC 31 at [36].
197 *Re C (A child) (No 2)* [2014] EWFC 44, Munby P.

suggesting that LAA assistance may have been found for the father in that case too. In relation to both *Q v Q* and *Re C* Sir James Munby P had set out that if LAA funding was not forthcoming HMCTS would be likely to have to foot the bill,[198] which the reader may think is likely to have assisted the LAA to reach a positive decision about funding.

6.149 Not many months later the same problem arose before Sir James Munby P again,[199] where the facts of the case put the lack of legal representation for the parents in even sharper focus, they being unable to effectively represent themselves and in the case of the father not competent to do so. The judge put the responsibilities of the court as follows

> '[27] In *Q v Q (Funding of Representation and Expert Attendance)* [2014] EWFC 7, [2015] 1 FLR 318, at paras [12], [15]–[16], I pointed out that r 1.1 of the FPR 2010 requires the court to deal with matters such as those with which I am here concerned "justly" and ensuring "so far as is practicable" that the case is dealt with "fairly" and also "that the parties are on an equal footing." That, as I observed, is the obligation of the court under domestic law, but it is also the obligation of the court under arts 6 and 8 of the European Convention. I went on to make the point that as long ago as 1979, in the well-known case of *Airey v Ireland* (Application No 6289/73) (1979–80) 2 EHRR 305, (1980) 2 EHRR 305, [1979] ECHR 3, the European Court of Human Rights had held that there could be circumstances in which, without the assistance of a legally qualified representative, a litigant might be denied her art 6 right to be able to present her case properly and satisfactorily. I referred to *Mantovanelli v France* (Application No 21497/93) [1997] ECHR 14, (1997) 24 EHRR 370 as indicating the significance of the right to an adversarial hearing guaranteed by art 6 specifically in the context of an expert's report which (as here with Ms Randall's report) is "likely to have a preponderant influence on the assessment of the facts by [the] court". See further *Q v Q; Re B; Re C (Private Law: Public Funding)* [2014] EWFC 31, [2015] 1 FLR 324, at paras [45]–[49].'

6.150 Sir James Munby P then cited the following European Court of Human Rights judgment[200] relating to a UK case where a mother with learning difficulties who lacked capacity to litigate had lacked legal representation:[201]

> '67. In light of the above, and bearing in mind the requirement in the UN Convention that State parties provide appropriate accommodation to facilitate disabled persons' effective role in legal proceedings, the court considers that it was not only appropriate but also necessary for the

198 [2014] EWFC 31 at [82] and [88].

199 *Re D (Non-availability of legal aid)* [2014] EWFC 39; [2015] 1 FLR 531.

200 *RP and Others v United Kingdom* (Application No 38245/08) [2008] ECHR 1124, [2013] 1 FLR 744.

201 *Re D* at [29].

United Kingdom to take measures to ensure that RP's best interests were represented in the childcare proceedings. Indeed, in view of its existing case-law the court considers that a failure to take measures to protect RP's interests might in itself have amounted to a violation of art 6(1) of the European Convention.'

6.151 In *Re D*, the case before Sir James Munby P, following his judgment and an invitation for the Lord Chancellor (re HMCTS and the LAA), the Legal Aid Agency, HMCTS and the Association of Directors of Children's Services (on behalf of local authorities) to make submissions, legal aid was in fact granted.[202] The case, however, sets out clearly the responsibilities on courts to comply with the Human Rights Act, as well as the other options for funding, namely: by HMCTS; by legal aid by requiring the legal costs to be met from public funding of the child, who did have legal aid; by requiring the local authority to pay.[203] None of those other options in fact had to be further explored in that case, as public funding was subsequently provided. (The application of the relevant public funding rules is dealt with in Chapter 7.)

6.152 In subsequent cases the questions have arisen of how intermediaries are to be paid for[204] and how cross-examination is to be conducted when it would be likely to be harmful for the child to be directly questioned by the alleged abuser, and where indeed it was accepted on the father's behalf as inappropriate for him to do so, but where there was no public funding made available through the LAA.[205] This problem of cross-examination had received judicial attention 8 years earlier[206] and the position had become more acute since then as a result of the further restrictions on legal aid under LASPO 2012.

6.153 The touchstone in relation to the need to provide litigation support in all these cases has been the Human Rights Act, specifically Art 6 (the right to a fair trial) and Art 8 (the right to respect for private and family life) of the ECHR. Article 6 provides that 'In the determination of his civil rights and obligations … everyone is entitled to a fair hearing'. In the cases cited above it was held that a hearing is not fair if:

(a) a person lacks capacity to engage in the proceedings which could be remedied by having an intermediary;[207]

(b) experts who have provided written reports are unable to be called to give evidence;[208]

202 *Re D* at [41].
203 *Re D* at [36].
204 Considered in *Re D (A Child) (No 2)* [2015] EWFC 2, [2015] 1 FLR 1247, per Munby P.
205 *Re K and H (Children: Unrepresented Father: Cross-Examination of Child)* [2015] EWHC 1, per HHJ Bellamy.
206 *H v L and R* [2006] EWHC 3099 (Fam), [2007] 2 FLR 162, per Roderic Wood J.
207 *Re D.*
208 *Q v Q (Funding of Representation and Expert Attendance)* [2014] EWFC 7, [2015] 1 FLR 318, per Munby P.

(c) a witness cannot be effectively cross-examined;[209]

(d) a party is unable to prepare the documents required to properly present their case.[210]

6.154 The issue of payment of intermediaries, which was resolved in relation to criminal proceedings following s 29 of the Youth Justice and Criminal Evidence Act 1999, seems now to be settled in family proceedings too. Intermediaries have been held to be 'a type of interpretation service',[211] and it is accepted that interpretation services are provided by HMCTS as an essential part of access to the court. HMCTS now accept that, on the appropriate order being made, they will fund intermediaries in family proceedings. Intermediary firms routinely do an assessment of the person's needs before providing their services, and it is now the practice of HMCTS also to pay for that assessment (rather than the LAA paying for it).

6.155 FPR PD12B (*The Child Arrangements Programme*) provides that 'Where both parties are Litigants in Person, the court may direct HMCTS to produce a Litigant in Person bundle'. More widely, on the authority of the judgment in *Re K and H* 'In any case in which the parties are litigants in person, HMCTS has agreed to respond to a judicial direction that HMCTS staff should prepare a hearing bundle'.[212] Whether, with the competing demands on the time of court staff, that will always happen, is doubted.

6.156 While in many cases it may be entirely straightforward for a judge to ask a witness questions expressed neutrally in order to elicit information, where a party's case involves a substantial challenge to a witness's evidence and where the issues are serious and central not only to the court's fact-finding but to the nature of the final order, it is much more questionable for a judge to do it. Is it really possible? Lord Bingham of Cornhill CJ considered, in the context of criminal proceedings, that[213]

> 'Without either descending into the arena on behalf of the defence or, generally speaking, putting any sort of positive case on behalf of the defence, this is a difficult tightrope for the trial judge to walk.'

6.157 The most contentious sort of HMCTS assistance recently has been with advocacy. The Lord Chancellor's submission in relation to HMCTS being asked to fund advocacy was that the legal funding code is a comprehensive code and 'constitutionally the court has no power to circumvent the statutory code'.[214] At first instance it was held, to the contrary, as follows:[215]

209 *Re K and H; H v L and R.*
210 *Re K and H.*
211 *Wiltshire County Council v N* [2013] EWHC 3502 at [79] per Baker J.
212 At [63].
213 *R v Brown (Milton)* [1998] 2 Cr App Rep 364 at [370].
214 *Re K and H* at [50].
215 *Re K and H* at [73].

> 'I do not accept that the comprehensive nature of the legal aid scheme precludes the State from providing, or the courts from requiring the State to provide, aspects of representation for those who are not able to benefit from the scheme set out by LASPO in circumstances where this is necessary, appropriate and proportionate in order to safeguard their Convention rights and to ensure compliance by the court with its own duty to act in a way which is compatible with convention rights.'

6.158 The option of the judge undertaking examination or cross-examination is specifically permitted by s 31G(6) of the Matrimonial and Family Proceedings Act 1984 which provides:

> 'Where in any proceedings in the family court it appears to the court that any party to the proceedings who is not legally represented is unable to examine or cross-examine a witness effectively, the court is to – (a) ascertain from that party the matters about which the witness may be able to depose or on which the witness ought to be cross-examined, and (b) put, or cause to be put, to the witness such questions in the interests of that party as may appear to the court to be proper.'

Sir James Munby P drew from the phrase 'or cause to be put' in s 31G(6)(b) the authority for a judge to provide, with HMCTS funding, an advocate instructed for the purpose of putting questions, such power to be used where the LAA was not providing funding for legal representation.

6.159 The Court of Appeal has however put a stop to this use of HMCTS funds, rejecting the use of either s 1 of the Courts Act 2003 or s 31G(6) of the Matrimonial and Family Proceedings Act 1984 as giving any power for such use. The court agreed with the Lord Chancellor's submissions as to the comprehensive nature of the statutory provisions for public funding, saying:[216]

> 'The court must respect the boundaries drawn by Parliament for public funding of legal representation. In my view, the interpretation adopted by the judge is impermissible: it amounts to judicial legislation.'

6.160 In the case under appeal 'the judge should probably have decided to conduct the questioning himself'.[217] This does, though, leave the question of how more difficult situations are to be handled such as where complex medical or other expert evidence, or confused evidence from a vulnerable witness, need to be tested. The Court of Appeal listed a number of ways in which evidence can be adduced, and then suggested consideration of a new statutory provision that would allow the appointment of a legal representative to conduct the cross-examination where necessary to comply with Articles 6 (right to a fair trial) or 8 (right to family life) of the European Convention on Human Rights.[218] Until

216 *Re K and H (Children)* [2015] EWCA Civ 543 at [31], per Lord Dyson MR.
217 *Ibid* at [61], Lord Dyson MR.
218 *Ibid* at [62], Lord Dyson MR.

and unless such a statutory provision is introduced HMCTS cannot be ordered to meet the costs of such advocacy. The problem for a judge in conducting cross-examination continues to be a real one, and was considered by Hayden J. On an appeal from a case where the judge had conducted the cross-examination he carefully considered the scope for conducting it more effectively and concluded that:

> 'The case for a regime which replicates the strengths of that operating in the Criminal Courts is compelling. Indeed, as I have said previously, there is no coherent alternative. In recognition of this the Government committed to legislate in the Prison and Courts Bill which I understand to have had cross party support. However, it was abandoned due to Parliamentary time constraints. I can do no more than express the hope that a legislative will may be found, perhaps by way of a micro-bill, to address this lamentable situation urgently.'

While it is not difficult to identify other shortcomings in the provision of legal aid, as we have considered, this one is perhaps the most unsatisfactory.

6.161 HHJ Hammerton dealt with a case where the local authority, having applied for a care order, then having applied for permission to discharge the care order, then further applied for that permission to be withdrawn.[219] As the judge pointed out, the effect of the original application for a care order was just the same as the effect of the application for the permission to withdraw the care order to be discharged. Non-means and non-merits tested legal aid was available to the father for the original application but none for the withdrawal application. The judge was unable to see any rational basis for that.[220] As a result much otherwise unnecessary court time was spent on the case and the father was unable to do himself justice. Only when he was finally represented pro bono was the case able to be concluded with the result that he had always wanted. The judge described the pro bono contribution as 'invaluable; indeed without their assistance, the court faces an almost impossible task'.[221] Pro bono help may be welcome to the Lord Chancellor, but it is an unreliable resource.

6.162 A similar situation arose before MacDonald J where, because proceedings were taken for wardship rather than under Part IV of the Children Act, the case was not a 'Special Children Act case' and so public funding was not provided for the parents. It was argued on the mother's behalf that the applicant local authority should pay for her representation. It was held that 'the court does not have power to require a local authority to incur expenditure to fund the legal representation of a litigant who has been lawfully refused legal aid'.[222] The lengthy judgment refers to the 'strict statutory controls' on local government expenditure, with

219 *Medway Council v EL and others* LTL 12/5/2015 (Judgment 14 April 2015).
220 At [91].
221 At [95].
222 *HB v A Local Authority and The Local Government Association* [2017] EWHC 524 (Fam), [2018] 1 FLR 538 at [108], also [94].

the implication that even if it wanted to a local authority has no power to fund a litigant in Children Act proceedings.[223]

6.163 None of these contortions would be necessary with readier access to legal aid. In particular greater use of the power under s 10 of LASPO 2012 to make an 'exceptional case determination' could provide representation in many of these particularly difficult cases. Between his hearing of two judicial reviews of the use of s 10 of LASPO 2012, one in June 2014 and one in June 2015,[224] Collins J found that the success rate of applications for exceptional case determinations had increased from 1% (in June 2014) to 13% (in June 2015). He comments that 'That remains a very low figure'.[225]

6.164 Collins J went on to hold that s 10 of LASPO 2012 is being operated in a way that does not provide the required safety net and that there must be changes to the scheme. This is considered in more detail at **7.39–7.43**. In the first edition of this book, we expressed the expectation that there would be an increase in the percentage of successful applications for exceptional case funding. That has indeed happened and the Public Law Project reported in its review of exceptional case funding in May 2018 that over half the applications received are granted[226]. The PLP review however concluded that exceptional case funding remains inaccessible for many people, particularly those who try to apply for it without the assistance of a legal aid provider. The position has continued to improve and in the last quarter at the time of going to press 68% of exceptional funding applications were granted. The percentage has improved but the number of applications is still low and there is a case for the number to grow in the light of the various needs discussed above.

6.165 In both public and private law children cases the parentage of a child may be in issue. The Family Law Reform Act 1969 sets out the procedure for such testing and provides that 'the party on whose application the direction [for testing] is given shall pay the cost of taking and testing the bodily samples'.[227] The problem has arisen in several such cases that neither parent has the means to pay for the testing and the court cannot make a decision without the test result. Various means have been resorted to in order to get round this problem, including for the Local Authority to pay where one is involved, and for the child to be made a party and the testing fee to be paid on the child's legal aid certificate. The necessary samples may now be obtained by Cafcass officers and Welsh family proceedings officers.[228] For a 12-month period in 2015–16 Cafcass agreed to pay

223 *Ibid* at [95].

224 *R (on the application of Gudanaviciene) v DLAC and Lord Chancellor* [2014] EWHC 1840 (Admin), decision upheld on appeal in *R (on the application of Gudanaviciene) v DLAC and Lord Chancellor* [2014] EWCA Civ 1622, [2015] 1 WLR 2247, and *IS (by the Official Solicitor as Litigation Friend) v DLAC and Lord Chancellor* [2015] EWHC 1965 (Admin).

225 *IS v DLAC and Lord Chancellor* at [29].

226 Katy Watts, *Exceptional Case Funding* (PLP Research Briefing Paper, May 2018).

227 Family Law Reform Act 1969, s 20(6).

228 The Blood Tests (Evidence of Paternity) (Amendment) Regulations 2015, SI 2015/1834 and explanatory note.

the fee for analysis in such cases. There can be little doubt that a child's Article 8 rights are infringed by a failure to fund a test to establish the child's parentage, and an impasse may be most readily circumvented by making the child a party so that the LAA can be ordered to pay the testing fee.

TAGGING

6.166 Electronic tagging is an order by which a device, usually an anklet, is fitted to the person whose movements are to be monitored in accordance with a court order. It is frequently ordered in criminal courts, but rarer in family courts. It was established in 2009 that tagging is available in family cases where it is also funded by the MoJ [229]. The usual form of tagging is Electronic Monitoring Services (EMS) tagging which is ordered in accordance with Guidance,[230] which includes a draft order. EMS is 'passive' tagging in which an alarm is raised if there is a breach of the conditions attached to the tag. GPS tagging, which is more expensive, is active tagging which reports the whereabouts of the person tagged at prescribed intervals. GPS tagging is not covered by the Guidance and will be approved and funded only in exceptional circumstances.[231]

6.167 Scram X bracelets are used for monitoring alcohol use. The LAA will pay for them on the usual sharing of costs for expert evidence basis 'if this has been ordered by the court and the testing does not form part of therapy or a support programme'[232].

TRANSLATIONS

6.168 Parties may have English which is too limited to understand the documents in the proceedings. In any proceedings there may be documents in a foreign language which need to be translated into English. The first principle, established by Munby P[233] and approved by the Court of Appeal, is that only those documents which are necessary should be translated, and that if there is disagreement as to which documents are necessary that disagreement should be resolved by the judge.[234]

229 *Re A (Family Proceedings: Electronic Tagging)* [2009] EWHC 710 (Fam), [2009] 2 FLR 891, Parker J at [8].

230 *Electronic Monitoring and Tagging in Family Cases* April 2015, HMCTS, set out at *Re X (Children) and Y (Children) (No 1)* [2015] EWHC 2265 (Fam), [2015] 2 FLR 1487 at [100]–[101].

231 *Re X (Children) and Y (Children) (No 2)* [2015] EWHC 2358 (Fam), [2015] 2 FLR 1515. Munby P at [7].

232 *LAA Guidance on the Remuneration of Expert Witnesses*, April 2019 [6.15].

233 In *Re L (Procedure: Bundles: Translation)* [2015] EWFC 15, [2015] 1 FLR 1417 at [33] and [35].

234 *Z (A Child)* [2017] EWCA Civ 157, [2018] 1 FLR 956 at [14], Macur LJ.

6.169 The Court of Appeal was required to address the question of who should pay for the translation of documents. There were two decisions at first instance by designated family judges: one had directed that the translation costs be met by the local authority as the party relying on the evidence; the other had directed that the parents (that is to say the LAA) bear the translation costs as the parties needing the translation. The Court of Appeal concluded that neither of those general rules was correct; it will all depend on the context, so that in some cases 'the party bearing the burden of proof shall be responsible for translation costs', while 'The circumstances of other cases may reasonably inform a view that the party which requires the translation should bear the cost.'[235] A third option is that more than one party contributes to the cost. This position, while pragmatic, leaves the parties to proceedings to make the case as to who should pay from first principles each time the translation of documents is needed.

6.170 The Court of Appeal however did hold, at [35], that it is reasonable for translation costs to be dealt with in the same way as the costs of experts and referred to 'clear authority for the apportionment of the costs of experts (*Calderdale Metropolitan Borough Council v S and the Legal Services Commission* [2005] 1 FLR 751).' The *Calderdale* case was heard by Bodey J (thus not, strictly, an authority). He considered the factors to be taken into account when determining who should pay the costs of experts and came to an 'it depends' conclusion similar to that in *Z (A child)* at **6.169** above.[236]

6.171 *Calderdale* was referred to and, at least arguably, to an extent overruled in *JG v Lord Chancellor*, discussed elsewhere at **7.80–7.83**.[237] In that case the Court of Appeal considered the rule in the FPR that 'Unless the court directs otherwise, the relevant parties are jointly and severally liable for the payment of the expert's fees and expenses'[238] and found it to be 'a default position as to liability in the event that the court does not direct otherwise'[239]. That rule had not been considered in *Calderdale*. We suggest that where translation costs are at issue, as the rationale in both *Z (A child)* and *Calderdale* is for translation fees to be approached in the way that expert fees are, FPR r 25.12(6) should be considered as well as the case law.

PAYMENT OF EXPERTS AND OTHER PROFESSIONALS

6.172 Although FPR r 25.12(6) states that 'Unless the court directs otherwise, the parties are jointly and severally liable for the payment of the expert's fees and expenses', that does not address any dispute that may arise as to whether the expert should be paid in full or at all. The question of the court's power to

235 *Z (A Child)* at [36], Macur LJ.
236 See [35] of *Calderdale*
237 *JG v Lord Chancellor and others* [2014] EWCA Civ 656, [2014] 2 FLR 1218, discussed at **7.80-7.83**.
238 FPR r 25.12(6).
239 *JG v Lord Chancellor* at [92] Black LJ.

resolve a dispute between a party and a professional – in that case an independent social worker who had been employed to supervise contact – was considered by the Court of Appeal.[240] The Court decided that while a court may, under s 11(7) of the Children Act 1989, specify conditions for the payment of the costs of supervision, a family court does not have jurisdiction to resolve a subsequent dispute about those costs. If the matter has to be resolved in court it must be as a small claim before a county court with the appropriate jurisdiction.[241] In the absence of any enforcement provision in Part 25 of the FPR, it seems that the same issue could arise in relation to an expert's fees.

240 *Re D (Children)* [2016] EWCA Civ 89.
241 At [55]–56]

CHAPTER 7

Public Funding

7.01 Three-and-a-half clauses of Magna Carta remain: one of them is Clause 40 which prohibits selling, denying or delaying justice. Some have suggested that the very much increased fees for civil justice amount to a breach of Clause 40. The reduction in access to courts resulting from the introduction of Part 1 of the Legal Aid, Sentencing and Punishment of Offenders Act 2012 (LASPO 2012) has generated much ill-feeling in the legal profession generally. Its practical effects in family proceedings have included an increase in litigants in person, in requests for pro bono help, in the growth of cheaper forms of legal assistance (direct access, unqualified legal support, professional McKenzie friends) and in many people deciding, for example, that there is no affordable way of getting to see their children regularly, or of enforcing a maintenance order. Though regrettably too long to include here, in a judgment following his departure as President of the Family Division, Sir James Munby delivered an excoriating condemnation of the public funding arrangements, together with praise for the pro bono support that solicitors and counsel provide to try to fill some of the glaring gaps. It is therapeutic.[1]

1 *M v P (Queen's Proctor Intervening)* [2019] EWFC 14 at [116]–[122].

LASPO 2012

7.02 There is no better way of introducing the intention of the Act than the Government's policy statement:[2]

> 'The Act gives effect to the Government's policy position on Legal Aid. The Government believes that legal aid has expanded far beyond its original intentions and is available for a wide range of issues, many of which need not be resolved through the courts. Irrespective of the current economic situation, a wide ranging programme of reform is required to ensure that legal aid is targeted to those who need it most, for the most serious cases in which legal advice and representation is justified.'

Thus the purpose of the Act is not solely to reduce the scope of legal aid, but also to encourage out of court resolution of disputes (MIAMs[3] and subsequent mediation), for which LASPO 2012 also makes public funding available.

7.03 Publicly funded services for family proceedings thus survive but in more restricted ways than before. LASPO 2012, particularly at ss 8–11 and in Sch 1 to the Act and in regulations growing out of those and guidance growing out of the regulations (someone in the Legal Aid Agency must keep account, perhaps by a large picture of a tree, of how all this fits together) provides a scheme of which there is too much dense detail to be recited here. What follows is an overview and the reader is referred to the Act, the Regulations and the Guidance for fuller detail. In doing so the reader should beware that, for example, there are at the time of writing 15 amending regulations to the means criteria regulations alone[4] and there will no doubt be more by the time this is read.

7.04 'Legal services' under the Act include advice, representation and mediation: advice as to how the law applies, advice and assistance in relation to legal proceedings, including the resolution of disputes outside court, and the enforcement of orders and other decisions.[5]

7.05 Part 1 of and Sch 1 to LASPO 2012 set out the proceedings for which legal services are available:

- the 'general cases': legal services are to be available 'if they are civil legal services described in Part 1 of Schedule 1 and the Director [of Legal Casework] has determined that the individual has qualified for the services';[6]
- the 'exceptional cases': where the Director has made an 'exceptional case determination'.[7]

2 As set out in the Explanatory Memoranda to LASPO 2012 and its statutory instruments.
3 Mediation Information and Assessment meetings, see **4.01–4.13**.
4 The principal regulations being the Civil Legal Aid (Financial Resources and Payment for Services) Regulations 2013, SI 2013/480.
5 LASPO 2012, s 8 and in more detail at regs 12–19 of the Civil Legal Aid (Merits Criteria) Regulations 2013, SI 2013/104.
6 LASPO 2012, s 9(1).
7 LASPO 2012, s 10.

7.06 When deciding whether a person qualifies for civil legal services the Director has to consider the individual's financial resources and the merit of the case in accordance with the merits criteria (where the financial and merits criteria apply).[8]

7.07 The structure of this chapter will take the following path through the statutory provisions, regulations and guidance:

(a) the merits tests;

(b) the means test;

(c) the statutory charge;

(d) prior authority (and experts);

(e) costs against publicly funded parties: cost protection;

(f) costs in favour of publicly funded parties.

THE MERITS TEST

7.08 In order to be eligible for legal aid a case has to pass the merits test[9] or to be determined to be an exceptional case.[10] Exceptional cases are less rare than they were and will be considered further below. In setting the criteria for the merits test the Lord Chancellor has to consider how they reflect a number of factors. Those factors provide a proportionality test: cost; appropriateness of funding that case rather than another case; the seriousness of the case both objectively and to the person applying for funding; the prospects of success; whether the applicant could obtain the service otherwise than by public funding; the applicant's conduct; and the public interest.[11]

7.09 The 'standard criteria' for the merits test in civil proceedings are:[12]

> '(a) the individual does not have access to other potential sources of funding (other than a conditional fee agreement) from which it would be reasonable to fund the case;
>
> (b) the case is unsuitable for a conditional fee agreement;
>
> (c) there is no person other than the individual, including a person who might benefit from the proceedings, who can reasonably be expected to bring the proceedings;

8 LASPO 2012, s 11, referring to s 21 of the Act, the Civil Legal Aid (Merits Criteria) Regulations 2013, SI 2013/104 and the Civil Legal Aid (Financial Resources and Payment for Services) Regulations 2013, SI 2013/480.

9 LASPO 2012, ss 9 and 11(1)(b).

10 LASPO 2012, s 10.

11 LASPO 2012, s 11(3).

12 The Civil Legal Aid (Merits Criteria) Regulations 2013, SI 2013/104 ('the Merits Regs'), reg 39.

(d) the individual has exhausted all reasonable alternatives to bringing proceedings including any complaints system, ombudsman scheme or other form of alternative dispute resolution;

(e) there is a need for representation in all the circumstances of the case including—
   (i) the nature and complexity of the issues;
   (ii) the existence of other proceedings; and
   (iii) the interests of other parties to the proceedings; and

(f) the proceedings are not likely to be allocated to the small claims track.'

7.10 The standard criteria for family proceedings are the same except they exclude conditions (b) and (f).[13] These standard criteria are supplemented by 'specific merits criteria' and together they provide six classes of family proceedings for the purpose of public funding, described at **7.20**. Each class applies a subset of the standard criteria, and then adds its own specific criteria. Each class will be considered separately below.

7.11 In addition to the standard and specific criteria two other criteria apply to all decisions on public funding:

- the conduct of the individual in relation to an application for publicly funded legal services, publicly funded legal services provided to the individual, and any civil proceedings for resolving rights and duties;[14] and
- 'Having had regard to the present and likely future demands for the provision of [publicly funded] legal services, it is reasonable to provide the individual or legal person with civil legal services in all the circumstances of the case including, but not limited to, the particular circumstances of the individual or legal person.'[15]

This last criterion allows the Legal Aid Agency (LAA) to include or exclude cases on the basis of the budget it is given. That is to say, it has no reference to the merits of funding any particular case and so is in a different category from the other criteria.

7.12 As well as the fact that the merits criteria are applied differently to each of the six classes of family proceedings, there is a seventh class of cases to which legal aid is available without regard to the merits criteria, namely:

(a) assessment by a mediator of whether a case is suitable for mediation (the first stage in the MIAM process);

(b) applications about child maintenance under Art 56 of the EU Maintenance Regulation;[16]

13 Merits Regs, reg 64 but see Class E at **7.33–7.38** in relation to condition (b).
14 Merits Regs, reg 11(6).
15 Merits Regs, reg 11(8).
16 Council Regulation (EU) No 4.2009 of 18 December 2008 on jurisdiction, applicable law, recognition and enforcement of decisions and co-operation in matters relating to maintenance obligations.

(c) applications under the 1980 Hague Convention[17] about a child abducted to England and Wales;

(d) applications about child maintenance under Article10 of the 2007 Hague Convention.[18]

7.13 The international cases at (b) above are excluded from the merits criteria because the UK is signatory to an EU Directive which sets minimum standards of legal aid for disputes which cross borders.[19] That Directive provides that member states must grant legal aid without discrimination to EU citizens and third country nationals lawfully residing in any EU member state if they are entitled to it in the jurisdiction where they are habitually resident.[20] Such cross-border cases are also likely to be excluded from the means criteria[21] (as are some others), so that a party to them will always be entitled to public funding unless the application is 'manifestly unfounded'.[22] That wording is found in the EU Maintenance Regulation which otherwise requires 'free legal aid' for any application under that Regulation to recover cross-border maintenance for a child.[23] The means and merits criteria do apply to cross-border disputes which relate to adults rather than to children, which fall into Class F below.[24] MIAMs are subject to the means criteria.

7.14 The international cases at (c) above are eligible for free non-means and non-merits tested legal aid by virtue of Article 26 of the 1980 Hague Convention which provides; 'Central Authorities and other public services of Contracting States shall not impose any charges in relation to applications submitted under this Convention. In particular, they may not require any payment from the applicant towards the costs and expenses of the proceedings or, where applicable, those arising from the participation of legal counsel or advisers'. We comment in **Chapter 4** on the inequality of arms that results from the applicant in Hague abduction proceedings having free legal aid and the respondent usually not having any.

7.15 The international cases at (d) above may be for enforcement or variation of an order, or for a new order. Applications for enforcement are eligible for free non-means and non-merits tested legal aid by virtue of Article 15 of the

17 The Convention on the Civil Aspects of International Child Abduction which was signed at the Hague on 25 October 1980, adopted into domestic law as Sch 1 to the Child Abduction and Custody Act 1985.

18 Merits Regs, regs 11(9), 70 and 71 as amended by the Civil Legal Aid (Financial resources and payment for Services) (Amendment) Regulations 2013, SI 2013/753.

19 The European Union Legal Aid Directive (2002/8/ESC) of 27 January 2003 which came into operation across the EU on 30 November 2004.

20 EU Legal Aid Directive, Art 4.

21 The Civil Legal Aid (Financial Resources and Payment for Services) Regulations 2013, SI 2013/480 ('the Financial Regs'), reg 5(1)(ja) and (ka) and para 44 of Sch 1 to LASPO 2012.

22 Merits Regs, reg 70(2).

23 Council Regulation (EC) No 4/2009 ('the Maintenance Regulation'), Art 46.

24 Merits Regs, reg 72 and see **7.32–7.33** below.

2007 Hague Convention[25] which provides that the state in which the request for enforcement is made shall provide free legal aid to the applicant, unless the claim is 'manifestly unfounded'. Applications for variation to an order or for a new order are effectively subject to the same means and merits tests as a domestic application.

7.16 The list of international instruments in relation to which legal aid is available does not however include the 1996 Hague Convention.[26] That Convention provides for the registration of judgments, as do the international Regulations and Convention above for which legal aid is available. There is no logic in the 1996 Hague Convention not being in this list, and this omission has been drawn to the LAA's attention.[27] Pending an amendment to the Merits Regulations there is a precedent for the LAA providing exceptional case funding to plug this gap as, arguably, they are obliged to in accordance with Article 47 of the Charter of Fundamental Rights of the European Union (see below at para **7.17**), at least while the UK remains a member of the EU.

7.17 There is also a general provision in EU law for legal aid. Article 47 of the Charter of Fundamental Rights of the European Union[28] makes more specific provision than Article 6 of the ECHR for public funding of legal aid. It provides a

> 'Right to an effective remedy and to a fair trial
>
> Everyone whose rights and freedoms guaranteed by the law of the Union are violated has the right to an effective remedy before a tribunal in compliance with the conditions laid down in this Article.
>
> Everyone is entitled to a fair and public hearing within a reasonable time by an independent and impartial tribunal previously established by law. Everyone shall have the possibility of being advised, defended and represented.
>
> Legal aid shall be made available to those who lack sufficient resources in so far as such aid is necessary to ensure effective access to justice.'

7.18 The LAA recognises that there may be cases which are not eligible for public funding within the Merits Regulations but where representation is required in order not to breach Article 47. Such cases will require to be classified as exceptional, and we discuss below under that heading the LAA's approach to such cases.

25 Hague Convention of 23 November 2007 on the International Recovery of Child Support and Other Forms of Family Maintenance, which was to have entered into force in the UK on 1 April 2019, though ratification is suspended subject to Brexit changes at the time of writing.

26 The Convention on Jurisdiction, Applicable Law, Recognition, Enforcement and Cooperation in Respect of Parental Responsibility and Measures for the Protection of Children of 19 October 1996.

27 By Anne-Marie Hutchinson of Dawson Cornwell Solicitors.

28 2012/C 326/02.

7.19 Representation of a respondent to a committal application in family proceedings is dealt with not under the rules for public funding in civil cases, but under those for public funding in criminal proceedings.[29] We discuss the position under those rules in **Chapter 4**.

7.20 The six classes of family proceedings are:

A. Special Children Act 1989 cases

B. Public law children cases

C. Domestic violence and forced marriage cases

D. Private law children cases

E. Financial and other proceedings

F. Proceedings for international spousal maintenance etc.

The different merits tests for each class of proceedings are now set out.

A. Special Children Act 1989 cases

7.21 These are proceedings under ss 25 (secure accommodation orders), 31 (care and supervision orders), 43 (child assessment orders) and 44–45 (emergency protection orders) of the Children Act 1989. As well as the child concerned, any parent or other person with parental responsibility comes within this class except for s 25, where only the child does. The list of proceedings included with this class ends with the words 'does not include appeals from final orders made under any of the provisions of the Children Act'.[30] This implies that appeals from interim orders in such proceedings (for example from interim care orders and refusals of assessment) are included in this class.

7.22 This definition applies to both the merits criteria[31] and to the financial criteria.[32] The financial position is simple – there is no means test.[33] That applies equally to other proceedings being heard with the proceedings in this list (for example, applications for a special guardianship order or for an injunction, for an assessment under s 38(6), for contact under s 34 or for a child arrangements order).[34] Although discovery and recovery orders in relation to emergency protection orders are not explicitly included in this class, in practice they will only be heard with applications for emergency protection orders, and so legal aid will be provided. The application of the merits test to associated proceedings

29 LASPO 2012, s 14(g) and (h) and Criminal Legal Aid (General) Regulations 2013, reg 9(v); see *Kings Lynn and West Norfolk Council v Bunning* [2013] EWHC 3390 (QB), [2014] 2 All ER 1095, [2015] 1 WLR 531, Blake J.

30 Merits Regs, reg 2.

31 Merits Regs, reg 2.

32 Financial Regs, reg 5(2).

33 Financial Regs, reg 5(1)(c).

34 Financial Regs, reg 5(1)(d).

is not made explicit in the Merits Regulations, and the combined effect of the provisions as to merits is that associated proceedings are in class B below.[35]

7.23 The merits test for special Children Act cases is set out at reg 39(e) only,[36] which states that there must be a need for representation in all the circumstances of the case including the nature and complexity of the issues, the existence of other proceedings, and the interests of other parties to the proceedings. It is hard to see any circumstances in which this criterion will not be met. The effect is that in these cases legal aid will always be provided.

B. Public law children cases

7.24 These are proceedings under s 25 of the Children Act (secure accommodation orders) for parents, the child's representation being covered under class A above, placement, recovery and adoption proceedings (including orders for contact under s 26 of the Adoption and Children Act 2002, removal from custody orders under s 36 of that Act and orders for parental responsibility prior to overseas adoption under s 84 of that Act), proceedings under the inherent jurisdiction of the High Court, proceedings for the discharge or variation of a care or supervision order (s 39 of the Children Act), and proceedings which would have the effect of discharging a care order (for example an application for a child arrangements order for a child in care). Also included in this class are orders under s 37 of the Children Act,[37] which are made in private law children proceedings, and which may involve the making of an interim care order[38]. It is suggested that when an interim care order is made under s 37 the proceedings in which that order is made, which up to that point would probably have been subject to the merits criteria at class D below, enter this class – as public law is then involved. It is arguable that when a court makes an order for a local authority to provide a report under s 37 the parents then become entitled to legal aid under this class.

7.25 The inherent jurisdiction is by its nature an open-ended category of proceedings. The Lord Chancellor's Guidance issued to the LAA suggests that where the inherent jurisdiction is invoked to secure the return of a child from a country with which there is no judicial protocol (North Cyprus springs to mind) the merits criteria may not be met as 'any order is likely to be ineffective'.[39] This is mentioned as typical of the Guidance, the principal purpose of which appears to be to assist staff to find ways of restricting the availability of public funding or, as might be said on the Lord Chancellor's behalf, to target it to those who need it most. The Guidance is substantial (65 pages, though not all applicable to family proceedings) and worth consulting if in disagreement with the LAA about funding, as it shows the thinking that is intended to inform the LAA's decisions.

35 Paragraph 1(2)(b) of Sch 1 to LASPO 2012, Merits Regs, regs 2 and 66.
36 Merits Regs, reg 65.
37 By the definition at para 1(1)(b) of Sch 1 to LASPO 2012.
38 By reg 2 of the Merits Regs and LASPO Sch 1, paras 1 and 9.
39 Paragraph 10.26 of the Lord Chancellor's Guidance under section 4 of LASPO, January 2018.

7.26 Criteria (a) and (e) of the merits criteria at reg 39 apply to public law children cases. That is to say, in addition to the fact that representation is necessary under (e), the individual does not have other sources of funding which it is reasonable to use for the class, criterion (a). Although one of the merits criteria, this is actually a means criterion. The means criteria also apply to this class, as to D and E below, and none of classes B, D or E is exempted from the application of the means criteria.[40] The means criteria however set levels of income and capital above which the individual has to meet his or her own legal costs. 'Where the gross monthly income of the individual exceeds £2,657, the Director must determine that the individual's financial resources are such that the individual is not eligible for legal services'[41] and 'If the individual's disposable capital exceeds £8,000, the Director must determine that the individual's financial resources are such that the individual is not eligible for civil legal services'.[42] No discretion is available in those provisions. The question is then what reg 39(a) of the Merits Regulations adds to these provisions: what discretion does it allow? In order to be read consistently with the Financial Regulations it must refer to other sources of funding than income and capital, for example a litigation loan, a mortgage or further mortgage, and whether it is reasonable to expect the individual to access such a source of funding.

7.27 There are two other specific merits criteria for this class of case: it has to be reasonable for representation to be provided having regard to the importance of the case for the individual; and if it is the application of the individual, then the prospects of success in the application must be very good, good or moderate,[43] that is to say they must be better than 50%. Following the judgment of Collins J in the case of *IS v Director of Legal Aid Agency*[44] the Ministry of Justice lost no time in amending this Regulation and others[45] which were found to be unlawful in that judgment.[46] For a short period the amendment meant that prospects of success could also be borderline or poor (but not very poor) if a refusal to provide legal aid would risk being a breach of the applicant's rights under either the European Convention on Human Rights or enforceable EU rights (as to which see **7.13–7.18** above). The LAA's appeal against this decision was however successful.[47] Following the appeal, rather than reinstating the position as it had been before the judgment of Collins J, the Regulations added a category of 'borderline or marginal' cases, defined as cases with a 45 to 50 per cent chance of success, as being eligible for public funding. Such borderline or marginal cases are now eligible for public funding but only if:

40 The exemptions are at reg 5(1) of the Financial Regs.
41 Financial Regs, reg 7(4).
42 Financial Regs, reg 6(4)(a).
43 Merits Regs, reg 66(2) applying Merits Regs, reg 64 and the definition of domestic violence at Merits Regs, reg 2 which relies on paras 11 and 16 of Schedule 1 to LASPO 2012.
44 [2015] EWHC 1965 (Admin), [2015] 1 WLR 5283.
45 The same amendment was made to regs 66(2), 67, 68 and 69(3).
46 The amending Regulations were made only 6 working days after the judgment: The Civil Legal Aid (Merits Criteria) (Amendment) (No 2) Regulations 2015, SI 2015/1571.
47 *Director of Legal Aid Casework v IS (through the Official Solicitor)* [2016] EWCA Civ 464, [2016] 2 FLR 392.

(i) the case is of significant wider public interest;

(ii) the case is one with overwhelming importance to the individual; or

(iii) the substance of the case relates to a breach of Convention rights.[48]

C. Domestic violence and forced marriage

7.28 This class comprises occupation orders and non-molestation orders under Part 4 of the Family Law Act 1996; applications for injunctions including use of the inherent jurisdiction following 'assault, battery or false imprisonment'; female genital mutilation (FGM) protection orders[49] and applications for forced marriage protection orders under Part 4A of the Family Law Act 1996.

7.29 The merits criteria for this class are (a), (c), (d) and (e) of the standard criteria plus two additional criteria that the prospects of success are very good, good or moderate,[50] and that the proportionality test is met.[51] The effect is to bring in three criteria not previously considered.

- First, reg 39(c) – no one else can be expected to bring the proceedings. While non-molestation orders and occupation orders are likely to be brought by the only person affected or by the person principally affected, an application for an FGM protection order or a forced marriage protection order may be made by a third party as well as by the person to be protected.[52] The LAA would no doubt prefer that a local authority be the applicant in forced marriage cases.
- Second, reg 39(d) – all forms of alternative dispute resolution have been exhausted. No MIAM is required when there has been a criminal report or civil proceedings in relation to domestic violence in the last 12 months, when the application is without notice to the other party or when the application is urgent.[53] In the majority of circumstances where a FGM, Part 4 or Part 4A application is made alternative dispute resolution will not be appropriate.
- Third, the proportionality test. The proportionality test is met if 'the likely benefits of the proceedings to the individual and others justify the likely costs, having regard to the prospects of success and all the other circumstances of the case'.[54] In the majority of cases for FGM Protection Orders and under Parts 4 and 4A of the Family Law Act 1996 there will be little difficulty in showing that this test is met. Indeed domestic violence is the one field in which the merits criteria and the Lord Chancellor's Guidance are sympathetic in terms of funding. This test is meant to be less stringent than the reasonable privately paying individual test applied to Class D.[55]

48 Civil Legal Aid (Merits Criteria) (Amendment) Regulations 2016, SI 2016/781, reg 2(5).
49 Added by the Civil Legal Aid (Merits Criteria) (Amendment) Regulations 2015, SI 2015/1414.
50 Or borderline or marginal, see **7.23** above
51 Merits Regs, reg 67.
52 Female Genital Mutilation Act 2003, Sch 2, para 2(2)(b) and Family Law Act 1996, s 63C(2).
53 Annex C to FPR PD 3A.
54 Merits Regs, reg 8.
55 Paragraph 4.2.8 of the Lord Chancellor's Guidance under s 4 LASPO and see **7.31**.

D. Private law children cases

7.30 This category includes:

A. applications to prevent removal of children either overseas or within the jurisdiction;

B. *arising out of domestic violence:* applications (other than those included in class C above) for child custody orders made under the inherent jurisdiction (which are rare), for declarations of status (marital status, parentage, legitimacy and overseas adoptions), for parental responsibility, for any order under s 8 of the Children Act, for monitoring and enforcement of contact under child arrangements orders, for orders for post-adoption contact,[56] for special guardianship orders and for family assistance orders;

C. *where a child is or would be at risk of abuse:* applications for special guardianship orders, removal of parental responsibility, termination of appointment of a guardian, any order under s 8 of the Children Act, and for Family Law Act 1986 disclosure of whereabouts and recovery orders;[57]

D. applications for recognition or enforcement of a foreign decision relating to the custody of children (in as far as it is not a case to which the merits criteria do not apply – under reg 11(9) of the Merits Regulations, see above at **7.12**) and of a foreign maintenance order – in both cases where an international agreement applies.[58]

7.31 Domestic violence means any incident of or pattern of incidents of controlling, coercive or threatening behaviour, violence or abuse (whether psychological, physical, sexual, financial or emotional) between individuals who are associated with each other.[59] There is a long and detailed list of the documentary evidence to be supplied to the LAA in support of an application for legal aid on the basis of domestic violence.[60] This long list was found by a unanimous Court of Appeal to frustrate the purposes of LASPO in that it required the domestic violence to be within 24 months of the date of the application, and in that it did not cater for victims of financial abuse.[61] Two months later the Procedure Regulations were amended so that the period has been increased to five years and 'abuse which relates to financial matters' is added.[62] There is a shorter

56 Section 51A of the Adoption and Children Act 2002, added by the Civil Legal Aid (Merits Criteria and Information about Financial Resources) (Amendment) Regs 2015, SI 2015/2005.

57 Merits Regs, reg 68(3)(a) relying on definitions in Merits Regs, reg 2 and paras 10, 12 and 13 of Sch 1 to LASPO 2012.

58 Merits Regs, reg 68(3)(b) and (c) relying on definitions at paras 17 and 18 of Sch 1 to LASPO 2012.

59 Paragraph 12(9) of Sch 1 to LASPO 2012, as amended.

60 The Civil Legal Aid (Procedure) Regulations 2012, SI 2012/3098, reg 33.

61 *R (Rights of Women) v Secretary of State for Justice* [2016] EWCA Civ 91, [2017] 1 FLR 615 at [51].

62 Regulation 2 of the Civil Legal Aid (Procedure) (Amendment) Regulations 2016, SI 2016/516. A new reg 33(2)(o) of the Procedure Regulations adds financial abuse, which is not further defined.

list of documentary evidence to be supplied in support of an application on the basis of child abuse.[63] It is worth mentioning that this documentary evidence requirement does not apply to Class C above, where the primary evidence will relate to domestic violence, nor indeed to Class B.

7.32 The merits criteria for Class D are (a), (c), (d) and (e) of the standard criteria, and in addition that the prospects of success are better than 50%[64] and that the reasonable privately paying individual test is met.[65] This final test is met where 'the potential benefit to be gained from the provision of civil legal services justifies the likely costs, such that a reasonable privately paying individual would be prepared to start or continue the proceedings having regard to the prospects of success and all the other circumstances of the case'.[66] The reasonable person would consider whether they are prepared to risk their own money in paying for the proceedings and, where appropriate, risk paying the other side's costs. This imaginary individual is one who has sufficient funds to take or respond to the proceedings, but not unlimited funds, so that the cost would be 'something of a sacrifice'.[67]

E. Financial and other proceedings

7.33 This category includes:

A. any family proceedings arising out of domestic violence which are not included in Classes C or D, including financial proceedings arising out of a family relationship where there has been domestic violence,[68] and including in particular Sch 1 to the Children Act proceedings (the only part of the Children Act included in this Class). For this purpose there is a broad definition of matters arising out of a family relationship, including all possible financial proceedings, save where dealt with under other classes;[69]

B. representation of a child in as far as not covered by another class;[70]

C. recognition and enforcement of spousal maintenance decisions in other jurisdictions signatory to the 2007 Hague Convention on Maintenance;[71]

D. recognition and enforcement of spousal maintenance decisions in other jurisdictions under Council Regulation (EC) 4/2009 ('the Maintenance Regulation').[72]

63 The Civil Legal Aid (Procedure) Regulations 2012, reg 34.
64 Or 45–50% if borderline or marginal and the eligibility test is satisfied see **7.27** above.
65 Merits Regs, reg 68.
66 Merits Regs, reg 7.
67 Paragraph 4.2.6 of the Lord Chancellor's Guidance under s 4(5) LASPO.
68 Merits Regs, reg 69(4)(a).
69 Merits Regs, reg 69(4)(a) and para 12(9) of Sch 1 to LASPO 2012.
70 Merits Regs, reg 69(4)(a), (b) and (ba).
71 Merits Regs, reg 69(4)(d) and para 18(3A) of Sch 1 to LASPO 2012 and Article 17(a) of the Convention on the international recovery of child support and other forms of family maintenance concluded at the Hague on 23 November 2007.
72 Merits Regs, reg 69(4)(c) and 70 and para 18(2) of Sch 1 to LASPO 2012 and Art 56 of the EU Maintenance Regulation.

7.34 The merits criteria for Class E are (a), (b), (c), (d) and (e) of the standard criteria.[73] That is to say, in addition to the other criteria previously discussed criterion (b) is applicable – that the case is not suitable for a CFA. As we consider elsewhere, there is a limited class of family proceedings in which a CFA is allowed, and CFAs are certainly available in relation to Trusts of Land Act and Inheritance Act applications – financial proceedings which often relate to families. Arguably CFAs are also available in Children Act, Sch 1 applications. In such proceedings the LAA might enquire whether a case was suitable for a CFA before giving a legal aid certificate for which an individual would otherwise be eligible.

7.35 In addition to these standard criteria there are three further criteria:

A. the reasonable privately paying individual test must be met; and

B. the prospects of success must be very good, good or moderate (ie better than 50%);[74] or

C. if the prospects of success are unclear then the case must be either of significant wider public interest, of overwhelming importance to the individual or relate to a breach of Convention rights.[75]

7.36 For the prospects of success to be unclear means that it is not possible without further information to estimate the prospects of success.[76]

F. International spousal maintenance, etc

7.37 This category[77] of cross-border cases includes solely the applications in relation to which public funding is required to be provided by the EU Council Directive,[78] or by the EC Maintenance Regulation,[79] other than those to which the merits criteria do not apply.[80] That Directive covers all cross-border proceedings by individuals, including family proceedings. Its tone, emphasising access to justice,[81] is similar to the former provisions of the Access to Justice Act 1999, now replaced by LASPO 2012. It provides for means testing but not for merits testing. In Brussels IIA proceedings there is also specific provision that a person receiving legal aid in one jurisdiction will receive it in the other.[82]

7.38 The general merits criteria are to be applied to cross-border disputes,[83] which we take to mean the criteria that are applicable to the sort of application

73 Merits Regs, reg 69(1).
74 Or 45–50% if borderline or marginal and the eligibility test is satisfied see **7.27** above.
75 Merits Regs, reg 69(2) and (3).
76 Merits Regs, reg 5(2).
77 Merits Regs, reg 72.
78 The European Union Legal Aid Directive (2002/8/ESC) of 27 January 2003.
79 Article 47 of Council Regulation (EC) No 4/2009.
80 Because the merits criteria are disapplied by Merits Regs, reg 11(9).
81 See, for example preambles (5) and (8) and Art 3.1.
82 Article 50 of Council Regulation (EC) No 2201/2003.
83 Merits Regs, reg 72(3)(a).

being made. Thus if it is a financial matter they will include criterion (b), while a private law children case will not include that criterion. There is, however, a large caveat to the result of the application of those criteria, which is that if they are not met then representation will be provided in any event in order to guarantee access to justice, to ensure the equality of the parties or in view of the complexity of the case, taking into account the importance of the case to the individual.[84] Cross-border cases are very often legally complex and compliance with this EU Council Directive will in practice mean that the merits test for representation is met in almost every case. The application must also not be 'manifestly unfounded'.[85]

EXCEPTIONAL CASES

7.39 If the merits test is not met in relation to a case then public funding can still be provided if the case is decided to be exceptional.[86] There is only one reason why a family case may be considered exceptional: that it is appropriate to do so having regard to the fact that a failure to provide legal services through public funding would breach or risk breaching the individual's rights under either the Human Rights Act or 'enforceable EU rights'.[87]

7.40 If a case is exceptional then the merits criteria applicable to that type of case will be applied.[88] The means criteria will also apply.[89] But not all family proceedings come within the merits criteria – that is to say if they are not proceedings included in Sch 1 to LASPO 2012 then they are not eligible for public funding at all; financial proceedings with no domestic violence or cross-border issues would be an example. In those cases the merit test to be applied is simply what is most appropriate in all the circumstances of the case.[90] The LAA has sought to argue from the wording of s 10(1) of LASPO 2012 that exceptional funding is available only for civil legal services not covered by the standard criteria. This (perverse) interpretation has been found to require 'urgent review'[91] so perhaps no more will be heard of it.

7.41 The Lord Chancellor has issued Exceptional Funding Guidance and on 1 June 2014 provided an application form for exceptional funding. The application form requires the applicant to address the matters that the LAA is required to consider before granting or refusing such an application.[92] They are:

84 Merits Regs, reg 72(3)(b).
85 Merits Regs, reg 72(2).
86 LASPO 2012, s 10.
87 LASPO 2012, s 10(3). 'Enforceable EU rights' are not defined but must include the European Union Legal Aid Directive (2002/8/ESC) of 27 January 2003 and Art 50 of Council Regulation (EC) No 2201/2003, referred to above.
88 Merits Regs, reg 49.
89 LASPO 2012, s 10(2)(b) and (4)(c).
90 Merits Regs, reg 50.
91 *R (on the application of Rights of Women) v Lord Chancellor* [2015] EWHC 35 (Admin), [2015] 2 FLR 823, Lang J, this point not challenged in the Court of Appeal [2016] EWCA Civ 91, [2017] 1 FLR 615.
92 Form CIV ECF1.

A. How important are the issues at stake for the client?

B. How complex are the procedures, the area of law or the evidence in question?

C. How capable is the client of presenting their case effectively?

D. If Art 6 ECHR is involved:
   i. Does the case involve a determination of the applicant's civil rights and obligations? And
   ii. Would the failure to provide legal aid be a breach of the client's rights under Art 6?

E. If any other ECHR Article is involved, would the failure to provide legal aid be a breach of that Article?

F. Would the failure to provide legal aid be a breach of the client's enforceable EU rights to legal services? (Article 47 of the Charter of Fundamental Rights of the European Union,[93] as set out above, goes further than Art 6 ECHR in requiring legal representation) If so supporting case-law is requested.

7.42 In relation to Art 47 of the 2012 Charter the LAA will also consider:

A. Does the case involve the determination of civil rights and obligations?

B. Does the case determine the rights guaranteed by or otherwise falling within the scope of EU law? And

C. What are the minimum services required to meet the legal obligation to provide legal aid?[94]

This final condition emphasises the approach the LAA is required to take.

7.43 In 2015, shortly before the first edition of this book, Collins J delivered a blistering attack on the way the LAA was managing exceptional funding under s 10 of LASPO.[95] He found that there was one single instance of a person making an application without legal assistance being granted exceptional funding, and of the applications made through solicitors only 13% were granted. The LAA appealed Collins J's judgment and the Court of Appeal very much toned down the criticism[96] but the judgment has had its effect: as we have seen, borderline cases are now eligible for funding under the merits test and the test for the grant of exceptional funding in the Lord Chancellor's Guidance has changed to 'whether the withholding of legal aid would mean the applicant will be unable to present his or her case effectively or lead to an obvious unfairness in the proceedings'.[97] Previously rather than 'would mean the applicant would be unable to present his or her case effectively' the test had been 'would make the assertion of the

93 2012/C 326/02, applicable throughout the EU.

94 Paragraphs 35–38 of the Lord Chancellor's Exceptional Funding Guidance (Non-Inquests).

95 *IS (by the Official Solicitor as Litigation Friend) v DLAC and Lord Chancellor* [2015] EWHC 1965 (Admin).

96 *Director of Legal Aid Casework v IS (through the Official Solicitor)* [2016] EWCA Civ 464, [2016] 2 FLR 392.

97 Lord Chancellor's Exceptional Funding Guidance (Non-Inquests) para 42.

claim practically impossible'. Perhaps just as importantly an independent tier of appeal has been introduced into what was previously an entirely internal LAA process. The adjudicators are independent solicitors and barristers with relevant experience. In the last quarter at the time of going to press the proportion of applications for exceptional funding which was granted was 68%. The fact that more than two thirds of such applications are now granted makes the unclaimable time filling up the fairly complex 11-page application form less unattractive.
In relation to private family proceedings four specific questions are raised: are the proceedings likely to be particularly emotive for the applicant? How complex are the proceedings in relation to *Airey v Ireland*?[98] Does the case involve unusually complex issues of law? What other support is the applicant likely to receive?[99]

REVIEW

7.44 The broad picture that emerges from the detail of the statutory provisions on merits and, more strongly, from the Lord Chancellor's Guidance, is that public funding will be very tightly limited with the exception of:

A. representation of parents and children in care proceedings;

B. domestic violence cases (though the provisions are extremely detailed);

C. mediation; and

D. cross-border cases.

THE MEANS TEST

7.45 Some family proceedings are exempted from the means test. They are, as far as relevant to family proceedings:

(a) special Children Act cases, as set out at Class A above in relation to the merits criteria, for a parent, a person with parental responsibility or a child;[100]

(b) proceedings heard with special Children Act cases, again only for a parent, a person with parental responsibility or a child;[101]

(c) a MIAM where the other party passes the means test;[102]

(d) a first mediation session where the other party passes the means test;[103]

(e) recognition and enforcement in the UK of a custody decision under either the 1980 European Convention on Child Custody or the 1980 Hague Convention;[104]

98 (1979) 2 EHRR 305 – a judicial separation case in Ireland without any particular complicating features, usually cited in applications for judicial review of public funding.
99 Paragraph 43 of the Lord Chancellor's Exceptional Funding Guidance (Non-Inquests).
100 Financial Regs, reg 5(1)(c).
101 Financial Regs, reg 5(1)(d).
102 Financial Regs, reg 5(1)(ga).
103 Financial Regs, reg 5(1)(gb).
104 Financial Regs, reg 5(1)(h).

(f) recognition and enforcement of EU maintenance judgments under any Convention or Regulation where the applicant would have been entitled to public funding in the member state of origin;[105]

(g) recognition and enforcement of cross-border decisions on child maintenance under Art 56 of the EU Maintenance Regulation or the 2007 Hague Convention.[106]

7.46 There is a differently worded test for entitlement to legal aid in cross-border disputes, drawn from the relevant EC Directive. In any cross-border dispute where the individual would be entitled to legal aid in their home jurisdiction,[107] they are also entitled to it in the UK. If the person is not so entitled in their home country then the means test applied is being 'unable to pay the costs of proceedings in England and Wales in relation to the dispute as a result of differences in the cost of living'.[108]

7.47 The final exception to the standard means test is in relation to:

A. applications for non-molestation or occupation orders for protection from physical harm;[109] or

B. applications for forced marriage protection orders;[110] and

C. committal for breach of any such order.

In relation to these cases the means test 'may' be disapplied. In practice it is, so that such applications, which will usually also pass the merits test (see class C above), are likely to attract public funding.

7.48 For all other family proceedings a means test is applied. While the details which follow are believed to be accurate as far as they go, there is considerable further detail in the Regulations particularly in relation to the evidence of income the LAA requires, and the reader needing that detail is referred in the first instance to the 'Guide to Determining Financial Eligibility for Controlled Work and Family Mediation'.

The elements of the means test

7.49 Means may be either income or capital, and the eligibility rules apply to both.

105 Financial Regs, reg 5(1)(i), (j) and (ja).
106 Financial Regs, reg 5(1)(k) and (ka).
107 Financial Regs, reg 11 and para 44 of Part 1 of Sch 1 to LASPO 2012 and Council Directive 2003/8/EC of 27 January 2003. Preamble (18) to the Council Directive states 'The complexity of and differences between the legal systems of the Member States and the costs inherent in the cross-border dimension of a dispute should not preclude access to justice. Legal aid should accordingly cover costs directly connected with the cross-border dimension of a dispute.' No such broad provision appears in the national legislation.
108 Financial Regs, reg 11(2).
109 Financial Regs, reg 12 and para 11 of Part 1 of Sch 1 to LASPO 2012.
110 Financial Regs, reg 12 and para 16 of Part 1 of Sch 1 of LASPO 2012.

Eligibility in relation to income

7.50 An applicant who is in receipt of state benefits in the form of income support, job-seekers allowance, guarantee credit, income-related employment support allowance, universal credit or, no doubt, any other such allowance to meet basic living needs that may be introduced in the future, will, unless that person has capital (see below) be entitled to legal aid and will make a zero contribution to it.[111] The same applies to an applicant from another EU country who is in receipt of such an allowance in their own country.[112]

7.51 For an applicant not in receipt of those state benefits their gross income is calculated. Gross income is calculated:

A. net of any sort of disability payment including personal independence payments, of carer's or attendance allowance, of housing benefit and council tax benefit and of any financial support being paid in relation to a foster-child;[113]

B. net of maintenance of any partner and any child calculated at the level at which state benefits are paid. At the time of writing the additional amount for a partner is £41.30 per week (£179 per month) and for each dependent child £66.33 per week (£274.43 per month). That maintenance may be reduced by the income of the partner or the child;[114]

C. net of rent or mortgage payments (capital and interest);[115]

D. net of any contribution order made in criminal proceedings.[116]

7.52 If gross monthly income so calculated is less than £733 per month then the applicant is entitled to legal aid (subject to not having capital in excess of £8,000) and if it is more than £2,657 per month (plus £222 for each additional child if the applicant has more than four children) then the applicant is ineligible for legal aid.[117] Between those two levels the applicant is entitled to legal aid, but may be required to make a contribution towards it. There is a sliding scale of contributions. (It is not apparent what purpose the lower figure of £733 serves, as an individual with a gross income below that level may still be liable to make a contribution by reg 44).

Contribution

7.53 Having calculated eligibility by reference to gross income, contribution is calculated by reference to disposable income.[118] For that calculation, in addition to the deductions listed at **7.51** above, also deducted are:

111 Regulation 6(2) Financial Regs.
112 Regulation 6(3) Financial Regs.
113 Regulations 7(1) and 24 Financial Regs.
114 Regulation 25 Financial Regs.
115 Regulation 28 Financial Regs.
116 Regulation 29 Financial Regs.
117 Regulation 8(2), 7(4) and 7(5) Financial Regs. Unchanged since the Regs were introduced in 2013, though RPI has increased by 18% in the subsequent six years, so the equivalent cash bracket should now be £865 to £3135.
118 Regulation 44 Financial Regs.

A. income tax and national insurance;[119]

B. deductions for the maintenance of a former partner or child, that is to say under a court order, an agreement, or a CSA[120] assessment;[121]

C. if the applicant is employed, £45 per month;[122]

D. if the applicant is employed, self-employed or has study-related income, childcare costs.[123]

E. housing costs, that is to say mortgage or rent payable, net of housing benefit.[124]

7.54 If disposable income is:

A. less than £311 per month, there is no contribution;

B. between £311 and £465 per month, the contribution is 35%;

C. between £466 and £616 per month, the contribution is 45%;

for any remaining income, the contribution is 70%.

7.55 A worked example would be: an applicant with a partner and two children who earns £1,500 per month gross (part-time, perhaps) will have a gross income for legal aid purposes of £1,500, less £179 (non-working partner) less £548.86 (two children) = £772.14, less rent or mortgage payments. An applicant with that income (and no capital) would pass the means test and being below the £2,657 per month figure would be eligible for legal aid. This eligibility is subject to the rules about capital, see below.

7.56 A person on such an income would be liable to pay £133 per month income tax, their national insurance contribution of (at this income level) £8 per month would be deducted, as well as the £45 per month for being employed. Assuming no other deductions their disposable income would be £586 per month, which would mean a contribution of £108 per month to their legal aid. It is likely however that there would be deductions for rent or mortgage which would mean that the applicant would be assessed to make no contribution.

Capital

7.57 If an applicant has capital in excess of £8,000 then he or she will be ineligible for means-tested legal aid.[125] Capital less than £3,000 is ignored, and

119 Regulation 23 Financial Regs.

120 The Child Maintenance Service, as it now is, continues to use the alternative name of Child Support Agency and the initials CSA.

121 Regulation 26 Financial Regs.

122 Financial Regs, reg 27(1)(a).

123 Financial Regs, reg 27.

124 Financial Regs, reg 28. There is also a specific exclusion of any payment made in relation to the Grenfell Tower fire: the Civil Legal Aid (Financial Resources and Payment for Services) (Amendment) Regulations 2017, SI 2017/745.

125 Financial Regs, reg 6(4).

between those two amounts the applicant is eligible for legal aid by the means test and will contribute as much of the amount of their capital above £3,000 as is necessary to pay for the legal services, the LAA meeting the rest of the bill.[126]

7.58 Capital is calculated excluding home contents, personal belongings, tools of a person's trade[127] and the first £100,000 of the net equity in an applicant's home[128] and other land.[129] Any capital subject of the proceedings (for example in financial remedy proceedings a share of the family home) is disregarded for the purpose of this calculation. If an applicant aged 60 or over has a small disposable income (less than £315 per month) there is a further capital disregard on a sliding scale between £10,000 (for a monthly income of £226-315) and £100,000 (for a monthly income of £25 or less). The income is calculated as above, so that, for example, the applicant whose sole income is from benefits has an income for these purposes of nil.[130]

7.59 The requirement for a person who is eligible for legal aid to make a contribution towards legal aid appears to be the exception rather than the rule under the primary statute.[131] The relevant regulation however reverses that position so that the individual 'must' pay the sum assessed in accordance with the criteria above.[132] The assessed sum 'must' be paid monthly.[133]

THE STATUTORY CHARGE

7.60 The cost of legal aid can be recovered from the individual by placing a charge in favour of the Lord Chancellor on any property recovered or preserved in the proceedings.[134] There is provision in rare circumstances for the charge to be in favour of the solicitor who has provided the legally aided services,[135] but otherwise the money recovered is payable to the LAA who are responsible for paying the solicitor. The Act makes it a 'first charge'.[136] The question arises whether as a 'first charge' it has priority over a pre-existing mortgage. The Legal Services Commission (the LAA's predecessor) accepted that such a mortgage has priority to the statutory charge.[137]

126 Financial Regs, reg 44(3).
127 Financial Regs, reg 34.
128 Financial Regs, reg 39.
129 Financial Regs, reg 37.
130 Financial Regs, reg 41 and Table 1.
131 Section 23(1) LASPO 'An individual to whom services are made available under this Part is not to be required to make a payment in connection with the provision of the services, except where regulations provide otherwise'.
132 Regulation 44(2) Financial Regs.
133 Regulation 44(4) Financial Regs.
134 Section 25(1) LASPO and reg 7 of the Civil Legal Aid (Statutory Charge) Regulations 2013, SI 2013/503 ('Statutory Charge Regs').
135 Regulation 7(2) Statutory Charge Regs.
136 Section 25(1) LASPO.
137 *McPherson v Legal Services Commission* [2008] EWHC 2865 (Ch) Morgan J at [45], [49] and [95].

Finance cases

7.61 Typically the charge is on land. In a financial remedy case it may well be on the former matrimonial home. The statutory charge cannot be applied to periodical payments, pensions or redundancy payments, nor to clothes, furniture or tools of the individual's trade.[138] It can be applied to cash in an account, investments of any kind (other than pensions) or valuable possessions such as jewellery or vehicles.

7.62 The question has arisen from time to time as to whether, where a spouse or other partner was the 50% beneficial owner of a home before the proceedings, that 50% has been 'recovered or preserved' in the proceedings. The House of Lords held in a divorce case that 'property has been recovered or preserved if it has been in issue in the proceedings … In property adjustment proceedings, in my view, it is only property the ownership or transfer of which has been in issue which has been "recovered or preserved" so as to be the subject of a Legal Aid charge'.[139] That left the loose end of whether all the assets in a financial remedy case are 'in issue' or not, since they are all taken into account when a judicial decision is made, but the subsequent possession of some of them may have been agreed between the parties. The Court of Appeal has subsequently held that the fact that a party to legal proceedings recovered in the proceedings that to which he or she was already entitled cannot by itself prevent the attachment of the statutory charge.[140] The weight of the authorities is to the effect that the statutory charge may be attached to any formerly matrimonial property which the publicly funded individual possesses after a final financial remedy order.

7.63 In practice if cash is recovered by a legally aided party that party's solicitor will use that cash first to pay the individual's publicly funded costs – effectively to meet the solicitor's own invoice.[141] Where money is paid to the LAA, it will be used to pay the solicitor's invoice.[142] Any remaining money must of course be returned to the individual. It is important that clients who receive public funding in proceedings where assets may be transferred to them are made aware that while their representation may be through public funding, they are likely to end up footing their own bill. It is particularly important to make this clear to a client who has made little or no contribution to their legal aid in relation to a dispute over children – in a financial dispute they will in contrast be likely to have to pay their legal costs in due course.

7.64 The LAA can enforce the charge like any other such creditor,[143] except where enforcement is postponed. If a charge on land is postponed it will be

138 Regulation 5 Statutory Charge Regs.

139 *Hanlon v Law Society* [1981] AC 124, [1980] 2 All ER 199, [1980] 2 WLR 756 at [180H], Lord Simon.

140 *Curling v Law Society* [1985] 1 All ER 705, [1985] FLR 831, [1985] 1 WLR 470 at [477G] (Neill J) and [483D–E] (Oliver LJ). See also a discussion of the authorities in *McPherson v Legal Services Commission* [2008] EWHC 2865 (Ch) by Morgan J at [54]–[71].

141 Regulations 13 and 15(3) Statutory Charge Regs.

142 Regulation 17 Statutory Charge Regs.

143 Regulation 21 Statutory Charge Regs.

registered at the Land Registry.[144] Enforcement of the statutory charge will be postponed (the language of the regulation is 'may') if there is a court order saying that the property is to be lived in by the individual or their dependants, or that the money received is to be used for the purpose of purchasing such a property.[145] That money has to be used for the purchase of a property within 12 months unless the LAA allows an extension of the period,[146] as they would if a purchase is in progress. Where a property bearing such a charge is sold and replaced by another property, the charge can be transferred to the new property[147] rather than being required to be repaid at that time.

7.65 This might seem a liberal provision since it allows the charge effectively to lie on the property for many years until, perhaps, the death of the individual. Regrettably the liberality is only apparent as immediately upon the charge being registered simple interest becomes due at the rate of 8% per year.[148] As this is a higher rate than has been available through mortgages in recent years, this rate is an encouragement to any individual who owns a property with a statutory charge to re-mortgage and pay off the LAA as soon as possible. If part of the debt is being paid off, the amount paid will be set against the interest due first, and only when the interest is paid off will the capital be reduced by such a payment.[149]

Human Rights Act damages

7.66 The LAA takes the view that the statutory charge applies to amounts awarded in damages for human rights breaches in relation to Children Act proceedings, typically against Local Authorities which have acted wrongly. In as far as such damages are not exempt from the statutory charge[150] the LAA is clearly right about that, as was acknowledged by Mostyn J.[151] The result of the application of the statutory charge in these circumstances has been, however, that the damages awards were absorbed by the costs and the client received nothing. That is clearly not what the court would consider just and Keehan J strained every muscle to prevent a statutory charge clawback by separating the Human Rights Act claim from the Children Act proceedings and finding that there was no separate LAA funding for the Human Rights Act claim: the child could keep his damages award.[152] Cobb J provided a full analysis of the interplay between the statutory charge and damages in public law proceedings and concluded that the position as found by Keehan J is the exception and that the Human Rights Act

144 Regulation 22(2) Statutory Charge Regs.
145 Regulation 22(1) Statutory Charge Regs.
146 Regulation 23(6) Statutory Charge Regs.
147 Regulation 22(3) Statutory Charge Regs.
148 Regulation 25(1)(c) Statutory Charge Regs.
149 Regulation 25(2) Statutory Charge Regs.
150 The exemptions are listed at reg 5 of the Civil Legal Aid (Statutory Charge) Regulations 2013.
151 *R (Faulkner) v Director of Legal Aid Casework* [2016] EWHC 717 at [37]–[38].
152 *P v A Local Authority* [2016] EWHC 2779 (Fam), [2017] 1 FLR 1589 at [79].

damages will not usually be exempt from the statutory charge.[153] In a subsequent case he acknowledged that 'It seems overwhelmingly likely that any award of damages which I make will be swallowed up by the statutory charge.'[154] The effect was that the Human Rights Act claim was not financially worthwhile.

7.67 Cobb J also made clear that, as Human Rights claims are not family proceedings, the relevant costs rules are those in the CPR, including the rule that the unsuccessful party pays the costs of the successful party. If anything, this makes the absorption of a costs award by the LAA even more unjust.

7.68 In *Faulkner* the Court of Appeal considered the power (now) under reg 9 of the Statutory Charge Regulations to waive all or part of the statutory charge. There are two parts to the test:

(a) the Director was satisfied, in determining that a legally aided party qualified for legal representation, that the proceedings had a significant wider public interest; and

(b) the Director in making the determination took into account that there were other claimants or potential claimants who might benefit from the proceedings.

The Court of Appeal held that the discretion must be exercised at the time the decision is made to provide or extend legal aid, and cannot be exercised in retrospect. It follows that if an application for legal aid is being made in a case where there may be damages awarded, the argument that there is a wider public interest must be made at the time of the application. [155]

7.69 The European Court of Human Rights (ECtHR) has been troubled by this issue of providing an 'effective, adequate and accessible remedy' when 'the State takes away with one hand what it has awarded with the other to repair a breach of the Convention'[156]. In *Scordino v Italy* the ECtHR awarded substantially more in compensation and costs than the national court had awarded in order that there would be an effective remedy. That was a case where the proceedings had taken unreasonably long because of failure of the court system. That case has been considered by the Court of Appeal[157] in the context of the application of the statutory charge. In not deciding that the statutory charge should be waived the Court of Appeal took a narrow approach to what the European Court had decided, though in that case the rejection of the claimant's claim to be exempted from the statutory charge was refused partly on the merits.

7.70 The perceived injustice and the degree of judicial concern expressed had their effect. In 2018 the LAA issued a 'Position as to the Application of the

153 *AZ, BZ and CZ v Kirklees Council* [2017] EWFC 11, [2018] 1 FLR 23 at [44]–[77].
154 *SW and TW (Human Rights Claim: Procedure) (No 1)* [2017] EWHC 450 (Fam), [2017] 2 FLR 1609 at [40].
155 *R (Faulkner) v Director of Legal Aid Casework* at [20].
156 *Scordino v Italy (No 1)* [2007] 45 EHRR 7 at [195] and [201].
157 *R (Faulkner) v Director of Legal Aid Casework* [2018] EWCA Civ 1656 at [25]–[36].

Statutory Charge in Relation to Care Costs and Human Rights Act Applications', which has been published as an appendix to *Northamptonshire County Council v Lord Chancellor (via the LAA).*[158] The LAA's position as set out in that Appendix is that 'The application of the statutory charge in respect of legally aided costs of care or other family law proceedings to HRA damages can be avoided by ensuring damages are not awarded within the care and other family proceedings and by keeping the costs of pursuing the damages claim separate.' This is welcome clarity, which also emphasises the care which those making such claims need to take in order to keep the costs incurred and ideally the hearings separate.

7.71 The earlier guidance given by Keehan J, prior to the LAA's Position being formally clarified in the *Northamptonshire* case, provides broad advice as to the management of such claims and so remains relevant to those making HRA claims which arise from public law Children Act cases.[159]

PRIOR AUTHORITY

7.72 Solicitors' contracts for legal aid are subject to the LAA's (copious) published Guidance. Legal aid certificates specify the work to be done under them in general terms, and specify a cost limit. Thus if the certificate is for legal representation and the costs are within the amount of the certificate then it might be assumed that the LAA will pay those costs. The relevant Guidance however specifies that is not the case when the LAA must give prior authority for certain items of costs. The area requiring such prior authority which is most frequently at issue is where a report is required from an expert charging more than the scheduled remuneration rates. Specific prior authority is also required for an expert in a field for which there is no specified rate and for a number of hours work by an expert in excess of the specified level,[160] for Queen's Counsel or for a second counsel,[161] and it is advisable to obtain prior authority for an item of costs in excess of £5,000.[162]

7.73 Prior authority is always required for an expert if the expert is charging more than the statutory remuneration rates. The rates cover the types of experts that will be needed in most cases. On 2 December 2013 the rates were reduced to 80% of their previous level,[163] with the dual effects that some experts have reduced their fee rates and that more applications for prior authority have had to be made. (On 22 April 2014 a 10% reduction was made to standard legal fee limits in family cases – further illustrative of the Government's determination to

158 [2018] EWHC 1628 (Fam), [2019] 1 FLR 169.

159 *H v A Local Authority* [2017] EWHC 282 (Fam) at [117].

160 *Ibid* at para 4.11.

161 LAA 'Guidance on authorities and legal aid for cases in courts outside England and Wales'.

162 LAA 'Guidance on the Remuneration of Expert Witnesses' at para 4.3.

163 Regulation 2(6) and Sch 2 to the Civil Legal Aid (Remuneration) (Amendment) Regulations 2013, SI 2013/2877.

drive down legal aid costs.[164]) As to prior authority when an expert's costs are not equally apportioned, see the section on 'Experts' below.

7.74 If the statutory remuneration rates for an expert are exceeded without prior authority then the LAA will disallow the amount of the excess.[165] The detail of the rules about prior authority mean that advocates are often uncertain whether it is necessary or advisable to apply for such authority. The main rules are:

A. while it is not required it is advisable to seek prior authority if it is known that the number of hours to be worked by the expert will exceed the maximum hours specified. The fact that the hours actually spent by the expert actually exceed that level may only become apparent after the expert has started work, and such an excess can always be sought to be justified on later assessment;

B. prior authority is not normally necessary for the expert's court attendance;

C. experts are not entitled to cancellation fees from the LAA if cancellation is more than 72 hours before the hearing or appointment;

D. drug and alcohol testing for periods longer than 3 months will not be allowed unless the longer period is specified in the court order. Testing segmented by months, which is more expensive, will also not be allowed unless specified in the order. The order must state which sort of testing (hair, blood or liver) is required;

E. interpreters away from court are funded by the LAA, and interpreters in court are funded by HMCTS. The position in relation to interpreting at court other than interpretation in the hearing is that the LAA will fund interpreting at court outside the hearing, and such an interpreter may go into court to be informed sufficiently to interpret between lawyer and client outside the courtroom;[166]

F. advice on foreign law needed for proceedings in England and Wales is funded, but advice on law for proceedings in another jurisdiction is not;[167]

G. a client's travel to see an expert or to attend court is funded if the client is 'impecunious'; as are any loss of income, hotel expenses and subsistence for a party or a witness attending court. A client's travel to his solicitors' office or to a conference with counsel is claimable similarly;

H. residential assessments are not funded by the LAA;

I. child contact centre fees are not funded, and so if the contact centre makes a charge it will be paid either by the client, by the local authority or sometimes by Cafcass.[168]

164 The Civil Legal Aid (Remuneration) (Amendment) (No 2) Regulations 2014, SI 2014/586.

165 'Guidance on the Remuneration of Expert Witnesses' at para 2.3.

166 'Guidance on the Remuneration of Expert Witnesses' at para 6.29.

167 These rules A to F are in the LAA's 'Guidance on the Remuneration of Expert Witnesses'.

168 These rules G to I are in the LAA's 'Guidance on authorities and legal aid for cases in courts outside England and Wales'.

EXPERT WITNESSES

7.75 Expert witnesses are not of course confined to proceedings which are publicly funded. The effects of controlling costs in publicly funded cases, particularly care proceedings, have however had major effects on the rules governing the instruction of expert witnesses in all family proceedings. Those effects have included a new Part 25 to the FPR with five Practice Directions replacing the previous one, new controls in primary legislation,[169] new and regularly updated Guidance from the LAA,[170] and case-law. As the costs of experts are of particular significance in publicly funded cases they are dealt with here.

7.76 The court's stricter control on the employment of experts is not principally about their funding but about case management. The statutory requirement in a children case is that 'the expert evidence is necessary to assist the court to resolve the proceedings justly' and the court may only give permission for an expert when that is the case.[171] 'Necessary' was used for the same purpose in the FPR when it was interpreted by Sir James Munby P as having 'a meaning lying somewhere between "indispensable" on the one hand and "useful", "reasonable" or "desirable" on the other hand', having 'the connotation of the imperative, what is demanded rather than what is merely optional or reasonable or desirable'.[172] It is conventional now to use the statutory words 'necessary to assist the court to resolve the proceedings justly'[173] in the paragraph of an order dealing with public funding for an expert. But the requirement is the same whether the expert is publicly or privately funded. And while the LAA may make an issue of those words being included, in fact the court may only make an order for an expert where that condition is satisfied, so that the fact that there is an order for an expert should be enough without more.

7.77 There is a difference in the statutory position for children proceedings and for financial proceedings in that the requirement for the instruction of the expert to be 'necessary' is in primary legislation in relation to children proceedings and in the FPR in relation to financial and other proceedings. The wording is identical in the two provisions save that the statute adds the word 'justly'.[174]

7.78 Part 25 makes a number of provisions about the cost of experts. The cost of the expert evidence is always a factor to be considered in deciding whether to give permission for an expert.[175] Although the costs of the expert are not required by the relevant rule to be included with the application for permission to instruct

169 Children and Families Act 2014, s 13.
170 Guidance on the Remuneration of Expert Witnesses, LAA and other Guidance.
171 Children and Families Act 2014, s 13(6).
172 *Re H-L (A child)* [2013] EWCA 655, [2013] 2 FLR 1434 at [3], quoting *Re P (Placement Orders: Parental Consent)* [2008] EWCA Civ 535, [2008] 2 FLR 625, [120], [125].
173 Children and Families Act 2014, s 13(6).
174 Children and Families Act 2014, s 13(6) and FPR r 25.4(3).
175 FPR r 25.5(1)(h) and r 25.5(2)(e).

the expert,[176] the Practice Directions do require the expert's hourly or other charging rates to be included with any application[177] and require the expert to have provided the likely hours needed before the application is considered by the court.[178] Where legal aid rates apply the party proposing the expert must inform the expert of the applicable legal aid rates.[179]

7.79 The application also has to state the proposed apportionment of the expert's fee between the parties.[180] The parties should agree how the expert's fee is to be funded before the application is made[181] and have obtained agreement for public funding, if applicable.[182] This suggests that prior authority should be obtained before the application is made, though in practice the LAA does not always provide prior authority quickly enough for that to be possible. It has been commented by the Court of Appeal that for the instruction of an expert to await an agreement or court order on apportionment 'would or may import harmful delay into the proceedings and in which there is no option but to adopt the Law Society's solution of requiring [one party] to instruct the expert in the first instance, but with the intention of revisiting the question of cost, on proper financial information, later by means of a conventional costs order'.[183] That there continue to be cases of delay by the LAA is illustrated by a case which came before Sir James Munby P in which the delays were 'unconscionable'.[184] A chronology in that case showed that the LAA took 9 months just to grant the parents' application for legal representation resulting in the proceedings taking a 'manifestly excessive' period of time during which the child was separated from his parents.[185]

7.80 This area of apportionment of the expert's fee and the public funding of a proportion or all of the fee has caused considerable difficulty, which has to some extent been laid to rest by the Court of Appeal in *JG*.[186] That case dealt with whether a child's public funding should pay the whole of an expert's costs when neither of the parents could afford it: 'a real issue of very considerable importance in private law proceedings relating to children in the wake of the severe restriction on public funding for those involved in such proceedings'.[187] In that case the court decided that as the suggestion for the expert came from the children's guardian it was appropriate for the whole cost to fall on the child's public funding certificate, but the court stressed repeatedly that: 'there is no

176 FPR r 25.7.
177 FPR PD25C para 3.10(g) and FPR PD25D para 3.11(g).
178 FPR PD25B para 8.1(c).
179 FPR PD25C para 3.2(n) and FPR PD25D para 3.3(k).
180 FPR PD25C para 3.10(h) and PD25D para 3.11(h).
181 FPR PD25C para 2.6(c) and PD25D para 2.6(c).
182 FPR PD25C para 2.6(d) and PD25D para 2.6(d).
183 *JG v Lord Chancellor and others* [2014] EWCA Civ 656, [2014] 2 FLR 1218 at [119].
184 *Re D (A child) (No 2)* [2015] EWFC 2, [2015] 1 FLR 1247.
185 *Ibid* at [11].
186 In *JG v Lord Chancellor and others* [2014] EWCA Civ 656, [2014] 2 FLR 1218.
187 At [64] Black LJ.

universally applicable answer and everything will depend on the facts of the case'.[188]

7.81 In the course of the judgment the court considered the rule which states that[189]

> 'Unless the court directs otherwise, the relevant parties are jointly and severally liable for the payment of the expert's fees and expenses.'

Having commented that it is odd to find a procedural rule concerning itself with 'the contractual relationship between the parties and the expert' the court concluded that that rule does not set up a 'normal rule' but creates 'a default position as to liability in the event that the court does not direct otherwise'.[190] The correct approach is for the court to ask what decision it would make on the facts of the case, leaving aside any resources problems. That may lead to equal apportionment of the costs, or it may lead to the conclusion that the publicly funded party 'should be paying a greater share of the costs in any event'.[191]

7.82 The court then addressed the question of when a court should depart from the order it would otherwise have made because of a resources problem. The only reason to depart from the order that the court would otherwise have made was whether a party's Art 6 or Art 8 rights under the ECHR would be infringed if the expert were not instructed. The court concluded from a consideration of ECtHR cases that Art 6 and Art 8 rights could be infringed by an inability to obtain expert evidence.[192] In such cases it would be right to order that the party who could afford it must pay a disproportionate share – perhaps all – of the costs of the expert, at least in the first instance. The court considered that 'By the time the guardian has endorsed the instruction of an expert as appropriate and the court itself has approved it as necessary, there will be the beginnings of a strong foundation for an argument that the child's Art 8/Art 6 rights will be violated if the court cannot be provided with that expert assistance'.[193]

7.83 Although not considered in the judgment, exceptional case determinations for legal aid are determinations that it is necessary to make legal services available to the individual because failure to do so would be a breach of the individual's Convention rights under the Human Rights Act.[194] The LAA should therefore go through the same reasoning process when deciding whether to provide exceptional public funding for an expert as the court has to when deciding how the costs of an expert should be apportioned in a case where not all the parties can afford the expert's fees.

188 At [66] Black LJ.
189 FPR r 25.12(6).
190 At [92] Black LJ.
191 At [93] Black LJ.
192 At [96]-[109] Black LJ, citing in particular *Elsholz v Germany* (Application No 25735/94) (2002) 34 EHRR 58, [2000] 2 FLR 486.
193 At [109] Black LJ.
194 LASPO 2012, s 10(2) and see **7.39–7.43** above.

SPECIAL ADVOCATES

7.84 The role of special advocates is to represent a person in proceedings in which some of the evidence is of such sensitivity that it should not be seen by one or more of the parties. The special advocate sees the material and puts forward his or her party's case without being able to disclose the sensitive material to the party.

7.85 In *Re R (Closed Material Procedure: Special Advocates: Funding)*[195] Cobb J considered how special advocates should be funded in family proceedings. The parties included for the purpose of this issue were not only the parties to the care proceedings but also the police (who objected to the sensitive material being disclosed), the Legal Aid Agency and the Attorney General. The parties' positions covered all the options: for payment to be either by the police, by the Attorney General, by the LAA, by the Local Authority, or split between the LA and the police.

7.86 Recognising that a special advocate was necessary to uphold the relevant Article 6 and 8 rights under the ECHR, Cobb J found no steer from authority as to the right source of funding. He decided it should be the police, on the basis they were the ones wishing the material to be withheld, although it was on the basis that it had been found that their position was a reasonable one. The Ministry of Justice chose to make written submissions only. That may have limited the extent to which there was an exploration of options for payment of special advocates under LASPO, for example by an application for exceptional funding.[196]

COSTS AGAINST PUBLICLY FUNDED PARTIES: COST PROTECTION

7.87 It is sometimes said that cost protection does not apply to family proceedings.[197] Well, yes and no. There is a distinctive definition of 'family proceedings' which complicates things.[198] In fact we conclude that cost protection is fairly widely available in publicly funded family proceedings, so that consideration of its operation is relevant here.

7.88 'Cost protection' is defined. It 'means the limit on costs awarded against a legally aided party in relevant civil proceedings'.[199] Where costs protection applies there is a very important corollary: a costs order may be made against the Lord Chancellor, as the person responsible for the Legal Aid Agency who have

195 [2017] EWHC 1793 (Fam), [2018] 1 FLR 460.

196 On which the Lord Chancellor's position was accepted fairly uncritically at [19]–[22].

197 *Halsbury's Laws* Vol 11 (Civil Procedure) at [1814].

198 See **7.99ff** below.

199 Regulation 2 of The Civil Legal Aid (Costs) Regulations 2013, SI 2013/611 and LASPO 2012, s 26(2).

provided the legal aid to the party against whom the costs order would otherwise be made. The Lord Chancellor has to 'stand behind' the legally aided party.[200]

The conditions for making an order

7.89 The usual rules on the making of costs orders against a party are first applied, that is to say either the CPR (in High Court non-family proceedings), the factors in the CPR (in clean sheet cases), or the FPR factors (in no order cases). Where a legally aided party has cost protection there are four additional circumstances which have to be taken into account, two in the statute:

A. the financial resources of all the parties to the proceedings; and

B. their conduct in connection with the dispute to which the proceedings relate.[201]

And there are two further regulatory requirements that:

C. the non-legally aided party will suffer financial hardship unless the order is made; and

D. it is just and equitable in the circumstances that provision for the costs should be made out of public funds.[202]

These four further conditions will be dealt with in turn.

7.90 Dealing first with the financial conditions A and C – 'the financial resources of all the parties to the proceedings' and financial hardship of the receiving party. It is likely that a legally aided party will have limited financial resources which would make him or her unable to pay a costs order, or perhaps able to pay only a proportion of the costs ordered. The Regulations contain detailed provision for assessment of the publicly funded party's ability to pay personally.[203] They include power to charge any equity in the party's home above £100,000.[204] Separately, the Regulations also contain provision for the receiving party's resources to be assessed[205] so that the court can determine, as required, whether the party in whose favour it is proposed the costs order be made would otherwise suffer financial hardship.

200 Note that cost protection is not the same thing as a protective costs order. In proceedings in which there is a public interest – and all the cases in which such orders have so far been made have been proceedings for judicial review – an order may be made capping the amount in costs a party can be ordered to pay to the other side(s) if unsuccessful. The rationale is that otherwise the matter in which there is a public interest could not be brought to court. The rules for such orders have been established by *R (on the application of Corner House Research) v Secretary of State for Trade and Industry* [2005] EWCA Civ 192, but as they are not applicable to family proceedings they are not considered here. A protective costs order was made in *IS v LAA* – see above at **7.43**.

201 LASPO 2012, s 26(1).

202 Regulation 10(3)(c)(iii) and 3(d) of the Civil Legal Aid (Costs) Regulations 2013.

203 Regulations 13 and 14(1)(b) of the Civil Legal Aid (Costs) Regulations 2013.

204 Regulation 13(1) of the Civil Legal Aid (Costs) Regulations 2013.

205 Regulation 14(1)(a) of the Civil Legal Aid (Costs) Regulations 2013.

7.91 Condition C received attention in a costs appeal following an order that the Legal Services Commission (LSC), in place of the wife, who was publicly funded, pay costs on the indemnity basis to the husband and to the interveners in the total sum of £680,000.[206] It had been determined by a costs judge (sitting as a deputy district judge of the Family Court – then the Principal Registry of the Family Division) that the husband and the interveners would each suffer financial hardship if a costs order in their favour were not made. Sharp J reviewed the previous case-law where the test had been 'severe financial hardship' rather than the present test of 'financial hardship' and concluded that it is 'a fact-specific question' and the fact that a party 'is comfortably or even well off by ordinary standards is not a bar to an order being made'.[207] The LSC's appeal was dismissed.

7.92 As will be seen shortly, a number of the reported cases relate to payment by the public funding authority – then the LSC – to public bodies (Government departments, local authorities, NHS trusts). The Regulations have since 2001 prevented such payments: an order for payment by the Lord Chancellor can only be made where 'as regards costs incurred in a court of first instance … the non-legally aided party is an individual'.[208] It must always have been difficult to justify a costs order in favour of a public authority on the basis of hardship, though there are several reported cases of such orders being made. We note that a public body is not prevented from getting an order for the Lord Chancellor to pay its costs on appeal.

7.93 Dealing next with B, we have discussed elsewhere[209] that in relation to costs orders in family proceedings generally, under any of the three regimes, while conduct in the litigation will be relevant to any costs order made, the conduct which gave rise to the litigation is not relevant to a costs order. The provision above thus appears to be anomalous in the context of the other provisions for costs orders in that it requires consideration of 'conduct in connection with the dispute to which the proceedings relate'. This suggests that if, for example, the person liable to pay is found to have been violent in the dispute which gave rise to the proceedings, then that behaviour will be reflected in the costs order. As the authorities previously discussed exclude such behaviour from consideration in relation to costs orders, that might imply that this provision should be interpreted in a similar way: to refer only to conduct in relation to the proceedings. However, conduct in relation to the proceedings will already have been taken into account in deciding on the appropriate costs order in any event, which means that there would be no purpose in the provision being re-stated in relation to cost protection. That would suggest that s 26(1)(b) of LASPO 2012 does require conduct which led to the proceedings to be taken into account.

206 *Legal Services Commission v F, A and V* [2011] EWHC 899 (QB), [2011] 2 FLR 1105.
207 At [49].
208 Regulation 10(2)(c)(ii) of the Civil Legal Aid (Costs) Regulations 2013, the change having been made by the Community Legal Service (Cost Protection) (Amendment No 2) Regulations 2001, SI 2001/3812.
209 At **2.36–2.39**.

7.94 The relevant Regulation does not help resolve this dilemma of interpretation. Where a court is not in a position to specify the amount of costs to be paid by the legally aided party, perhaps because the court does not have information about that person's financial resources as required,[210] the court may 'make findings of fact (as to the parties' conduct in connection with the dispute to which the proceedings relate or otherwise) relevant to the determination of the amount'.[211]

7.95 Under the previous costs protection regime[212] the wording of the statute was identical to that now in LASPO 2012, s 26(1)(a). Its effect was considered by the Court of Appeal, in a judgment intended to set out the principles relating to cost protection.[213] That was a judicial review case, in which the conduct of the parties, while relevant to the court's decision, did not require separate consideration. The court held in that case that 'it must also be open to the trial court to make any findings in relation to the conduct of the parties or facts that have emerged in the course of the proceedings that have relevance to the task to be performed by the costs judge or district judge'.[214]

7.96 *Wyatt* was a case on appeal from the Family Division where a costs order was made against the public funder (then the Legal Services Commission) under the cost protection provisions. In that case the receiving party was an NHS Trust. The Court of Appeal did not have the information needed to make the costs order but observed that: 'There are, however, aspects of parental behaviour in the instant case – such as reporting the Trust's medical staff to the police for alleged assaults on Charlotte and refusing to agree to her being sedated when her leg was accidentally broken – which, if investigated fully, might well warrant censure. If the costs judge takes the view that the Wyatts' conduct (as found by the judge) is in any way relevant to his determination of the Trust's application for costs against the LSC he will no doubt say so.'[215] The clear implication of these comments is that it is indeed conduct in relation to the dispute leading to the proceedings, and not just conduct in the proceedings, which is to be taken into account when making a costs decision in relation to a cost protection case.

7.97 The final condition – D above – is that it must be just and equitable to make a costs award out of public funds. The principle is that 'Costs judges should proceed on the premise that it is just and equitable that the [Legal Services] Commission should stand behind their 'client', by definition under the regulations the individual who receives funded services, unless they are aware

210 By s 26(1)(a) of LASPO 2012 and regs 13, 14 and 16 of the Civil Legal Aid (Costs) Regulations 2013.

211 Regulation 15(7) of the Civil Legal Aid (Costs) Regulations 2013.

212 Section 26 of LASPO 2012 replaced s 11 of the Access to Justice Act 1999.

213 *R v Secretary of State for the Home Department (ex parte Gunn)* [2001] EWCA Civ 891, [2001] 3 All ER 481.

214 *Ibid* at [34].

215 *Re Wyatt (A Child) (Medical Treatment: Continuation of Order) (Costs)* [2006] EWCA Civ 529 at [47]–[48].

of facts which render that result unjust or inequitable'.[216] In such circumstances it would be for the Lord Chancellor to make the case that it would be unjust or inequitable, perhaps where a client had been shown to have obtained public funding by dishonesty. A specific point at issue in *Wyatt* was whether a government department could have a costs order made in its favour against the agency which had provided the public funding (then the LSC) – it was decided that it could,[217] but that is no longer the case under the current regulations.

Payment by the Lord Chancellor

7.98 When the limited resources of a legally aided party are taken into account (as required) the privately funded party in whose favour the costs order is made may be unable to obtain their costs from the losing party directly. So provision is made for the Lord Chancellor (the person responsible for public funding through the Legal Aid Agency) to be ordered to pay the costs instead.[218] There is provision, where appropriate, for the legally aided person to pay the sum in costs that they can afford (and provision to determine what that sum is[219]) and for the Lord Chancellor to pay the remainder. Thus the successful privately funded litigant has also an element of 'cost protection' since he can recover his costs against the Lord Chancellor.

Application to family proceedings

7.99 However, there is also provision for exceptions to cost protection to legally aided parties.[220] The principal exception is for 'family proceedings':

> '6. Costs protection does not apply in relation to –
> (a) Parts of proceedings for which civil legal services are provided in the form of
> (i) Help at court;
> (ii) Legal help, help with family mediation or family help (lower), except in the circumstances described in regulation 7;
> (b) Parts of family proceedings for which civil legal services are provided in the form of –
> (i) Family help (higher);
> (ii) Legal representation.'[221]

Regulation 6(a)(ii) provides for cost protection as at reg 7, which is:

216 *R v Secretary of State for the Home Department (ex parte Gunn)* [2001] EWCA Civ 891, [2001] 3 All ER 481 at [50].
217 *Ibid* at [51].
218 LASPO 2012, s 26(6)(d) and reg 10 of the Civil Legal Aid (Costs) Regulations 2013.
219 Regulation 13 of the Civil Legal Aid (Costs) Regulations 2013.
220 Section 26(3) LASPO.
221 Regulation 6 of The Civil Legal Aid (Costs) Regulations 2013.

'7. Costs protection applies where a legally aided party receives legal help, help with family mediation or family help (lower) in relation to proceedings (other than family proceedings) and later receives, in respect of the same proceedings –
   (a) Family help (higher); or
   (b) Legal representation.'[222]

7.100 This begs the question: what is the relevant definition of family proceedings? 'Family proceedings' in this context (and only this context) means proceedings arising out of domestic violence (principally Family Law Act 1996, Part 4 proceedings for non-molestation and occupation orders) and arising out of private law children proceedings where the child is alleged to be at risk of abuse; and also include the occasions where the Director has made an exceptional case determination.[223]

7.101 The combined effect of these provisions is that there is no costs protection in relation to that narrow definition of family proceedings where legal aid is provided at any stage, but that if legal representation or family help (higher) are provided in other family proceedings, then there is costs protection. By providing such a narrow definition of family proceedings which are exempt from costs protection, the consequence is that costs protection is available for the other family proceedings in Part 1 of Sch 1 to LASPO 2012, which is all other family proceedings in which legal aid can be granted.

7.102 Where does that leave costs against publicly funded parties in other family cases – such as public law children proceedings and financial proceedings, and indeed private law proceedings where there is no allegation of child abuse by the legally aided party? Consider public law children proceedings first: the parties are typically a local authority, parents and child, sometimes with another party or intervener, often a family member. The parents and the child are themselves fully publicly funded so cannot apply for costs against another publicly funded party. As the courts have said, it is never unreasonable to oppose a care order which might involve losing your child,[224] and on that basis no-one can make a successful application for costs against the parents. Other relatives, often grandparents, may be privately funded and may wish to apply for costs.

7.103 It would therefore appear to be the case that: if the child's position (through the children's guardian) was to oppose unreasonably the grandparents as carers for the child; and as a result of that opposition the grandparents incurred legal costs; and the court determined that the child should live with the grandparents; then costs protection would apply. As the child would not usually have any financial resources the grandparents could claim their costs from the

222 Regulation 7 of The Civil Legal Aid (Costs) Regulations 2013

223 Regulation 2 of The Civil Legal Aid (Costs) Regulations 2013, s 10 of and paras 12 and 13, Pt 1 of Sch 1 to LASPO, and see earlier discussion as to applications for and awards of exceptional funding.

224 *Re S (A Child)* [2015] UKSC 20 at [33].

Lord Chancellor. This jurisdiction was potentially invoked where a foster-carer applied unsuccessfully for the child's guardian – legally funded by the LAA – to pay her costs following her successful appeal to the Court of Appeal.[225]

7.104 Consider next financial remedy proceedings – a party may be publicly funded in such proceedings, though rarely now. In many such cases the publicly funded party will obtain a share of the assets sufficient to pay their own costs (perhaps through the operation of the statutory charge[226]) and sufficient to pay any adverse costs order made. But there are cases where the money recovered by a publicly funded party is not sufficient to pay an adverse costs order, and in such cases costs protection will apply and the party with the order in their favour will be able to claim costs against the Lord Chancellor.

7.105 Cost protection received consideration in a long-running case before Munby J.[227] They were financial remedy proceedings to which a company and the parties' children were parties because of the asset structure. The wife was ordered to pay the company's and the children's costs and the husband was ordered to pay the wife's costs, including those liabilities to the children and the company. The wife had been legally aided through much of the proceedings and found to be eligible for cost protection.[228] The application of cost protection was found to be subject to a provision which survives without significant change in LASPO 2012:[229]

> 30 Position of other parties, courts and tribunals
>
> (1) Except as expressly provided by regulations, any rights conferred by or under this Part on an individual for whom services are provided under this Part for the purposes of proceedings do not affect –
> a. the rights or liabilities of other parties to the proceedings, or
> b. The principles on which the discretion of a court or tribunal is normally exercised.'

There is no explicit alteration to an individual's rights in the Costs Regulations, so this principle applies to cost protection.

7.106 The wife was ordered to pay costs to the company, but the company was ordered to pay a sum of money in the proceedings to the wife. As the costs payable by the wife to the company arose out of proceedings in which the company was ordered to make the lump sum payment to the wife, there was 'a nexus' between the financial orders so that they could be set off against each other.[230] The following authority of the Court of Appeal in relation to the set off

225 *Re B (A child)* [2019] EWCA Civ 680.
226 See Civil Legal Aid (Statutory Charge) Regulations 2013, SI 2013/503.
227 *Ben Hashem v Ali Shayif and Radfan* [2009] EWHC 864 (Fam) at [42]–[80].
228 *Ibid* at [50].
229 LASPO 2012, s 30(1).
230 *Ibid* at [77].

of costs against a sum due was cited as an 'accurate and succinct summary of the principles':[231]

> '(1) A direction for the set-off of costs against damages or costs to which a legally aided person has become or becomes entitled in the action may be permissible.
>
> (2) The set-off is no different from and no more extensive than the set-off available to or against parties who are not legally aided.
>
> (3) The broad criterion for the application of set-off is that the plaintiff's claim and the defendant's claim are so closely connected that it would be inequitable to allow the plaintiff's claim without taking into account the defendant's claim. As it has sometimes been put, the defendant's claim must, in equity, impeach the plaintiff's claim.
>
> (4) Set-off of costs or damages to which one party is entitled against costs or damages to which another party is entitled depends upon the application of the equitable criterion I have endeavoured to express. It was treated by May J in *Currie & Co v The Law Society* [1977] Q.B. 990, 1000, as a "question for the court's discretion." It is possible to regard all questions regarding costs as being subject to the statutory discretion conferred on the court by section 51 of the Supreme Court Act 1981. But I would not have thought that a set-off of damages against damages could properly be described as a discretionary matter, nor that a set-off of costs against damages could be so described.
>
> (5) If and to the extent that a set-off of costs awarded against a legally aided party against costs or damages to which the legally aided party is entitled, cannot be justified as a set off (i) the liability of the legally aided party to pay the costs awarded against him will be subject to section 17(1) of the Act of 1988 and regulation 124(1) of the Regulations of 1989[232]; and (ii) the section 16(6)[233] charge will apply to the costs or damages to which the legally aided party is entitled.'[234]

The effect of these principles continues to be that a set-off may be ordered in relation to costs ordered to be paid to or by a publicly funded party. Such a set-off is not, however, automatic, and it is dependent on an exercise of the court's discretion by an application of the above principles.[235]

7.107 It follows that in that case the wife did not have cost protection in relation to the costs she was due to pay the company, but did have cost protection in relation to the costs order against her for the benefit of the children.[236] Whether she would be able to benefit from cost protection would depend, at a subsequent hearing if necessary, on consideration of the factors at **7.89**.

231 *Ibid* at [66].
232 Now s 26 of LASPO 2012 and reg 9 of the Costs Regs.
233 Now s 25 of LASPO 2012.
234 *Lockley v National Blood Transfusion Service* [1992] 1 WLR 492 at [496], Scott LJ.
235 *Ben Hashem v Ali Shayif* at [67]–[77].
236 *Ibid* at [78].

7.108 Consider finally private law proceedings in which there is no allegation of child abuse. Costs orders where the parties are privately funded in such proceedings are not routine, but are not very uncommon either. It appears that, where a costs order would be appropriate between privately funded parties, but in fact one of the parties is publicly funded and the four conditions set out above are satisfied, cost protection will work for the benefit of both the publicly funded party and the party to whom the costs are awarded, so that the Lord Chancellor may be ordered to pay the successful privately funded party's costs.

7.109 Or so it seems to us. But we are very conscious of the fact that what is here set out is not the usual understanding of the position, which is that costs protection is not generally available in family proceedings. There is limited judicial authority on which to base these conclusions, which rely on a reading of the statutory provisions. We look forward to further judicial consideration of the subject.

No cost protection

7.110 In family proceedings where a publicly funded party has no cost protection, that is to say principally in proceedings for non-molestation and occupation orders where there are allegations of domestic violence, or in private law cases where the publicly funded party has made allegations of child abuse, a costs order can be made against the publicly funded party personally without the court having to consider whether he or she can afford it. In many cases he or she will not be able to. There is no reason why publicly funded parties should be dealt with differently: 'the question of whether it is just to make an order for costs should as a matter of principle be determined irrespective of whether any of the parties are publicly funded.'[237] The court can respond to this situation by adding to the end of the costs order the words 'not to be enforced without the leave of the court', but there is no requirement to do so and it is not always done.[238] Such an order is in principle enforceable, but the cost of enforcement will be just money down the drain if the formerly publicly funded party does not have the means to pay. For that reason such costs orders against publicly funded parties have been called 'football pools orders' – perhaps 'lottery orders' now – because the costs will only ever be paid if the publicly funded party wins the pools (or the lottery).

COSTS IN FAVOUR OF PUBLICLY FUNDED PARTIES

7.111 The counterpart of the restrictions on public expenditure in legal aid is the generosity of the costs to be paid to the Lord Chancellor where a costs order is made in favour of a publicly funded client. The amount of costs must

237 *Re S* [2015] UKSC 20 at [25].
238 See, for example, *Re G (Contact Proceedings: Costs)* [2013] EWCA Civ 1017, [2014] 1 FLR 517 at [14] and [18].

be determined as if the party were not legally aided.[239] It follows that the costs schedule to be provided on behalf of a legally aided party for the purposes of a claim for costs must be at the rates that would be charged for a privately paying client. The rules require detailed assessment of costs paid in favour of a publicly funded client,[240] though in the interest of minimising any further costs that requirement is not always observed in practice.

7.112 Where such a costs order is made the solicitor will wish to be authorised by the Lord Chancellor to take payment of the full amount of the costs.[241] The solicitor and any counsel will then be paid at the private client rate for work which they had done in the expectation of payment at publicly funded rates. Indeed there is no bar to a costs order in favour of a publicly funded client being on the indemnity basis, though the beneficiaries are solely the lawyers representing the publicly funded party.[242] Mostyn J has gone so far as to say that 'Legal aid firms depend for their survival on inter partes costs orders being made.'[243] As costs orders are the exception in children proceedings, that remark should presumably be taken to apply to financial remedy proceedings, like those before the Judge in that case.

239 Regulation 21 of the Civil Legal Aid (Costs) Regulations 2013. Courts do not always follow this rule in practice. In awarding a publicly-funded party her costs in a wardship case Baker J made an order that costs, to be assessed if not agreed, were to be 'limited to those sums recoverable by the applicant under the terms of the public finding certificate' *Re SO (Wardship: Extension of protective injunction orders)* [2015] EWHC 935 (Fam), [2016] 1 FLR 1144 at [29].

240 CPR PD44 para 9.8.

241 Regulation 21(2) of the Civil Legal Aid (Costs) Regulations 2013 and LASPO 2012, s 28(2)(b).

242 *Brawley v Marczynski (No 2)* [2002] EWCA Civ 1453, [2002] 4 All ER 1067, [2003] 1 WLR 813 and *Kaur v Randhawa* [2015] EWHC 1592 (Fam) at [20]–[21], Mostyn J.

243 *Veluppillai v Velupillai* [2015] EWHC 3095 (Fam), [2016] 2 FLR 681 at [14].

CHAPTER 8

Assessment of Costs

8.01 Costs may be assessed for two purposes: first, to determine the costs to be paid by one party to another; and second, to determine how much a client (or the Lord Chancellor in a publicly funded case) should pay their solicitor.

ASSESSMENT PROCEDURE

8.02 FPR r 28.2 adopts CPR rr 44.3 and 44.6. Therefore, on deciding to make an order for costs (other than for costs that fall under the fixed costs regime), the court must elect whether the costs should be assessed on a summary basis or after a detailed review.[1] For the purposes of CPR Parts 44 to 47, 'summary assessment' is defined as the procedure whereby costs are assessed by the judge who has heard the case, and in a 'detailed assessment' the amount of costs is determined by a costs officer in accordance with CPR Part 47.[2]

1 CPR r 44.6(1); CPR PD44 [9.1].
2 CPR r 44.1(1).

8.03 If a costs order does not specify summary assessment, then a detailed assessment will follow if the costs are not agreed.[3] However, costs cannot be assessed without the court making an order in respect to costs. If the order is silent as to costs, there will be no assessment.

Summary assessment

8.04 Summary assessment is 'the procedure whereby costs are assessed by the judge who has heard the case or application.'[4] The assessment is performed either at the end of a hearing or at a subsequent hearing before the same judge,[5] but must not be conducted by a costs officer.[6]

Circumstances in which summary assessment is appropriate

8.05 The Practice Direction to CPR Part 44 states the court should consider whether to summarily assess the costs *whenever* a costs order is to be made outside the fixed costs regime (emphasis added).[7] It goes on to set out the general rule that costs should be summarily assessed at the end of a hearing that lasts not more than one day and the costs assessed should relate either to the costs of that hearing or, if the hearing has disposed of the matter, may relate to the costs of the entire proceedings.[8] The Practice Direction adds the proviso, 'unless there is a good reason not to do so', and cites (as an example of when detailed assessment may be appropriate) a situation in which the paying party has substantial grounds to dispute the sum of costs claimed and which require detailed investigation and so are not appropriate to be considered summarily.

8.06 In *Edwards v Devon and Cornwall Constabulary*, the Court of Appeal considered an appeal against the lower court's decision to assess costs summarily and the procedure adopted by that court to do so.[9] The court found that the decision to carry out a summary assessment was within the judge's discretion, but that the claimant's counsel had been given insufficient time to make submissions on the details of the costs schedule. Thus, the court allowed the appeal and adjourned for 30 minutes to allow the parties to attempt to agree the costs award, otherwise the court would re-sit to conduct a summary assessment. The court's view, in this case, was that the costs of a detailed assessment would be disproportionate.[10]

3 CPR PD44 [8.2].

4 CPR r 44.1(1); CPR PD44 [9] makes general provisions as to the summary assessment procedure.

5 CPR PD44 [9.7]; *Mahmood v Penrose* [2002] EWCA Civ 457, [2002] All ER (D) 227 (Mar), 13 per Sir Swinton Thomas. However, there are circumstances in which a judge may have the jurisdiction to summarily assess the costs of a hearing or an order made by a different judge: *Transformers and Rectifiers Ltd v Needs Ltd* [2015] EWHC 1687 (TCC) per Coulson J.

6 CPR PD44 [9.7]; 'costs officer' means a costs judge, a District Judge, or an authorised court officer: CPR r 44.1(1).

7 CPR PD44 [9.1].

8 CPR PD44 [9.2].

9 [2001] EWCA Civ 388, [2001] All ER (D) 143 (Mar) per Sir Andrew Morritt V-C.

10 At [31].

8.07 In *Contractreal Ltd v Davies and another,*[11] Arden LJ acknowledged that summary assessment may be 'rough and ready'[12] but, nevertheless, the sum of costs ordered would only be amended at appeal in exceptional cases. In fact, the court found the judge had erred whilst exercising his discretion in the course of summarily assessing the costs, and the matter was ordered to be dealt with by detailed assessment.

8.08 In *Q v Q*, Wilson J[13] considered whether or not costs could be summarily assessed at the end of a ten day hearing. Mr Mostyn QC, on behalf of the payer husband, advanced the submission that there was a general rule that, 'unless there is good reason to the contrary, an award of costs referable to a hearing which has lasted more than one day should be the subject of detailed assessment.'[14] Wilson J carefully reviewed the Civil Procedure Rules and associated Practice Directions. The judge, however, denied such a rule, saying, 'there is now more of a steer than hitherto towards summary assessment even of the costs of longer hearings: for the exercise of the power to make a summary assessment, … *must* now be considered in *every* case'.[15] Wilson J concluded that summary assessment was appropriate in this case as he aimed to conclude all disputes between the parties and a detailed costs assessment was unnecessary since, 'I am confident of my ability to make a summary assessment which is fair to both parents'.[16] The mother had claimed costs of £336,000 and was awarded £150,000 after the summary assessment. The approach taken by Wilson J received the approval of the Court of Appeal in *Lemmens v Lemmens*[17] when the court also approved the dicta of Thorpe LJ in *Malialis v Malialis* that in financial remedy proceedings, a judge has a particularly wide discretion.'[18]

8.09 By contrast, Hayden J decided not to summarily assess costs in *SB v MB*,[19] having determined the habitual residence of a child. The judge referred to an earlier judgment (in a non-family matter) of Coulson J in which it was said: 'A degree of robustness is not only permitted by the CPR, it is positively encouraged.'[20] Rather than go through the costs item by item, Hayden J considered whether or not the overall proportionality of costs could be assessed, and advocates for both parties favoured a summary assessment. However, the judge concluded that a detailed assessment would be a better use of the court's time as he was not in a position to assess some individual items that warranted scrutiny and as the hearing had lasted over 3 days.

11 [2001] EWCA Civ 928, [2001] All ER (D) 231 (May).
12 At [51].
13 *Q v Q (Family Division: costs: summary assessment)* [2002] 2 FLR 668, [2002] All ER (D) 07 (Jul).
14 At [1].
15 At [33]. NB. since the revocation of CPR Part 43 on 1 April 2013, the surviving rules from that Part are now found at CPR r 44.1. Old Rule 44.7 is now CPR r 44.6. Section 13 of the Practice Direction About Costs is at PD44 [9].
16 At [34].
17 [2018] EWCA Civ 2963, at [25-26] and [29] per Moylan LJ.
18 *Malialis v Malialis* [2012] EWCA Civ 1748, 13.
19 [2014] EWHC 3721 at [9], (Fam).
20 [2011] EWHC 1412 at [14], QB.

8.10 Holman J summarily assessed the final costs bill in *Vilinova v Vilinov and Hinaly Company Limited* to avoid the risk of the payee not receiving the costs of a detailed assessment.[21]

Duties of legal representatives and parties

8.11 In order to assist a judge to summarily assess the costs, the Practice Direction says a written statement of costs should be provided to the court by each party to the proceedings, or by their respective legal representatives.[22] The Practice Direction lists precisely the information that must be provided in a costs schedule and advises the completion of Form N260 to facilitate this task.[23] Generally, a party's statement of costs must be signed by that party or by that party's legal representative.[24] In *A local Authority v A Mother and others*,[25] Knowles J observed that FPR Pt 28 did not specify how parties (whether or not publicly funded) in children proceedings seeking costs should provide information to the court and suggested the rule at CPR PD44, para 9.5 should be followed.

8.12 In financial remedy proceedings there is a requirement to inform the court of the costs incurred at each stage of the proceedings.[26] The costs forms used for that purpose (Forms H and H1)[27] are not appropriate for detailed assessment, for which Form N260 is required. In practice, if the court decides to depart from the general rule of no costs in financial remedy proceedings, summary assessment may be carried out on the basis of Form H1.

8.13 The statement of costs must be filed and served on any party against whom a costs order is sought no later than 24 hours before the time at which the hearing has been fixed.[28] Any failure, without reasonable excuse, to comply with the duties described at CPR PD44, para 9 will be considered by the court when determining what order for costs to make, and may adversely affect that party's position as to costs.[29] Therefore, it is worth taking care to complete Form N260 fully and correctly rather than submitting a bespoke costs schedule or an incomplete Form N260.

21 [2019] EWHC 1107 (Fam), see **8.112**.
22 CPR PD44 [9.5].
23 CPR PD44 [9.5(2)] and [9.5(3)] and emphasised at FPR PD28 [4.5]. Form N260 can be found at: **Appendix 1** and http://hmctsformfinder.justice.gov.uk/HMCTS/GetForm.do?court_forms_id=517.
24 The certificate at the end of Form N260 need not be completed where the party is: an assisted person; a LAA funded client; a person for whom civil legal services (within the meaning of LASPO 2012, Pt 1) are provided under arrangements made for the purposes of that Part of that Act; or represented by a person in the party's employment: CPR PD44 [9.5(3)].
25 [2018] EWHC 1841 at [61-62], (Fam).
26 FPR r 9.27.
27 See **Appendix 1**.
28 CPR PD44 [9.5(4)].
29 CPR PD44 [9.6].

8.14 Neuberger J considered this issue in *MacDonald v Taree Holdings*[30] and said the court should respond in a proportionate way to a party's failure to serve a statement of costs according to the provisions of the Practice Direction. Where there were no 'aggravating factors', the court should consider what, if any, prejudice had been suffered by the paying party.[31] Either: a brief adjournment should be granted to enable the paying party to consider the statement, followed by the summary assessment of the costs; a direction should be made for detailed assessment; or the summary assessment should be listed at a later date or be dealt with on the papers and on written submissions.[32] He stated that, 'where there is a failure to apply plus some aggravating factor, then it may very well be right to deprive the party who would otherwise be entitled to his costs, of all or a significant proportion of his costs'.[33]

8.15 In *R (A Child)*,[34] Thorpe LJ agreed with counsel for the paying party that detailed assessment of the wasted costs order was appropriate, if the parties were unable to agree quantum. A statement of costs had been filed at court but had not been served on the paying party, and therefore that party had not had an opportunity to consider the sums claimed. It is to be hoped the parties reached an agreement as the statement of costs valued the wasted costs at just £4,022, and the costs of a further hearing would have been disproportionate.

8.16 The courts have looked at this point since the revision of the CPR in April 2013. In *Group M Ltd v Cabinet Office*[35] the court considered the payment of an interested party's costs by the losing party in proceedings. The court noted the stricter attitude to compliance with rules following *Mitchell*[36] and applied the three stage test described in *Denton*.[37] As the interested party had served a statement of costs only three hours before judgment was handed down, the issue of costs had to be adjourned to another day. Akenhead J decided that the interested party should not be entirely deprived of his costs due to a failure to file a statement of costs in time and a failure to provide a breakdown of the major item on the bill of costs.[38] The judge said that it would be disproportionate to disallow all costs when the effect of the non-compliance had only a minimal effect on those costs. After summary assessment, the costs were valued at £40,127.50 which included a reduction of £2,240 due to the interested party's failure to comply with the rule.

8.17 Lord Neuberger considered the information provided by solicitors in a statement of costs in the case of *Drake and another v Fripp*[39] and gave the

30 (2000) All ER (D) 2204, [2001] 1 Costs LR 147.
31 'Paying party' is defined as a party liable to pay costs: CPR 44.1(1).
32 At [23]–[26].
33 At [27].
34 [2012] EWCA Civ 1903.
35 [2014] EWHC 3863 (TCC).
36 *Mitchell v News Group Newspapers Ltd* [2013] EWCA Civ 1537, [2014] 2 All ER 430.
37 *Denton v TH White and others* [2014] EWCA Civ 906 at [24] per Lord Dyson MR and Vos LJ.
38 At [13].
39 [2011] EWCA Civ 1282 at [14].

following guidance which practitioners would be well-advised to follow in a suitable case:

> 'I would like to commend Mr Fripp's representatives for accompanying their schedule of costs with an explanatory three page note, which very helpfully and clearly explains how the various components of pre-costs hearing as set out in the pro forma schedule are actually made up. Such an explanatory note, provided that it is short and clear, can be very helpful to the court when assessing costs, and is regrettably very rare in my experience. In many cases where the solicitors' costs may require to be explained to the court such a note should be provided, albeit only in cases where it is proportionate and where an explanation of solicitors' costs may reasonably expected to be necessary.'

Performing the summary assessment

8.18 A summary assessment of costs is generally carried out fairly quickly at the end of the hearing and, as mentioned at **8.07**, it may be done in a rough and ready way.[40] However, it is wrong merely to compare the parties' schedules in terms of costs and hours worked and, where they are similar, to assume they are both reasonable. This can have the effect of awarding costs on the indemnity basis.[41]

8.19 The court should begin the assessment by determining whether or not the costs are reasonable in amount and have been reasonably incurred.[42] The assessing judge will also decide whether or not costs (or some costs) should be awarded on the indemnity basis rather than the standard basis, taking into account the conduct of the parties. This decision affects the assessment procedure adopted and is considered in more detail at **8.80–8.115**. In particular, indemnity costs are not subject to the rule that they must be proportionate.

The indemnity principle

8.20 Whilst the use of conditional fee agreements (CFAs) in family proceedings is limited, such agreements are available in proceedings under TLATA 1996 and I(PFD)A 1975. Where a party is funded under a CFA, that party's liability to their solicitor for costs will depend upon success (as defined under the agreement). The indemnity principle, that a receiving party cannot receive a greater sum of costs than they are liable to pay their legal representative, does not apply to legal aid and to CFAs; such costs are recoverable.[43]

40 *Bryen & Langley Ltd v Boston* [2005] EWCA Civ 973 at [53] per Rimer J.

41 *Bryen & Langley Ltd v Boston* [2005] EWCA Civ 973 at [54] per Rimer J.

42 CPR r 44.3(1).

43 *The Senior Courts Costs Office Guide 2018*, 2.6; https://www.judiciary.uk/wp-content/uploads/2018/11/6.4764_JO_SCCO-Guide-2018_WEB_2.pdf.

8.21 Form N260 includes the statement, 'The costs stated above do not exceed the costs which the (party) is liable to pay in respect of the work which this statement covers' and must be signed by the party or the party's legal representative. This provision is generally taken to relate to the indemnity principle.[44]

Consent orders

8.22 On sending a consent order to court for approval without further attendance by the parties, that order should include an agreed costs award or a statement that there shall be no order as to costs.[45]

8.23 Whenever the parties agree the terms of a costs order, that order must record that it has been made by consent.[46]

Restrictions on summary assessment

8.24 Summary assessment of the costs to be paid to a publicly funded party[47] by another party is prohibited by the Practice Direction and, rather, those costs must be subject to detailed assessment.[48] Though, as such costs are assessed on the same basis as any other costs it is difficult to see the rationale for this rule. However, where the parties consent to summary assessment of such costs, the court may well agree.

8.25 The court may summarily assess the costs to be paid to a child[49] or a protected party,[50] but will only make a costs order in favour of such a party if that party's legal representative waives the right to receive any further costs.[51]

Payment of costs

8.26 After summary assessment, the sum of costs awarded must be paid within 14 days of the date of the order or judgment specifying the award, unless the court specifies some other period.[52]

44 *The Senior Courts Costs Office Guide 2018*, 2.6(iii).
45 CPR PD44 [9.4].
46 CPR PD44 [9.10].
47 For example, one funded under the civil legal services provisions of LASPO 2012, Pt 1.
48 CPR PD44 [9.8].
49 'Child' defined for the purposes of this provision, at CPR r 21.1(2)(b), as a person under 18.
50 'Protected party' defined for the purposes of this provision, at CPR r 21.1(2)(d), as a party or an intended party who lacks the capacity to conduct the proceedings.
51 CPR PD44 [9.9] and CPR PD46 [2.1].
52 CPR r 44.7.

If costs are not paid within the prescribed period, then the receiving party may commence enforcement procedures.[53]

Appeals against summary assessment

8.27 An appeal from a summary assessment is conducted under the general provisions of FPR Pt 30 or CPR Pt 52 and permission to appeal is required.[54]

Detailed assessment

8.28 As discussed above at **8.02–8.03**, on making a costs order the court has the power to order a detailed assessment of costs.[55] The CPR Pt 47 sets out the procedure for such an assessment, and this Part is adopted by FPR r 28.2(1) in respect to family proceedings. 'Detailed assessment' is described in the CPR as 'the procedure by which the amount of costs is decided by a costs officer in accordance with CPR Part 47.'[56] For these purposes, a 'costs officer' means a costs judge,[57] a District Judge, or an authorised court officer[58] (the latter includes any officer of the Family Court, the High Court, or the Costs Office[59] who has been authorised by the Lord Chancellor to assess costs).[60]

Payments on account

8.29 When a court directs that costs should be subject to detailed assessment, then (provided there is no good reason not to do so) an order to pay a reasonable sum on account of costs will be made.[61] Thus, it is important to have filed and served a statement of costs (in Form N260) 24 hours before the hearing to enable the court to calculate the payment on account. Directing a payment on account may make the prospect of detailed assessment less attractive to the payer as it removes the advantage of postponing the date of payment but reduces the final interest payment.

8.30 Christopher Clarke LJ looked at what a 'reasonable sum' might be for a payment on account in *Excalibur Ventures LLC v Texas Keystone Inc.*[62] He noted that the rule had changed, in April 2013, from being permissive to creating a presumption that a payment on account would be made. The judge reviewed

53 **Chapter 9**.
54 FPR r 30.3 and CPR r 52.3.
55 CPR r 44.6(1)(b).
56 CPR r 44.1(1).
57 'Costs judge' defined as a taxing master of the Senior Courts: CPR r 44.1(1).
58 'Court officer' defined as 'member of the court staff': CPR r 2.3(1).
59 'Costs Office' defined as the Senior Courts Costs Office: CPR r 44.1(1).
60 CPR r 44.1(1).
61 CPR r 44.2(8).
62 [2015] EWHC 566 (Comm), [2015] All ER (D) 109 (Mar).

the case law but noted that the revision to the rule had changed the test and the relevance of past cases.[63] He stated:

> '23. What is a reasonable amount will depend on the circumstances, the chief of which is that there will, by definition, have been no detailed assessment and thus an element of uncertainty, the extent of which may differ widely from case to case as to what will be allowed on detailed assessment.
>
> Any sum will have to be an estimate. A reasonable sum would often be one that was an estimate of the likely level of recovery subject, as the costs claimants accept, to an appropriate margin to allow for error in the estimation. This can be done by taking the lowest figure in a likely range or making a deduction from a single estimated figure or perhaps from the lowest figure in the range if the range itself is not very broad.
>
> 24. In determining whether to order any payment and its amount, account needs to be taken of all relevant factors including the likelihood (if it can be assessed) of the claimants being awarded the costs that they seek or a lesser [sic] and if so what proportion of them; the difficulty, if any, that may be faced in recovering those costs; the likelihood of a successful appeal; the means of the parties; the imminence of any assessment; any relevant delay and whether the paying party will have any difficulty in recovery in the case of any overpayment.'

He concluded by ordering the payment on account of 80% of the costs (payable on the indemnity basis) and the interest claimed.[64]

8.31 Blair J decided not to order a payment on account in a financial remedies matter in which he had ordered the wife and her half-sister to pay 25% of the husband's costs as assessed on the standard basis.[65] The judge stated the costs should be subject to detailed assessment if the parties were unable to settle the figures, and he encouraged them to reach agreement. Blair J's reason for refusing to grant an order for payment on account was that the issue had not been raised in advance of the hearing and thus it could not 'be dealt with fairly.'[66]

Authorised court officers' powers

8.32 Authorised court officers who are at the level of a senior executive officer may conduct assessment proceedings where the base costs[67] excluding

63 At [22].

64 At [25], cf *Royal Bank of Scotland plc v Highland Financial Partners LP and others* [2013] EWCA Civ 472 at [21] where the court established 'starting figures' for the receiving parties' costs and ordered payment on account of 70 per cent of those costs.

65 *W v W and another* [2015] EWHC 1652 (Fam).

66 At [28].

67 Costs other than the amount of any additional liability: The Costs Practice Direction (CPR PD43.1 [2.2]) [before 1 April 2013].

VAT are £35,000 or less, and those at the level of a principal officer may conduct proceedings where the base costs excluding VAT are £100,000 or less.[68]

8.33 An authorised court officer may not exercise all the powers of the other costs officers, and may not:

(a) award wasted costs under the provisions of CPR r 46.8;

(b) make orders in relation to misconduct under CPR r 44.11;

(c) impose a sanction for delaying the commencement of detailed assessment proceedings under CPR r 47.8;

(d) order detailed assessment to be carried out by a costs judge or a District Judge where a party has objected to the assessment being performed by an authorised court officer under CPR r 47.3(2); or

(e) make a detailed assessment of the costs to be paid by a client to their solicitor unless costs are assessed under CPR r 46.4 as money is to be paid to a child or a protected party.[69]

8.34 If one party objects to the performance of the detailed assessment by an authorised court officer, an application must be made under CPR Pt 23 to the costs judge or the District Judge explaining their position.[70] That judge may then order the assessment to be conducted by a costs judge or District Judge.[71] If the parties to the detailed assessment proceedings agree that an authorised court officer should not be the assessor, then the receiving party should state this position to the court when a hearing date is requested and the court will list the hearing accordingly.[72]

Timing of the detailed assessment

8.35 The general rule is that detailed assessment is performed when proceedings have ended, irrespective of any appeal,[73] unless the court orders otherwise or the parties agree in writing.[74] Nevertheless, a party may apply to stay the detailed costs assessment pending an appeal, and should make that application either to the court whose decision is to be appealed or to the appeal court under FPR Pt 18 or CPR Pt 23 or as an application within the appeal notice.[75] If there is no realistic prospect of the case continuing, then a District Judge or a costs judge may order the commencement of detailed assessment proceedings.[76] The parties might agree to a detailed assessment in long-running

68 CPR PD47 [3.1].
69 CPR r 47.3(1).
70 CPR PD47 [3.3].
71 CPR r 47.3(2).
72 CPR PD47 [3.2].
73 CPR r 47.2.
74 CPR r 47.1; CPR PD47 [1.1] and [1.2].
75 CPR PD47 [2].
76 CPR PD47 [1.4].

private law children proceedings at the end of the main hearing, even though there is to be a subsequent review.

Venue for the proceedings

8.36 The CPR sets out the venue for applications and requests related to detailed assessment proceedings.[77] The FPR clarifies that under CPR r 47.4(1), 'the 'appropriate office' means the court office of the Designated Family Court for the Designated Family Judge area in which the case was being dealt with when the judgment or order was made, or the event occurred which gave rise to the right to assessment, or to which the case has subsequently been moved.'[78]

8.37 The Costs Office will also deal with cases heard by the Court of Appeal.[79] It is only appropriate for non-Court of Appeal and non-London county court matters to be considered by the Costs Office where:

(a) the sum of costs is high;

(b) difficult issues are involved;

(c) a lengthy hearing is anticipated;

(d) the cost to the parties is significant; or

(e) there is some other relevant factor.[80]

Commencement of the proceedings

Procedure

8.38 The receiving party instigates proceedings by serving the paying party (and any other relevant persons[81]) with a notice of commencement[82] and a copy of the bill of costs.[83] In addition, the Practice Direction states:

(a) copies of fee notes from counsel and experts for whom fees are claimed;

(b) written evidence of other disbursements valued at more than £500; and

(c) a statement providing the names and addresses of all persons the receiving party intends to serve with the notice of commencement

should be served with the commencement notice.[84] Any non-party served in this way becomes a party to the detailed assessment proceedings.[85]

77 CPR r 47.4.
78 CPR PD47 [4.1] as modified by FPR PD28A [2.8].
79 CPR PD47 [4.1].
80 CPR PD47 [4.3(2)].
81 See CPR PD47 [5.5(1)] for the definition of a 'relevant person'.
82 In Form N252 at https://www.gov.uk/government/publications/form-n252-notice-of-commencement-of-assessment.
83 CPR r 47.6(1) and (2).
84 CPR PD47 [5.2].
85 CPR r 47.6(3).

8.39 Further information as to service and the precise form and content of the bill of costs is provided in the Practice Direction,[86] which also provides precedents for the bill of costs (Precedents A to D).[87] The bill of costs will include the costs of preparing and checking the bill of costs itself, but will include no other costs that are related only to the detailed assessment proceedings.[88]

8.40 In *A Local Authority v A Mother and Child*,[89] Lady Hale gave the leading judgment addressing the issue of what a solicitor may claim for preparing the bill of costs for a legal aid detailed assessment. The court concluded that such costs were allowable up to the maximum permitted by the relevant regulations[90] which set a '"reasonable cost" in the context in which the Regulations apply' (and which take precedence over the Practice Direction).[91] The permitted cost included the preparation, checking and verification of the bill.[92]

Time of commencement

8.41 Detailed assessment proceedings should be commenced within three months of the event which gave rise to the entitlement to detailed assessment. Thus, proceedings should be started no more than three months after the date of judgment or order, or three months after the date of an order lifting the stay of the detailed assessment pending an appeal.[93] However, either the parties (by agreement)[94] or the court[95] may extend or shorten the time for commencement.[96] It is not necessary to receive permission to commence assessment proceedings out of time, although the sanction of loss of interest may apply.[97]

8.42 If the receiving party fails to commence proceedings within the prescribed timescales, then the paying party may apply to the court[98] for an order that the receiving party must begin detailed assessment proceedings by a date specified by the court.[99]

86 CPR PD47 [5.7]–[5.22].
87 CPR PD47 [21]–[24]: Precedent A – model form of bill of costs; Precedent B – detailed assessment of additional liability only; Precedent C – payable by defendant and the LSC (now LAA); Precedent D – alternative form, single column for amounts claimed, separate parts for costs payable by the LSC (now LAA) only.
88 CPR PD47 [5.19].
89 [2001] 1 Costs LR 136, CA.
90 Then the Legal Aid in Family Proceedings (Remuneration) Regulations 1991, SI 1991/2038, reg 3(4)(c) and Sch 1 Part V and now the Civil Legal Aid (Remuneration) Regulations 2013, SI 2013/422.
91 At [30].
92 At [33].
93 CPR r 47.7.
94 CPR r 2.11.
95 CPR r 3.1(2)(a).
96 CPR PD47 [6.1].
97 CPR PD47 [6.2].
98 In writing and serving the application notice at least seven days before the hearing: CPR PD47 [7].
99 CPR r 47.8(1).

Sanctions

8.43 After the paying party has applied for an order requiring the receiving party to commence proceedings, that order may state that the receiving party's failure to comply with such an order may lead to some or all of the receiving party's costs being disallowed.[100] Further, if the receiving party has failed to commence detailed assessment proceedings within the three month period set out at CPR r 47.7 and the paying party has not applied for an order regarding commencement, the receiving party may be penalised by a reduction in the interest awarded or an award of costs against the relevant legal representative on grounds of misconduct. No other sanction is permitted.[101]

8.44 These sanctions apply when the Lord Chancellor is the paying party (under the LASPO 2012, Pt 1) and the receiving party is the publicly funded solicitor to whom the costs are payable.[102]

8.45 In *Haji-Ioannou v Frangos and others*,[103] leave to appeal had been granted to enable the court to provide guidance on exercising the discretion provided under the old CPR r 44.14(2)(a).[104] The case concerned the failure to commence detailed assessment proceedings within the times prescribed under CPR r 47.8; in fact there had been a delay of almost five years.[105] Longmore LJ gave the leading judgment and noted that non-compliance with a rule triggered the power to penalise for misconduct, under what is now r 44.11(2)(a), but that the court should exercise its discretion in determining the extent of any misconduct and whether or not it was sufficiently serious to warrant the use of the power to disallow costs. In particular, Longmore LJ said that every failure to commence detailed assessment proceedings could not be considered to be misconduct.[106] Two examples were provided to illustrate the types of behaviour that might be considered: first, an inordinate and inexcusable delay in commencing may be classed as misconduct; and second, an inordinate, excusable delay which had not prejudiced the receiving party may not be symptomatic of misconduct.[107] The judge provided further guidance:

> 'where the relevant rule not only gives to the party at the receiving end of the delay the option of preventing further delay by himself taking the initiative but also spells out the normal sanction for penalising such delay (as r 47.8 does), it seems to me that the court should be hesitant to exercise further powers to impose further penalties by way of reducing otherwise allowable costs.' [108]

100 CPR r 47.8(2).
101 CPR r 47.8(3) and CPR r 44.11.
102 CPR r 47.8(5).
103 [2006] EWCA Civ 1663, [2007] 3 All ER 938.
104 Now CPR r 44.11(2)(a).
105 At [6].
106 At [9].
107 At [10].
108 At [17].

Points of dispute

8.46 Once the notice of commencement has been served, parties to the detailed assessment proceedings have 21 days to serve points of dispute in respect to any items in the receiving party's bill of costs.[109] Points of dispute must be 'short and to the point'[110] and must be served on all parties to the detailed assessment proceedings[111] with an open letter from the paying party to state the total sum that party offers to pay to settle the total costs claimed. At this time, the paying party may also make a Part 36 offer.[112]

8.47 If points of dispute are served by a party out of time, that party may not be heard without the court's permission in the subsequent proceedings.[113]

Default costs certificate

8.48 If points of dispute are not served within the prescribed period, the receiving party may file a request for the issue of a default costs certificate according to the procedure set out in the Practice Direction.[114] However, the court may not issue that certificate if points of dispute are served (out of time) by any party before the certificate has been issued.[115]

8.49 The default costs certificate[116] orders payment of the total costs to which it relates,[117] and includes the fixed costs for commencing the detailed assessment proceedings.[118] Payment is due by 14 days from the date of that certificate or the date specified by the court.[119]

8.50 A default costs certificate may be set aside or varied, following an application from either the receiving or the paying party, where:

(a) the receiving party was not entitled to the certificate;[120] or

109 CPR r 47.9(2).

110 CPR PD47 [8.2] and must follow the Schedule of Costs Precedents, Precedent G – points of dispute and reply at CPR PD47 [27].

111 CPR r 47.9(1).

112 CPR PD47 [8.3].

113 CPR r 47.9(3).

114 CPR PD47 [10] and CPR r 47.9(4); in Form N254 at https://www.gov.uk/government/publications/form-n254-request-for-a-default-costs-certificate.

115 CPR r 47.9(5).

116 In the County Court in Form N255(CC) at https://www.gov.uk/government/publications/form-n255cc-default-costs-certificate-county-court, and in the High Court in Form N255(HC) at https://www.gov.uk/government/publications/form-n255hc-default-costs-certificate-high-court.

117 CPR r 47.11(2).

118 CPR r 47.11(3) and CPR PD47 [10.7]-[10.8]: Fixed costs of £80 plus a sum to reimburse the court fee payable on issue of the certificate.

119 CPR r 44.7(1).

120 CPR r 47.12(1); for example, if the certificate is issued before the expiry of the 21 day period allowed for service of points of dispute.

(b) the court is of the view that there is some good reason why the detailed assessment proceedings should continue.[121]

Settlement

8.51 Probably because of the cost, complexity and time involved in detailed assessment proceedings, many parties agree a settlement in respect to those costs in advance of the assessment hearing. In such cases, either party may apply[122] to the court[123] for a costs certificate in the amount agreed.[124] The application will be either for a final or for an interim certificate depending upon, respectively, whether all or some of the costs have been agreed. CPR PD47 para 9 sets out the procedure on discontinuance.

8.52 Alternatively, the parties may wish to agree a settlement in writing and forego the opportunity to obtain a costs certificate; in which case, the receiving party need only inform the court of this in writing to ensure the hearing is vacated.

Detailed assessment proceedings

8.53 Once a party to proceedings serves points of dispute, if there is no agreement, the matter will progress to a detailed assessment. First, the receiving party may elect to serve a reply to those points of dispute on the other parties,[125] and should do so within 21 days of service of the points of dispute.[126] The reply should refer only to points of principle and concessions (without mere repetition of the bill of costs) and, where feasible, should follow the format of Precedent G.[127]

8.54 The receiving party must file a request for a detailed assessment hearing[128] within three months of the expiry of the period for commencing such proceedings (either under CPR r 47.7 or as specified by the court).[129] If this is not done, then:

(a) the paying party may prompt the process by applying for an order that directs the receiving party to file the request within a specified time. That order may take the form of an unless order, and may state that failure to comply with

121 CPR r 47.12(2).
122 CPR PD47 [9.1]: application to be made under CPR r 40.6 (Consent judgments and orders).
123 This will be the court which gave the judgment or made the order (or to which the matter has been transferred) if detailed assessment proceedings have not begun. If proceedings have begun, then see **8.36–8.37**. Applications in cases that have been proceeding in the Royal Courts of Justice should be sent to the Senior Courts Costs Office.
124 CPR r 47.10.
125 CPR r 47.13(1).
126 CPR r 44.11(2)(a) and see **6.115–6.116**.
127 CPR PD47 [12.1]-[12.2] and Precedent G at CPR PD47 [27].
128 In Form N258 with specified supplementary documents: CPR PD47 [13.2]; https://www.gov.uk/government/publications/form-n258-request-for-provisional-general-detailed-assessment.
129 CPR r 47.14(1); this will usually be within six months of the judgment or order awarding costs.

its terms will result in the court disallowing some or all of the costs to which the receiving party would otherwise be entitled;[130] or

(b) if the paying party has not applied to the court and the receiving party has requested a detailed assessment hearing out of time, the court may disallow some or all of the interest otherwise due to the receiving party, but will not impose any other sanction unless there is misconduct that falls under CPR r 44.11 (Court's powers in relation to misconduct).[131]

8.55 The reader will notice that the sanctions against the receiving party for delay in commencing detailed assessment proceedings are similar to those for failing to file a request for a detailed assessment hearing in time.[132]

Interim costs certificate

8.56 After requesting a hearing date, the receiving party may apply for an interim costs certificate under CPR Pt 23[133] or FPR Pt 18.[134] As the court should have already exercised its power to order a payment on account, an interim certificate may be unnecessary. Additionally, if the case is suitable for provisional assessment, then the timing of that assessment may mean that an interim certificate is of little relevance. Nevertheless, the court is empowered to issue, amend or cancel such a certificate and may order the costs certified by the certificate to be paid to the receiving party or to be paid into court within 14 days[135] of issue of the certificate.[136]

Provisional assessment

8.57 On receipt of a request for a detailed assessment hearing, the court will consider whether or not the criteria for provisional assessment (a hearing only on the papers which the parties are not allowed to attend)[137] are made out.[138] These criteria include the value of the bill of costs being £75,000 or less (excluding VAT)[139] and it being unnecessary to hear live evidence due to a dispute over the facts. Some of the, fairly obvious, advantages of a provisional assessment are that the matter is likely to be dealt with more quickly[140] and that the costs of the

130 CPR r 47.14(2) and (3).
131 CPR r 47.14(4) and see *Haji-Ioannou v Frangos and others* [2006] EWCA Civ 1663, [2007] 3 All ER 938 at [43].
132 See **8.43–8.45**.
133 CPR PD47 [15].
134 FPR PD28A [3.2].
135 CPR r 44.7(1).
136 CPR r 47.16.
137 PD47 [14.4(1)].
138 CPR r 47.15 and PD47 [14].
139 *The Senior Courts Costs Office Guide 2018*, 13.1.
140 The court uses its best endeavours to carry out the assessment within six weeks of receiving the request for assessment and documents in support: CPR PD47 [14.4(1)].

assessment are reduced as there is no hearing.[141] However, the court may at any time resolve that the matter is unsuitable for provisional assessment and should be dealt with by a full detailed assessment hearing.[142]

8.58 On completion of the provisional assessment, the court will send to the parties a copy of Precedent G (points of dispute) and any reply annotated with the court's decisions or the annotated bill of costs or both. The parties may challenge all or part of the assessment within 21 days of its receipt by filing and serving a written request for an oral hearing.[143] No permission is required to challenge the provisional assessment. Before making a challenge, the parties should consider CPR r 47.15(10), which specifies how the costs of such an oral hearing are to be met. The challenging party will be liable for the costs of that hearing unless it results in the costs being adjusted in favour of that party by at least 20 per cent of the sum provisionally assessed or unless the court orders differently (having considered the parties' conduct and any offers made).[144] This is a powerful incentive to agree a provisional assessment determination.

8.59 If the assessment goes unchallenged, the parties are bound by the court's assessment (other than in unspecified exceptional circumstances)[145] and a final costs certificate is unnecessary but will be provided if requested.[146]

Detailed assessment hearing

8.60 At least 14 days' notice of the assessment hearing will be given by the court.[147] At that hearing, only the receiving and paying parties and any party who has served points of dispute may be heard without the court's permission.[148] Furthermore, submissions will be limited to the points of dispute, unless the court permits otherwise.[149] The procedure relating to detailed assessment proceedings is set out at CPR PD47, para 13. If the parties simply disagree as to the sum of disbursements, then usually the court will deal with the matter on the papers and will issue a written decision.[150]

8.61 The detailed assessment hearing differs from other court hearings in some respects. A helpful and practical guide to such a hearing is given in *Cook on Costs 2019*.[151] Some of the main distinctions that a legal representative unaccustomed to such hearings would notice are:

141 CPR r 47.15(5) and *The Senior Courts Costs Office Guide 2018*, 13.3: The maximum award is £1,500 (excluding the cost of drafting the bill of costs – see **8.39** plus VAT and court fees.
142 CPR r 47.15(6).
143 CPR r 47.15(7).
144 CPR PD47 [14.5].
145 CPR r 47.15(7).
146 Middleton and Rowley *Cook on Costs 2019* (LexisNexis, 2019), 30.12.
147 CPR PD47 [13.6].
148 CPR r 47.14(5).
149 CPR r 47.14(6).
150 CPR PD47 [13.5].
151 Middleton and Rowley *Cook on Costs 2019* (LexisNexis, 2019), 28.42–28.45.

(a) the paying party will be expected to have considered any replies to the points of dispute and whether the issues have been narrowed and/or whether any concessions can be agreed;

(b) the receiving party must lodge the papers at court from seven to 14 days before the hearing[152] and the documents to be included and the order of presentation is set out in the practice direction;[153]

(c) documents may be amended without permission before the hearing and at the hearing the court will decide whether those amendments are to be allowed or penalised by payment of costs or both;[154]

(d) the parties and their legal representatives do not have an agreed bundle as papers lodged by the receiving party or requested by the court are protected by privilege unless that party decides to rely upon them and allows their disclosure;[155]

(e) if the court determines the overall costs are disproportionate, then each item of the bill may be considered by the judge, whether or not it relates to a point of dispute.

8.62 When making a detailed assessment of costs, the judge should begin by allowing costs that are reasonable or that were reasonably incurred. Then, the total of those costs will be assessed as to whether or not it seems proportionate and, if necessary, the sum will be adjusted accordingly. Attention is likely to be paid to hourly rates, seniority and location of fee earners, number of hours worked, disbursement costs and counsel's fees.

Proportionality

8.63 The CPR provides guidance on whether or not the costs incurred are proportionate:

> 'Costs incurred are proportionate if they bear a reasonable relationship to –
>
> (a) the sums in issue in the proceedings;
>
> (b) the value of any non-monetary relief in issue in the proceedings;
>
> (c) the complexity of the litigation;
>
> (d) any additional work generated by the conduct of the paying party; and
>
> (e) any wider factors involved in the proceedings, such as reputation or public importance.' [156]

152 CPR PD47 [13.11].
153 CPR PD47 [13.12].
154 CPR PD47 [13.10].
155 CPR PD47 [13.13].
156 CPR r 44.3(5).

8.64 This rule has, since 1 April 2013, replaced the guidance given by Lord Woolf in *Home Office v Lownds*[157] and the case law prior to that date concerning proportionality must be considered in the light of this change.

8.65 In *K v K*,[158] MacDonald J considered the need for costs to be proportionate and reasonably incurred, and significantly reduced the father's costs bill from £38,813 to £3,737.50. The case had involved a straightforward single issue on a legal point. The judge set out the principle (taken from *Khazakstan Kagazy PLC v Zhunus*[159]) that, 'the concept of proportionality concerns not the amount of costs which it was in the party's best interests to incur but the lowest amount which he or she could reasonably be expected to spend in order to have his or her case conducted and presented proficiently having regard to all the relevant circumstances'.[160] Summarily assessing the father's schedule of costs, the judge drastically reduced the hourly rates and the hours expended and disallowed costs that had not been particularised.[161]

Final costs certificate

8.66 After the detailed assessment hearing, the receiving party has 14 days in which to complete the bill to show the amount due (as a result of that detailed assessment) and to file that bill at court.[162] The court will then issue and serve on the parties a final costs certificate[163] which will include an order for the paying party to pay what is due.[164] As with all costs orders, the sum must be paid within 14 days of the order, unless a different period is specified in the order.[165] In many cases, however, the parties will agree the sum and it will be paid without recourse to the court for a costs certificate.[166]

8.67 In order to stay the enforcement of either an interim or a final costs certificate, an application should be made to a costs judge or a District Judge of the court office which issued the certificate or to the court office with jurisdiction to enforce the certificate, where this is different.[167] Costs certificates may be enforced as if they were money judgments,[168] but enforcement proceedings may not be issued in the Costs Office.[169]

157 [2002] 2 Costs LR 279.
158 *K v K (Family Proceedings: Costs)* [2016] EWHC 2002 (Fam), [2016] 4 WLR 143 and **9.64**.
159 [2015] EWHC 404 (Comm).
160 At [43].
161 At [44].
162 CPR r 47.17(2).
163 CPR r 47.17(3); in the County Court in Form 256(CC) at https://www.gov.uk/government/publications/form-n256cc-final-costs-certificate-county-court, and in the High Court in Form 256(HC) at https://www.gov.uk/government/publications/form-n256hc-final-costs-certificate-high-court.
164 CPR r 47.17(5).
165 CPR r 44.7.
166 Middleton and Rowley *Cook on Costs 2019* (LexisNexis, 2019), 28.55.
167 CPR PD47 [16.11].
168 See **Chapter 9**.
169 CPR PD47 [16.12].

Procedure when the costs are to be paid by the Lord Chancellor[170]

8.68 The procedure for detailed assessment (described above) is varied when the applicant is a publicly funded solicitor and the assessed costs are to be paid by the Lord Chancellor from the legal aid fund.[171] In such cases the claiming solicitor must file a detailed assessment request within three months of the right to detailed assessment crystallising.[172] The assisted person (who is the solicitor's publicly funded client) must also be served with the request for assessment if the court has previously been given notice of that person's financial interest in the hearing (which happens when, after assessment, it has been decided the person must make a contribution to the solicitor's legally aided costs). Otherwise, the assisted person should not be involved.[173]

8.69 A hearing will be listed if the assisted person has a financial interest and wishes to attend an assessment hearing or the court sees the need for a hearing.[174] Otherwise, the matter will be provisionally assessed on the papers.[175] After provisional assessment, the bill is returned to the solicitor[176] and the solicitor has 14 days to inform the court if an assessment hearing is required because the assessment is disputed.[177]

8.70 The Practice Direction provides further details of procedure.[178]

8.71 Where a publicly funded client is claiming their costs from another party, then the bill of costs must be compiled at private client rates;[179] however, where a solicitor is preparing a bill of costs for a claim against the Legal Aid Agency, it must be based upon the publicly funded rates prescribed in the costs regulations. A schedule of fee rates is set out in the regulations, and some flexibility to enhance these rates is allowed.[180]

Procedure when the costs are to be paid from a private fund[181]

8.72 The CPR sets out the procedure for detailed assessment when the assessed costs are to be paid from a private fund;[182] this might apply to a trustee's

170 Under LASPO 2012, Pt 1 (as amended).
171 CPR r 47.18(1).
172 CPR r 47.18(2); in form N258A at https://www.gov.uk/government/publications/form-n258a-request-for-detailed-assessment-legal-aid-legal-services-commission-only.
173 CPR r 47.18(3) and *The Senior Courts Costs Office Guide 2019*, 33.2 .
174 CPR r 47.18(4).
175 CPR r 47.18(5).
176 Middleton and Rowley *Cook on Costs 2019* (LexisNexis, 2019) at [28.42]–[28.45].
177 CPR r 47.18(7).
178 CPR PD47 [17].
179 Civil Legal Aid (Costs) Regulations 2013, SI 2013/611, reg 21.
180 Civil Legal Aid (Remuneration) Regulations 2013, SI 2013/422, reg 6(2)-(3) and Sch 1.
181 'Fund' is defined as including any estate or property held for the benefit of any person or class of person and any fund to which a trustee or personal representative is entitled in that capacity: CPR r 44.1(1).
182 CPR r 47.19 and PD47 [18].

claim or where there is a protected party. The receiving party commences proceedings by filing a request[183] within three months of obtaining the right to detailed assessment.[184] The receiving party may be directed by the court to serve a copy of the request on anyone with a financial interest in the result of the assessment (such as a trustee).[185] Unless a hearing is thought necessary, the court will provisionally assess the costs on the papers and return the bill to the receiving party.[186] An assessment hearing will then be arranged only if the receiving party makes such a request within 14 days of receiving the provisionally assessed bill.[187] The receiving party's legal representative, if appointed, must complete the bill so that a final certificate can be issued.[188]

8.73 It has long been established that costs payable from a fund in an action for administration of an estate do not attract interest since the costs order is granted on the basis of non-contentious litigation.[189]

The costs of detailed assessment proceedings

8.74 The general rule is that the receiving party is entitled to receive the costs of the detailed assessment proceedings.[190] However, the court may order otherwise[191] and that rule may be displaced by statute (none is mentioned in the rules) or by other CPR rules or Practice Directions.[192] A party who has benefited from pro bono representation in the proceedings will not receive an order for the costs of the detailed assessment proceedings other than if, in the usual way, an application is made under the Legal Services Act 2007[193] for a payment to the prescribed charity.[194] Costs will be summarily assessed, with interest running from the date of either the default, the interim certificate or the final costs certificate.[195] In order to claim the costs of a detailed assessment, it is necessary to file and serve a statement of costs at least 24 hours before the hearing.[196]

8.75 Since 1 April 2013, the court has been able to consider any offer made under Part 36 in respect to the costs of detailed assessment.[197] Any such offer will

183 In form N258B at https://www.gov.uk/government/publications/form-n258b-request-for-detailed-assessment-costs-payable-out-of-a-fund-other-than-the-community-legal-service-fund.
184 CPR r 47.19(1)-(2).
185 CPR r 47.19(3).
186 CPR r 47.19(4)-(5).
187 CPR r 47.19(6).
188 CPR PD47 [18.9].
189 *In re Marsden's Estate. Withington v Neumann* [1886-90] All ER Rep 1119 at [1121], (1889) 40 Ch D, 475 per Chitty J.
190 CPR r 47.20(1).
191 Having considered all the circumstances including conduct, any reduction to the bill of costs and whether the parties' claims and disputes as to particular items were reasonable: CPR r 47.20(3)
192 CPR r 47.20(1).
193 Section 194(3).
194 CPR r 47.20(2) and **5.94–5.102** . The prescribed charity is the Access to Justice Foundation.
195 CPR r 47.20(5) and (6).
196 The full procedure is set out at CPR PD44 [9.5].
197 CPR r 47.20(4)

be taken to include the cost of preparation of the bill, interest and VAT unless a contrary position is clearly specified. Other offers to settle (including *Calderbank* offers) may also be considered under CPR r 47.20.[198]

Cost assessment appeals

8.76 Any party[199] may appeal the decision of an authorised court officer in detailed assessment proceedings, without permission,[200] by filing an appeal notice[201] within 21 days of the decision.[202] The appeal is to a costs judge or District Judge of the High Court[203] who will then re-hear the proceedings and order or direct as is deemed appropriate.[204]

8.77 If the detailed assessment decision was made by a costs judge or a District Judge, then any appeal falls under the general provisions of CPR Pt 52 or FPR Pt 30 and permission to appeal is required.[205]

8.78 In appeals related to costs assessment proceedings, the court may wish to obtain the assistance of an assessor. FPR r 25.20 makes provisions for the court to appoint an assessor to aid the court by taking part in proceedings[206] and, under the court's direction, to prepare a report or to attend a hearing to advise the court. Unless the court decides otherwise, the assessor's fees will be paid at the rate of a fee-paid deputy district judge of the Central Family Court and those costs will be included in the costs of the proceedings.[207] As such, the court may direct a party to deposit a sum in court to cover the fees before an assessor becomes involved in the matter.[208]

8.79 FPR PD25F sets out the procedure to be followed when appointing an assessor. The court begins the process by informing the parties of the matters upon which assistance is required and the name and qualifications of the proposed expert. Such notification must be provided not less than 21 days before an appointment is made and the parties then have 7 business days in which to object, in writing, to the selection of the assessor either personally or on the basis

198 CPR PD47 [19].
199 CPR r 47.21.
200 CPR PD47 [20.2].
201 In Form N161 at https://www.gov.uk/government/publications/form-n161-appellants-notice-all-appeals-except-small-claims-track-appeals-and-appeals-to-the-family-division-of-the-high-court.
202 CPR r 47.23.
203 CPR r 47.22.
204 CPR r 47.24.
205 CPR PD47 [20.1].
206 Under the Senior Courts Act 1981, s 70(1), (2) and (5) as amended by the Crime and Courts Act 2013, s 17(6), Sch 10, Pt 2, paras 54, 62 and the Matrimonial and Family Proceedings Act 1984, s 31J(e).
207 FPR r 25.20(5).
208 FPR r 25.20(6).

of their qualifications. The court will consider any objections before deciding whether or not to make the appointment.

BASIS OF ASSESSMENT

8.80 When making an order for costs (other than for fixed costs), the court must also choose whether the costs should be assessed on the standard or the indemnity basis. CPR rr 44.3 and 44.4 set out the rules for such assessments but, regardless of which method of assessment is adopted, costs which have been unreasonably incurred or which are unreasonable in amount will not be allowed.[209]

8.81 Where the costs are assessed on the standard basis, the court can only allow costs which are proportionate to the matters in issue and it will resolve any doubt it has as to whether costs were either reasonably incurred or were reasonable in favour of the paying party.[210] Thus, a successful party in receipt of a costs order in their favour (which is assessed on a standard basis) is still likely to have to pay a proportion of their solicitor's fees himself.[211] In contrast, where costs are assessed on an indemnity basis, the rules do not mention proportionality and the court will resolve any doubt it may have as to whether the costs were reasonably incurred or were reasonable in amount in favour of the receiving party.[212]

8.82 It is wrong for the court to combine the assessments of reasonableness and proportionality. Since the amendment of the CPR on 1 April 2013,[213] the position established by the Court of Appeal in *Lownds v Home Office (Practice Note)*[214] on proportionality has been overruled. However, it is still likely that the court will consider the matters set out by Lord Neuberger in *Drake* (although that case was decided under the *Lownds* regime) such as: hourly rates, the seniority and location of fee earners, the number of hours worked, disbursement costs, and counsel's fees. CPR r 44.3(5) relating to proportionality is set out at **8.63**.

8.83 In exercising its discretion to determine costs, the court is also required to consider:

(a) court orders that have already been made;

(b) the parties' conduct both before and during the proceedings and, in particular, any attempts made to settle their differences;

(c) the value of any money or property involved;

209 CPR rr 44.3(1) and 44.4(1).
210 CPR r 44.3(2).
211 *McPhilemy v Times Newspapers Ltd* [2001] EWCA Civ 933 at [20] per Chadwick LJ.
212 CPR r 44.3(3).
213 By the Civil Procedure (Amendment) Rules 2013, SI 2013/262.
214 [2002] EWCA Civ 365.

(d) the significance of the issues to the parties;

(e) the complexity, novelty or difficulty of the issues;

(f) the level of skill, effort, specialised knowledge and responsibility required to conduct the case;

(g) the amount of time spent on the proceedings;

(h) where and in what circumstances the work (or part of the work) was done; and

(i) the receiving party's last approved or agreed budget.[215]

8.84 Under CPR r 44.3(4), if an order for costs is silent as to the basis for assessing the costs (or states that costs are to be assessed on some other basis than the standard or indemnity basis), then costs are to be assessed on the standard basis.

8.85 It follows that:

(a) where costs can be shown to have been reasonably and proportionately incurred, then there is no difference between the result of an assessment on the standard basis and one on the indemnity basis;

(b) in practice, any contested costs bill will contain sums which the paying party can take issue with as to whether or not they are reasonable and/or proportionate;

(c) the main difference between standard and indemnity costs is the approach the court will take to resolve those disagreements: in the payer's favour on the standard basis and in the receiver's favour on the indemnity basis;

(d) where costs are to be paid on an indemnity basis, the bill will be paid in full save where the costs are found to have been unreasonably incurred or are unreasonable in amount.[216]

8.86 Choosing whether to apply standard or indemnity costs depends upon the court finding a reason as to why one or the other regime is appropriate. As has been observed, that is not something on which the rules assist and the practitioner must rely upon the case law which is considered below.

Standard basis costs

Proportionality

8.87 The rules do not define what is classed as 'reasonable' or 'unreasonable', but 'proportionate' is defined at CPR r 44.3(5):

215 CPR r 44.4(2)–(3).

216 CPR r 44.3(1) 'the court will not in either case allow costs which have been unreasonably incurred or are unreasonable in amount'.

'Costs incurred are proportionate if they bear a reasonable relationship to –

(a) the sums at issue in the proceedings;

(b) the value of any non-monetary relief in issue in the proceedings;

(c) the complexity of the litigation;

(d) any additional work generated by the conduct of the paying party; and

(e) any wider factors involved in the proceedings, such as reputation or public importance.'

This list is the basis for challenging or defending a challenge to a bill of costs awarded on the standard basis.

8.88 In *Quan v Bray*,[217] Holman J considered the proportionality of costs. The wife had applied to enforce maintenance sums of around £38,000 by such method of enforcement as the court may consider appropriate. The husband failed to attend the hearing and the wife's advisors pragmatically accepted that none of the means of enforcement would be effective. Holman J considered the wife's costs of the application. The judge allowed counsel's fees in full as he found they were not excessive given the complexity of the case and the considerable amount of preparation carried out. However, Holman J said,

> 'incurring costs of over 40 per cent of the actual arrears in issue at the time of issue of this application is the kind of profligate legal expenditure which discredits the practice of family law and is out of all proportion. It is simply not proportionate to incur these sorts of costs on behalf of a client, who claims herself to be penniless, in pursuit of the amount of arrears as they were at the date of issue.'[218]

The solicitor's costs of £13,801 were summarily assessed at £6,000, and therefore the total costs (including counsel's fees and VAT) came to £9,300. Holman J weighed the husband's failure to attend court and to pay anything towards the maintenance order against the wife's forlorn application and determined that the husband should pay 50% of the wife's costs. The order was not to be enforced without leave of the court.

Indemnity costs

The test for indemnity costs

8.89 Prior to the launch of the CPR, the precedents suggested that some sort of moral condemnation was necessarily associated with an indemnity costs order. After the CPR was introduced, in *Reid Minty (a firm) v Taylor*, the Court of Appeal held that 'litigation can readily be conducted in a way which is

217 [2019] EWFC 46.
218 At [15].

unreasonable and which justifies an award of costs on an indemnity basis, where the conduct could not properly be regarded as lacking moral probity or deserving moral condemnation.'[219]

8.90 In that case Kay LJ held that:

> 'The approach of the CPR is a relatively simple one: namely, if one party has made a real effort to find a reasonable solution to the proceedings and the other party has resisted that sensible approach, then the latter puts himself at risk that the order for costs may be on an indemnity basis.' [220]

8.91 However, in *Kiam v MGN Ltd* Simon Brown LJ rejected the approach that the refusal of an offer, later found by the court to be reasonable, would lead to an indemnity costs order. He explained that:

> 'I for my part, understand the court there to have been deciding no more than that conduct, albeit falling short of misconduct deserving of moral condemnation, *can* be so unreasonable as to justify an order for indemnity costs. With that I respectfully agree. To my mind, however, such conduct would need to be unreasonable to a high degree; unreasonable in this context certainly does not mean merely wrong or misguided in hindsight. An indemnity costs order made under r 44 (unlike one made under r 36) does, I think, carry at least some stigma. It is of its nature penal rather than exhortatory.'[221]

He concluded that:

> 'It follows from all this that in my judgment it will be a rare case indeed where the refusal of a settlement offer will attract under r 44 not merely an adverse order for costs, but an order on an indemnity rather than standard basis.'[222]

8.92 A few months later, Lord Justice Waller (who had been a party to the judgment in *Kiam*) condensed the issue to be determined by the court when considering the appropriateness of an order for indemnity costs into one query:

> 'The question will always be: is there something in the conduct of the action or the circumstances of the case which takes the case out of the norm in a way which justifies an order for indemnity costs?' [223]

8.93 The position thus established, it was possible for the rules in relation to indemnity costs orders to be set out comprehensively by Tomlinson J in the

219 *Reid Minty (a firm) v Taylor* [2001] EWCA Civ 1723, [2002] 2 All ER 150 at [28] per May LJ.
220 *Reid Minty (a firm) v Taylor* at [27].
221 *Kiam v MGN Ltd (No 2)* [2002] EWCA Civ 66 at [12].
222 *Kiam v MGN Ltd (No 2)* at [13].
223 *Excelsior Commercial & Industrial Holdings Ltd v Salisbury Hamer Aspden & Johnson (a firm) and another* [2002] EWCA Civ 879, [2002] All ER (D) 39 (Jun) at [39].

monstrous case in which the liquidators for the Bank of Credit and Commerce International accused dozens of Bank of England staff of dishonesty; allegations which became, over 255 days, increasingly implausible until they were abandoned on day 256 of the trial.[224]

8.94 In awarding indemnity costs the judge summarised the jurisdiction as follows:[225]

> 'The following principles should guide the court's determination whether the Claimants should be required to pay the Bank's costs of the action on an indemnity basis: –
>
> (1) The court should have regard to all the circumstances of the case and the discretion to award indemnity costs is extremely wide.
>
> (2) The critical requirement before an indemnity order can be made in the successful Defendant's favour is that there must be some conduct or some circumstance which takes the case out of the norm.
>
> (3) Insofar as the conduct of the unsuccessful Claimant is relied on as a ground for ordering indemnity costs, the test is not conduct attracting moral condemnation, which is an a fortiori ground, but rather unreasonableness.
>
> (4) The court can and should have regard to the conduct of an unsuccessful Claimant during the proceedings, both before and during the trial, as well as whether it was reasonable for the Claimant to raise and pursue particular allegations and the manner in which the Claimant pursued its case and its allegations.
>
> (5) Where a claim is speculative, weak, opportunistic or thin, a Claimant who chooses to pursue it is taking a high risk and can expect to pay indemnity costs if it fails.
>
> (6) A fortiori, where the claim includes allegations of dishonesty, let alone allegations of conduct meriting an award to the Claimant of exemplary damages, and those allegations are pursued aggressively inter alia by hostile cross examination.
>
> (7) Where the unsuccessful allegations are the subject of extensive publicity, especially where it has been courted by the unsuccessful Claimant, that is a further ground.
>
> (8) The following circumstances take a case out of the norm and justify an order for indemnity costs, particularly when taken in combination with

224 *Three Rivers District Council and others v Bank of England* [2006] EWHC 816 (Comm), [2006] All ER (D) 175 (Apr) at [1] .

225 *Three Rivers District Council and others v Bank of England* [2006] EWHC 816 (Comm), [2006] All ER (D) 175 (Apr) at [25] and approved by the Court of Appeal in *Royal Bank of Scotland plc v Highland Financial Partners LP and others* [2013] EWCA Civ 472 at [10] per Aikens LJ.

the fact that a Defendant has discontinued only at a very late stage in proceedings;

(a) Where the Claimant advances and aggressively pursues serious and wide ranging allegations of dishonesty or impropriety over an extended period of time;
(b) Where the Claimant advances and aggressively pursues such allegations, despite the lack of any foundation in the documentary evidence for those allegations, and maintains the allegations, without apology, to the bitter end;
(c) Where the Claimant actively seeks to court publicity for its serious allegations both before and during the trial in the international, national and local media;
(d) Where the Claimant, by its conduct, turns a case into an unprecedented factual enquiry by the pursuit of an unjustified case;
(e) Where the Claimant pursues a claim which is, to put it most charitably, thin and, in some respects, far-fetched;
(f) Where the Claimant pursues a claim which is irreconcilable with the contemporaneous documents;
(g) Where a Claimant commences and pursues large-scale and expensive litigation in circumstances calculated to exert commercial pressure on a Defendant, and during the course of the trial of the action, the Claimant resorts to advancing a constantly changing case in order to justify the allegations which it has made, only then to suffer a resounding defeat.'

8.95 Some of these principles will have little application to a family case, and they reflect the judge's displeasure at the particular case before him. They are focused on the misconduct of a claimant, but most of the principles (perhaps with the exceptions of (8)(c) and (8)(g)) can be rephrased for an applicant or a respondent. Filtered through the facts of a particular family case, they do, we suggest, include all the matters that a court is likely to need to consider.

8.96 The Court of Appeal in a judgment handed down by Lord Woolf CJ held that, 'In particular [the court] can reflect its disapproval in the orders for costs which it makes'.[226] In that personal injury claim the insurers had sent a private investigator into the claimant's home under a pretext, and whilst there the investigator took a video of the claimant which the insurers wished to use in evidence. The Court of Appeal called this action improper and unjustified[227] but decided to allow the video to be used but (by implication at least) even if the claim was dismissed, there should be a costs order against the insurers as, 'In giving effect to the overriding objective, and taking into account the wider interests of the administration of justice, the court must, while doing justice between the parties, also deter improper conduct of a party while conducting litigation'.[228] If

226 *Jones v University of Warwick* [2003] EWCA Civ 151, [2003] 1 WLR 954, [2003] 3 All ER 760 at [30].
227 At [29].
228 *Jones v University of Warwick* [2003] EWCA Civ 151, [2003] 1 WLR 954, [2003] 3 All ER 760 at [30].

the claim was successful then the court suggested that at the conclusion of the hearing an order for the defendants to pay the costs throughout on the indemnity basis should be considered.

8.97 In the well-known financial remedy case, *Imerman*, there had similarly been an invasion of privacy to obtain evidence. In order to mark the court's disapproval and 'to discourage similar conduct in the course of other ancillary relief applications', costs were awarded on the indemnity basis against the party who had invaded the other party's privacy.[229]

8.98 The case of *Brawley v Marczynski (No 2)*[230] provides authority for the principle that costs may be awarded on the indemnity basis to a party in receipt of legal aid. In such a case, it is recognised that the publicly funded party's lawyers will be the only beneficiaries of the penalty imposed upon the paying party.

Examples of indemnity costs in family proceedings

8.99 The appropriateness of an indemnity costs order has been considered in several reported family cases. In a case under the Hague Convention jurisdiction concerning the alleged abduction of a child, Ryder J described the difference between the court deciding to order costs on the standard or the indemnity basis, saying:

> 'The difference between the bases is the burden of proof in respect of any doubt as to its reasonableness. In the overall context of the conduct of proceedings, costs on the standard basis mark the unreasonableness while giving scope in an appropriate case where the unreasonable conduct persists through a contested hearing to be marked by indemnity costs.'[231]

In that case, indemnity costs were found not to be appropriate because although the applicant mother's behaviour had been unreasonable, she had withdrawn her unfounded allegations 'albeit at a late stage'.[232]

8.100 A case in which, unusually, an indemnity costs order had been made against the mother in Children Act 1989 proceedings came before the Court of Appeal in 2007.[233] The court granted permission to appeal and went on to set aside the indemnity costs order. Thorpe LJ considered the judgment of the lower court, in which it had been said that the mother's unreasonable litigation conduct in failing to participate had caused a significant increase in the costs of the proceedings. In fact, correspondence properly sent to the court by the mother had not been placed in front of the District Judge at that hearing. Thorpe LJ concluded, 'an

229 *Imerman v Tchenguiz (Costs)* [2010] EWHC 64 (Fam), [2010] 2 FLR 802 at [49] per Moylan J.
230 [2002] EWCA Civ 1453, [2002] 4 All ER 1067 at [4] and [18] per Longmore LJ.
231 *EC-L v DM (Child Abduction: Costs)* [2005] EWHC 588 (Fam), [2005] 2 FLR 772 at [71].
232 At [71].
233 *Re B (children)* [2007] EWCA Civ 921, [2008] 1 FLR 205.

indemnity order against the mother was simply unthinkable. Should any order be made against her, bearing in mind that orders for costs particularly in CA 1989 cases are extremely uncommon …?'[234] Wall LJ reiterated this position: 'In my view an order for indemnity costs is a wholly exceptional order to make in family proceedings and needs to be very carefully thought through and justified.'[235] The appeal court made no order as to costs in the proceedings both in the lower court and in relation to the appeal.

8.101 *Fisher Meredith v JH and PH (Financial Remedy: Appeal: Wasted Costs)*[236] is a case in which Mostyn J was referred to the 'very high threshold established' regarding indemnity costs in *Kiam v MGN* and decided the standard basis for assessment was appropriate.[237]

8.102 Jonathan Cohen QC sat as a Deputy Judge of the High Court in *CR v MZ, FZ and IU Limited* to determine a preliminary issue as to the beneficial ownership of a company.[238] He stated that in such hearings costs should follow the event[239] and ordered indemnity costs for the applicant wife, having found that the respondents (the husband and an intervener) had sought to mislead the court and the wife and had relied upon documents which had been found to be a sham. The judge did not consider the respondents' litigation misconduct, including a failure to comply with directions, sufficient by itself to warrant an order for indemnity costs.

8.103 Eleanor King J also had little difficulty in deciding that indemnity costs were appropriate where a number of findings amounting to serious litigation misconduct were made against a husband and the companies whose case presented at trial was 'a fantastic charade with the husband a shady puppet master in the background'.[240]

8.104 In *Maughan v Wilmot*, Mostyn J adopted the principles set out in the *Three Rivers District Council* case above, in as far as applicable to a family case before him.[241] The husband had repeatedly made allegations of corruption against his wife's legal team which were found to be 'completely baseless' and his application was described as being 'totally without merit'.[242] The judge made an order for costs in the wife's favour on the indemnity basis. Further, an order in accordance with CPR r 44.2(8)[243] was made for the husband to pay the wife

234 At [9].
235 At [12].
236 [2012] EWHC 408 (Fam).
237 At [69]–[70].
238 [2013] EWHC 295 (Fam), [2014] 1 FLR 22.
239 At [91].
240 *M v M and others (Costs)* [2013] EWHC 3372 (Fam), [2014] 1 FLR 499 at [4].
241 [2014] EWHC 1288 at [30] (Fam).
242 [2014] EWHC 1288 at [30] (Fam).
243 CPR r 44.2(8): 'Where the court orders a party to pay costs subject to detailed assessment, it will order that party to pay a reasonable sum on account of costs, unless there is good reason not to do so.'

£45,000 on account within 14 days. In spite of this case, it seems, from other reported cases in family proceedings, that the presumption under r 44.2(8) that a payment of a reasonable sum on account will be ordered whenever a costs order is made subject to detailed assessment, is frequently overlooked.

8.105 Sir Peter Singer determined the final hearing in the financial remedy proceedings of *Thiry v Thiry*.[244] As to the husband, the judge concluded, 'he is an unprincipled rogue who has acted in financially predatory fashion to prey on his wife for his own profit and to her substantial detriment'.[245] The judge performed a summary assessment and noted, 'that this is a case for the indemnity basis of assessment is, in my judgment, indisputable'.[246] Approving of the wife's bill of costs as reasonable, the judge awarded those costs against the husband in the sum of £456,000. The wife's costs schedule had been drawn up by a firm of costs draughtsmen and provided far greater detail than a judge making a summary assessment would usually receive.

8.106 McFarlane LJ heard an application for permission to appeal from an order of indemnity costs, amongst other things, against a husband and his two sisters (who had been joined to the financial remedy proceedings).[247] In the court below, Parker J had found a series of sham transactions had been performed by the husband and his sisters to frustrate the legally-aided wife's claim for a financial remedy. She found their behaviour unreasonable to such a high degree (based upon their dishonesty and their litigation conduct) that she carried out a summary assessment and awarded the wife 90% of her costs on an indemnity basis and totalling some £126,000. The costs were calculated on the basis of the legal representatives' private rates.[248] The husband made submissions that:

(a) the wife's position throughout had been that she would not seek an order for costs and yet, on hearing Parker J's findings, she changed her position;

(b) in such proceedings the appropriate order was that there be no order as to costs;

(c) on the wife's case, as she expected to receive a lump sum that would avoid the statutory charge, she was not concerned with costs;

(d) the order had been determined on a top down basis without due consideration of those elements of the litigation in which the wife's conduct had justified an order in favour of the husband;

(e) the adverse findings against the husband were not sufficiently serious to warrant the assessment of costs on the indemnity basis.[249]

244 [2014] EWHC 4046 (Fam).
245 At [26].
246 At [49].
247 *K v K* [2014] EWCA Civ 1746.
248 At [7] and [9]. See **8.71**.
249 At [19]-[21].

8.107 Of these arguments, McFarlane LJ stated that only the first point had any merit as an arguable ground of appeal. Nevertheless, he refused permission to appeal the costs order, having concluded that the wife had been entitled to change her mind on her position as to costs. The judge stated that the husband had received notice of her costs application, albeit that it had been made rather late, and he had been given the opportunity to make submissions.[250]

8.108 Sir Peter Singer again addressed the issue of indemnity costs in the case of *Joy v Joy-Morancho & Others (No 3)*.[251] This lengthy financial remedies case had included numerous applications, some of which fell within the no order regime and others within the clean sheet regime. The judge described the husband as displaying 'scandalous and outrageous conduct and attitude',[252] conducting 'an elaborate charade, the stage management of which has been conducted ruthlessly and without regard to cost'.[253] Further, the husband's case 'was a rotten edifice founded on concealment and misrepresentation and therefore a sham, a charade, bogus, spurious and contrived. I do not shrink from applying to it the description fraud, a deliberate design to deceive, inflicted on W and on the court, and found by the court so to be.'[254]

8.109 The reader will not be surprised to learn, based upon these findings, that the husband was ordered to pay all the wife's costs on the indemnity basis after detailed assessment.[255] In addition, he was to pay 80% of the wife's costs bill on account within 14 days of judgment. The judge stated that at a detailed assessment the husband would be unlikely to achieve as much as a 20% reduction. Sir Peter Singer also noted that it was unlikely that the costs order would be complied with as the husband claimed his assets were already encumbered.[256]

8.110 Roberts J awarded a husband costs on the indemnity basis in *AB v CD*.[257] The husband had succeeded in his application to set aside a consent order in financial remedy proceedings due to his wife's non-disclosure. The judge noted: the husband's successful application; both parties had been guilty of litigation misconduct; and the wife had made a sensible offer to settle the proceedings some two and a half years earlier. Balancing those findings, the judge ordered the wife to pay 50% of the costs of the set aside application. However, to balance the 'benefit of a substantial discount' the costs were to be assessed on the indemnity basis.[258]

8.111 In *Timokhina v Timokhin*,[259] the Court of Appeal considered whether the judge in the lower court had been wrong to order costs on the indemnity basis and

250 At [22].
251 [2015] EWHC 2507 (Fam).
252 At [231].
253 At [170].
254 At [215].
255 At [238].
256 At [240]–[242].
257 [2016] EWHC 2482 (Fam).
258 At [74].
259 [2019] EWCA Civ 1284.

to carry out a summary assessment without the necessary information before the Court. Following the principles set out in *Three Rivers District Council v Bank of England*,[260] the Court found the decision to order payment on the indemnity basis was within the scope of the judge's discretion and was warranted on both the evidence and the mother's conduct in choosing to appeal a hopeless case. The decision of the judge to carry out a summary assessment was also upheld. The Court did, however, make a hefty reduction in the sum of costs awarded having determined that the respondent's counsel's fees were unreasonable in amount. King LJ noted that both parties had been skilfully represented by counsel, yet there was a marked disparity between the appellant's counsel's brief fee of £1,500 and that of the respondent's counsel (a silk attended by a junior barrister) of £37,500. Accordingly, the latter sum was assessed and somewhat reduced to £31,250.[261]

8.112 In 2019, Holman J ordered a husband and a company with which he had been involved (and that had been joined as second respondent) to pay indemnity costs to a wife in proceedings under MFPA 1984, Pt III.[262] From the start, the husband had failed to engage in the proceedings, and he had disobeyed every order. The company's participation in the proceedings had increased the costs, complexity, number and length of hearings. The company then breached several orders against them and abandoned the claim without formality. The wife's total costs bill came to around £270,500. At the request of the wife's counsel, Holman J agreed to assess costs summarily, whilst noting that this was an exceptional decision as the size and scale of the bill were beyond the norm for summary assessment. The judge noted the wife might struggle to recover the costs of a detailed assessment from the respondents and he gave a significant discount to compensate from the facts that he lacked a detailed, itemised bill and was not experienced in assessing the reasonableness of the rates or work done by lawyers of different seniority. Discounting the wife's bill by around 30%, costs were assessed at £170,000.[263]

Comparison of the value of standard and indemnity costs

8.113 What is the monetary difference between an order for costs to be paid on the standard basis and one that is to be paid on the indemnity basis? We have seen that a bill assessed on the indemnity basis will be paid in full, provided the costs have been reasonably incurred and are reasonable in amount. However, the proportion of the bill of costs ordered to be paid after a summary assessment on the standard basis has been addressed in several family cases. Moor J has considered standard costs to be about 75% of the total bill of costs.[264] Having

260 See [**8.94**]–[**8.95**].
261 At [74]–[77].
262 *Vilinova v Vilinov and Hinaly Company Limited* [2019] EWHC 1107 (Fam) at [94–97].
263 At [99].
264 *Re R (Costs: Contact Enforcement)* [2011] EWHC 2777 (Fam), [2012] 1 FLR 445 at [41] and *WD v HD* [2015] EWHC 1547 (Fam) at [72].

canvassed counsel's views, Mostyn J chose a figure of 70% (the payer's counsel had suggested 66% and the payee's counsel 70 to 80%),[265] which was the same percentage that he had adopted as a 'rule of thumb'[266] in a case in the previous year. This level of costs recovery of 70% has been approved by the Court of Appeal when considering another of Mostyn J's judgments.[267] The effect is that a judge summarily assessing a bill, if there are no items to be excluded entirely from the assessment, may be likely to assess costs on the standard basis at around 70 to 75% of the bill of costs. Although Mostyn J set out the basis for summary assessment under CPR r 44.3 in his judgment,[268] that judgment reflects only that he adopted 'a percentage yardstick … of 70%' to assess the costs, and any direct consideration given to reasonableness or proportionality of costs is not mentioned.[269]

8.114 We suggest that some caution should be exercised in adopting the civil case law on indemnity costs in family proceedings. That is because of the different starting point in making a costs order in civil proceedings, where costs follow the event.[270] Civil courts merely have to decide who has won (albeit that is not always a straightforward task) and do not otherwise have to consider the merits of a claim or of a defence when making a standard costs order. In family proceedings, though, with a clean sheet or no order starting point, the merits have to be considered in relation to every costs order.

8.115 Family judges must have regard to the CPR r 44.2 clean sheet factors[271] or the FPR r 28.3 no order factors every time they consider making an order for costs. Those factors are principally concerned with conduct,[272] and conduct is also the principal consideration in deciding whether or not an indemnity costs order is appropriate. Accordingly, in the Family Court a finer judgment is required in relation to conduct. First, is it sufficiently bad (taking all the relevant factors into account)[273] to make an order for costs at all? Second, if bad conduct warrants the making of a costs order, is that conduct so bad that an order on the indemnity basis is required? And, we wonder, does that mean that the threshold for indemnity costs in family proceedings is or should be higher than that in civil proceedings?

GUIDELINE HOURLY RATES

8.116 During 2014, the Civil Justice Council Costs Committee performed a review of guideline solicitors' charge out hourly rates and made recommendations to the Master of the Rolls.[274] Nevertheless, due to the difficulties found by the

265 *JM v CZ (Costs: Ex Parte Order)* [2014] EWHC 1125 (Fam) at [26], [2015] 1 FLR 559.
266 *KS v ND (Schedule 1: Appeal: Costs)* [2013] EWHC 464 (Fam) at [35], [2013] 2 FLR 698.
267 *R (on the application of Faulkner) v Director of Legal Aid Casework* [2018] EWCA Civ 1656, per Asplin LJ at [35].
268 *JM v CZ (Costs: Ex Parte Order)* [2014] EWHC 1125 (Fam) at [25].
269 At [26].
270 CPR r 44.2(2).
271 Subject to the exceptions at FPR r 28.2(1).
272 See **Chapter 2**.
273 For which see particularly *Re S (A Child)* [2015] UKSC 20, discussed at **2.19–2.33**.
274 https://www.judiciary.uk/wp-content/uploads/2014/07/ghr-final-report.pdf.

Committee in recommending revised rates, on 28 July 2014 the Master of the Rolls determined to leave the rates unchanged until further evidence could be gathered and assessed. Those rates, set in 2010, remain applicable at the time of writing.[275] The guideline solicitors' rates are intended to be used in the summary assessment of costs but are described as 'broad approximations' only.[276]

8.117 Guideline fees for counsel are no longer published within the guidelines; perhaps as they were rarely referred to.

VAT

8.118 VAT has been set at 20% since 4 January 2011. The Practice Direction to CPR Pt 44 offers guidance as to claims for VAT on costs.[277] VAT should not be claimed on the bill of costs if the receiving party can recover the VAT sum as input tax.[278] If only a proportion of the VAT can be accounted for as an input tax that gains credit from HMRC, then the remaining proportion of VAT should be included as part of the costs claim. If, however, none of the VAT can be recovered then it may be claimed in full on the bill of costs. It is the receiving party's duty to ensure that only VAT sums that cannot be recovered as input tax are claimed.[279]

Changes in the VAT rate

8.119 Should the rate of VAT change, then the presumption is that an election to charge the lower rate of VAT has been made where the supply has crossed the period of the rate change. That presumption may be rebutted by writing to inform HMRC of the election, but the decision to do so should be justified to the court when costs are subsequently assessed.[280]

8.120 On such a change in the VAT rate, it is necessary to identify items on the bill of costs separately according to whether or not the work was done before, or after the date of the VAT rate change, or whether it bridged the VAT change. Where a piece of work has been carried out over the time of the VAT change and has been charged as a lump sum, it may be necessary to refer to the guidance provided by HMRC.[281] This approach avoids the paying party overpaying if the rate has risen or, in the alternative case, underpaying.

275 https://www.gov.uk/guidance/solicitors-guideline-hourly-rates.

276 Guide to Summary Assessment of Costs, 2005 edn, 41: https://www.gov.uk/government/publications/summary-assessment-of-court-costs-a-guide-for-judges.

277 CPR PD44.2.

278 Input VAT is the VAT added to the price of goods or services liable to VAT. Buyers who have registered to pay VAT may deduct the input VAT they have paid from the output VAT they have received, thereby reducing the settlement due to HMRC: Value Added Tax Act 1994, s 24.

279 CPR PD44 [2.3]-[2.4].

280 CPR PD44 [2.7]-[2.8].

281 VAT Guide (Notice 700) at https://www.gov.uk/guidance/vat-guide-notice-700, 30.

8.121 Should the VAT rate change after a detailed assessment has been performed but before the final costs certificate has been issued, then any interested party may apply to vary the assessment according to the new rate of VAT. The Practice Direction does not allow any such variation once the certificate has been issued.[282]

VAT on disbursements

8.122 The Practice Direction sets out, at para 2.11, the circumstances in which VAT on disbursements should be included in a claim for costs.

8.123 Third party payments which are treated as an overhead of the legal representative are not dealt with as disbursements. Such payments might include the costs of postage, DX, telephone and stationery. The legal representative's bill for legal services should include such costs and VAT must be charged on that bill.[283]

8.124 The situation becomes more complicated when dealing with payments which are classed as disbursements in some circumstances, but not for VAT purposes.[284] Those disbursements must be dealt with according to **8.122** and should be included in the bill for legal services upon which VAT is charged. This is the case regardless of whether or not the third-party supplier charged VAT for those items.[285]

8.125 According to the VAT Guide, where a third party supplied the legal representative directly, and that supply was then included in the general supply of legal services (such as the travel and subsistence costs of the legal representative) then VAT would be charged by the legal representative on the third party supply according to **8.122**.[286] The supply, though, may be made directly to the receiving party with the legal representative acting as merely the receiving party's agent by paying for the supply (for example in the case of court fees or fees to expert witnesses). Such supplies are classed as disbursements in respect to VAT and the legal representative should not claim VAT on those costs.[287]

Circumstances in which VAT cannot be claimed

8.126 VAT cannot be claimed:

(a) on the costs of work done by a litigant in person;[288]

282 CPR PD44 [2.10].
283 CPR PD44 [2.11(2)].
284 VAT Guide (Notice 700) at https://www.gov.uk/guidance/vat-guide-notice-700, 25.1.
285 CPR PD44 [2.11(3)].
286 CPR PD44 [2.11(4)(a)] and [2.11(5)].
287 CPR PD44 [2.11(4)(b)] and [2.11(6)].
288 CPR PD44 [2.12].

(b) on the costs paid to a government department for legal services provided by the department's own staff;[289]

(c) on a costs bill that is to be agreed or assessed under the pro bono representative's payment provisions of the Legal Services Act 2007, s 194(3);[290]

(d) when the receiving party is registered as a VAT taxable person and the supply of legal services was obtained for the purpose of their business;[291]

(e) when the receiving party is domiciled outside the European Union;[292] and

(f) when the receiving party is domiciled outside the UK but is domiciled in the European Union and received the supply of legal services for the purposes of their business.[293]

VAT on costs to be paid from the legal aid fund[294]

8.127 The rule is that supplies made under a legal aid certificate are subject to VAT, provided: the solicitor is a VAT registered taxable person; and the party receiving legal aid belongs in the UK or in another European Union member state and is a private individual or receives the supplies for purposes not related to business.

8.128 If the party in receipt of legal aid belongs outside the European Union then, unless the supply relates to land within the UK, VAT is usually not payable.

8.129 VAT on legal services provided to a legally aided party is payable out of the legal aid fund regardless of whether or not the legally aided party is registered for VAT and the legal services were supplied in relation to that party's business.

FORMS OF COSTS ORDERS

8.130 A list of the more usual costs orders made in interim hearings is given at CPR PD44,[295] and that table is reproduced below.

289 CPR PD44 [2.13].
290 CPR PD44 [2.14].
291 *The Senior Courts Costs Office Guide 2018*, 2.23(i); https://www.judiciary.uk/wp-content/uploads/2018/11/6.4764_JO_SCCO-Guide-2018_WEB_2.pdf .
292 *The Senior Courts Costs Office Guide 2018* at [2.23(ii)]; https://www.judiciary.uk/wp-content/uploads/2018/11/6.4764_JO_SCCO-Guide-2018_WEB_2.pdf.
293 *The Senior Courts Costs Office Guide 2018* at [2.23(iii)]; https://www.judiciary.uk/wp-content/uploads/2018/11/6.4764_JO_SCCO-Guide-2018_WEB_2.pdf.
294 *The Senior Courts Costs Office Guide 2018* at [33.10]; https://www.judiciary.uk/wp-content/uploads/2018/11/6.4764_JO_SCCO-Guide-2018_WEB_2.pdf.
295 At [4.2].

Term	**Effect**
Costs Costs in any event	The party in whose favour the order is made is entitled to that party's costs in respect of the part of the proceedings to which the order relates, whatever other costs orders are made in the proceedings.
Costs in the case Costs in the application	The party in whose favour the court makes an order for costs at the end of the proceedings is entitled to that party's costs of the part of the proceedings to which the order relates.
Costs reserved	The decision about costs is deferred to a later occasion, but if no later order is made the costs will be costs in the case.
Applicant's/respondent's costs in case/application	If the party in whose favour the costs order is made is awarded costs at the end of the proceedings, that party is entitled to that party's costs of the part of the proceedings to which the order relates. If any other party is awarded costs at the end of the proceedings, the party in whose favour the final costs order is made is not liable to pay the costs of any other party in respect of the part of the proceedings to which the order relates.
Costs thrown away	Where, for example, a judgment or order is set aside, the party in whose favour the costs order is made is entitled to the costs which have been incurred as a consequence. This includes the costs of: • preparing for and attending any hearing at which the judgment or order which has been set aside was made; • preparing for and attending any hearing to set aside the judgment or order in question; • preparing for and attending any hearing at which the court orders the proceedings or the part in question to be adjourned; • any steps taken to enforce a judgment or order which has subsequently been set aside.

Term	Effect
Costs of and caused by	Where, for example, the court makes this order on an application to amend a statement of case, the party in whose favour the costs order is made is entitled to the costs of preparing for and attending the application and the costs of any consequential amendment to their own statement of case.
Costs here and below	The party in whose favour the costs order is made is entitled not only to that party's costs in respect of the proceedings in which the court makes the order but also to that party's costs of the proceedings in any lower court. In the case of an appeal from a Divisional Court the party is not entitled to any costs incurred in any court below the Divisional Court.
No order as to costs Each party to pay own costs	Each party is to bear that party's own costs of the part of the proceedings to which the order relates whatever costs order the court makes at the end of the proceedings.

FAMILY PROCEEDINGS FEES FOR ASSESSMENT PROCEEDINGS

8.131 The table below sets out the court fees payable in relation to assessment proceedings:[296]

Determination of costs	
Where the party filing the request for detailed assessment is legally aided	£200
Where the amount of the costs claimed are:	
up to £15,000	£335
£15,000.01 – £50,000	£675
£50,000.01 – £100,000	£1,005
£100,000.01 – £150,000	£1,345
£150,000.01 – £200,000	£1,680
£200,000.01 – £300,000	£2,520

296 Taken from Form EX50, Civil and Family Court Fees, HM Courts and Tribunals Service, March 2019 and Form EX50A, Ministry of Justice, July 2019.

£300,000.01 – £500,000	£4,200
£500,000.01 or more	£5,600
Appeal (detailed assessment proceedings)	£210
Issue of default costs certificate	£60
Request or application to set aside a default costs certificate	£110

CHAPTER 9

The Costs of Enforcing Orders and Enforcement of Costs Orders

INTRODUCTION

9.01 Unfortunately, the granting of a final order may not be the end of the matter. What happens if a party does not comply with the terms of the order and, for example, does not pay what is due or allow the other party to spend time with the child? Practitioners will be well aware that there are various ways in which the party benefiting from a judgment or an order may seek to enforce that judgment or order, depending upon whether the order relates to financial[1] or non-financial matters.

9.02 Costs orders cannot be enforced until they have been assessed,[2] but interest on the costs due runs from the date of judgment or order (at the judgment

1 Under FPR Pt 33, which adopts CPR Pt 70 with some modifications set out at FPR r 33.2.
2 *Chohan v Times Newspapers Ltd* [2001] EWCA Civ 964 at [33] per Aldous LJ.

rate of 8 per cent), unless the court makes an alternative provision.[3] Once assessed, a costs order is an enforceable judgment debt.[4]

9.03 Applications to enforce orders in family proceedings are dealt with under FPR r 28.2, and therefore generally the clean sheet rule applies to costs on enforcement. However, some applications for enforcement fall under the CPR fixed costs provisions. It is also important to note that an enforcement application concerning an order made in financial remedy proceedings (to which the no costs order regime of FPR r 28.3 relates) will be dealt with under r 28.2, and so the clean sheet rule applies to such enforcement proceedings.

9.04 Following a consultation, The Law Commission reported on the enforcement of financial orders in family proceedings in 2016.[5] National data on enforcement applications were not available, but the Commission noted that between August 2015 and August 2016 the Central Family Court found 9% of cases resulting in a family financial order required enforcement action to be taken.[6] Further, 28% of those enforcement applications concluded without an enforcement order. Generally, this was either because: the debt was paid; the debtor was unable to pay; the creditor had made the wrong application; there was insufficient information about the debtor; or the available methods of enforcement could not reach the debtor's assets. The Commission's report recommended:

(a) simplification of the procedural rules;

(b) enhanced guidance and information for litigators;

(c) greater debtors' duties as to disclosure of their financial position;

(d) granting the court increased powers to obtain information from third parties;

(e) widening enforcement methods to catch additional assets; and

(f) allowing courts to prohibit debtors from certain rights (such as driving or leaving the jurisdiction) whilst judgment debts are outstanding.

9.05 The Government responded to the report on 23 July 2018. Many of the proposed reforms were non-statutory and the Government agreed to progress those changes. As to changes requiring primary legislation, the Government decided to consider those after implementation of the non-statutory reforms. The Government was unable to indicate how long implementation of the reforms might take 'due to the complexity of this area of law'.[7] As we write, none of the promised reforms have been made, but we look forward to the availability of a more comprehensive and effective set of procedural rules on enforcement.

3 CPR r 44.2(6)(g), adopted by FPR r 28.2(1).
4 CPR r 70.1(2)(d).
5 The Law Commission, Enforcement of Family Financial Orders, Law Com No 370, 2016.
6 The Law Commission, Enforcement of Family Financial Orders, Law Com No 370, 2016 at [1.21].
7 https://s3-eu-west-2.amazonaws.com/lawcom-prod-storage-11jsxou24uy7q/uploads/2016/12/2018.07.23-Government-final-response-on-enforcement-of-family-financial-orders.pdf

ENFORCING FINANCIAL ORDERS (INCLUDING ORDERS FOR COSTS)

9.06 Under FPR Pt 33:

(a) CPR Pt 50 (Application of the Schedules);[8]

(b) CPR Pt 69 (Court's power to appoint a receiver);[9]

(c) CPR Pt 71 (Orders to obtain information from judgment debtors);[10]

(d) CPR Pt 83 (Writs and warrants – general provisions);[11]

(e) CPR Pt 84 (Enforcement by taking control of goods);[12] and

(f) Schs 1 (RSC provisions) and 2 (CCR provisions) to the CPR,[13]

apply (with some necessary modifications) in applications to the High Court or the Family Court to enforce orders made in family proceedings.

9.07 In addition, CPR Pt 70 (General rules about enforcement of judgments and orders) is adopted by FPR r 33.2 with amendments. CPR r 70.1(2)(d)[14] states that in Pts 71 to 73, a 'judgment or order for the payment of money includes a judgment or order for the payment of costs, but does not include a judgment or order for the payment of money into court'. The notes to the CPR[15] record that before enforcing a costs order, the amount payable should have been assessed and that, if this is not the case then CPR r 44.2(8)[16] or CPR r 44.16 should be used as orders made under these provisions may be enforced. FPR r 28.2(1) adopts those CPR rules.

9.08 The Practice Direction to CPR Pt 70 sets out ways in which financial orders or judgments (including costs orders) may be enforced, and a judgment creditor may use more than one enforcement method concurrently or consecutively.[17] FPR r 33.3(2)(b) goes further, in that an enforcement application need not specify the method of enforcement sought and, rather, the court may determine the appropriate enforcement method. Indeed, in many cases the most appropriate enforcement method is best determined by the court.[18] The methods of enforcement described in the CPR are:[19]

8 FPR r 33.1(2).
9 FPR r 33.22.
10 FPR r 33.23.
11 FPR r 33.1(2).
12 *Ibid.*
13 *Ibid.*
14 As modified by FPR r 33.2(a).
15 *Civil Procedure 2018* (Thompson Reuters, 2018) Vol 1, 70.1.3.
16 'Where the court orders a party to pay costs subject to detailed assessment, it will order that party to pay a reasonable sum on account of costs, unless there is good reason not to do so.'
17 CPR r 70.2(2)(b).
18 *Quan v Bray* [2019] EWFC 46 shows that even this more flexible application may be ineffective.
19 CPR PD70 [1.1].

(a) a writ or warrant of control;

(b) a third party debt order;

(c) a charging order, stop order or stop notice;

(d) the appointment of a receiver;[20]

(e) an attachment of earnings order;[21] and

(f) sequestration.[22]

These methods are discussed in more detail below.

9.09 The court does not have the power to commit for contempt of court for breach of an order to pay money (including costs) other than in the breach of a maintenance order.[23]

Fixed costs of legal representatives' charges

9.10 From the CPR fixed costs rules, at Pt 45, the FPR incorporates only r 45.8 which sets out fixed costs of enforcement in particular circumstances.[24] Table 5 under that rule lists the various fixed enforcement costs of legal representatives when:

(a) questioning a judgment debtor;

(b) making a third party debt order;

(c) making a charging order;

(d) issuing and registering a certificate awarded under the Civil Jurisdiction and Judgments Act 1982, Sch 6;[25]

(e) requesting permission under CPR r 83.13 to enforce a judgment or order granting possession of land;

(f) issuing and enforcing a writ or warrant of control; and

(g) making an attachment of earnings order.

9.11 It is notable that the fixed costs system provides for recovery of costs at an extremely low rate and one which is most unlikely to cover the actual costs incurred. Solicitors may, of course, charge their lay client costs over and above these rates. Also of note is that FPR r 28.1 allows the court to make 'such order as to costs as it thinks just'. Therefore, experience suggests that (when making a costs order) the court may be persuaded to step outside the fixed costs regime, but that such occasions are likely to be very limited.

20 CPR Pt 69.
21 CPR Pt 39.
22 CPR PD70 [1.2(2)].
23 CPR PD70 [1.2(1)].
24 FPR r 28.2(1).
25 In order to enforce a money judgment made elsewhere in the UK.

9.12 VAT is not charged on an order for fixed costs, but it is recoverable from the lay client by the solicitor.[26]

9.13 The parts of Table 5 which are relevant to family proceedings are specified in the table below and those enforcement methods are described in the following text:[27]

A	
On attendance to question a judgment debtor (or officer of a company or other corporation) who has been ordered to attend court under r 71.2[28] where the questioning takes place before a court officer, including attendance by a responsible representative of the legal representative	for each half hour or part, £15.00
B	
On the making of a final third party debt order under r 72.8(6)(a):[29]	
if the amount recovered is less than £150	one-half of the amount recovered
otherwise	£98.50
C	
On the making of a final charging order under FPR r 40.8(2)(a)[30]	£110.00 The court may also allow reasonable disbursements in respect of search fees and the registration of the order.
D	
Where a certificate is issued and registered under Sch 6 to the Civil Jurisdiction and Judgments Act 1982,[31] the costs of registration	£39.00

26 Middleton and Rowley, *Cook on Costs 2019* (Lexis Nexis, 2019) 2.19.

27 FPR r 33.2(b) omits CPR r 70.5 (Enforcement of decisions of bodies other than the High Court and the County Court and compromises enforceable by enactment).

28 CPR Pt 71 as amended by FPR r 33.23(2).

29 FPR r 33.24 incorporates CPR Pt 72 with amendments, including the omission of CPR r 72.10. As the introduction of FPR Pt 40 has removed the application of CPR Pt 73 to proceedings under FPR 33, the reference to costs associated with charging orders have been removed from this table.

30 FPR PD28A [3.2] states, 'References in CPR Parts 44 to 47 to other rules or Parts of the CPR shall be read, where there is an equivalent rule or Part in these Rules, to that equivalent rule or Part.' Thus, FPR r 40 applies here.

31 Enforcement of UK Judgments (Money Provisions).

E	
Where permission is given under r 83.13[32] to enforce a judgment or order giving possession of land and costs are allowed on the judgment or order, the amount to be added to the judgment or order for costs[33]	
(a) basic costs	£42.50
(b) where notice of the proceedings is to be to more than one person, for each additional person	£2.75
F	
Where a writ of control as defined in r 83.1(2)(k) is issued against any party	£51.75
G	
Where a writ of execution as defined in r 83.1(2)(l) is issued against any party	£51.75
H	
Where a request is filed for the issue of a warrant of control under r 83.15 for a sum exceeding £25	£2.25
I	
Where a request is filed for the issue of a warrant of delivery under r 83.15 for a sum exceeding £25	£2.25
J	
Where an application for an attachment of earnings order is made and costs are allowed under r 89.10 or CCR Order 28, r 10, for each attendance on the hearing of the application[34]	£8.50

A. Obtaining information from judgment debtors

9.14 In order to determine a judgment debtor's ability to pay sums due under an order or judgment, the judgment creditor may apply for an order to obtain information from the debtor. On request, the judgment creditor must pay the judgment debtor's reasonable expenses of travelling to court for the hearing.[35] CPR Pt 71 (with modifications) applies to such applications.[36]

9.15 According to Table 5 above, the fixed costs regime only applies when questioning takes place before a court officer. Therefore, on occasions when the questioning hearing is before a judge, there are no fixed costs for the hearing itself and the clean sheet rule will apply.

32 Enforcement in the High Court of a judgment or order for possession of land.
33 FPR r 33.1(2) incorporates CPR Pt 83 with amendments.
34 FPR r 33 Chapter 3 incorporates CCR Order 27 with amendments.
35 CPR r 71.4.
36 FPR r 33.23.

B. Third party debt orders

9.16 A third party debt order instructs a third party (typically a bank or building society) to pay out funds from the judgment debtor's account or accounts to the judgment creditor in order to satisfy the debt. FPR r 33.24 adopts CPR Pt 72 (with modifications) in respect to third party debt orders.

9.17 On succeeding in an application for a third party debt order, the fixed costs of the application are allowed and, if awarded, those costs may be recovered by the judgment creditor under the final third party debt order and they take precedence over the judgment debt.[37]

9.18 When served with an interim third party debt order, the deposit-taker (the bank or the building society) may deduct a sum from the debt towards its administrative and clerical costs[38] (thereby further reducing the sum received by the creditor). The maximum value of that sum is prescribed and stands currently at £55.[39]

C. Charging orders

9.19 A charging order is based upon statute and is now granted under the procedure set out at FPR Pt 40 Chapter 2; prior to 6 April 2016, CPR Pt 73 procedure was used. The order places a charge on the property (such as land, stocks or other funds) of the judgment debtor in respect to the outstanding sum owed to the judgment creditor under a judgment or order (including an order for costs) of the High Court or the Family Court.[40] Thus, the grant of a charging order serves to secure the debt[41] rather than to achieve its repayment. A judgment creditor may apply to enforce a charging order by sale of the charged property.

9.20 Under the Charging Orders Act 1979, a judgment or order of the High Court or the Family Court includes a judgment, order, decree or award of any court or arbitrator in the jurisdiction of England and Wales or in an overseas jurisdiction which is enforceable (whether in whole or in part) as if it were a judgment or order of the High Court or the Family Court.[42]

9.21 There is a limit to the extent to which a charging order may be granted when securing a costs order against a legally aided party's main or only dwelling in which they live. The order must secure an amount payable under the costs order (and including any interest due) only to the extent that the proceeds of

37 CPR r 72.11.

38 Senior Courts Act 1981, s 40A(1); County Courts Act 1984, s 109(1).

39 Attachment of Debts (Expenses) Order 1996, SI 1996/3098, art 2.

40 Charging Orders Act 1979, s 1(1).

41 *Re Exchange Travel (Holdings) Ltd (in liq) (No 3); Katz and others v McNally and others* [1997] 2 BCLC 579 at [590], CA per Phillips LJ: costs must be assessed before they may be secured by a charging order.

42 Charging Orders Act 1979, s 6(2).

sale of the legally aided party's interest after mortgage debts exceed £100,000. Further, the court must not make an order for sale of the dwelling in favour of the party who obtained the charging order.[43] These restrictions do not apply to property held in the name of a party who is not legally aided.

9.22 In addition to the fixed costs of a charging order, the court may award costs in respect to the reasonable disbursements paid to Her Majesty's Land Registry in respect to search fees and the registration of the charge. Even though not expressly stated in the order, the costs of enforcement (when assessed) may be added to the original debt, along with any interest that has accrued on that original debt, to calculate the value of the charge.[44] Enforcement of a charging order and the interest that accrues on the order are not affected by any limitation period.[45]

9.23 Under the Solicitors Act 1974,[46] a solicitor may secure the payment of their costs by applying for a charging order over a client's property. Under that Act, the definition of 'property' which may be subject to a charging order includes an order for costs which has not been assessed.[47] In *Harrison v Harrison*,[48] three Court of Appeal judges agreed that a sum ordered to be paid annually by a husband to a wife on their divorce was 'property' liable to a charging order in respect to the wife's solicitors' unpaid fees. However, the order was not granted as the court found the solicitors could not show that they had contracted with the wife to bind her separate estate and, therefore, the solicitors' costs were the husband's debt. The High Court also has an inherent jurisdiction to protect a solicitor, which enables a charging order to be granted to secure unpaid solicitors' costs and is helpful when those costs fall outside the provisions of the Solicitors Act 1974.[49]

E to I. Writs and warrants of control and writs of execution

9.24 CPR Pt 83 makes general provisions for writs and warrants (of control,[50] of execution,[51] of delivery and of possession) and Pt 84 deals specifically with enforcement by taking control of goods. Those Parts are adopted (with necessary modifications) by the FPR[52] to apply to applications made in the High Court and the Family Court to enforce orders granted in family proceedings.

43 Civil Legal Aid (Costs) Regulations 2013, SI 2013/611, reg 11.
44 *Ezekiel v Orakpo* [1997] 1 WLR 340, CA per Millett LJ.
45 *Ezekiel v Orakpo* [1997] 1 WLR 340, CA per Millett LJ.
46 Section 73.
47 *Fairfold Properties Ltd v Exmouth Docks Co Ltd (No 2)* [1993] Ch 196, [1992] 4 All ER 289.
48 (1888) 36 WR 748, [1886-90] All ER Rep Ext 1460, CA.
49 *Campbell v Campbell and Lewis* [1941] 1 All ER 274, CA, at [276–277] per Sir Wilfred Greene MR; *Re Fuld (deceased)* [1967] 2 All ER 649, P, D and Admlty, at [656].
50 CPR r 83.1(2)(j) and (k), read in accordance with the Tribunals, Courts and Enforcement Act 2007, s 62. 'Warrant of execution' is renamed 'warrant of control' under the Tribunals, Courts and Enforcement Act 2007, s 62(4)(b).
51 'Writ of execution' is defined at CPR r 83.1(2)(l) to include, amongst others, writs of possession, delivery and sequestration.
52 FPR r 33.1(2).

9.25 Since 6 April 2014,[53] the Tribunals, Courts and Enforcement Act 2007, s 62 and Sch 12 have specified the procedure to be used when taking control of goods to enforce an order or judgment for payment of money (including an assessed costs order) on the issue of a writ or warrant of control.

9.26 Writs may be issued by the Family Division of the High Court and warrants by the Family Court[54]. These measures enable an enforcement officer or bailiff, respectively, to seize and sell goods belonging to a debtor in order to repay the debt and to cover the costs of execution of the writ or warrant.

9.27 If the writ or warrant is issued for a debt before the costs element of that debt has been assessed then, after assessment, a further writ may be issued for the recovery of the costs.[55]

9.28 A party who is entitled to enforce a High Court judgment or order for the delivery of property (other than money) or for the possession of property may issue a separate writ of control to enforce the payment of costs due under that judgment or order.[56] Similarly, a party who is entitled to enforce a Family Court judgment or order by warrant of delivery may issue a separate warrant of control to enforce the payment of costs due under that judgment or order.[57]

9.29 Sequestration is considered at **9.53**.

J. Attachment of earnings orders

9.30 An attachment of earnings order may be appropriate if the judgment debtor is employed as it requires the debtor's employer to deduct a prescribed sum from the debtor's salary, on the payment date, and to remit that sum to the court.

9.31 The Attachment of Earnings Act 1971, gives the High Court and the Family Court the power to order an attachment of earnings to secure payments under a maintenance order.[58] Further, the Act specifies that references in the 'Act to sums payable under a judgment or order, or to the payment of such sums, includes a reference to costs and the payment of them'.[59]

9.32 The term 'maintenance order' is defined in the Attachment of Earnings Act 1971, s 2(a) as:

53 Tribunals, Courts and Enforcement Act 2007 (Commencement No 11) Order 2014, SI 2014/768, art 2(1).
54 MFPA 1984, s 31E(2).
55 CPR r 83.5(1) and (2).
56 CPR r 83.5(3).
57 CPR r 83.5(4).
58 Attachment of Earnings Act 1971, s 1(1) and (1A).
59 Section 25(2).

'any order, decision, settlement, arrangement or instrument specified in Schedule 1 to this Act and includes one which has been discharged or has otherwise ceased to operate if any arrears are recoverable thereunder.'

9.33 The Children Act 1989, Sch 1 specifies the following orders (in family proceedings) as applicable to the Attachment of Earnings Act 1971:

(a) An order for periodical or other payments made for a spouse or a child, or having effect as if made, under MCA 1973, Pt II (and any surviving orders made under the preceding provisions of Matrimonial Causes Act 1965, Pts II and III).

(b) An order for maintenance or other payments to or in respect of a spouse or child, made under the Domestic Proceedings and Magistrates' Court Act 1978, Pt I.

(c) An order for periodical or other payments made or having effect as if made under CA 1989, Sch 1.

(d) An order under CA 1989, Sch 2, Pt III, para 23 (contribution orders).

(e) An order to which the Maintenance Orders Act 1950, s 16 applies by virtue of ss (2)(b) or (c) of that section and which has been registered in a court in England and Wales under Pt II of that Act.

(f) A maintenance order within the meaning of the Maintenance Orders (Facilities for Enforcement) Act 1920 registered in, or confirmed by, a court in England and Wales under that Act.

(g) A maintenance order within the meaning of Pt I of the Maintenance Order (Reciprocal Enforcement) Act 1972 which has been registered in the Family Court under Pt I.

(h) A maintenance order within the meaning of Pt I of the Civil Jurisdiction and Judgments Act 1982 which is registered in the Family Court under that Part.

(i) A decision, court settlement or authentic instrument[60] which falls to be enforced by the Family Court by virtue of the Maintenance Regulation[61] and the Civil Jurisdiction and Judgments (Maintenance) Regulations 2011.

(j) An order made under CPA 2004, Sch 5 (for periodical or other payments) or Sch 6 (for maintenance or other payments to or in respect of a civil partner or child).

9.34 Under FPR r 33.19, the procedure set out in Pt 39 applies to applications for attachment of earnings orders to secure payments under a maintenance order. FPR r 39.12 sets out the position on costs:

60 'Decision', 'court settlement' and 'authentic instrument' have the meanings given by Article 2 of that Regulation.

61 'The Maintenance Regulation' means Council Regulation (EC) No 4/2009 including as applied in relation to Denmark by virtue of the Agreement made on 19 October 2005 between the European Community and the Kingdom of Denmark.

'(1) Where costs are allowed to the creditor on an application for an attachment of earnings order, there may be allowed —
   (a) a charge of a legal representative for preparing the application, attending the hearing and, if applicable, for serving the application; and
   (b) the court fee for issuing the application.

(2) The costs may be fixed and allowed without detailed assessment under CPR Pt 47.'

9.35 In addition to the judgment creditor's costs, an employer complying with the order may deduct from the debtor's earnings an additional £1 to cover administration and clerical costs.[62]

9.36 A judgment debtor who is employed by the armed forces may have maintenance payments due under a maintenance order (and the costs of enforcing the debt and any associated appeal) deducted from their earnings.[63]

Costs of service of documents

9.37 CPR r 45.8 also allows fixed sums for a legal representative's miscellaneous enforcement costs related to service of documents and these are listed at Table 4:[64]

For service by a party of any document other than the claim form required to be served personally including preparing and copying a certificate of service for each individual served	£15.00
Where service by an alternative method or at an alternative place is permitted by an order under r 6.15 for each individual served	£53.25
Where a document is served out of the jurisdiction –	
(a) in Scotland, Northern Ireland, the Isle of Man or the Channel Islands;	£68.25
(b) in any other place	£77.00

Enforcement costs outside the fixed costs regime

Appointment of a receiver

9.38 Where it is found to be just and convenient, the High Court and the Family Court may appoint a receiver to allow a judgment creditor to enforce a

62 Attachment of Earnings Act 1971, s 7(4)(a) as amended by Attachment of Earnings (Employer's Deduction) Order 1991, SI 1991/356, art 2.

63 Armed Forces Act 2006, s 342; Armed Forces (Forfeitures and Deductions) Regulations 2009, SI 2009/1109, regs 7–11.

64 CPR r 45.7.

debt.[65] The costs must have been assessed before enforcing a costs order in this way.[66] The receiver may collect sums to which the judgment debtor is entitled due to their interest in a property, and those sums may be paid to the judgment creditor. FPR r 33.22 adopts CPR Pt 69 in respect to the court's power to appoint receivers. Under CPR r 69.7, a receiver may only charge for their services if so directed by the court. The court may specify who shall pay the receiver's charges and the amount of those charges. Alternatively, the court may refer the determination of a receiver's fee to a costs judge. Such an appointment is expensive and, in most cases, is unlikely to be suitable to recover sums due under a costs order.

9.39 Mostyn J heard the case of *Maughan v Wilmot*[67] in which, amongst other things, the wife applied for the appointment of a receiver. The husband owed over £75,000 in respect to child maintenance and costs of just over £66,000 (which had been estimated by a costs draftsman but had still to be assessed).[68] The judge found the husband's reason for failing to pay was 'inexcusable'.[69] Accordingly, a receiver was appointed over the husband's assets, despite the judge noting that a receiver was usually an accountant charging sizeable hourly rates.[70]

Stop orders and notices

9.40 A judgment creditor can apply to the High Court for a stop order to prevent the judgment debtor dealing with the securities specified in the order.[71] The objective of such an order is to provide the creditor time to apply to the court to secure a judgment debt.

9.41 When served with a 'stop notice', the recipient must not take any of the steps identified in the notice in respect to the securities listed in the notice without first informing the person who has served the notice. This allows the judgment creditor an opportunity to assert their claim.[72]

Judgment summons and committal

9.42 When a judgment creditor is sure the judgment debtor has the means to pay sums due under an order or judgment, then it may be appropriate to apply to issue a judgment summons which can result in the debtor's committal to prison for a period of up to six weeks.[73] A successful application will not, of itself, lead

65 Senior Courts Act 1981, s 37(1) and (6).
66 *Willis v Cooper* (1900) 44 Sol Jo 698, CA.
67 [2014] EWHC 1288 (Fam), [2015] 1 FLR 567.
68 At [19].
69 At [20].
70 At [18].
71 Charging Orders Act 1979, s 5; FPR Pt 40, Chapter 3.
72 Charging Orders Act 1979, s 5; FPR Pt 40, Chapter 4.
73 Debtors Act 1869, s 5(1).

to payment of the debt but it may provide the debtor with a strong inducement to pay up.

9.43 The Family Court's power of committal due to failure to pay a debt or an instalment of a debt due under a judgment or order comes from the Debtors Act 1869, s 5 and is restricted by the Administration of Justice Act 1970 ('AJA 1979'), s 11. The power may only be exercised in respect to enforcement of a High Court or Family Court maintenance order[74] as specified in AJA 1970, Sch 8. However, FPR Pt 39, Chapter 2 sets out the procedure rules for committal by way of judgment summons and interprets 'order' as, 'an order made in family proceedings for the payment of money'.[75] Further, as FPR r 33.16(1)(a) refers to the hearing of a judgment summons in respect to an order for costs, this point must be arguable. Indeed, in *Migliaccio* Mostyn J sets out a comprehensive argument in support of enforcing a costs order by judgment summons.[76]

9.44 The Debtors Act 1869, s 5, allows a judgment creditor to apply for a judgment debtor to attend court. At the consequent hearing, the judgment creditor will be required to prove to the criminal standard[77] that the judgment debtor has the means to pay what is due and has refused or neglected to do so and maintains that stance.[78] Under the County Courts Act 1984, s 110(4) and FPR r 33.14A, if a debtor fails to attend court after being summoned by judgment summons and the judgment creditor has not paid or offered to pay the debtor's reasonable costs of travelling to and from the court, the debtor may not be committed for their failure to attend.

9.45 At the hearing of the judgment summons, the court may order the debtor to pay the costs of the judgment summons (along with any unpaid sums due under the original order) to the creditor by a prescribed time or by instalments.[79] The court may also make an attachment of earnings order at the hearing.[80] In the High Court, at the hearing of a judgment summons attended by the debtor and at which the court does not make an order for committal, the court may grant the debtor their 'proper costs including compensation for any loss of earnings'.[81]

9.46 After the Court of Appeal's judgment in *Prest v Prest*,[82] Mostyn J determined the case of *Migliaccio*[83] and disagreed with McFarlane LJ's obiter

74 Defined at Administration of Justice Act 1970, s 28(1) as 'a maintenance order enforceable by the High Court and the family court', where a 'maintenance order' means 'any order, decision, settlement, arrangement or instrument specified in Schedule 8 to this Act and includes one which has been discharged or has otherwise ceased to operate, if any arrears are recoverable thereunder'.

75 FPR r 33.9.

76 *Migliaccio v Migliaccio* [2016] EWHC 1055 (Fam), at [30–42].

77 *Prest v Prest* [2014] EWHC 3430 (Fam), at [61].

78 Debtors Act 1869, s 5; FPR r 33.14(1) and *Quan v Bray* [2019] EWFC 46, at [11] per Holman J.

79 FPR r 33.16(1) and (2).

80 Family Proceedings Fees Order 2008, SI 2008/1054, Sch 1, Fee 12.5.

81 FPR r 33.17(3).

82 [2015] EWCA Civ 714.

83 *Migliaccio v Migliaccio* [2016] EWHC 1055 (Fam).

comments about the standard of proof to be applied in determining the debtor's ability to pay. McFarlane LJ opposed the position that:

> 'it is simply sufficient to rely upon findings as to wealth made on the civil standard of proof in the original proceedings and that those findings, coupled with proof of non-payment, is sufficient to establish a "burden" on the respondent which can only be discharged if he or she enters the witness box and proffers a credible explanation.'[84]

9.47 Rather, McFarlane LJ set out the matters the court must consider as:

> 'a) The fact that the respondent has or has had, since the date of the order or judgment, the means to pay the sum due must be proved to the criminal standard of proof;
>
> b) The fact that the respondent has refused or neglected, or refuses or neglects, to pay the sum due must also be proved to the criminal standard;
>
> c) The burden of proof is at all times on the applicant; and
>
> d) The respondent cannot be compelled to give evidence.'[85]

9.48 These cases have led to some interesting commentary scrutinising the Court of Appeal judgments in *Prest* and the earlier case of *Karoonian v CMEC*[86] and concluding that, whilst there may be need for further legal clarification regarding judgment summons procedure, practitioners may be best advised to follow the principles set out in *Prest*.[87]

Statutory demands and bankruptcy proceedings

9.49 A statutory demand may be made for a payment (of £750 or more) overdue under a court order or judgment.[88] If either:

(a) the debt is not paid within 21 days of service of the demand;

(b) the debtor has not agreed a settlement with the creditor; or

(c) the debtor has not applied to set aside the demand

then the creditor may petition for bankruptcy.

9.50 Since Insolvency Rule 12.3(2)(a) was amended on 1 April 2005, 'an obligation to pay a lump sum or to pay costs arising under an order made in family proceedings' is provable and may therefore found a petition for bankruptcy.[89]

84 At [55].
85 At [55].
86 *Karoonian v CMEC; Gibbons v CMEC* [2012] EWCA Civ 1379.
87 Murray, 'The evidential burden in judgment summons hearings: *Migliaccio*' [2016] Fam Law 1017.
88 Insolvency Act 1986, s 268(1)(a).
89 Insolvency (Amendment) Rules 2005, SI 2005/527, r 44; debts related to periodical payments ordered in family proceedings remain unprovable unless it is shown that exceptional circumstances exist.

9.51 On discharge from bankruptcy, the bankrupt is not discharged from arrears of the unpaid costs of family proceedings.[90] A costs order is therefore both provable in bankruptcy and, if unpaid, survives bankruptcy.

9.52 At a creditors' meeting to discuss an Individual Voluntary Arrangement (IVA), a creditor whose claim relates to unassessed costs may vote[91] as their claim is for an unliquidated sum.[92]

Sequestration

9.53 Sequestration is the act of seizing assets belonging to a judgment debtor when that debtor is in contempt of court by failing to comply with an order. This form of enforcement may be used to enforce an assessed costs order. An application for a writ of sequestration should be made in the High Court under FPR Pt 37, Chapter 6.[93]

Enforcement of financial undertakings and recitals

9.54 Undertakings may be subject to enforcement procedures such as third party debt orders[94] and judgment summonses,[95] but not by committal for contempt of court.[96]

Enforcing the debt of a deceased judgment debtor

9.55 An order for costs, whether or not it has been assessed, may be enforced against a deceased debtor's estate.[97]

Enforcing costs in a publicly funded case

9.56 Under LASPO 2012, provisions are made[98] for the creation of regulations to enforce obligations to pay for legal aid services.[99] Such regulations may allow for the recovery of costs incurred in enforcing such obligations[100] and may state

90 Insolvency Act 1986, s 281(5)(b).
91 Insolvency Act 1986, s 257.
92 *Re Bradley-Hole (a bankrupt)* [1995] 4 All ER 865, Ch.
93 See also CPR r 83.2A, adopted by FPR r 33.1(2).
94 *Gandolfo v Gandolfo* [1981] QB 359, 367 per Browne LJ.
95 Where the undertaking is an integral and indivisible part of the order: *Symmons v Symmons* [1993] 1 FLR 317 Fam, 321 per Hunter J.
96 *Buckley v Crawford* [1893] 1 QB 105, 107 per Wills J.
97 *Mosey v Mosey and Barker* [1956] P 26, 40.
98 LASPO 2012, s 24(1).
99 LASPO 2012, s 23.
100 LASPO 2012, s 24(2).

that overdue payments and sums can be recovered summarily as a civil debt[101] or as if they were to be paid under a High Court order.[102] The regulations may also require the provision of information and documents.[103] As yet, no such regulations have been made in respect to payment for civil legal aid services.

COSTS OF ENFORCING NON-FINANCIAL ORDERS

9.57 A review of the reported cases may lead to the conclusion that costs are rarely ordered in applications to enforce non-financial orders. Clearly though, such applications for costs may be made and they can succeed. In circumstances where the offending party is not impecunious (and therefore the order will not adversely affect the child's welfare) and the offence is serious, a court may be persuaded to grant the order.

Enforcement of non-financial orders and undertakings by committal

9.58 The court may commit a party to prison for failure to comply with an order or undertaking.[104] The procedure in applying for committal for a failure to comply with an order made under the FPR, is set out at FPR Pt 37[105] and is augmented by PD37. Otherwise, CPR Pt 81 relates to an application made during civil proceedings, say in relation to the Protection from Harassment Act 1997 or TLATA 1996.

9.59 In *Re A Solicitor (Disclosure of Confidential Records)*,[106] Johnson J ordered a firm of solicitors to pay the costs (on an indemnity basis) of the Official Solicitor in making the committal application. This followed an application for committal brought by the Official Solicitor due to the firm of solicitors having breached a court order by wrongly disclosing medical records.

Child arrangements orders

9.60 The rules of enforcement of child arrangement orders are provided for in the Children Act 1989, ss 11J–11P. A party's failure to comply with the terms of a child arrangements order may result in the court making an enforcement order against that party which requires compensation to be paid for any financial loss caused as a result of the breach.[107]

101 LASPO 2012, s 24(3)(a).
102 LASPO 2012, s 24(3)(b).
103 LASPO 2012, s 24(4).
104 FPR r 37.4(1) and (4).
105 FPR r 33.5.
106 [1997] 1 FLR 101.
107 CA 1989, s 110(2).

Enforcement of execution of documents

9.61 A court may order that a document must be executed by a nominee if a person previously ordered to do so has neglected or refused to comply with the order or cannot reasonably be found.[108] The non-compliant person may also be liable for the associated costs.

ENFORCING INTERNATIONAL ORDERS

Enforcement of international orders under statute

9.62 The field of international enforcement of orders and judgments is far from straightforward (and not the subject of this book), therefore what follows is merely a brief summary as to the main methods of enforcing international orders and some of the cost implications of so doing.

9.63 Orders (including maintenance orders) from one jurisdiction may be enforced in a different jurisdiction. However, the procedure used to do so differs according to the countries concerned, the circumstances of the judgment debtor, the nature of the order and when the judgment was handed down, amongst other things.[109] Foreign orders should be registered in England and Wales, where possible, and they may then be enforced in the same manner as an order originally made in this jurisdiction. Where such registration is not possible, then the common law may provide an alternative means of enforcement. In other instances, MFPA 1984, Pt III may enable enforcement of a foreign order.[110] There are provisions in FPR Pts 31 and 34 and CPR Pt 74 regarding international enforcement.

9.64 Clearly, understanding how to enforce a foreign order can be complicated. The danger of misinterpreting the rules and procedures was illustrated in *K v K*,[111] where a mother sought to enforce a Russian order in this jurisdiction under the provisions of the 1996 Hague Convention. However, the Russian order was made just over two months before the date from which the Convention was in force between the two jurisdictions. Despite receiving advice to withdraw from her English solicitors, the mother relied upon advice from a Russian lawyer and continued to pursue the enforcement action for some time. As a result, MacDonald J ordered her to pay the father's costs which he summarily assessed at £3,737.50. Perhaps surprisingly, although the matter related to a single issue of law, the father's statement of costs came to over £38,000 and that of the mother nearly £23,000.

9.65 The Reciprocal Enforcement of Maintenance Orders (REMO) Unit is the central authority which helps those in England and Wales to register and to enforce child maintenance orders internationally.[112]

108 Senior Courts Act 1981, s 39 and MFPA, s 31E(1).
109 See also FPR Pt 34 and the associated PDs.
110 *Jordan v Jordan* [2000] 1 WLR 210, [1999] 2 FLR 1069, CA at [214] per Thorpe LJ.
111 [2016] EWHC 2002 (Fam) and **8.65**.
112 https://www.gov.uk/child-maintenance-if-one-parent-lives-abroad/other-partner-lives-abroad.

9.66 As to which foreign enforcement procedures may be classed as family proceedings in the High Court, the Senior Courts Act 1981[113] refers only to:

'(f) …

(v) Council Regulation (EC) No 2201/2003 of 27th November 2003[114] concerning jurisdiction and the recognition and enforcement of judgments in matrimonial matters and matters of parental responsibility, so far as that Regulation relates to jurisdiction, recognition and enforcement in parental responsibility matters;

(vi) the Convention on Jurisdiction, Applicable Law, Recognition, Enforcement and Co-Operation in respect of Parental Responsibility and Measures for the Protection of Children that was signed at The Hague on 19 October 1996;[115] …

(l) proceedings under Regulation (EU) No 606/2013 of the European Parliament and of the Council of 12 June 2013 on mutual recognition of protection measures in civil matters, so far as relating to the recognition and enforcement in England and Wales of a protection measure (within the meaning of that Regulation) ordered in a Member State other than the United Kingdom.'

9.67 These and a number of other statutes, rules and precedents relate to the reciprocal enforcement of foreign orders, and the most common of these are described briefly in the table below.

Statutory provision:	**What is enforced:**	**Provision as to enforcing costs orders and costs of enforcement:**
Administration of Justice Act 1920 (AJA 1920), Pt II	The Act allows reciprocal enforcement between certain Commonwealth countries of judgments or orders made in superior courts[116] and requiring a money payment (or of arbitration awards where they are enforceable in the same manner as a court judgment); thus, maintenance and lump sum payments may be enforced.[117]	An application must be made to register a foreign judgment in England and Wales and 'the reasonable costs of and incidental to the registration of the judgment (including the costs of obtaining a certified copy of the judgment from the original court and of the application for registration) are recoverable in like manner as if they were sums payable under the judgment.'[118]

113 Sch 1, para 3.

114 Known as 'Brussels IIA'.

115 Known as the 'Hague Convention 1996'.

116 'Any of the higher courts of the legal system, whose jurisdiction is not limited, for example, by geography or by value of claim and whose decisions have weight as precedents': Law, A Dictionary of Law (9th edn, Oxford University Press, 2018).

117 AJA 1920, s 12(1).

118 AJA 1920, s 9(3)(c).

Statutory provision:	**What is enforced:**	**Provision as to enforcing costs orders and costs of enforcement:**
		A creditor may prefer to enforce a foreign judgment under the common law; however, they will not generally be entitled to recover the costs of that action.[119]
Maintenance Orders (Facilities for Enforcement) Act 1920 (MO(FE)A 1920)	The Act is to be repealed at a date to be appointed by the Maintenance Orders (Reciprocal Enforcement) Act 1972 (MO(RE)A 1972)[120] and, in the meantime, applies to maintenance orders (periodical payments only)[121] and to Commonwealth countries not yet reciprocating under MO(RE)A 1972.[122]	No fee is charged for applications under this Act.
Foreign Judgments (Reciprocal Enforcement) Act 1933 (FJ(RE)A 1933), Pt I	The Act allows reciprocal enforcement of judgments for a sum of money (thus a lump sum but not maintenance payments)[123] between this jurisdiction and a number of others.	The costs of applying to register the judgment and incidental costs, ie of obtaining a certified copy of the judgment from the original court, are added to the original judgment debt.[124] The applicant may be required to pay security for costs.[125] Final costs orders may be enforced.
Maintenance Orders Act 1950 (MOA 1950)	The Act enables reciprocal enforcement of maintenance orders (periodical payments and lump sum orders)[126] between England and Wales, Scotland and Northern Ireland.	An application for registration of an order under may be made by a court officer at the request of the person entitled to payments under the order. However, the person at whose request the application is made shall be liable for costs properly incurred as if they had made the application.[127]

119 AJA 1920, s 9(5).
120 MO(RE)A 1972, s 22(2)(a).
121 MO(RE)A 1972, s 10.
122 Reciprocating countries listed in the Maintenance Orders (Facilities for Enforcement) Order 1959, SI 1959/377, Sch 1 (as amended).
123 FJ(RE)A 1933, s 11(1).
124 FJ(RE)A 1933, s 2(6).
125 FJ(RE)A 1933, s 3(1)(a).
126 MOA 1950, s 16(2) and see procedure at FPR Pt 32, Ch 2.
127 MOA 1950, s 17(6).

Statutory provision:	**What is enforced:**	**Provision as to enforcing costs orders and costs of enforcement:**
1968 Brussels Convention[128] Convention on jurisdiction and the enforcement of judgments in civil and commercial matters (as amended by various Accession Conventions) signed at Brussels on 27 September 1968 (known as the 'Brussels Convention').	The Brussels Convention was largely replaced by Brussels I[129] such that it applies only to territories of EU member states that are excluded from the European Community and the jurisdiction of Brussels I (ie Aruba and the French overseas territories).[130]	'Judgment' means any judgment given by a court or tribunal of a contracting state, whatever the judgment may be called, including the determination of costs or expenses by an officer of the court.[131]
Maintenance Orders (Reciprocal Enforcement) Act 1972 (MO(RE)A 1972) The Act largely replaces MO(FE)A 1920.	MO(RE)A 1972, Pt 1 provides for reciprocity of enforcement of maintenance orders relating to lump sum and periodical payments[132] between UK jurisdictions[133] and certain other countries (including parties to the 1973 Hague Convention and the USA[134]). MO(RE)A 1972, Pt 2 stipulates reciprocal principles for the enforcement of maintenance claims between UK residents and parties who reside in or have assets in a signatory state to the United Nations 1956 Convention on the Recovery Abroad of Maintenance[135] or another country specified by Order in Council.[136]	Not specified.

128 https://eur-lex.europa.eu/legal-content/SL/TXT/?uri=CELEX:41968A0927(01) .

129 Brussels I itself has been replaced by EU Regulation No 1215/2012.

130 Explanatory note to Civil Jurisdiction and Judgments Regulations 2007, SI 2007/1655.

131 Art 25.

132 MO(RE)A 1972, s 21(1)–(2).

133 England and Wales, Scotland and Northern Ireland: Interpretation Act 1978, s 5, Sch 1; and Jersey: Reciprocal Enforcement of Maintenance Orders (Designation of Reciprocating Countries) Order 2008, SI 2008/1202, art 3.

134 With some modifications: Reciprocal Enforcement of Maintenance Orders (United States of America) Order 2007 (SI 2007/2005). The 2007 Hague Convention, Article 48 replaces MO(RE)A 1972 in respect to the USA wherever the scope corresponds.

135 New York, 20 June 1956.

136 MO(RE)A 1972, s 25.

Statutory provision:	What is enforced:	Provision as to enforcing costs orders and costs of enforcement:
1980 European Convention on Child Custody European Convention on Recognition and Enforcement of Decisions concerning Custody of Children and on the Restoration of Custody of Children, signed in Luxembourg on 20 May 1980.	A Convention signed by the member states of the Council of Europe making provisions to enable the custody of children which has been arbitrarily interrupted to be restored. Mostly superseded by Brussels IIA and the 1996 Hague Convention, this Convention now has limited application in respect to Denmark only.	Other than the cost of repatriation, each contracting state will not claim any payment from an applicant in respect of any measures taken under Art 5, para 1 (to take or cause to be taken all steps which it considers to be appropriate, if necessary by instituting proceedings before its competent authorities, in order: to discover the whereabouts of the child; to avoid prejudice to the interests of the child or of the applicant; to secure the recognition or enforcement of the decision; to secure the delivery of the child to the applicant where enforcement is granted; to inform the requesting authority of the measures taken and their results)[137] by the central authority of that state on the applicant's behalf, including the costs of proceedings and, where applicable, the costs incurred by the assistance of a lawyer.[138]

137 European Treaty Series, No. 105, Art 5.1.
138 European Treaty Series, No. 105, Art 5.3.

Statutory provision:	**What is enforced:**	**Provision as to enforcing costs orders and costs of enforcement:**
1980 Hague Convention Convention on the Civil Aspects of International Child Abduction, signed at The Hague on 25 October 1980.[139]	A Convention to protect children internationally from the harmful effects of their wrongful removal or retention and to establish procedures to ensure their prompt return to the state of their habitual residence, as well as to secure protection for rights of access. There are over 100 contracting states to the Convention.[140]	No charges will be levied in relation to applications submitted under this Convention. The applicant is not required to pay towards the costs and expenses of the proceedings or, where applicable, those arising from the participation of legal counsel or advisers. Payment of the expenses incurred or to be incurred in implementing the return of the child may be required.[141] The UK has made a declaration that it shall not be bound to assume any costs referred to in Art 26, para 2 of the Convention resulting from the participation of legal counsel or advisers or from court proceedings, except insofar as those costs may be covered by its system of legal aid and advice. Upon ordering the return of a child or issuing an order concerning rights of access under this Convention, the person who removed or retained the child, or who prevented the exercise of rights of access, may be directed to pay necessary expenses incurred by or on behalf of the applicant, including travel expenses, any costs incurred or payments made for locating the child, the costs of legal representation of the applicant, and those of returning the child.[142]

139 https://www.hcch.net/en/instruments/conventions/full-text/?cid=24.
140 The current status table is at: https://www.hcch.net/en/instruments/conventions/status-table/?cid=24.
141 Article 26.
142 Article 26.

Statutory provision:	**What is enforced:**	**Provision as to enforcing costs orders and costs of enforcement:**
Civil Jurisdiction and Judgments Act 1982 (CJJA 1982)	CJJA 1982, Pt 1 allows enforcement of judgments and maintenance orders registered under the 2007 Lugano Convention and certain other European conventions.[143]	Pt 1: Where a judgment, other than a maintenance order, is registered under the Lugano Convention or the 1968 Brussels Convention, the reasonable costs or expenses of and incidental to its registration are recoverable as if they were sums recoverable under the judgment.[144] Where a certificate is issued and registered under the CJJA 1982, Sch 6, the costs of registration are fixed at £39.[145]
	CJJA, Pt 2 allows reciprocal enforcement of both money and non-money judgments and orders (including orders for costs) across the UK jurisdictions,[146] other than those (such as lump sum or periodical payment orders) which may be enforced under the MOA 1950.[147]	Pt 2: Once a certificate is registered under the CJJA 1982, the reasonable costs and expenses in relation to obtaining and registering the certificate (and, if required, to obtaining a certified copy of the judgment) are recoverable in addition to any original debt and on the same basis as if they had been ordered under the original order or judgment.[148]
1996 Hague Convention on Jurisdiction, Applicable Law, Recognition, Enforcement and Co-operation in Respect of Parental Responsibility and Measures for the Protection of Children	The Convention[149] deals with child protection and parental responsibility and allows the enforcement of measures between Contracting States.[150]	States must bear the costs of their own services and there is no provision for publicly funded legal aid.

143 CJJA 1982, ss 4A and 5A.
144 CJJA 1982, ss 4(1), 4A(1) and 7(3).
145 CPR r 45.8, Table 5.
146 CJJA 1982, s 18(1) and (2). UK jurisdictions: England and Wales, Scotland and Northern Ireland.
147 CJJA 1982, s 18(5)(a) and MOA 1950, s 16.
148 CJJA 1982, Sch 6, para 7 and Sch 7, para 7.
149 In force in the UK since 1 November 2012.
150 At the time of writing, there are 52 contracting parties. The current status table is at: https://www.hcch.net/en/instruments/conventions/status-table/?cid=70.

Statutory provision:	**What is enforced:**	**Provision as to enforcing costs orders and costs of enforcement:**
2003 Brussels Regulation Council Regulation (EC) No 2201/2003 of 27 November 2003 concerning jurisdiction and the recognition and enforcement of judgments in matrimonial matters and the matters of parental responsibility (known as 'Brussels IIA'), repealing Reg (EC) No 1347/2000 ('Brussels I').	The Regulation binds member states (other than Denmark)[151] and accession states and has been in force since 1 August 2004.[152] It enables the enforcement of orders related to matrimonial finance, contact and parental responsibility across the jurisdictions.	The provisions of Ch III (recognition and enforcement), except s 4 (rights of access and certain judgments requiring the return of the child), apply to the determination of the amount of costs and expenses of proceedings under this Regulation and to the enforcement of any order concerning such costs and expenses.[153]
European Enforcement Order (EEO Regulation) (EC) No 805/2004 of 21 April 2004 creating a European Enforcement Order for uncontested claims.	Since the EU Maintenance Regulation came into force, this no longer applies to maintenance orders. It applies to judgments obtained in default of a defence or an objection.	Under the Order, 'judgment' is defined as any judgment given by a court or tribunal of a Member State, whatever the judgment may be called, including a decree, order, decision or writ of execution, as well as the determination of costs or expenses by an officer of the court.[154] Where a judgment includes an enforceable decision on the amount of costs related to the court proceedings, including interest rates, it shall be certified as an EEO also with regard to the costs unless the debtor has specifically objected to their obligation to bear such costs in the course of the court proceedings, in accordance with the law of the Member State of origin.[155]

151 (EC) No 2201/2003, Preamble, para 31.
152 (EC) No 2201/2003, art 72.
153 (EC) No 2201/2003, art 49.
154 (EC) No 805/2004, art 4, para 1.
155 (EC) No 805/2004, art 7.

Statutory provision:	What is enforced:	Provision as to enforcing costs orders and costs of enforcement:
2007 Hague Convention Convention on the international recovery of child support and other forms of family maintenance concluded at The Hague on 23 November 2007.[156]	The Convention applies to the enforcement of family maintenance orders between the UK and non-EU contracting states.[157]	Determinations of costs or expenses may be enforced.[158] The recovery of costs incurred in the application do not take precedence over the recovery of maintenance.[159] Various other provisions are made as to costs.[160]
2007 Lugano Regulation[161] Convention on jurisdiction and the recognition and enforcement of judgments in civil and commercial matters, signed on behalf of the European Community on 30 October 2007, between the European Community, Iceland, Norway, and Switzerland.	The Regulation has been superseded by Brussels I,[162] but still applies to non-EU member states.[163]	Under the Convention, 'judgment' includes the determination of costs by a court officer.[164] There are provisions regarding entitlement to legal aid and exemption from costs.[165] Security for costs is not required.[166]

156 Replacing the 1973 Hague Convention.
157 The current status table is at: https://www.hcch.net/en/instruments/conventions/status-table/?cid=131. EU Member States rely upon the EU Maintenance Regulation.
158 Article 19(1).
159 Article 43(1).
160 Articles 8, 14, 45 and 46.
161 OJ L 339, 21.12.2007.
162 Brussels I itself has been replaced by EU Regulation No 1215/2012.
163 Iceland, Norway and Switzerland.
164 Article 32.
165 Article 50.
166 Article 51.

Statutory provision:	**What is enforced:**	**Provision as to enforcing costs orders and costs of enforcement:**
EU Maintenance Regulation Council Regulation (EC) No 4/2009 of 18 December 2008 on jurisdiction, applicable law, recognition and enforcement of decisions and co-operation in matters relating to maintenance obligations.[167]	On 18 June 2011,[168] this Regulation replaced the Brussels I maintenance obligations.[169] It applies to enforcement within the EU of orders and administratively made decisions,[170] and overrides domestic law and international conventions.	'Decision' includes a decision by an officer of the court determining the costs or expenses.[171] Recovery of costs incurred in the application do not take precedence over the recovery of maintenance.[172] There is an entitlement to non-means tested legal aid and exemption from costs. [173] Security for costs is not required.[174] Exceptionally, a Member State may recover costs from an unsuccessful party who has received free legal aid.[175]
EU Regulation No 1215/2012[176]	This Regulation applies from 10 January 2015 to all EU Member States and to money judgments other than: maintenance obligations; and rights in property arising out of a matrimonial relationship or out of a relationship deemed by the law applicable to such relationship to have comparable effects to marriage.[177]	Under the Regulation, 'judgment' means any judgment given by a court or tribunal of a Member State, whatever the judgment may be called, including a decree, order, decision or writ of execution, as well as a decision on the determination of costs or expenses by an officer of the court.[178] The applicant must provide the enforcement authority with relevant information on the recoverable costs of the proceedings.[179]

167 (EC) No 4/2009, art 1, para 1: Applies to maintenance relationship, parentage, marriage or affinity. See also FPR Pt 38.
168 (EC) No 4/2009, art 76.
169 Preamble, para 44, art 68(1).
170 (EC) No 4/2009, art 2(1)(1).
171 (EC) No 4/2009, art 2(1)(1).
172 (EC) No 4/2009, art 43.
173 (EC) No 4/2009, art 45.
174 (EC) No 4/2009, art 44(5).
175 (EC) No 4/2009, art 67.
176 Replacing (EC) No 44/2001 (which was known as 'Brussels I').
177 (EC) No 1215/2012, art 1, para 2.
178 (EC) No 1215/2012, art 2(a).
179 (EC) No 1215/2012, art 42, para 1(b).

Statutory provision:	**What is enforced:**	**Provision as to enforcing costs orders and costs of enforcement:**
EU Regulation No 606/2013 of 12 June 2013 on mutual recognition of protection measures in civil matters.	The Regulation has been in force since 11 January 2015, and allows a person with the benefit of a protective measure to enforce that measure in other EU Member States (except Denmark)[180] (eg non-molestation orders, occupation orders and forced marriage protection orders made under the FLA 1996, Pt 4, and undertakings accepted under that Act and injunctions granted in family proceedings under the Protection from Harassment Act 1997).	Not specified.

Enforcement of international orders under the common law

9.68 The jurisdiction of England and Wales does not have statutory reciprocal arrangements with all foreign jurisdictions. Nevertheless, a foreign costs order may be enforced without the need of any reciprocal procedure, under the common law.[181] There are two conditions for enforcement:

(a) the foreign judgment must be for a definite sum of money;[182] and

(b) the foreign judgment must be final and conclusive.[183]

9.69 Therefore, an order for costs must have been assessed or be capable of calculation by a straightforward mathematical computation.[184]

9.70 Enforcement under the common law is prohibited if the judgment could be registered under FJ(RE)A 1933, s 6. Further, if the judgment could be registered under AJA 1920, s 9(5) and common law enforcement is sought, then costs are not usually awarded unless the registration application was refused or the court ordered otherwise.

180 (EC) No 606/2013, Preamble, para 41.

181 *Schibsby v Westenholz* (1870) LR 6 QB 155 at [158–159].

182 *Beatty v Beatty* [1924] 1 KB 807, CA, at [816] per Scrutton LJ .

183 *Joint Stock Company 'Aeroflot-Russian Airlines' v Berezovsky and another* [2014] EWCA Civ 20, at [2] per Arden LJ.

184 *Beatty v Beatty* [1924] 1 KB 807, CA,at [816] per Scrutton LJ in respect to costs in divorce proceedings.

COURT FEES FOR ENFORCEMENT PROCEEDINGS

9.71 The table below sets out the court fees payable in relation to enforcement in family proceedings:[185]

Application to question a judgment debtor or other person	£50
Application for a third party debt order[186] or appointment of a receiver	£100
Application for a charging order[187]	£100
Application for a judgment summons	£100
Application for an attachment of earnings order[188]	£100
Enforcement in the Family Court Application for enforcement of a judgment or order	£100
Application for an order for such method of enforcement as the court may consider appropriate	£50
Request for attempt at execution of a warrant at a new address	£30
Issue for a warrant of possession or a warrant of delivery[189]	£110
To issue a warrant of control (recovery of a sum of money)	£100
Enforcement in the High Court Sealing a writ of control or possession or delivery[190]	£60
Request or application to register a judgment or order	£60
Permission to enforce an arbitration award	£60
Certified copy of a judgment or order for use abroad	£60
Method of enforcement as the court may consider appropriate – application	£50
Request for service by a bailiff of a document subject to exceptions listed in the order	£110
An application for an enforcement order under Children Act 1989 or an order for compensation for financial loss, due to the breakdown of a child arrangement order	£215

185 Taken from: Form EX50 Civil and Family Court Fees From March 2019, HMCTS and Form EX50A: July 2019, Ministry of Justice.

186 Payable in respect of each third party against whom the order is sought.

187 Payable in respect of each charging order applied for.

188 Payable in respect of each defendant against whom an order is sought. Not payable where the attachment of earnings order is made on the hearing of a judgment summons.

189 Where the recovery of a sum of money is sought in addition, no further fee is payable.

190 Where the recovery of a sum of money is sought in addition to a writ of possession or delivery, no further fee is payable.

APPENDIX 1

Statutes, Procedural Rules and Practice Directions

MATRIMONIAL CAUSES ACT 1973

22ZA Orders for payment in respect of legal services

(1) In proceedings for divorce, nullity of marriage or judicial separation, the court may make an order or orders requiring one party to the marriage to pay to the other ('the applicant') an amount for the purpose of enabling the applicant to obtain legal services for the purposes of the proceedings.

(2) The court may also make such an order or orders in proceedings under this Part for financial relief in connection with proceedings for divorce, nullity of marriage or judicial separation.

(3) The court must not make an order under this section unless it is satisfied that, without the amount, the applicant would not reasonably be able to obtain appropriate legal services for the purposes of the proceedings or any part of the proceedings.

(4) For the purposes of subsection (3), the court must be satisfied, in particular, that—
   (a) the applicant is not reasonably able to secure a loan to pay for the services, and
   (b) the applicant is unlikely to be able to obtain the services by granting a charge over any assets recovered in the proceedings.

(5) An order under this section may be made for the purpose of enabling the applicant to obtain legal services of a specified description, including legal services provided in a specified period or for the purposes of a specified part of the proceedings.

(6) An order under this section may—
   (a) provide for the payment of all or part of the amount by instalments of specified amounts, and
   (b) require the instalments to be secured to the satisfaction of the court.

(7) An order under this section may direct that payment of all or part of the amount is to be deferred.

(8) The court may at any time in the proceedings vary an order made under this section if it considers that there has been a material change of circumstances since the order was made.

(9) For the purposes of the assessment of costs in the proceedings, the applicant's costs are to be treated as reduced by any amount paid to the applicant pursuant to an order under this section for the purposes of those proceedings.

(10) In this section 'legal services', in relation to proceedings, means the following types of services—

(a) providing advice as to how the law applies in the particular circumstances,

(b) providing advice and assistance in relation to the proceedings,

(c) providing other advice and assistance in relation to the settlement or other resolution of the dispute that is the subject of the proceedings, and

(d) providing advice and assistance in relation to the enforcement of decisions in the proceedings or as part of the settlement or resolution of the dispute,

and they include, in particular, advice and assistance in the form of representation and any form of dispute resolution, including mediation.

(11) In subsections (5) and (6) 'specified' means specified in the order concerned.

22ZB Matters to which court is to have regard in deciding how to exercise power under section 22ZA

(1) When considering whether to make or vary an order under section 22ZA, the court must have regard to—

(a) the income, earning capacity, property and other financial resources which each of the applicant and the paying party has or is likely to have in the foreseeable future,

(b) the financial needs, obligations and responsibilities which each of the applicant and the paying party has or is likely to have in the foreseeable future,

(c) the subject matter of the proceedings, including the matters in issue in them,

(d) whether the paying party is legally represented in the proceedings,

(e) any steps taken by the applicant to avoid all or part of the proceedings, whether by proposing or considering mediation or otherwise,

(f) the applicant's conduct in relation to the proceedings,

(g) any amount owed by the applicant to the paying party in respect of costs in the proceedings or other proceedings to which both the applicant and the paying party are or were party, and

(h) the effect of the order or variation on the paying party.

(2) In subsection (1)(a) 'earning capacity', in relation to the applicant or the paying party, includes any increase in earning capacity which, in the opinion of the court, it would be reasonable to expect the applicant or the paying party to take steps to acquire.

(3) For the purposes of subsection (1)(h), the court must have regard, in particular, to whether the making or variation of the order is likely to—

(a) cause undue hardship to the paying party, or
(b) prevent the paying party from obtaining legal services for the purposes of the proceedings.

(4) The Lord Chancellor may by order amend this section by adding to, omitting or varying the matters mentioned in subsections (1) to (3).

(5) An order under subsection (4) must be made by statutory instrument.

(6) A statutory instrument containing an order under subsection (4) may not be made unless a draft of the instrument has been laid before, and approved by a resolution of, each House of Parliament.

(7) In this section 'legal services' has the same meaning as in section 22ZA.

SENIOR COURTS ACT 1981

51 Costs in civil division of Court of Appeal, High Court and county courts

[1](1) Subject to the provisions of this or any other enactment and to rules of court, the costs of and incidental to all proceedings in –
(a) the civil division of the Court of Appeal;
(b) the High Court;
(ba) the family court; and
(c) the county court,

shall be in the discretion of the court.

(2) Without prejudice to any general power to make rules of court, such rules may make provision for regulating matters relating to the costs of those proceedings including, in particular, prescribing scales of costs to be paid to legal or other representatives or for securing that the amount awarded to a party in respect of the costs to be paid by him to such representatives is not limited to what would have been payable by him to them if he had not been awarded costs.

(3) The court shall have full power to determine by whom and to what extent the costs are to be paid.

(4) In subsections (1) and (2) 'proceedings' includes the administration of estates and trusts.

(5) Nothing in subsection (1) shall alter the practice in any criminal cause, or in bankruptcy.

[2,3](6) In any proceedings mentioned in subsection (1), the court may disallow, or (as the case may be) order the legal or other representative concerned

1 INDEX_Costs:Senior Courts, in:discretion as to
2 INDEX_Costs:Senior Courts, in:wasted costs order
3 INDEX_Wasted costs order

to meet, the whole of any wasted costs or such part of them as may be determined in accordance with rules of court.

(7) In subsection (6), 'wasted costs' means any costs incurred by a party –
 (a) as a result of any improper, unreasonable or negligent act or omission on thc part of any legal or other representative or any employee of such a representative; or
 (b) which, in the light of any such act or omission occurring after they were incurred, the court considers it is unreasonable to expect that party to pay.

(7A) Where the court exercises a power under subsection (6) in relation to costs incurred by a party, it must inform such of the following as it considers appropriate—
 (a) an approved regulator;
 (b) the Director of Legal Aid Casework.

(8) Where –
 (a) a person has commenced proceedings in the High Court; but
 (b) those proceedings should, in the opinion of the court, have been commenced in the county court or family court in accordance with any provision made

under section 1 of the Courts and Legal Services Act 1990 or by or under any other enactment,

the person responsible for determining the amount which is to be awarded to that person by way of costs shall have regard to those circumstances.

(9) Where, in complying with subsection (8), the responsible person reduces the amount which would otherwise be awarded to the person in question –
 (a) the amount of that reduction shall not exceed 25 per cent; and
 (b) on any taxation of the costs payable by that person to his legal representative, regard shall be had to the amount of the reduction.

(10) The Lord Chancellor may by order amend subsection (9)(a) by substituting, for the percentage for the time being mentioned there, a different percentage.

(11) Any such order shall be made by statutory instrument and may make such transitional or incidental provision as the Lord Chancellor considers expedient.

(12) No such statutory instrument shall be made unless a draft of the instrument has been approved by both Houses of Parliament.

(12A) In subsection (7A)—

'approved regulator' has the meaning given by section 20 of the Legal services Act 2007;

'the Director of Legal Aid Casework' means the civil servant designated under section 4 of the Legal Aid, sentencing and Punishment of Offenders Act 2012.

(13) In this section 'legal or other representative', in relation to a party to proceedings, means any person exercising a right of audience or right to conduct litigation on his behalf.

LEGAL AID, SENTENCING AND PUNISHMENT OF OFFENDERS ACT 2012

Sections 9–12, 21–32

Part 1
Legal Aid

[…]

Civil legal aid

[…]

9 General cases

(1) Civil legal services are to be available to an individual under this Part if—
   (a) they are civil legal services described in Part 1 of Schedule 1, and
   (b) the Director has determined that the individual qualifies for the services in accordance with this Part (and has not withdrawn the determination).

(2) The Lord Chancellor may by order—
   (a) add services to Part 1 of Schedule 1, or
   (b) vary or omit services described in that Part,

(whether by modifying that Part or Part 2, 3 or 4 of the Schedule).

10 Exceptional cases

(1) Civil legal services other than services described in Part 1 of Schedule 1 are to be available to an individual under this Part if subsection (2) or (4) is satisfied.

(2) This subsection is satisfied where the Director—
   (a) has made an exceptional case determination in relation to the individual and the services, and
   (b) has determined that the individual qualifies for the services in accordance with this Part,

(and has not withdrawn either determination).

(3) For the purposes of subsection (2), an exceptional case determination is a determination—
   (a) that it is necessary to make the services available to the individual under this Part because failure to do so would be a breach of—
      (i) the individual's Convention rights (within the meaning of the Human Rights Act 1998), or
      (ii) any rights of the individual to the provision of legal services that are enforceable EU rights, or
   (b) that it is appropriate to do so, in the particular circumstances of the case, having regard to any risk that failure to do so would be such a breach.

(4) This subsection is satisfied where—

(a) the services consist of advocacy in proceedings at an inquest under the Coroners Act 1988 into the death of a member of the individual's family,

(b) the Director has made a wider public interest determination in relation to the individual and the inquest, and

(c) the Director has determined that the individual qualifies for the services in accordance with this Part,

(and neither determination has been withdrawn).

(5) For the purposes of subsection (4), a wider public interest determination is a determination that, in the particular circumstances of the case, the provision of advocacy under this Part for the individual for the purposes of the inquest is likely to produce significant benefits for a class of person, other than the individual and the members of the individual's family.

(6) For the purposes of this section an individual is a member of another individual's family if—

(a) they are relatives (whether of the full blood or half blood or by marriage or civil partnership),

(b) they are cohabitants (as defined in Part 4 of the Family Law Act 1996), or

(c) one has parental responsibility for the other.

11 Qualifying for civil legal aid

(1) The Director must determine whether an individual qualifies under this Part for civil legal services in accordance with—

(a) section 21 (financial resources) and regulations under that section, and

(b) criteria set out in regulations made under this paragraph.

(2) In setting the criteria, the Lord Chancellor—

(a) must consider the circumstances in which it is appropriate to make civil legal services available under this Part, and

(b) must, in particular, consider the extent to which the criteria ought to reflect the factors in subsection (3).

(3) Those factors are—

(a) the likely cost of providing the services and the benefit which may be obtained by the services being provided,

(b) the availability of resources to provide the services,

(c) the appropriateness of applying those resources to provide the services, having regard to present and likely future demands for the provision of civil legal services under this Part,

(d) the importance for the individual of the matters in relation to which the services would be provided,

(e) the nature and seriousness of the act, omission, circumstances or other matter in relation to which the services are sought,

(f) the availability to the individual of services provided other than under this Part and the likelihood of the individual being able to make use of such services,

(g) if the services are sought by the individual in relation to a dispute, the individual's prospects of success in the dispute,
(h) the conduct of the individual in connection with services made available under this Part or an application for such services,
(i) the conduct of the individual in connection with any legal proceedings or other proceedings for resolving disputes about legal rights or duties, and
(j) the public interest.

(4) In setting the criteria, the Lord Chancellor must seek to secure that, in cases in which more than one form of civil legal service could be provided for an individual, the individual qualifies under this Part for the form of service which in all the circumstances is the most appropriate having regard to the criteria.

(5) The criteria must reflect the principle that, in many disputes, mediation and other forms of dispute resolution are more appropriate than legal proceedings.

(6) Regulations under subsection (1)(b) may provide that no criteria apply in relation to a prescribed description of individual or services.

12 Determinations

(1) A determination by the Director that an individual qualifies under this Part for civil legal services must specify—
(a) the type of services, and
(b) the matters in relation to which the services are to be available.

(2) Regulations may make provision about the making and withdrawal of determinations under sections 9 and 10.

(3) Regulations under subsection (2) may, in particular, include—
(a) provision about the form and content of determinations and applications for determinations,
(b) provision permitting or requiring applications and determinations to be made and withdrawn in writing, by telephone or by other prescribed means,
(c) provision setting time limits for applications and determinations,
(d) provision for a determination to be disregarded for the purposes of this Part if made in response to an application that is made otherwise than in accordance with the regulations,
(e) provision about conditions which must be satisfied by an applicant before a determination is made,
(f) provision about the circumstances in which a determination may or must be withdrawn,
(g) provision requiring information and documents to be provided,
(h) provision requiring individuals who are the subject of a determination to be informed of the reasons for making or withdrawing the determination, and
(i) provision for giving information to individuals who do not qualify for civil legal services under this Part about alternative ways of obtaining or funding civil legal services.

(4) The circumstances prescribed under subsection (3)(f) may, in particular, relate to whether the individual who is the subject of the determination has complied with requirements imposed by or under this Part.

(5) Regulations under subsection (2) must make provision establishing procedures for the review of determinations under sections 9 and 10 and of the withdrawal of such determinations.

(6) Regulations under subsection (2) may make provision for appeals to a court, tribunal or other person against such determinations and against the withdrawal of such determinations.

[…]

Financial resources

21 Financial resources

(1) A person may not make a relevant determination that an individual qualifies under this Part for services unless the person has determined that the individual's financial resources are such that the individual is eligible for the services (and has not withdrawn the determination).

(2) Regulations may—
   (a) make provision about when an individual's financial resources are such that the individual is eligible under this Part for services, and
   (b) make provision for exceptions from subsection (1).

(3) Regulations may provide that an individual is to be treated, for the purposes of regulations under subsection (2), as having or not having financial resources of a prescribed description.

(4) Regulations under subsection (3) may, in particular, provide that the individual is to be treated as having prescribed financial resources of a person of a prescribed description.

(5) Regulations may make provision about the making and withdrawal of determinations under this section.

(6) Regulations under subsection (5) may, in particular, include—
   (a) provision about the form and content of determinations,
   (b) provision permitting or requiring determinations to be made and withdrawn in writing, by telephone or by other prescribed means,
   (c) provision setting time limits for determinations,
   (d) provision about conditions which must be satisfied before a determination is made,
   (e) provision about the circumstances in which a determination may or must be withdrawn,
   (f) provision requiring information and documents to be provided,
   (g) provision requiring individuals who are the subject of a determination to be informed of the reasons for making or withdrawing the determination, and

(h) provision for the review of a determination in respect of an individual's financial resources.

(7) The circumstances prescribed under subsection (6)(e) may, in particular, relate to whether the individual who is the subject of the determination has complied with requirements imposed by or under this Part.

(8) In this section 'relevant determination' means a determination that is required to be carried out in accordance with this section by—
(a) section 11 or 17, or
(b) regulations under section 15 or paragraph 4 of Schedule 3.

22 Information about financial resources

(1) The relevant authority may make an information request to—
(a) the Secretary of State,
(b) a relevant Northern Ireland Department, or
(c) the Commissioners for Her Majesty's Revenue and Customs ('the Commissioners').

(2) An information request may be made only for the purposes of facilitating a determination about an individual's financial resources for the purposes of this Part.

(3) An information request made to the Secretary of State or a relevant Northern Ireland Department under this section may request the disclosure of some or all of the following information—
(a) a relevant individual's full name and any previous names;
(b) a relevant individual's address and any previous addresses;
(c) a relevant individual's date of birth;
(d) a relevant individual's national insurance number;
(e) a relevant individual's benefit status at a time specified in the request;
(f) information of a prescribed description.

(4) An information request made to the Commissioners under this section may request the disclosure of some or all of the following information—
(a) whether or not a relevant individual is employed or was employed at a time specified in the request;
(b) the name and address of the employer;
(c) whether or not a relevant individual is carrying on a business, trade or profession or was doing so at a time specified in the request;
(d) the name under which it is or was carried on;
(e) the address of any premises used for the purposes of carrying it on;
(f) a relevant individual's national insurance number;
(g) a relevant individual's benefit status at a time specified in the request;
(h) information of a prescribed description.

(5) The information that may be prescribed under subsections (3)(f) and (4)(h) includes, in particular, information relating to—
(a) prescribed income of a relevant individual for a prescribed period, and
(b) prescribed capital of a relevant individual.

(6) Information may not be prescribed under subsection (4)(h) without the Commissioners' consent.

(7) The Secretary of State, the relevant Northern Ireland Departments and the Commissioners may disclose to the relevant authority information specified in an information request made under this section.

(8) In this section—

'benefit status', in relation to an individual, means whether or not the individual is in receipt of a prescribed benefit or benefits and, if so—

(a) which benefit or benefits the individual is receiving,
(b) whether the individual is entitled to the benefit or benefits alone or jointly,
(c) in prescribed cases, the amount the individual is receiving by way of the benefit (or each of the benefits) ('the benefit amount'), and
(d) in prescribed cases, where the benefit consists of a number of elements, what those elements are and the amount included in respect of each element in calculating the benefit amount;

'the relevant authority' means—

(a) a prescribed person, or
(b) in relation to circumstances for which no person is prescribed, the Director;

'a relevant individual', in relation to an information request for the purposes of a determination about an individual's financial resources, means—

(a) that individual, and
(b) any other individual whose financial resources are or may be relevant for the purposes of the determination;

'relevant Northern Ireland Department' means the Department for Social Development in Northern Ireland or the Department of Finance and Personnel in Northern Ireland.

Contributions and costs

23 Payment for services

(1) An individual to whom services are made available under this Part is not to be required to make a payment in connection with the provision of the services, except where regulations provide otherwise.

(2) The regulations may, in particular, provide that in prescribed circumstances an individual must do one or more of the following—

(a) pay the cost of the services;
(b) pay a contribution in respect of the cost of the services of a prescribed amount;
(c) pay a prescribed amount in respect of administration costs.

(3) The regulations may, in particular, provide that where—

(a) civil legal services are provided to an individual under this Part in relation to a dispute, and
(b) prescribed conditions are met,

the individual must pay a prescribed amount which may exceed the cost of the civil legal services provided.

(4) The regulations may, in particular, make provision about the determination of the cost of services for the purposes of the regulations.

(5) The regulations may, in particular—
 (a) provide for an individual's liability under the regulations to make a payment to change or cease in prescribed circumstances,
 (b) provide for an individual's liability under the regulations to arise on a determination by a prescribed person,
 (c) provide for such a determination to be varied or withdrawn by a prescribed person, and
 (d) provide for the review of such a determination in respect of an individual's liability to make a payment.

(6) The regulations may, in particular, provide that an individual is to be treated, for the purposes of the regulations, as having or not having financial resources of a prescribed description.

(7) Regulations under subsection (6) may, in particular, provide that the individual is to be treated as having prescribed financial resources of a person of a prescribed description.

(8) The regulations may, in particular, include provision for an amount to be payable entirely or partly—
 (a) by periodical payments;
 (b) by one or more lump sums;
 (c) out of income;
 (d) out of capital.

(9) The regulations may, in particular, include—
 (a) provision requiring information and documents to be provided,
 (b) provision about the time and manner in which payments must be made,
 (c) provision about the person to whom payments must be made, and
 (d) provision about what that person must do with the payments.

(10) The regulations may, in particular, make provision for the payment by an individual of interest, on such terms as may be prescribed, in respect of—
 (a) a loan made to the individual under this Part,
 (b) a payment in connection with the provision of services which is not required by the regulations to be made by the individual until after the time when the services are provided, and
 (c) so much of a payment as remains unpaid after the time when it is required by the regulations to be made by the individual.

(11) The regulations—
 (a) must make provision for the repayment to an individual of any amount in excess of the individual's liability under the regulations or under section 24, and
 (b) may make provision for the payment of interest on the excess.

(12) In this section—

'administration costs' means costs in connection with the administration of legal aid, including the administration of charges arising under section 25;

'prescribed amount' includes an amount calculated in a prescribed manner.

24 Enforcement

(1) Regulations may make provision about the enforcement of an obligation to make a payment imposed under section 23.

(2) The regulations may, in particular, make provision for costs incurred in connection with the enforcement of an individual's obligation to make a payment to be recovered from the individual.

(3) Regulations under this section may, in particular—
- (a) provide that overdue amounts are recoverable summarily as a civil debt;
- (b) provide that overdue amounts are recoverable as if they were payable under an order of the High Court or [the county court], if the court in question so orders on the application of the person to whom the amounts are due.

(4) Regulations under this section may include provision requiring information and documents to be provided.

(5) Schedule 2 (criminal legal aid: motor vehicle orders) has effect.

25 Charges on property in connection with civil legal services

(1) Where civil legal services are made available to an individual under this Part, the amounts described in subsection (2) are to constitute a first charge on—
- (a) any property recovered or preserved by the individual in proceedings, or in any compromise or settlement of a dispute, in connection with which the services were provided (whether the property is recovered or preserved for the individual or another person), and
- (b) any costs payable to the individual by another person in connection with such proceedings or such a dispute.

(2) Those amounts are—
- (a) amounts expended by the Lord Chancellor in securing the provision of the services (except to the extent that they are recovered by other means), and
- (b) other amounts payable by the individual in connection with the services under section 23 or 24.

(3) Regulations may make provision for exceptions from subsection (1).

(4) Regulations may make provision about the charge under subsection (1) including, in particular—
- (a) provision as to whether the charge is in favour of the Lord Chancellor or a person by whom the services were made available,

(b) provision modifying the charge for the purposes of its application in prescribed cases or circumstances, and
(c) provision about the enforcement of the charge.

(5) Regulations under subsection (4)(c) may, in particular, include—
(a) provision requiring amounts recovered by the individual in proceedings or as part of a compromise or settlement of a dispute, and costs payable to the individual, to be paid to the Lord Chancellor or a person by whom the services were made available,
(b) provision about the time and manner in which the amounts must be paid,
(c) provision about what the Lord Chancellor or the person by whom the services were made available must do with the amounts,
(d) provision for the payment of interest on all or part of the amounts,
(e) provision for the payment to the individual concerned of any amount in excess of the amounts described in subsection (2), and
(f) provision for the enforcement of requirements described in paragraph (a).

(6) Regulations under this section may include provision requiring information and document to be provided.

26 Costs in civil proceedings

(1) Costs ordered against an individual in relevant civil proceedings must not exceed the amount (if any) which it is reasonable for the individual to pay having regard to all the circumstances, including—
(a) the financial resources of all of the parties to the proceedings, and
(b) their conduct in connection with the dispute to which the proceedings relate.

(2) In subsection (1) 'relevant civil proceedings', in relation to an individual, means—
(a) proceedings for the purposes of which civil legal services are made available to the individual under this Part, or
(b) if such services are made available to the individual under this Part for the purposes of only part of proceedings, that part of the proceedings.

(3) Regulations may make provision for exceptions from subsection (1).

(4) In assessing for the purposes of subsection (1) the financial resources of an individual to whom civil legal services are made available, the following must not be taken into account, except so far as prescribed—
(a) the individual's clothes and household furniture, and
(b) the implements of the individual's trade.

(5) Subject to subsections (1) to (4), regulations may make provision about costs in relation to proceedings for the purposes of which civil legal services are made available under this Part.

(6) Regulations under subsection (5) may, in particular, make provision—

(a) specifying the principles to be applied in determining the amount of any costs which may be awarded against a party to whom civil legal services are made available under this Part,
(b) limiting the circumstances in which, or the extent to which, an order for costs may be enforced against such a party,
(c) as to the cases in which, and the extent to which, such a party may be required to give security for costs and the manner in which it is to be given,
(d) requiring the payment by the Lord Chancellor of the whole or part of any costs incurred by a party to whom civil legal services are not made available under this Part,
(e) specifying the principles to be applied in determining the amount of costs which may be awarded to a party to whom civil legal services are made available under this Part,
(f) as to the court, tribunal or other person by whom the amount of any costs is to be determined, and
(g) as to the extent to which any determination of that amount is to be final.

(7) Regulations may provide that an individual is to be treated, for the purposes of subsection (1) or regulations under subsection (3) or (5), as having or not having financial resources of a prescribed description (but such regulations have effect subject to subsection (4)).

(8) Regulations under subsection (7) may, in particular, provide that the individual is to be treated as having prescribed financial resources of a person of a prescribed description.

(9) Regulations under this section may include provision requiring information and document

Providers of services etc

27 Choice of provider of services etc

(1) The Lord Chancellor's duty under section 1(1) does not include a duty to secure that, where services are made available to an individual under this Part, they are made available by the means selected by the individual.

(2) The Lord Chancellor may discharge that duty, in particular, by arranging for the services to be provided by telephone or by other electronic means.

(3) The Lord Chancellor's duty under section 1(1) does not include a duty to secure that, where services are made available to an individual under this Part, they are made available by a person selected by the individual, subject to subsections (4) to (10).

(4) An individual who qualifies under this Part for representation for the purposes of criminal proceedings by virtue of a determination under section 16 may select any representative or representatives willing to act for the individual, subject to regulations under subsection (6).

(5) Where an individual exercises that right, representation by the selected representative

(6) Regulations may provide that in prescribed circumstances—
   (a) the right conferred by subsection (4) is not to apply in cases of prescribed descriptions,
   (b) an individual who has been provided with advice or assistance in accordance with section 13 or regulations under section 15 by a person selected by the individual is to be taken to have selected that person under subsection (4),
   (c) the right conferred by subsection (4) is not to include a right to select a representative of a prescribed provision,
   (d) that right is to select only a representative located in a prescribed area or of a prescribed description,
   (e) that right is to select not more than a prescribed number of representatives to act at any one time, and
   (f) that right is not to include a right to select a representative in place of a representative previously selected.

(7) Regulations under subsection (6)(b) may prescribe circumstances in which an individual is to be taken to have selected a person to provide advice or assistance.

(8) Regulations may provide that in prescribed circumstances the Lord Chancellor is not required to make available representation for an individual by a prescribed representative.

(9) Provision made under subsection (8) does not prejudice any right of the individual to select another representative.

(10) The circumstances which may be prescribed under this section include that a determination has been made by a prescribed person.

28 Position of providers of services

(1) The fact that services provided for an individual are or could be provided under arrangements made for the purposes of this Part does not affect—
   (a) the relationship between the individual and the person by whom the services are provided,
   (b) any privilege arising out of that relationship, or
   (c) any right which the individual may have to be indemnified by another person in respect of expenses incurred by the individual,

   except to the extent that regulations provide otherwise.

(2) A person who provides services under arrangements made for the purposes of this Part must not take any payment in respect of the services apart from—
   (a) payment made in accordance with the arrangements, and
   (b) payment authorised by the Lord Chancellor to be taken.

(3) Regulations may provide that the withdrawal of a determination that an individual qualifies for prescribed services under this Part does not affect

the right of any person who has provided such services to the individual under arrangements made for the purposes of this Part to remuneration for work done before the date of the withdrawal.

29 Code of conduct

(1) The Lord Chancellor must publish a code of conduct to be observed by the following persons when providing services to an individual under arrangements made for the purposes of this Part—
  (a) civil servants, and
  (b) employees of a body established and maintained by the Lord Chancellor.

(2) The code must include—
  (a) duties to avoid discrimination,
  (b) duties to protect the interests of the individuals for whom services are provided,
  (c) duties to courts and tribunals,
  (d) duties to avoid conflicts of interest,
  (e) duties of confidentiality, and
  (f) duties on persons who are members of a professional body to comply with the rules of the body.

(3) The Lord Chancellor must lay the code, and any revision of the code, before Parliament.

(4) The persons described in subsection (1)(a) and (b) are not subject to the direction of the Lord Chancellor when providing services to an individual under arrangements made for the purposes of this Part.

30 Position of other parties, courts and tribunals

(1) Except as expressly provided by regulations, any rights conferred by or under this Part on an individual for whom services are provided under this Part for the purposes of proceedings do not affect—
  (a) the rights or liabilities of other parties to the proceedings, or
  (b) the principles on which the discretion of a court or tribunal is normally exercised.

(2) Regulations may make provision about the procedure of a court or tribunal in relation to services made available under this Part.

(3) Regulations under subsection (2) may, in particular, authorise the exercise of the functions of a court or tribunal by—
  (a) a member or officer of that court or tribunal, or
  (b) another court or tribunal.

Supplementary

31 Legal aid for legal persons

Schedule 3 (legal aid for legal persons) has effect.

32 Foreign law

(1) The civil legal services described in Part 1 of Schedule 1 do not include services relating to any law other than the law of England and Wales, except—
  (a) where express provision to the contrary is made by or under Part 1 of Schedule 1;
  (b) where such law is relevant for determining any issue relating to the law of England and Wales;
  (c) in other circumstances specified by the Lord Chancellor by order.

(2) A determination by the Director or a court under section 13, 15 or 16 that an individual qualifies for advice, assistance or representation under this Part does not impose a duty on the Lord Chancellor to secure that services relating to any law other than the law of England and Wales are made available, except—
  (a) where such law is relevant for determining any issue relating to the law of England and Wales;
  (b) in other circumstances specified by the Lord Chancellor by order.

(3) The Lord Chancellor may not make an order under subsection (1) or (2) unless the Lord Chancellor considers—
  (a) that it is necessary to make the order because failure to do so would result in a breach of—
    (i) an individual's Convention rights (within the meaning of the Human Rights Act 1998), or
    (ii) any rights of an individual to the provision of legal services that are enforceable EU rights, or
  (b) that it is appropriate to make the order having regard to any risk that failure to do so would result in such a breach.

[…]

FAMILY PROCEDURE RULES 2010

FPR Pt 28

Part 28
Costs

28.1 Costs

The court may at any time make such order as to costs as it thinks just.

28.2 Application of other rules

(1) [4]Subject to rule 28.3, Parts 44 (except rules 44.2(2) and (3) and 44.10(2) and (3)), 46 and 47 and rule 45.8 of the CPR apply to costs in proceedings, with the following modifications –
  (a) in the definition of 'authorised court officer' in rule 44.1(1), for the words in sub-paragraph (i) substitute 'the family court';

4 INDEX_Costs:family proceedings, in

(b) (*revoked*)
(c) in accordance with any provisions in Practice Direction 28A; and
(d) any other necessary modifications.

(2) (*revoked*)

28.3 Costs in financial remedy proceedings

(1) [5]This rule applies in relation to financial remedy proceedings.

(2) Rule 44.2(1), (4) and (5) of the CPR do not apply to financial remedy proceedings.

(3) Rules 44.2(6) to (8) and 44.12 of the CPR apply to an order made under this rule as they apply to an order made under rule 44.3 of the CPR.

(4) In this rule –
(a) 'costs' has the same meaning as in rule 44.1(1)(c) of the CPR; and
(b) 'financial remedy proceedings' means proceedings for –
(i) a financial order except an order for maintenance pending suit, an order for maintenance pending outcome of proceedings, an interim periodical payments order, an order for payment in respect of legal services or any other form of interim order for the purposes of rule 9.7(1)(a), (b), (c) and (e);
(ii) an order under Part 3 of the 1984 Act;
(iii) an order under Schedule 7 to the 2004 Act;
(iv) an order under section 10(2) of the 1973 Act;
(v) an order under section 48(2) of the 2004 Act.

(5) Subject to paragraph (6), the general rule in financial remedy proceedings is that the court will not make an order requiring one party to pay the costs of another party.

(6) The court may make an order requiring one party to pay the costs of another party at any stage of the proceedings where it considers it appropriate to do so because of the conduct of a party in relation to the proceedings (whether before or during them).

(7) In deciding what order (if any) to make under paragraph (6), the court must have regard to –
(a) any failure by a party to comply with these rules, any order of the court or any practice direction which the court considers relevant;
(b) any open offer to settle made by a party;
(c) whether it was reasonable for a party to raise, pursue or contest a particular allegation or issue;
(d) the manner in which a party has pursued or responded to the application or a particular allegation or issue;
(e) any other aspect of a party's conduct in relation to proceedings which the court considers relevant; and
(f) the financial effect on the parties of any costs order.

5 INDEX_Costs:financial remedy (ancillary relief) proceedings

(8) No offer to settle which is not an open offer to settle is admissible at any stage of the proceedings, except as provided by rule 9.17.

(9) For the purposes of this rule "financial remedy proceedings" do not include an application under rule 9.9A.

28.4 (*revoked*)

Practice Direction 28A – Costs

FPR PD 28

This Practice Direction supplements FPR Part 28

Application and modification of the CPR

1.1 [6,7]Rule 28.2 provides that subject to rule 28.3 of the FPR, Parts 44 (except rules 44.2(2) and (3) and 44.10(2) and (3)), 46 and 47 and rule 45.8 of the CPR apply to costs in family proceedings with the modifications listed in rule 28.2(1)(a), (c) and (d). Rule 28.2(1)(c) refers to modifications in accordance with this Practice Direction.

1.2–1.3 (*omitted*)

Application and modification of the Practice Direction supplementing CPR Parts 43 to 48

2.1 For the purpose of proceedings to which these Rules apply, the Practice Directions which supplement Parts 44 to 47 of the CPR will apply, but with the exclusions and modifications explained below to reflect the exclusions and modifications to those Parts of the CPR as they are applied by Part 28 of these Rules.

2.2 Rule 28.2(1) applies, with modifications and certain exceptions, Parts 44 to 47 of the CPR to costs in family proceedings. Rule 28.3, by way of exception, disapplies CPR rule 44.2(1), (4) and (5) in the case of financial remedy proceedings.

2.3 CPR Practice Directions 44 to 47 do not, therefore, apply in their entirety but with the exclusion of Practice Direction 45 and of certain sections of the other Practice Directions, reflecting the non-application of Part 45 and of certain rules of the CPR which those sections of the other Practice Directions supplement.

2.4 CPR Practice Directions 44, 46 and 47 apply as follows –

- to family proceedings including financial remedy proceedings with the exception of paragraphs 3.1 to 3.5 of Practice Direction 44 and paragraphs 7.1 and 9.1 to 9.12 of Practice Direction 46.

6 CPRPRACTICEDIRECTIONS_FPR Pt 28:Costs (PD28A)
7 INDEX_Costs:Practice Direction

2.5 All subsequent editions of CPR Practice Directions 44, 46 and 47 as and when they are published and come into effect shall in the same way extend to all family proceedings.

2.6 CPR Practice Directions 44, 46, 47 and 48 include provisions applicable to proceedings following changes in the manner in which legal services are funded pursuant to the Access to Justice Act 1999. It should be noted that family proceedings (within section 58A(2) of the Courts and Legal Services Act 1990) cannot be the subject of an enforceable conditional fee agreement.

2.7 Paragraph 1.1 of CPR Practice Direction 44 shall be modified as follows–
in the definition of 'counsel' for 'High Court or in the county courts' substitute 'High Court or in the family court'.

2.8 Paragraphs 4.1 and 4.2 of CPR Practice Direction 47 shall be modified as follows:
– for paragraphs 4.1 and 4.2 substitute:

'4.1 For the purposes of rule 47.4(1), "appropriate office" means the court office of the Designated Family Court for the Designated Family Judge area in which the case was being dealt with when the judgment or order was made, or the event occurred which gave rise to the right to assessment, or to which the case has subsequently been moved.

(Her Majesty's Courts and Tribunals Service will publish information to enable Designated Family Judge areas and Designated Family Courts to be identified).'

General interpretation of references in CPR

3.1 References in the costs practice direction to 'claimant' and 'defendant' are to be read as references to equivalent terms used in proceedings to which these Rules apply and other terms and expressions used in the costs practice direction shall be similarly treated.

3.2 References in CPR Parts 44 to 47 to other rules or Parts of the CPR shall be read, where there is an equivalent rule or Part in these Rules, to that equivalent rule or Part.

Costs in financial remedy proceedings

4.1 [8]Rule 28.3 relates to the court's power to make costs orders in financial remedy proceedings. For the purposes of rule 28.3, 'financial remedy proceedings' are defined in accordance with rule 28.3(4)(b). That definition, which is more limited than the principal definition in rule 2.3(1), includes:

(a) an application for a financial order, except:

(i) an order for maintenance pending suit or an order for maintenance pending outcome of proceedings;

8 INDEX_Costs:financial remedy (ancillary relief) proceedings:Practice Direction

(ii) an interim periodical payments order or any other form of interim order for the purposes of rule 9.7(1)(a), (b), (c) and (e);

(iii) an order for payment in respect of legal services.

(b) an application for an order under Part 3 of the Matrimonial and Family Proceedings Act 1984 or Schedule 7 to the Civil Partnership Act 2004; and

(c) an application under section 10(2) of the Matrimonial Causes Act 1973 or section 48(2) of the Civil Partnership Act 2004.

4.2 Accordingly, it should be noted that:

(a) while most interim financial applications are excluded from rule 28.3, the rule does apply to an application for an interim variation order within rule 9.7(1)(d),

(b) rule 28.3 does not apply to an application for any of the following financial remedies:

(i) an order under Schedule 1 to the Children Act 1989;

(ii) an order under section 27 of the Matrimonial Causes Act 1973 or Part 9 of Schedule 5 to the Civil Partnership Act 2004;

(iii) an order under section 35 of the Matrimonial Causes Act 1973 or paragraph 69 of Schedule 5 to the Civil Partnership Act 2004; or

(iv) an order under Part 1 of the Domestic Proceedings and Magistrates' Courts Act 1978 or Schedule 6 to the Civil Partnership Act 2004.

4.3 Under rule 28.3 the court only has the power to make a costs order in financial remedy proceedings when this is justified by the litigation conduct of one of the parties. When determining whether and how to exercise this power the court will be required to take into account the list of factors set out in that rule. The court will not be able to take into account any offers to settle expressed to be 'without prejudice' or 'without prejudice save as to costs' in deciding what, if any, costs orders to make.

4.4 In considering the conduct of the parties for the purposes of rule 28.3(6) and (7) (including any open offers to settle), the court will have regard to the obligation of the parties to help the court to further the overriding objective (see rules 1.1 and 1.3) and will take into account the nature, importance and complexity of the issues in the case. This may be of particular significance in applications for variation orders and interim variation orders or other cases where there is a risk of the costs becoming disproportionate to the amounts in dispute. The court will take a broad view of conduct for the purposes of this rule and will generally conclude that to refuse openly to negotiate reasonably and responsibly will amount to conduct in respect of which the court will consider making an order for costs. This includes in a 'needs' case where the applicant litigates unreasonably resulting in the costs incurred by each party becoming disproportionate to the award made by the court. Where an order for costs is made at an interim stage the court will not usually allow any resulting liability to be reckoned as a debt in the computation of the assets.

4.5 Parties who intend to seek a costs order against another party in proceedings to which rule 28.3 applies should ordinarily make this plain in open correspondence or in skeleton arguments before the date of the hearing. In any case where summary assessment of costs awarded under rule 28.3 would be appropriate parties are under an obligation to file a statement of costs in CPR Form N260.

4.6 An order for payment in respect of legal services under section 22ZA of the Matrimonial Causes Act 1973 or paragraph 38A of Part 8 of Schedule 5 to the Civil Partnership Act 2004 is not a 'costs order' within the meaning of rule 28.3.

4.7 By virtue of rule 28.2(1), where rule 28.3 does not apply, the exercise of the court's discretion as to costs is governed by the relevant provisions of the CPR and in particular rule 44.2 (excluding r 44.2(2) and (3)).

CIVIL PROCEDURE RULES 1998

CPR Pt 44

Part 44
General Rules about Costs

Section I
General

44.1 Interpretation and application

(1) In Parts 44 to 47, unless the context otherwise requires –

'authorised court officer' means any officer or –
- (i) the County Court;
- (ii) a district registry;
- (iii) the Family Court; or
- (iiia) the High Court; or
- (iv) the Costs Office,

whom the Lord Chancellor has authorised to assess costs;

'conditional fee agreement' means an agreement enforceable under section 58 of the Courts and Legal Services Act 1990;
'costs' includes fees, charges, disbursements, expenses, remuneration, reimbursement allowed to a litigant in person under rule 46.5 and any fee or reward charged by a lay representative for acting on behalf of a party in proceedings allocated to the small claims track;
'costs judge' means a taxing master of the Senior Courts;
'Costs Office' means the Senior Courts Costs Office;
'costs officer' means –
- (i) a costs judge;
- (ii) a District Judge; or
- (iii) an authorised court officer;

'detailed assessment' means the procedure by which the amount of costs is decided by a costs officer in accordance with Part 47;

'the Director (legal aid)' means the person designated as the Director of Legal Aid Casework pursuant to section 4 of the Legal Aid, Sentencing and Punishment of Offenders Act 2012, or a person entitled to exercise the functions of the Director;

...

'free of charge' has the same meaning as in section 194(10) of the 2007 Act;

'fund' includes any estate or property held for the benefit of any person or class of person and any fund to which a trustee or personal representative is entitled in that capacity;

'HMRC' means HM Revenue and Customs;

'legal aid' means civil legal services made available under arrangements made for the purposes of Part 1 of the Legal Aid, Sentencing and Punishment of Offenders Act 2012;

'paying party' means a party liable to pay costs;

'the prescribed charity' has the same meaning as in section 194(8) of the 2007 Act;

'pro bono representation' means legal representation provided free of charge;

'receiving party' means a party entitled to be paid costs;

'summary assessment' means the procedure whereby costs are assessed by the judge who has heard the case or application;

'VAT' means Value Added Tax;

'the 2007 Act' means the Legal Services Act 2007.

('Legal representative' has the meaning given in rule 2.3).

(2) The costs to which Parts 44 to 47 apply include –
  (a) the following costs where those costs may be assessed by the court –
    (i) costs of proceedings before an arbitrator or umpire;
    (ii) costs of proceedings before a tribunal or other statutory body; and
    (iii) costs payable by a client to their legal representative; and
  (b) costs which are payable by one party to another party under the terms of a contract, where the court makes an order for an assessment of those costs.

(3) Where advocacy or litigation services are provided to a client under a conditional fee agreement, costs are recoverable under Parts 44 to 47 notwithstanding that the client is liable to pay the legal representative's fees and expenses only to the extent that sums are recovered in respect of the proceedings, whether by way of costs or otherwise.

44.2 Court's discretion as to costs

(1) The court has discretion as to –
  (a) whether costs are payable by one party to another;
  (b) the amount of those costs; and
  (c) when they are to be paid.

(2) If the court decides to make an order about costs –
  (a) the general rule is that the unsuccessful party will be ordered to pay the costs of the successful party; but
  (b) the court may make a different order.

(3) The general rule does not apply to the following proceedings –
  (a) proceedings in the Court of Appeal on an application or appeal made in connection with proceedings in the Family Division; or
  (b) proceedings in the Court of Appeal from a judgment, direction, decision or order given or made in probate proceedings or family proceedings.

(4) In deciding what order (if any) to make about costs, the court will have regard to all the circumstances, including –
  (a) the conduct of all the parties;
  (b) whether a party has succeeded on part of its case, even if that party has not been wholly successful; and
  (c) any admissible offer to settle made by a party which is drawn to the court's attention, and which is not an offer to which costs consequences under Part 36 apply.

(5) The conduct of the parties includes –
  (a) conduct before, as well as during, the proceedings and in particular the extent to which the parties followed the Practice Direction – Pre-Action Conduct or any relevant pre-action protocol;
  (b) whether it was reasonable for a party to raise, pursue or contest a particular allegation or issue;
  (c) the manner in which a party has pursued or defended the case or a particular allegation or issue; and
  (d) whether a claimant who has succeeded in the claim, in whole or in part, exaggerated its claim.

(6) The orders which the court may make under this rule include an order that a party must pay –
  (a) a proportion of another party's costs;
  (b) a stated amount in respect of another party's costs;
  (c) costs from or until a certain date only;
  (d) costs incurred before proceedings have begun;
  (e) costs relating to particular steps taken in the proceedings;
  (f) costs relating only to a distinct part of the proceedings; and
  (g) interest on costs from or until a certain date, including a date before judgment.

(7) Before the court considers making an order under paragraph (6)(f), it will consider whether it is practicable to make an order under paragraph (6)(a) or (c) instead.

(8) Where the court orders a party to pay costs subject to detailed assessment, it will order that party to pay a reasonable sum on account of costs, unless there is good reason not to do so.

44.3 Basis of assessment

(1) Where the court is to assess the amount of costs (whether by summary or detailed assessment) it will assess those costs –
(a) on the standard basis; or
(b) on the indemnity basis,

but the court will not in either case allow costs which have been unreasonably incurred or are unreasonable in amount.

(Rule 44.5 sets out how the court decides the amount of costs payable under a contract.)

(2) Where the amount of costs is to be assessed on the standard basis, the court will –
(a) only allow costs which are proportionate to the matters in issue. Costs which are disproportionate in amount may be disallowed or reduced even if they were reasonably or necessarily incurred; and
(b) resolve any doubt which it may have as to whether costs were reasonably and proportionately incurred or were reasonable and proportionate in amount in favour of the paying party.

(Factors which the court may take into account are set out in rule 44.4.)

(3) Where the amount of costs is to be assessed on the indemnity basis, the court will resolve any doubt which it may have as to whether costs were reasonably incurred or were reasonable in amount in favour of the receiving party.

(4) Where –
(a) the court makes an order about costs without indicating the basis on which the costs are to be assessed; or
(b) the court makes an order for costs to be assessed on a basis other than the standard basis or the indemnity basis,

the costs will be assessed on the standard basis.

(5) Costs incurred are proportionate if they bear a reasonable relationship to –
(a) the sums in issue in the proceedings;
(b) the value of any non-monetary relief in issue in the proceedings;
(c) the complexity of the litigation;
(d) any additional work generated by the conduct of the paying party; and
(e) any wider factors involved in the proceedings, such as reputation or public importance.

(6) Where the amount of a solicitor's remuneration in respect of non-contentious business is regulated by any general orders made under the Solicitors Act 1974, the amount of the costs to be allowed in respect of any such business which falls to be assessed by the court will be decided in accordance with those general orders rather than this rule and rule 44.4.

(7) Paragraphs (2)(a) and (5) do not apply in relation to –
(a) cases commenced before 1 April 2013; or
(b) costs incurred in respect of work done before 1 April 2013,

and in relation to such cases or costs, rule 44.4.(2)(a) as it was in force immediately before 1 April 2013 will apply instead.

44.4 Factors to be taken into account in deciding the amount of costs

(1) The court will have regard to all the circumstances in deciding whether costs were –
  (a) if it is assessing costs on the standard basis –
    (i) proportionately and reasonably incurred; or
    (ii) proportionate and reasonable in amount, or
  (b) if it is assessing costs on the indemnity basis –
    (i) unreasonably incurred; or
    (ii) unreasonable in amount.

(2) In particular, the court will give effect to any orders which have already been made.

(3) The court will also have regard to –
  (a) the conduct of all the parties, including in particular –
    (i) conduct before, as well as during, the proceedings; and
    (ii) the efforts made, if any, before and during the proceedings in order to try to resolve the dispute;
  (b) the amount or value of any money or property involved;
  (c) the importance of the matter to all the parties;
  (d) the particular complexity of the matter or the difficulty or novelty of the questions raised;
  (e) the skill, effort, specialised knowledge and responsibility involved;
  (f) the time spent on the case;
  (g) the place where and the circumstances in which work or any part of it was done; and
  (h) the receiving party's last approved or agreed budget.

(Rule 35.4(4) gives the court power to limit the amount that a party may recover with regard to the fees and expenses of an expert.)

44.5 Amount of costs where costs are payable under a contract

(1) Subject to Paragraphs (2) and (3), where the court assesses (whether by summary or detailed assessment) costs which are payable by the paying party to the receiving party under the terms of a contract, the costs payable under those terms are, unless the contract expressly provides otherwise, to be presumed to be costs which –
  (a) have been reasonably incurred; and
  (b) are reasonable in amount,

and the court will assess them accordingly.

(2) The presumptions in paragraph (1) are rebuttable. Practice Direction 44—General rules about costs sets out circumstances where the court may order otherwise.

Practice Direction 44 – General rules about costs sets out circumstances where the court may order otherwise.

(3) Paragraph (1) does not apply where the contract is between a solicitor and client.

44.6 Procedure for assessing costs

(1) Where the court orders a party to pay costs to another party (other than fixed costs) it may either –
   (a) make a summary assessment of the costs; or
   (b) order detailed assessment of the costs by a costs officer,

unless any rule, practice direction or other enactment provides otherwise.

(Practice Direction 44 – General rules about costs sets out the factors which will affect the court's decision under paragraph (1).)

(2) A party may recover the fixed costs specified in Part 45 in accordance with that Part.

44.7 Time for complying with an order for costs

A party must comply with an order for the payment of costs within 14 days of –
   (a) the date of the judgment or order if it states the amount of those costs;
   (b) if the amount of those costs (or part of them) is decided later in accordance with Part 47, the date of the certificate which states the amount; or
   (c) in either case, such other date as the court may specify.

(Part 47 sets out the procedure for detailed assessment of costs.)

44.8 Legal representative's duty to notify the party

Where –
   (a) the court makes a costs order against a legally represented party; and
   (b) the party is not present when the order is made,

the party's legal representative must notify that party in writing of the costs order no later than 7 days after the legal representative receives notice of the order.

(Paragraph 10.1 of Practice Direction 44 defines 'party' for the purposes of this rule.)

44.9 Cases where costs orders deemed to have been made

(1) Subject to paragraph (2), where a right to costs arises under—
   (a) rule 3.7 or 3.7A1 (defendant's right to costs where claim is struck out for non-payment of fees);
   (a1) rule 3.7B (sanctions for dishonouring cheque);
   (b) rule 36.13(1) or (2) (claimant's entitlement to costs where a Part 36 offer is accepted); or
   (c) rule 38.6 (defendant's right to costs where claimant discontinues),

a costs order will be deemed to have been made on the standard basis.

(2) Paragraph 1(b) does not apply where a Part 36 offer is accepted before the commencement of proceedings.

(3) Where such an order is deemed to be made in favour of a party with pro bono representation, that party may apply for an order under section 194(3) of the 2007 Act.

(4) Interest payable under section 17 of the Judgments Act 1838 or section 74 of the County Courts Act 1984 on the costs deemed to have been ordered under paragraph (1) will begin to run from the date on which the event which gave rise to the entitlement to costs occurred.

44.10 Where the court makes no order for costs

(1) Where the court makes an order which does not mention costs –
  (a) subject to Paragraphs (2) and (3), the general rule is that no party is entitled –
    (i) to costs; or
    (ii) to seek an order under section 194(3) of the 2007 Act,

  in relation to that order; but
  (b) this does not affect any entitlement of a party to recover costs out of a fund held by that party as trustee or personal representative, or under any lease, mortgage or other security.

(2) Where the court makes –
  (a) an order granting permission to appeal;
  (b) an order granting permission to apply for judicial review; or
  (c) any other order or direction sought by a party on an application without notice,

  and its order does not mention costs, it will be deemed to include an order for applicant's costs in the case.

(3) Any party affected by a deemed order for costs under paragraph (2) may apply at any time to vary the order.

(4) The court hearing an appeal may, unless it dismisses the appeal, make orders about the costs of the proceedings giving rise to the appeal as well as the costs of the appeal.

(5) Subject to any order made by the transferring court, where proceedings are transferred from one court to another, the court to which they are transferred may deal with all the costs, including the costs before the transfer.

44.11 Court's powers in relation to misconduct

(1) The court may make an order under this rule where –
  (a) a party or that party's legal representative, in connection with a summary or detailed assessment, fails to comply with a rule, practice direction or court order; or
  (b) it appears to the court that the conduct of a party or that party's legal representative, before or during the proceedings or in the assessment proceedings, was unreasonable or improper.

(2) Where paragraph (1) applies, the court may –
  (a) disallow all or part of the costs which are being assessed; or
  (b) order the party at fault or that party's legal representative to pay costs which that party or legal representative has caused any other party to incur.

(3) Where –
  (a) the court makes an order under paragraph (2) against a legally represented party; and
  (b) the party is not present when the order is made,

  the party's legal representative must notify that party in writing of the order no later than 7 days after the legal representative receives notice of the order.

44.12 Set Off

Where a party entitled to costs is also liable to pay costs, the court may assess the costs which that party is liable to pay and either –

(a) set off the amount assessed against the amount the party is entitled to be paid and direct that party to pay any balance; or

(b) delay the issue of a certificate for the costs to which the party is entitled until the party has paid the amount which that party is liable to pay.

****

Practice Direction 44 – General Rules About Costs

CPR PD 44

This Practice Direction supplements CPR Part 44

Section 1: General

Subsection 1 of this Practice Direction – Documents and Forms

Documents and Forms

1.1 [9]In respect of any document which is required by Practice Directions 44 to 47 to be signed by a party or that party's legal representative, the provisions of Practice Direction 22 relating to who may sign apply as if the document in question was a statement of truth. Statements of truth are not required in assessment proceedings unless a rule or Practice Direction so requires or the court so orders.

(Practice Direction 22 makes provision for cases in which a party is a child, a protected party or a company or other corporation and cases in which a document is signed on behalf of a partnership.)

9 CPRPRACTICEDIRECTIONS_CPR Pt 44:General Rules About Costs (PD44)

1.2 Form N260 is a model form of Statement of Costs to be used for summary assessments.

(Further details about Statements of Costs are given in paragraph 9.5 below.)

Precedents A, B and C in the Schedule of Costs Precedents annexed to this Practice Direction are model forms of bills of costs to be used for detailed assessments. A party wishing to rely upon a bill which departs from the model forms should include in the background information of the bill an explanation for that departure.

(Further details about bills of costs are given in Practice Direction 47.)

Subsection 2 of this Practice Direction – Special Provisions Relating to VAT

Scope of this subsection

2.1 This subsection deals with claims for VAT) which are made in respect of costs being dealt with by way of summary assessment or detailed assessment.

VAT Registration Number

2.2 The number allocated by HMRC to every person registered under the Value Added Tax Act 1994 (except a Government Department) must appear in a prominent place at the head of every statement, bill of costs, fee sheet, account or voucher on which VAT is being included as part of a claim for costs.

Entitlement to VAT on Costs

2.3 VAT should not be included in a claim for costs if the receiving party is able to recover the VAT as input tax. Where the receiving party is able to obtain credit from HMRC for a proportion of the VAT as input tax, only that proportion which is not eligible for credit should be included in the claim for costs.

2.4 The receiving party has responsibility for ensuring that VAT is claimed only when the receiving party is unable to recover the VAT or a proportion thereof as input tax.

2.5 Where there is a dispute as to whether VAT is properly claimed the receiving party must provide a certificate signed by the legal representatives or the auditors of the receiving party substantially in the form illustrated in Precedent F in the Schedule of Costs Precedents annexed to Practice Direction 47. Where the receiving party is a litigant in person who is claiming VAT, evidence to support the claim (such as a letter from HMRC) must be produced at the hearing at which the costs are assessed.

2.6 Where there is a dispute as to whether any service in respect of which a charge is proposed to be made in the bill is zero rated or exempt from VAT, reference should be made to HMRC and its view obtained and made known at the hearing at which the costs are assessed. Such enquiry should be made by the receiving party. In the case of a bill from a solicitor to the solicitor's legal representative's own client, such enquiry should be made by the client.

Form of bill of costs where VAT rate changes

2.7 Where there is a change in the rate of VAT, suppliers of goods and services are entitled by sections 88 (1) and 88(2) of the Value Added Tax Act 1994 in most circumstances to elect whether the new or the old rate of VAT should apply to a supply where the basic and actual tax points span a period during which the rate changed.

2.8 It will be assumed, unless a contrary indication is given in writing, that an election to take advantage of the provisions mentioned in paragraph 2.7 and to charge VAT at the lower rate has been made. In any case in which an election to charge at the lower rate is not made, such a decision must be justified to the court assessing the costs.

Apportionment

2.9 Subject to 2.7 and 2.8, all bills of costs, fees and disbursements on which VAT is included must be divided into separate parts so as to show work done before, on and after the date or dates from which any change in the rate of VAT takes effect. Where, however, a lump sum charge is made for work which spans a period during which there has been a change in VAT rates, and paragraphs 2.7 and 2.8 above do not apply, reference should be made to paragraphs 30.7 or 30.8 of the VAT Guide (Notice 700) (or any revised edition of that notice) published by HMRC. If necessary, the lump sum should be apportioned. The totals of profit costs and disbursements in each part must be carried separately to the summary.

Change in VAT rate between the conclusion of a detailed settlement and the issue of a final certificate

2.10 Should there be a change in the rate between the conclusion of a detailed assessment and the issue of the final costs certificate, any interested party may apply for the detailed assessment to be varied so as to take account of any increase or reduction in the amount of tax payable. Once the final costs certificate has been issued, no variation under this paragraph will be permitted.

Disbursements not classified as such for VAT purposes

2.11

(1) Legal representatives often make payments to third parties for the supply of goods or services where no VAT was chargeable on the supply by the third party: for example, the cost of meals taken and travel costs. The question whether legal representatives should include VAT in respect of these payments when invoicing their clients or in claims for costs between litigants should be decided in accordance with this Practice Direction and with the criteria set out in the VAT Guide (Notice 700).

(2) Payments to third parties which are normally treated as part of the legal representative's overheads (for example, postage costs and telephone costs) will not be treated as disbursements. The third party supply should be included as part of the costs of the legal representatives' legal services and VAT must be added to the total bill charged to the client.

(3) Disputes may arise in respect of payments made to a third party which the legal representative shows as disbursements in the invoice delivered to the receiving party. Some payments, although correctly described as disbursements for some purposes, are not classified as disbursements for VAT purposes. Items not classified as disbursements for VAT purposes must be shown as part of the services provided by the legal representative and, therefore, VAT must be added in respect of them whether or not VAT was chargeable on the supply by the third party.

(4) Guidance as to the circumstances in which disbursements may or may not be classified as disbursements for VAT purposes is given in the VAT Guide (Notice 700, paragraph 25.1). One of the key issues is whether the third party supply—

   (a) was made to the legal representative (and therefore subsumed in the onward supply of legal services); or

   (b) was made direct to the receiving party (the third party having no right to demand payment from the legal representative, who makes the payment only as agent for the receiving party).

(5) Examples of payments under subparagraph (4)(a) are: travelling expenses, such as an airline ticket, and subsistence expenses, such as the cost of meals, where the person travelling and receiving the meals is the legal representative. The supplies by the airline and the restaurant are supplies to the legal representative, not to the client.

(6) Payments under subparagraph (4)(b) are classified as disbursements for VAT purposes and, therefore, the legal representative need not add VAT in respect of them. Simple examples are payments by a legal representative of court fees and payment of fees to an expert witness.

Litigants in person

2.12 Where a litigant acts in person, that litigant is not treated for the purposes of VAT as having supplied services and therefore no VAT is chargeable in respect of work done by that litigant (even where, for example, that litigant is a solicitor or other legal representative). Consequently in such circumstances a bill of costs should not claim any VAT.

Government Departments

2.13 On an assessment between parties, where costs are being paid to a Government Department in respect of services rendered by its legal staff, VAT should not be added.

Payment pursuant to an order under section 194(3) of the 2007 Act

2.14 Where an order is made under section 194(3) of the 2007 Act, any bill presented for agreement or assessment pursuant to that order must not include a claim for VAT.

****

Subsection 4 of this Practice Direction – Court's Discretion as to Costs: Rule 44.2

Court's Discretion as to Costs

4.1 The court may make an order about costs at any stage in a case.

4.2 There are certain costs orders which the court will commonly make in proceedings before trial. The following table sets out the general effect of these orders. The table is not an exhaustive list of the orders which the court may make.

Term	Effect
Costs Costs in any event	The party in whose favour the order is made is entitled to that party's costs in respect of the part of the proceedings to which the order relates, whatever other costs orders are made in the proceedings.
Costs in the case Costs in the application	The party in whose favour the court makes an order for costs at the end of the proceedings is entitled to that party's costs of the part of the proceedings to which the order relates.
Costs reserved	The decision about costs is deferred to a later occasion, but if no later order is made the costs will be costs in the case.
Claimant's/defendant's costs in case/application	If the party in whose favour the costs order is made is awarded costs at the end the proceedings, that party is entitled to that party's costs of the part of the proceedings to which the order relates. If any other party is awarded costs at the end of the proceedings, the party in whose favour the final costs order is made is not liable to pay the costs of any other party in respect of the part of the proceedings to which the order relates.
Costs thrown away	Where, for example, a judgment or order is set aside, the party in whose favour the costs order is made is entitled to the costs which have been incurred as a consequence. This includes the costs of – (a) preparing for and attending any hearing at which the judgment or order which has been set aside was made;

Term	Effect
	(b) preparing for and attending any hearing to set aside the judgment or order in question; (c) preparing for and attending any hearing at which the court orders the proceedings or the part in question to be adjourned; (d) any steps taken to enforce a judgment or order which has subsequently been set aside.
Costs of and caused by	Where, for example, the court makes this order on an application to amend a statement of case, the party in whose favour the costs order is made is entitled to the costs of preparing for and attending the application and the costs of any consequential amendment to his own statement of case.
Costs here and below	The party in whose favour the costs order is made is entitled not only to that party's costs in respect of the proceedings in which the court makes the order but also to that party's costs of the proceedings in any lower court. In the case of an appeal from a Divisional Court the party is not entitled to any costs incurred in any court below the Divisional Court.
No order as to costs Each party to pay own costs	Each party is to bear that party's own costs of the part of the proceedings to which the order relates whatever costs order the court makes at the end of the proceedings.

Subsection 5 of this Practice Direction – Fees of Counsel

Fees of Counsel

5.1

(1) When making an order for costs the court may state an opinion as to whether or not the hearing was fit for the attendance of one or more counsel, and, if it does so, the court conducting a detailed assessment of those costs will have regard to the opinion stated.

(2) The court will generally express an opinion only where –
   (a) the paying party asks it to do so;
   (b) more than one counsel appeared for a party; or
   (c) the court wishes to record its opinion that the case was not fit for the attendance of counsel.

5.2

(1) Where the court refers any matter to the conveyancing counsel of the court the fees payable to counsel in respect of the work done or to be done will be assessed by the court in accordance with rule 44.2.

(2) An appeal from a decision of the court in respect of the fees of such counsel will be dealt with under the general rules as to appeals set out in Part 52. If the appeal is against the decision of an authorised court officer, it will be dealt with in accordance with rules 47.22 to 47.24.

Subsection 6 of This Practice Direction – Basis of Assessment: Rule 44.3

Costs on the indemnity basis

6.1 If costs are awarded on the indemnity basis, the court assessing costs will disallow any costs –

(a) which it finds to have been unreasonably incurred; or

(b) which it considers to be unreasonable in amount.

Costs on the standard basis

6.2 If costs are awarded on the standard basis, the court assessing costs will disallow any costs –

(a) which it finds to have been unreasonably incurred;

(b) which it considers to be unreasonable in amount;

(c) which it considers to have been disproportionately incurred or to be disproportionate in amount; or

(d) about which it has doubts as to whether they were reasonably or proportionately incurred, or whether they are reasonable and proportionate in amount.

Subsection 7 of this Practice Direction – Amount of costs where costs are payable pursuant to a contract rule 44.5

Application of rule 44.5

7.1 Rule 44.5 only applies if the court is assessing costs payable under a contract. It does not–

(a) require the court to make an assessment of such costs; or

(b) require a mortgagee to apply for an order for those costs where there is a contractual right to recover out of the mortgage funds.

Costs relating to a mortgage

7.2

(1) The following principles apply to costs relating to a mortgage.

(2) An order for the payment of costs of proceedings by one party to another is always a discretionary order: section 51 of the Senior Courts Act 1981 ('the section 51 discretion').

(3) Where there is a contractual right to the costs, the discretion should ordinarily be exercised so as to reflect that contractual right.

(4) The power of the court to disallow a mortgagee's costs sought to be added to the mortgage security is a power that does not derive from section 51, but from the power of the courts of equity to fix the terms on which redemption will be allowed.

(5) A decision by a court to refuse costs in whole or in part to a mortgagee may be –

(a) a decision in the exercise of the section 51 discretion;

(b) a decision in the exercise of the power to fix the terms on which redemption will be allowed;

(c) a decision as to the extent of a mortgagee's contractual right to add the mortgagee's costs to the security; or

(d) a combination of two or more of these things.

(6) A mortgagee is not to be deprived of a contractual or equitable right to add costs to the security merely by reason of an order for payment of costs made without reference to the mortgagee's contractual or equitable rights, and without any adjudication as to whether or not the mortgagee should be deprived of those costs

7.3

(1) Where the contract entitles a mortgagee to—

(a) add the costs of litigation relating to the mortgage to the sum secured by it; or

(b) require a mortgagor to pay those costs,

the mortgagor may make an application for the court to direct that an account of the mortgagee's costs be taken.

(Rule 25.1(1)(n) provides that the court may direct that a party file an account.)

(2) The mortgagor may then dispute an amount in the mortgagee's account on the basis that it has been unreasonably incurred or is unreasonable in amount.

(3) Where a mortgagor disputes an amount, the court may make an order that the disputed costs are assessed under rule 44.5.

Subsection 8 of This Practice Direction – Procedure for Assessing Costs: Rule 44.6

Procedure for Assessing Costs

8.1 Subject to paragraph 8.3, where the court does not order fixed costs (or no fixed costs are provided for) the amount of costs payable will be assessed by the court. Rule 44.6 allows the court making an order about costs either –

(a) to make a summary assessment of the amount of the costs; or

(b) to order the amount to be decided in accordance with Part 47 (a detailed assessment).

8.2 An order for costs will be treated as an order for the amount of costs to be decided by a detailed assessment unless the order otherwise provides.

8.3 Where a party is entitled to costs some of which are fixed costs and some of which are not, the court will assess those costs which are not fixed. For example, the court will assess the disbursements payable in accordance with rules 45.12 or 45.19. The decision whether such assessment should be summary or detailed will be made in accordance with paragraphs 9.1 to 9.10 of this Practice Direction.

Subsection 9 of This Practice Direction – Summary Assessment: General Provisions

When the court should consider whether to make a summary assessment

9.1 Whenever a court makes an order about costs which does not provide only for fixed costs to be paid the court should consider whether to make a summary assessment of costs.

Timing of summary assessment

9.2 The general rule is that the court should make a summary assessment of the costs –

(a) at the conclusion of the trial of a case which has been dealt with on the fast track, in which case the order will deal with the costs of the whole claim; and

(b) at the conclusion of any other hearing, which has lasted not more than one day, in which case the order will deal with the costs of the application or matter to which the hearing related. If this hearing disposes of the claim, the order may deal with the costs of the whole claim,

unless there is good reason not to do so, for example where the paying party shows substantial grounds for disputing the sum claimed for costs that cannot be dealt with summarily.

****

Consent orders

9.4 Where an application has been made and the parties to the application agree an order by consent without any party attending, the parties should seek to agree a figure for costs to be inserted in the consent order or agree that there should be no order for costs.

Duty of parties and legal representatives

9.5

(1) It is the duty of the parties and their legal representatives to assist the judge in making a summary assessment of costs in any case to which paragraph 9.2 above applies, in accordance with the following subparagraphs.

(2) Each party who intends to claim costs must prepare a written statement of those costs showing separately in the form of a schedule –

(a) the number of hours to be claimed;

(b) the hourly rate to be claimed;

(c) the grade of fee earner;

(d) the amount and nature of any disbursement to be claimed, other than counsel's fee for appearing at the hearing;

(e) the amount of legal representative's costs to be claimed for attending or appearing at the hearing;

(f) counsel's fees; and
(g) any VAT to be claimed on these amounts.

(3) The statement of costs should follow as closely as possible Form N260 and must be signed by the party or the party's legal representative. Where a party is –
(a) an assisted person;
(b) a LSC funded client;
(c) a person for whom civil legal services (within the meaning of Part 1 of the Legal Aid, Sentencing and Punishment of Offenders Act 2012) are provided under arrangements made for the purposes of that Part of that Act; or
(d) represented by a person in the party's employment,

the statement of costs need not include the certificate appended at the end of Form N260.

(4) The statement of costs must be filed at court and copies of it must be served on any party against whom an order for payment of those costs is intended to be sought as soon as possible and in any event –
(a) for a fast track trial, not less than 2 days before the trial; and
(b) for all other hearings, not less than 24 hours before the time fixed for the hearing.

9.6 The failure by a party, without reasonable excuse, to comply with paragraph 9.5 will be taken into account by the court in deciding what order to make about the costs of the claim, hearing or application, and about the costs of any further hearing or detailed assessment hearing that may be necessary as a result of that failure.

No summary assessment by a costs officer

9.7 The court awarding costs cannot make an order for a summary assessment of costs by a costs officer. If a summary assessment of costs is appropriate but the court awarding costs is unable to do so on the day, the court may give directions as to a further hearing before the same judge.

Assisted persons etc

9.8 The court will not make a summary assessment of the costs of a receiving party who is an assisted person or LSC funded client or who is a person for whom civil legal services (within the meaning of Part 1 of the Legal Aid, Sentencing and Punishment of Offenders Act 2012) are provided under arrangements made for the purposes of that Part of that Act.

Children or protected parties

9.9

(1) The court will not make a summary assessment of the costs of a receiving party who is a child or protected party within the meaning of Part 21 unless the legal representative acting for the child or protected

party has waived the right to further costs (see Practice Direction 46 paragraph 2.1).

(2) The court may make a summary assessment of costs payable by a child or protected party.

Disproportionate or unreasonable costs

9.10 The court will not give its approval to disproportionate or unreasonable costs. When the amount of the costs to be paid has been agreed between the parties the order for costs must state that the order is by consent.

Subsection 10 of this Practice Direction – Legal Representative's Duty to Notify Party: Rule 44.8

Legal Representative's Duty to Notify Party: Rule 44.8

10.1 For the purposes of rule 44.8 and paragraph 10.2, 'party' includes any person (for example, an insurer, a trade union or the LSC or Lord Chancellor) who has instructed the legal representative to act for the party or who is liable to pay the legal representative's fees.

10.2 A legal representative who notifies a party of an order under rule 44.8 must also explain why the order came to be made.

10.3 Although rule 44.8 does not specify any sanction for breach of the rule the court may, either in the order for costs itself or in a subsequent order, require the legal representative to produce to the court evidence showing that the legal representative took reasonable steps to comply with the rule.

Subsection 11 of this Practice Direction – Court's Powers In Relation To Misconduct: Rule 44.11

Court's Powers In Relation To Misconduct: Rule 44.11

11.1 Before making an order under rule 44.11, the court must give the party or legal representative in question a reasonable opportunity to make written submissions or, if the legal representative so desires, to attend a hearing.

11.2 Conduct which is unreasonable or improper includes steps which are calculated to prevent or inhibit the court from furthering the overriding objective.

11.3 Although rule 44.11(3) does not specify any sanction for breach of the obligation imposed by the rule the court may, either in the order under rule 44.11(2) or in a subsequent order, require the legal representative to produce to the court evidence that the legal representative took reasonable steps to comply with the obligation.

****

CPR Pt 45

Part 45
Fixed Costs

Section I – Fixed Costs

****

45.7 Miscellaneous fixed costs

Table 4 shows the amount to be allowed in respect of legal representative's charges in the circumstances mentioned.

TABLE 4

Miscellaneous Fixed Costs	
For service by a party of any document other than the claim form required to be served personally including preparing and copying a certificate of service for each individual served	£15.00
Where service by an alternative method or at an alternative place is permitted by an order under rule 6.15 for each individual served	£53.25
Where a document is served out of the jurisdiction—	
(a) in Scotland, Northern Ireland, the Isle of Man or the Channel Islands;	£68.25
(b) in any other place	£77.00

45.8 Fixed enforcement costs

Table 5 shows the amount to be allowed in respect of legal representative's costs in the circumstances mentioned. The amounts shown in Table 4 are to be allowed in addition, if applicable.

TABLE 5

Fixed Enforcement Costs	
For an application under rule 70.5(4) that an award may be enforced as if payable under a court order, where the amount outstanding under the award:	
exceeds £25 but does not exceed £250	£30.75
exceeds £250 but does not exceed £600	£41.00
exceeds £600 but does not exceed £2,000	£69.00
exceeds £2,000	£75.50

Fixed Enforcement Costs	
On attendance to question a judgment debtor (or officer of a company or other corporation) who has been ordered to attend court under rule 71.2 where the questioning takes place before a court officer, including attendance by a responsible representative of the legal representative	For each half hour or part, £15.00
On the making of a final third party debt order under rule 72.8(6)(a) or an order for the payment to the judgment creditor of money in court under rule 72.10(1)(b):	
if the amount recovered is less than £150	One-half of the amount recovered
otherwise	£98.50
On the making of a final charging order under rule 73.10(7)(a) or 73.10A(3)(a):	£110.00
	The court may also allow reasonable disbursements in respect of search fees and the registration of the order.
Where a certificate is issued and registered under Schedule 6 to the Civil Jurisdiction and Judgments Act 1982, the costs of registration	£39.00
Where permission is given under rule 83.13 to enforce a judgment or order giving possession of land and costs are allowed on the judgment or order, the amount to be added to the judgment or order for costs—	
(a) basic costs	£42.50
(b) where notice of the proceedings is to be to more than one person, for each additional person	£2.75
Where a writ of control as defined in rule 83.1(2)(k) is issued against any party	£51.75
Where a writ of execution as defined in rule 83.1(2)(l) is issued against any party	£51.75
Where a request is filed for the issue of a warrant of control under rule 83.15 for a sum exceeding £25	£2.25
Where a request is filed for the issue of a warrant of delivery under rule 83.15 for a sum exceeding £25	£2.25
Where an application for an attachment of earnings order is made and costs are allowed under rule 89.10 or CCR Order 28, rule 10, for each attendance on the hearing of the application	£8.50

****

CPR Pt 46

Part 46
Costs – Special Cases

Section I – Costs Payable by or to Particular Persons

46.1 Pre-commencement disclosure and orders for disclosure against a person who is not a party

(1) This paragraph applies where a person applies –
  (a) for an order under –
    (i) section 33 of the Senior Courts Act 1981; or
    (ii) section 52 of the County Courts Act 1984,

  (which give the court powers exercisable before commencement of proceedings); or
  (b) for an order under –
    (i) section 34 of the Senior Courts Act 1981; or
    (ii) section 53 of the County Courts Act 1984,

  (which give the court power to make an order against a non-party for disclosure of documents, inspection of property etc.).

(2) The general rule is that the court will award the person against whom the order is sought that person's costs –
  (a) of the application; and
  (b) of complying with any order made on the application.

(3) The court may however make a different order, having regard to all the circumstances, including –
  (a) the extent to which it was reasonable for the person against whom the order was sought to oppose the application; and
  (b) whether the parties to the application have complied with any relevant pre-action protocol.

46.2 Costs orders in favour of or against non-parties

(1) Where the court is considering whether to exercise its power under section 51 of the Senior Courts Act 19815 (costs are in the discretion of the court) to make a costs order in favour of or against a person who is not a party to proceedings, that person must –
  (a) be added as a party to the proceedings for the purposes of costs only; and
  (b) be given a reasonable opportunity to attend a hearing at which the court will consider the matter further.

(2) This rule does not apply –
  (a) where the court is considering whether to –
    (i) make an order against the Lord Chancellor in proceedings in which the Lord Chancellor has provided legal aid to a party to the proceedings;
    (ii) make a wasted costs order (as defined in rule 46.8); and

(b) in proceedings to which rule 46.1 applies (pre-commencement disclosure and orders for disclosure against a person who is not a party).

46.3 Limitations on court's power to award costs in favour of trustee or personal representative

(1) This rule applies where –
(a) a person is or has been a party to any proceedings in the capacity of trustee or personal representative; and
(b) rule 44.5 does not apply.

(2) The general rule is that that person is entitled to be paid the costs of those proceedings, insofar as they are not recovered from or paid by any other person, out of the relevant trust fund or estate.

(3) Where that person is entitled to be paid any of those costs out of the fund or estate, those costs will be assessed on the indemnity basis.

46.4 Costs where money is payable by or to a child or protected party

(1) This rule applies to any proceedings where a party is a child or protected party and–
(a) money is ordered or agreed to be paid to, or for the benefit of, that party; or
(b) money is ordered to be paid by that party or on that party's behalf.

('Child' and 'protected party' have the same meaning as in rule 21.1(2).)

(2) The general rule is that–
(a) the court must order a detailed assessment of the costs payable by, or out of money belonging to, any party who is a child or protected party; and
(b) on an assessment under paragraph (a), the court must also assess any costs payable to that party in the proceedings, unless –
(i) the court has issued a default costs certificate in relation to those costs under rule 47.11; or
(ii) the costs are payable in proceedings to which Section II or Section III of Part 45 applies.

(3) The court need not order detailed assessment of costs in the circumstances set out in paragraph (5) or in Practice Direction 46.

(4) Where –
(a) a claimant is a child or protected party; and
(b) a detailed assessment has taken place under paragraph (2)(a),

the only amount payable by the child or protected party is the amount which the court certifies as payable.

(5) Where the costs payable comprise only the success fee claimed by the child's or protected party's legal representative under a conditional fee agreement or the balance of any payment under a damages based agreement, the court may direct that—

(a) the assessment procedure referred to in rule 46.10 and paragraph 6 of Practice Direction 46 shall not apply; and
(b) such costs be assessed summarily.

(This rule applies to a counterclaim by or on behalf of a child or protected party by virtue of rule 20.3.)

46.5 Litigants in person

(1) This rule applies where the court orders (whether by summary assessment or detailed assessment) that the costs of a litigant in person are to be paid by any other person.

(2) The costs allowed under this rule will not exceed, except in the case of a disbursement, two-thirds of the amount which would have been allowed if the litigant in person had been represented by a legal representative.

(3) The litigant in person shall be allowed –
(a) costs for the same categories of –
(i) work; and
(ii) disbursements,

which would have been allowed if the work had been done or the disbursements had been made by a legal representative on the litigant in person's behalf;
(b) the payments reasonably made by the litigant in person for legal services relating to the conduct of the proceedings; and
(c) the costs of obtaining expert assistance in assessing the costs claim.

(4) The amount of costs to be allowed to the litigant in person for any item of work claimed will be –
(a) where the litigant can prove financial loss, the amount that the litigant can prove to have been lost for time reasonably spent on doing the work; or
(b) where the litigant cannot prove financial loss, an amount for the time reasonably spent on doing the work at the rate set out in Practice Direction 46.

(5) A litigant who is allowed costs for attending at court to conduct the case is not entitled to a witness allowance in respect of such attendance in addition to those costs.

(6) For the purposes of this rule, a litigant in person includes –
(a) a company or other corporation which is acting without a legal representative; and
(b) any of the following who acts in person (except where any such person is represented by a firm in which that person is a partner) –
(i) a barrister,
(ii) a solicitor,
(iii) a solicitor's employee,
(iv) a manager of a body recognised under section 9 of the Administration of Justice Act 1985; or

(v) a person who, for the purposes of the 2007 Act, is an authorised person in relation to an activity which constitutes the conduct of litigation (within the meaning of that Act).

46.6 Costs where the court has made a group litigation order

(1) This rule applies where the court has made a Group Litigation Order ('GLO').

(2) In this rule–

'individual costs' means costs incurred in relation to an individual claim on the group register;

'common costs' means–

(i) costs incurred in relation to the GLO issues;

(ii) individual costs incurred in a claim while it is proceeding as a test claim, and

(iii) costs incurred by the lead legal representative in administering the group litigation; and

'group litigant' means a claimant or defendant, as the case may be, whose claim is entered on the group register.

(3) Unless the court orders otherwise, any order for common costs against group litigants imposes on each group litigant several liability for an equal proportion of those common costs.

(4) The general rule is that a group litigant who is the paying party will, in addition to any liability to pay the receiving party, be liable for –

(a) the individual costs of that group litigant's claim; and

(b) an equal proportion, together with all the other group litigants, of the common costs.

(5) Where the court makes an order about costs in relation to any application or hearing which involved –

(a) one or more GLO issues; and

(b) issues relevant only to individual claims,

the court will direct the proportion of the costs that is to relate to common costs and the proportion that is to relate to individual costs.

(6) Where common costs have been incurred before a claim is entered on the group register, the court may order the group litigant to be liable for a proportion of those costs.

(7) Where a claim is removed from the group register, the court may make an order for costs in that claim which includes a proportion of the common costs incurred up to the date on which the claim is removed from the group register.

(Part 19 sets out rules about group litigation.)

46.7 Orders in respect of pro bono representation

(1) Where the court makes an order under section 194(3) of the 2007 Act –

(a) the court may order the payment to the prescribed charity of a sum no greater than the costs specified in Part 45 to which the party with pro bono representation would have been entitled in accordance with that Part and in respect of that representation had it not been provided free of charge; or

(b) where Part 45 does not apply, the court may determine the amount of the payment (other than a sum equivalent to fixed costs) to be made by the paying party to the prescribed charity by –

  (i) making a summary assessment; or

  (ii) making an order for detailed assessment,

of a sum equivalent to all or part of the costs the paying party would have been ordered to pay to the party with pro bono representation in respect of that representation had it not been provided free of charge.

(2) Where the court makes an order under section 194(3) of the 2007 Act, the order must direct that the payment by the paying party be made to the prescribed charity.

(3) The receiving party must send a copy of the order to the prescribed charity within 7 days of receipt of the order.

(4) Where the court considers making or makes an order under section 194(3) of the 2007 Act, Parts 44 to 47 apply, where appropriate, with the following modifications –

  (a) references to 'costs orders', 'orders about costs' or 'orders for the payment of costs' are to be read, unless otherwise stated, as if they refer to an order under section 194(3);

  (b) references to 'costs' are to be read, as if they referred to a sum equivalent to the costs that would have been claimed by, incurred by or awarded to the party with pro bono representation in respect of that representation had it not been provided free of charge; and

  (c) references to 'receiving party' are to be read, as meaning a party who has pro bono representation and who would have been entitled to be paid costs in respect of that representation had it not been provided free of charge.

Section II – Costs Relating to Legal representatives

46.8 Personal liability of legal representative for costs – wasted costs orders

(1) This rule applies where the court is considering whether to make an order under section 51(6) of the Senior Courts Act 19817 (court's power to disallow or (as the case may be) order a legal representative to meet, 'wasted costs').

(2) The court will give the legal representative a reasonable opportunity to make written submissions or, if the legal representative prefers, to attend a hearing before it makes such an order.

(3) When the court makes a wasted costs order, it will –

(a) specify the amount to be disallowed or paid; or
(b) direct a costs judge or a District Judge to decide the amount of costs to be disallowed or paid.

(4) The court may direct that notice must be given to the legal representative's client, in such manner as the court may direct –
(a) of any proceedings under this rule; or
(b) of any order made under it against his legal representative.

46.9 Basis of detailed assessment of solicitor and client costs

(1) This rule applies to every assessment of a solicitor's bill to a client except a bill which is to be paid out of the Community Legal Service Fund under the Legal Aid Act 1988 or the Access to Justice Act 1999 or by the Lord Chancellor under Part 1 of the Legal Aid, Sentencing and Punishment of Offenders Act 2012.

(2) Section 74(3) of the Solicitors Act 1974 applies unless the solicitor and client have entered into a written agreement which expressly permits payment to the solicitor of an amount of costs greater than that which the client could have recovered from another party to the proceedings.

(3) Subject to paragraph (2), costs are to be assessed on the indemnity basis but are to be presumed –
(a) to have been reasonably incurred if they were incurred with the express or implied approval of the client;
(b) to be reasonable in amount if their amount was expressly or impliedly approved by the client;
(c) to have been unreasonably incurred if –
(i) they are of an unusual nature or amount; and
(ii) the solicitor did not tell the client that as a result the costs might not be recovered from the other party.

(4) Where the court is considering a percentage increase on the application of the client, the court will have regard to all the relevant factors as they reasonably appeared to the solicitor or counsel when the conditional fee agreement was entered into or varied.

46.10 Assessment procedure

(1) This rule sets out the procedure to be followed where the court has made an order under Part III of the Solicitors Act 1974 for the assessment of costs payable to solicitor by the solicitor's client.

(2) The solicitor must serve a breakdown of costs within 28 days of the order for costs to be assessed.

(3) The client must serve points of dispute within 14 days after service on him of the breakdown of costs.

(4) The solicitor must serve any reply within 14 days of service on the solicitor of the points of dispute.

(5) Either party may file a request for a hearing date –
   (a) after points of dispute have been served; but
   (b) no later than 3 months after the date of the order for the costs to be assessed.

(6) This procedure applies subject to any contrary order made by the court.

Section IV – Costs-only Proceedings

46.14 Costs-only proceedings

(1) This rule applies where –
   (a) the parties to a dispute have reached an agreement on all issues (including which party is to pay the costs) which is made or confirmed in writing; but
   (b) they have failed to agree the amount of those costs; and
   (c) no proceedings have been started.

(2) Where this rule applies, the procedure set out in this rule must be followed.

(3) Proceedings under this rule are commenced by issuing a claim form in accordance with Part 8.

(4) The claim form must contain or be accompanied by the agreement or confirmation.

(5) In proceedings to which this rule applies the court may make an order for the payment of costs the amount of which is to be determined by assessment and/or, where appropriate, for the payment of fixed costs.

(6) Where this rule applies but the procedure set out in this rule has not been followed by a party –
   (a) that party will not be allowed costs greater than those that would have been allowed to that party had the procedure been followed; and
   (b) the court may award the other party the costs of the proceedings up to the point where an order for the payment of costs is made.

(7) Rule 44.5 (amount of costs where costs are payable pursuant to a contract) does not apply to claims started under the procedure in this rule.

Practice Direction 46 – Costs Special Cases

CPR PD 46

This Practice Direction supplements CPR Part 46

Awards of Costs in Favour of a Trustee or Personal Representative: Rule 46.3

1.1 [10]A trustee or personal representative is entitled to an indemnity out of the relevant trust fund or estate for costs properly incurred. Whether costs were

10 CPRPRACTICEDIRECTIONS_CPR Pt 46:Costs Special Cases (PD46)

properly incurred depends on all the circumstances of the case including whether the trustee or personal representative ('the trustee') –

(a) obtained directions from the court before bringing or defending the proceedings;
(b) acted in the interests of the fund or estate or in substance for a benefit other than that of the estate, including the trustee's own; and
(c) acted in some way unreasonably in bringing or defending, or in the conduct of, the proceedings.

1.2 The trustee is not to be taken to have acted for a benefit other than that of the fund by reason only that the trustee has defended a claim in which relief is sought against the trustee personally.

Costs Where Money Is Payable By Or To A Child Or Protected Party: Rule 46.4

2.1 The circumstances in which the court need not order the detailed assessment of costs under rule 46.4(2) are as follows –

(a) where there is no need to do so to protect the interests of the child or protected party or their estate;
(b) where another party has agreed to pay a specified sum in respect of the costs of the child or protected party and the legal representative acting for the child or protected party has waived the right to claim further costs;
(c) where the court has decided the costs payable to the child or protected party by way of summary assessment and the legal representative acting for the child or protected party has waived the right to claim further costs;
(d) where an insurer or other person is liable to discharge the costs which the child or protected party would otherwise be liable to pay to the legal representative and the court is satisfied that the insurer or other person is financially able to discharge those costs; and
(e) where the court has given a direction for summary assessment pursuant to rule 46.4(5).

Litigants In Person: Rule 46.5

3.1 In order to qualify as an expert for the purpose of rule 46.5(3)(c) (expert assistance in connection with assessing the claim for costs), the person in question must be a –

(a) barrister;
(b) solicitor;
(c) Fellow of the Institute of Legal Executives;
(d) Fellow of the Association of Costs Lawyers;
(e) law costs draftsman who is a member of the Academy of Experts;
(f) law costs draftsman who is a member of the Expert Witness Institute.

3.2 Where a self-represented litigant wishes to prove that the litigant has suffered financial loss, the litigant should produce to the court any written evidence relied on to support that claim, and serve a copy of that evidence on any party against whom the litigant seeks costs at least 24 hours before the hearing at which the question may be decided.

3.3 A self-represented litigant who commences detailed assessment proceedings under rule 47.5 should serve copies of that written evidence with the notice of commencement.

3.4 The amount, which may be allowed to a self-represented litigant under rule 45.39(5)(b) and rule 46.5(4)(b), is £19 per hour.

Orders in Respect of Pro Bono Representation: Rule 46.7

4.1 Where an order is sought under section 194(3) of the Legal Services Act 2007 the party who has pro bono representation must prepare, file and serve a written statement of the sum equivalent to the costs that party would have claimed for that legal representation had it not been provided free of charge.

Personal Liability of Legal Representative for Costs – Wasted Costs Orders: Rule 46.8

5.1 A wasted costs order is an order –
(a) that the legal representative pay a sum (either specified or to be assessed) in respect of costs to a party; or
(b) for costs relating to a specified sum or items of work to be disallowed.

5.2 Rule 46.8 deals with wasted costs orders against legal representatives. Such orders can be made at any stage in the proceedings up to and including the detailed assessment proceedings. In general, applications for wasted costs are best left until after the end of the trial.

5.3 The court may make a wasted costs order against a legal representative on its own initiative.

5.4 A party may apply for a wasted costs order –
(a) by filing an application notice in accordance with Part 23; or
(b) by making an application orally in the course of any hearing.

5.5 It is appropriate for the court to make a wasted costs order against a legal representative, only if –
(a) the legal representative has acted improperly, unreasonably or negligently;
(b) the legal representative's conduct has caused a party to incur unnecessary costs, or has meant that costs incurred by a party prior to the improper, unreasonable or negligent act or omission have been wasted;
(c) it is just in all the circumstances to order the legal representative to compensate that party for the whole or part of those costs.

5.6 The court will give directions about the procedure to be followed in each case in order to ensure that the issues are dealt with in a way which is fair and as simple and summary as the circumstances permit.

5.7 As a general rule the court will consider whether to make a wasted costs order in two stages –

(a) at the first stage the court must be satisfied –

(i) that it has before it evidence or other material which, if unanswered, would be likely to lead to a wasted costs order being made; and

(ii) the wasted costs proceedings are justified notwithstanding the likely costs involved;

(b) at the second stage, the court will consider, after giving the legal representative an opportunity to make representations in writing or at a hearing, whether it is appropriate to make a wasted costs order in accordance with paragraph 5.5 above.

5.8 The court may proceed to the second stage described in paragraph 5.7 without first adjourning the hearing if it is satisfied that the legal representative has already had a reasonable opportunity to make representations.

5.9 On an application for a wasted costs order under Part 23 the application notice and any evidence in support must identify –

(a) what the legal representative is alleged to have done or failed to do; and

(b) the costs that the legal representative may be ordered to pay or which are sought against the legal representative.

Assessment of Solicitor and Client Costs: Rules 46.9 and 46.10

6.1 A client and solicitor may agree whatever terms they consider appropriate about the payment of the solicitor's charges. If however, the costs are of an unusual nature, either in amount or the type of costs incurred, those costs will be presumed to have been unreasonably incurred unless the solicitor satisfies the court that the client was informed that they were unusual and that they might not be allowed on an assessment of costs between the parties. That information must have been given to the client before the costs were incurred.

6.2 Costs as between a solicitor and client are assessed on the indemnity basis. The presumptions in rule 46.9(3) are rebuttable.

6.3 If a party fails to comply with the requirements of rule 46.10 concerning the service of a breakdown of costs or points of dispute, any other party may apply to the court in which the detailed assessment hearing should take place for an order requiring compliance. If the court makes such an order, it may –

(a) make it subject to conditions including a condition to pay a sum of money into court; and

(b) specify the consequence of failure to comply with the order or a condition.

6.4 The procedure for obtaining an order under Part III of the Solicitors Act 1974 is by a Part 8 claim, as modified by rule 67.3 and Practice Direction 67. Precedent J of the Schedule of Costs Precedents is a model form of claim form. The application must be accompanied by the bill or bills in respect of which assessment is sought, and, if the claim concerns a conditional fee agreement, a copy of that agreement. If the original bill is not available a copy will suffice.

6.5 Model forms of order, which the court may make, are set out in Precedents K, L and M of the Schedule of Costs Precedents.

6.6 The breakdown of costs referred to in rule 46.10 is a document which contains the following information –

(a) details of the work done under each of the bills sent for assessment; and

(b) in applications under Section 70 of the Solicitors Act 1974, a cash account showing money received by the solicitor to the credit of the client and sums paid out of that money on behalf of the client but not payments out which were made in satisfaction of the bill or of any items which are claimed in the bill.

6.7 Precedent P of the Schedule of Costs Precedents is a model form of breakdown of costs. A party who is required to serve a breakdown of costs must also serve –

(a) copies of the fee notes of counsel and of any expert in respect of fees claimed in the breakdown, and

(b) written evidence as to any other disbursement which is claimed in the breakdown and which exceeds £250.

6.8 The provisions relating to default costs certificates (rule 47.11) do not apply to cases to which rule 46.10 applies.

6.9 The time for requesting a detailed assessment hearing is within 3 months after the date of the order for the costs to be assessed.

6.10 The form of request for a hearing date must be in Form N258C. The request must be accompanied by copies of –

(a) the order sending the bill or bills for assessment;

(b) the bill or bills sent for assessment;

(c) the solicitor's breakdown of costs and any invoices or accounts served with that breakdown;

(d) a copy of the points of dispute;

(e) a copy of any replies served;

(f) a statement signed by the party filing the request or that party's legal representative giving the names and addresses for service of all parties to the proceedings.

6.11 The request must include the estimated length of hearing.

6.12 On receipt of the request the court will fix a date for the hearing, or will give directions.

6.13 The court will give at least 14 days' notice of the time and place of the detailed assessment hearing.

6.14 Unless the court gives permission, only the solicitor whose bill it is and parties who have served points of dispute may be heard and only items specified in the points of dispute may be raised.

6.15 If a party wishes to vary that party's breakdown of costs, points of dispute or reply, an amended or supplementary document must be filed with the court and copies of it must be served on all other relevant parties. Permission is not required to vary a breakdown of costs, points of dispute or a reply but the court may disallow the variation or permit it only upon conditions, including conditions as to the payment of any costs caused or wasted by the variation.

6.16 Unless the court directs otherwise the solicitor must file with the court the papers in support of the bill not less than 7 days before the date for the detailed assessment hearing and not more than 14 days before that date.

6.17 Once the detailed assessment hearing has ended it is the responsibility of the legal representative appearing for the solicitor or, as the case may be, the solicitor in person to remove the papers filed in support of the bill.

6.18 If, in the course of a detailed assessment hearing of a solicitor's bill to that solicitor's client, it appears to the court that in any event the solicitor will be liable in connection with that bill to pay money to the client, it may issue an interim certificate specifying an amount which in its opinion is payable by the solicitor to the client.

6.19 After the detailed assessment hearing is concluded the court will –

(a) complete the court copy of the bill so as to show the amount allowed;
(b) determine the result of the cash account;
(c) award the costs of the detailed assessment hearing in accordance with Section 70(8) of the Solicitors Act 1974; and
(d) issue a final costs certificate.

****

Costs-only proceedings: rule 46.11

9.1 A claim form under rule 46.14 should not be issued in the High Court unless the dispute to which the agreement relates was of such a value or type that proceedings would have been commenced in the High Court.

9.2 A claim form which is to be issued in the High Court at the Royal Courts of Justice will be issued in the Costs Office.

9.3 Attention is drawn to rule 8.2 (in particular to paragraph (b)(ii)) and to rule 46.14(3). The claim form must –

(a) identify the claim or dispute to which the agreement relates;
(b) state the date and terms of the agreement on which the claimant relies;
(c) set out or attach a draft of the order which the claimant seeks;
(d) state the amount of the costs claimed.

9.4 Unless the court orders otherwise or Section II of Part 45 applies the costs will be treated as being claimed on the standard basis.

9.5 The evidence required under rule 8.5 includes copies of the documents on which the claimant relies to prove the defendant's agreement to pay costs.

9.6 A costs judge or a district judge has jurisdiction to hear and decide any issue which may arise in a claim issued under this rule irrespective of the amount of the costs claimed or of the value of the claim to which the agreement to pay costs relates. The court may make an order by consent under paragraph 9.8, or an order dismissing a claim under paragraph 9.10 below.

9.7 When the time for filing the defendant's acknowledgement of service has expired, the claimant may request in writing that the court make an order in the terms of the claim, unless the defendant has filed an acknowledgement of service stating the intention to contest the claim or to seek a different order.

9.8 Rule 40.6 applies where an order is to be made by consent. An order may be made by consent in terms which differ from those set out in the claim form.

9.9 Where costs are ordered to be assessed, the general rule is that this should be by detailed assessment. However when an order is made under this rule following a hearing and the court is in a position to summarily assess costs it should generally do so.

9.10 If the defendant opposes the claim the defendant must file a witness statement in accordance with rule 8.5(3). The court will then give directions including, if appropriate, a direction that the claim shall continue as if it were a Part 7 claim. A claim is not treated as opposed merely because the defendant disputes the amount of the claim for costs.

9.11 A claim issued under this rule may be dealt with without being allocated to a track. Rule 8.9 does not apply to claims issued under this rule.

9.12 Where there are other issues nothing in rule 46.14 prevents a person from issuing a claim form under Part 7 or Part 8 to sue on an agreement made in settlement of a dispute where that agreement makes provision for costs, nor from claiming in that case an order for costs or a specified sum in respect of costs but the 'costs only' procedure in rule 46.14 must be used where the sole issue is the amount of costs.

CPR Pt 47

Part 47
Procedure for Detailed Assessment of Costs and Default Provisions

Section I
General Rules about Detailed Assessment

47.1 Time when detailed assessment may be carried out

The general rule is that the costs of any proceedings or any part of the proceedings are not to be assessed by the detailed procedure until the conclusion of the proceedings but the court may order them to be assessed immediately.

(Practice Direction 47 gives further guidance about when proceedings are concluded for the purpose of this rule.)

47.2 No stay of detailed assessment where there is an appeal

Detailed assessment is not stayed pending an appeal unless the court so orders.

47.3 Powers of an authorised court officer

(1) An authorised court officer has all the powers of the court when making a detailed assessment, except –
   (a) power to make a wasted costs order as defined in rule 46.8;
   (b) power to make an order under –
      (i) rule 44.11 (powers in relation to misconduct);
      (ii) rule 47.8 (sanction for delay in commencing detailed assessment proceedings);
      (iii) paragraph (2) (objection to detailed assessment by authorised court officer); and
   (c) power to make a detailed assessment of costs payable to a solicitor by that solicitor's client, unless the costs are being assessed under rule 46.5 (costs where money is payable to a child or protected party).

(2) Where a party objects to the detailed assessment of costs being made by an authorised court officer, the court may order it to be made by a costs judge or a District Judge.

(Practice Direction 47 sets out the relevant procedure.)

47.4 Venue for detailed assessment proceedings

(1) [11]All applications and requests in detailed assessment proceedings must be made to or filed at the appropriate office.

(Practice Direction 47 sets out the meaning of 'appropriate office' in any particular case)

(2) The court may direct that the appropriate office is to be the Costs Office.

(3) In the County Court, a court may direct that another County Court hearing centre is to be the appropriate office.

(4) A direction under paragraph (3) may be made without proceedings being transferred to that court.

(Rule 30.2 makes provision for the transfer within the County Court of proceedings for detailed assessment of costs.)

Section II
Costs Payable by one Party to Another – Commencement of Detailed Assessment Proceedings

47.5 Application of this Section

This Section of Part 47 applies where a cost officer is to make a detailed assessment of –

11 INDEX_Costs:detailed assessment:venue for proceedings

(a) costs which are payable by one party to another; or
(b) the sum which is payable by one party to the prescribed charity pursuant to an order under section 194(3) of the 2007 Act.

47.6 Commencement of detailed assessment proceedings

(1) [12]Detailed assessment proceedings are commenced by the receiving party serving on the paying party –
(a) notice of commencement in the relevant practice form;
(b) a copy or copies of the bill of costs, as required by Practice Direction 47; and
(c) if required by Practice Direction 47, a breakdown of the costs claimed for each phase of the proceedings.

(Rule 47.7 sets out the period for commencing detailed assessment proceedings)

(2) The receiving party must also serve a copy of the notice of commencement, the bill and, if required by Practice Direction 47, the breakdown on any other relevant persons specified in Practice Direction 47.

(3) A person on whom a copy of the notice of commencement is served under paragraph (2) is a party to the detailed assessment proceedings (in addition to the paying party and the receiving party).

(Practice Direction 47 deals with –
- other documents which the party must file when requesting detailed assessment;
- the court's powers where it considers that a hearing may be necessary;
- the form of a bill; and
- the length of notice which will be given if a hearing date is fixed.)

(Paragraphs 7B.2 to 7B.7 of the Practice Direction – Civil Recovery Proceedings contain provisions about detailed assessment of costs in relation to civil recovery orders.)

47.7 Period for commencing detailed assessment proceedings

The following table shows the period for commencing detailed assessment proceedings.

Source of right to detailed assessment	Time by which detailed assessment proceedings must be commenced
Judgment, direction, order, award or other determination	3 months after the date of the judgment etc. Where detailed assessment is stayed pending an appeal, 3 months after the date of the order lifting the stay

12 INDEX_Costs:detailed assessment:commencement

Source of right to detailed assessment	Time by which detailed assessment proceedings must be commenced
Discontinuance under Part 38	3 months after the date of service of notice of discontinuance under rule 38.3; or 3 months after the date of the dismissal of application to set the notice of discontinuance aside under rule 38.4
Acceptance of an offer to settle under Part 36	3 months after the date when the right to costs arose

47.8 Sanction for delay in commencing detailed assessment proceedings

(1) [13]Where the receiving party fails to commence detailed assessment proceedings within the period specified –

(a) in rule 47.7; or

(b) by any direction of the court,

the paying party may apply for an order requiring the receiving party to commence detailed assessment proceedings within such time as the court may specify.

(2) On an application under paragraph (1), the court may direct that, unless the receiving party commences detailed assessment proceedings within the time specified by the court, all or part of the costs to which the receiving party would otherwise be entitled will be disallowed.

(3) If –

(a) the paying party has not made an application in accordance with paragraph (1); and

(b) the receiving party commences the proceedings later than the period specified in rule 47.7,

the court may disallow all or part of the interest otherwise payable to the receiving party under –

(i) section 17 of the Judgments Act 1838; or

(ii) section 74 of the County Courts Act 1984,

but will not impose any other sanction except in accordance with rule 44.11 (powers in relation to misconduct).

(4) Where the costs to be assessed in a detailed assessment are payable out of the Community Legal Service Fund, this rule applies as if the receiving party were the solicitor to whom the costs are payable and the paying party were the Legal Services Commission.

(5) Where the costs to be assessed in a detailed assessment are payable by the Lord Chancellor under Part 1 of the Legal Aid, Sentencing and Punishment of Offenders Act 2012, this rule applies as if the receiving party were the solicitor to whom the costs are payable and the paying party were the Lord Chancellor.

13 INDEX_Costs:detailed assessment:delay in

47.9 Points of dispute and consequence of not serving

(1) The paying party and any other party to the detailed assessment proceedings may dispute any item in the bill of costs by serving points of dispute on –
  (a) the receiving party; and
  (b) every other party to the detailed assessment proceedings.

(2) The period for serving points of dispute is 21 days after the date of service of the notice of commencement.

(3) If a party serves points of dispute after the period set out in paragraph (2), that party may not be heard further in the detailed assessment proceedings unless the court gives permission.

(Practice Direction 47 sets out requirements about the form of points of dispute)

(4) The receiving party may file a request for a default costs certificate if –
  (a) the period set out in paragraph (2) for serving points of dispute has expired; and
  (b) the receiving party has not been served with any points of dispute.

(5) If any party (including the paying party) serves points of dispute before the issue of a default costs certificate the court may not issue the default costs certificate.

(Section IV of this Part sets out the procedure to be followed after points of dispute have been served).

47.10 Procedure where costs are agreed

(1) If the paying party and the receiving party agree the amount of costs, either party may apply for a costs certificate (either interim or final) in the amount agreed.

(Rule 47.16 and rule 47.17 contain further provisions about interim and final costs certificates respectively)

(2) An application for a certificate under paragraph (1) must be made to the court which would be the venue for detailed assessment proceedings under rule 47.4.

Section III
Costs Payable by One Party to Another – Default Provisions

47.11 Default costs certificate

(1) [14]Where the receiving party is permitted by rule 47.9 to obtain a default costs certificate, that party does so by filing a request in the relevant practice form.

(Practice Direction 47 deals with the procedure by which the receiving party may obtain a default costs certificate.)

14 INDEX_Costs:detailed assessment:default costs certificate

(2) A default costs certificate will include an order to pay the costs to which it relates.

(3) Where a receiving party obtains a default costs certificate, the costs payable to that party for the commencement of detailed assessment proceedings will be the sum set out in Practice Direction 47.

(4) A receiving party who obtains a default costs certificate in detailed assessment proceedings pursuant to an order under section 194(3) of the 2007 Act must send a copy of the default costs certificate to the prescribed charity.

47.12 Setting aside a default costs certificate

(1) The court will set aside a default costs certificate if the receiving party was not entitled to it.

(2) In any other case, the court may set aside or vary a default costs certificate if it appears to the court that there is some good reason why the detailed assessment proceedings should continue.

(Practice Direction 47 contains further details about the procedure for setting aside a default costs certificate and the matters which the court must take into account)

(3) Where the court sets aside or varies a default costs certificate in detailed assessment proceedings pursuant to an order under section 194(3) of the Legal Services Act 2007, the receiving party must send a copy of the order setting aside or varying the default costs certificate to the prescribed charity.

Section IV
Costs Payable by One Party to Another – Procedure where Points of Dispute are Served

47.13 Optional Reply

(1) [15]Where any party to the detailed assessment proceedings serves points of dispute, the receiving party may serve a reply on the other parties to the assessment proceedings.

(2) The receiving party may do so within 21 days after being served with the points of dispute to which the reply relates.

(Practice Direction 47 sets out the meaning of 'reply'.)

47.14 Detailed assessment hearing

(1) Where points of dispute are served in accordance with this Part, the receiving party must file a request for a detailed assessment hearing within 3 months of the expiry of the period for commencing detailed assessment proceedings as specified –

15 INDEX_Costs:detailed assessment:optional reply

(a) in rule 47.7; or
(b) by any direction of the court.

(2) Where the receiving party fails to file a request in accordance with paragraph (1), the paying party may apply for an order requiring the receiving party to file the request within such time as the court may specify.

(3) On an application under paragraph (2), the court may direct that, unless the receiving party requests a detailed assessment hearing within the time specified by the court, all or part of the costs to which the receiving party would otherwise be entitled will be disallowed.

(4) If –
(a) the paying party has not made an application in accordance with paragraph (2); and
(b) the receiving party files a request for a detailed assessment hearing later than the period specified in paragraph (1),

the court may disallow all or part of the interest otherwise payable to the receiving party under –
(i) section 17 of the Judgments Act 1838; or
(ii) section 74 of the County Courts Act 1984,

but will not impose any other sanction except in accordance with rule 44.11 (powers in relation to misconduct).

(5) No party other than –
(a) the receiving party;
(b) the paying party; and
(c) any party who has served points of dispute under rule 47.9,

may be heard at the detailed assessment hearing unless the court gives permission.

(6) Only items specified in the points of dispute may be raised at the hearing, unless the court gives permission.

(7) If an assessment is carried out at more than one hearing, then for the purposes of rule 52.12 time for appealing shall not start to run until the conclusion of the final hearing, unless the court orders otherwise.

(Practice Direction 47 specifies other documents which must be filed with the request for hearing and the length of notice which the court will give when it fixes a hearing date.)

47.15 Provisional Assessment

(1) This rule applies to any detailed assessment proceedings commenced in the High Court or the County Court on or after 1 April 2013 in which the costs claimed are the amount set out in paragraph 14.1 of the practice direction supplementing this Part, or less.

(2) In proceedings to which this rule applies, the parties must comply with the procedure set out in Part 47 as modified by paragraph 14 Practice Direction 47.

(3) The court will undertake a provisional assessment of the receiving party's costs on receipt of Form N258 and the relevant supporting documents specified in Practice Direction 47.

(4) The provisional assessment will be based on the information contained in the bill and supporting papers and the contentions set out in Precedent G (the points of dispute and any reply).

(5) The court will not award more than £1,500 to any party in respect of the costs of the provisional assessment.

(6) The court may at any time decide that the matter is unsuitable for a provisional assessment and may give directions for the matter to be listed for hearing. The matter will then proceed under rule 47.14 without modification.

(7) When a provisional assessment has been carried out, the court will send a copy of the bill, as provisionally assessed, to each party with a notice stating that any party who wishes to challenge any aspect of the provisional assessment must, within 21 days of the receipt of the notice, file and serve on all other parties a written request for an oral hearing. If no such request is filed and served within that period, the provisional assessment shall be binding upon the parties, save in exceptional circumstances.

(8) The written request referred to in paragraph (7) must –
 (a) identify the item or items in the court's provisional assessment which are sought to be reviewed at the hearing; and
 (b) provide a time estimate for the hearing.

(9) The court then will fix a date for the hearing and give at least 14 days' notice of the time and place of the hearing to all parties.

(10) Any party which has requested an oral hearing, will pay the costs of and incidental to that hearing unless –
 (a) it achieves an adjustment in its own favour by 20% or more of the sum provisionally assessed; or
 (b) the court otherwise orders.

Section V
Interim Costs Certificate and Final Costs Certificate.

47.16 Power to issue an interim certificate

(1) [16]The court may at any time after the receiving party has filed a request for a detailed assessment hearing –
 (a) issue an interim costs certificate for such sum as it considers appropriate or
 (b) amend or cancel an interim certificate.

(2) An interim certificate will include an order to pay the costs to which it relates, unless the court orders otherwise.

16 INDEX_Costs:detailed assessment:interim certificate

(3) The court may order the costs certified in an interim certificate to be paid into court.

(4) Where the court –
(a) issues an interim costs certificate; or
(b) amends or cancels an interim certificate,

in detailed assessment proceedings pursuant to an order under section 194(3) of the 2007 Act, the receiving party must send a copy of the interim costs certificate or the order amending or cancelling the interim costs certificate to the prescribed charity.

47.17 Final costs certificate

(1) [17]In this rule a 'completed bill' means a bill calculated to show the amount due following the detailed assessment of the costs.

(2) The period for filing the completed bill is 14 days after the end of the detailed assessment hearing.

(3) When a completed bill is filed the court will issue a final costs certificate and serve it on the parties to the detailed assessment proceedings.

(4) Paragraph (3) is subject to any order made by the court that a certificate is not to be issued until other costs have been paid.

(5) A final costs certificate will include an order to pay the costs to which it relates, unless the court orders otherwise.

(Practice Direction 47 deals with the form of a final costs certificate)

(6) Where the court issues a final costs certificate in detailed assessment proceedings pursuant to an order under section 194(3) of the 2007 Act, the receiving party must send a copy of the final costs certificate to the prescribed charity.

Section VI
Detailed Assessment Procedure for Costs of a LSC Funded Client, an Assisted Person or Person to Whom Legal Aid is Made Available where Costs are Payable out of the Community Legal Service Fund or by the Lord Chancellor under Part 1 of the Legal Aid, Sentencing and Punishment of Offenders Act 2012

47.18 Detailed assessment procedure where costs are payable out of the Community Legal Services Fund or by the Lord Chancellor under Part 1 of the Legal Aid, Sentencing and Punishment of Offenders Act 2012

(1) [18]Where the court is to assess costs of a LSC funded client, an assisted person or a person to whom legal aid is provided which are payable out of the Community Legal Services Fund or by the Lord Chancellor under Part

17 INDEX_Costs:detailed assessment:final costs certificate
18 INDEX_Community Legal Service:costs:detailed assessment procedure

1 of the Legal Aid, Sentencing and Punishment of Offenders Act 2012, that person's solicitor may commence detailed assessment proceedings by filing a request in the relevant practice form.

(2) A request under paragraph (1) must be filed within 3 months after the date when the right to detailed assessment arose.

(3) The solicitor must also serve a copy of the request for detailed assessment on the LSC funded client, the assisted person or the person to whom legal aid is provided, if notice of that person's interest has been given to the court in accordance with community legal service or legal aid regulations.

(4) Where the solicitor has certified that the LSC funded client or that person wishes to attend an assessment hearing, the court will, on receipt of the request for assessment, fix a date for the assessment hearing.

(5) Where paragraph (3) does not apply, the court will, on receipt of the request for assessment provisionally assess the costs without the attendance of the solicitor, unless it considers that a hearing is necessary.

(6) After the court has provisionally assessed the bill, it will return the bill to the solicitor.

(7) The court will fix a date for an assessment hearing if the solicitor informs the court, within 14 days after receiving the provisionally assessed bill, that the solicitor wants the court to hold such a hearing.

47.19 Detailed assessment procedure where costs are payable out of a fund other than the community legal service fund

(1) Where the court is to assess costs which are payable out of a fund other than the Community Legal Service Fund, the receiving party may commence detailed assessment proceedings by filing a request in the relevant practice form.

(2) A request under paragraph (1) must be filed within 3 months after the date when the right to detailed assessment arose.

(3) The court may direct that the party seeking assessment serve a copy of the request on any person who has a financial interest in the outcome of the assessment.

(4) The court will, on receipt of the request for assessment, provisionally assess the costs without the attendance of the receiving party, unless the court considers that a hearing is necessary.

(5) After the court has provisionally assessed the bill, it will return the bill to the receiving party.

(6) The court will fix a date for an assessment hearing if the receiving party informs the court, within 14 days after receiving the provisionally assessed bill, that the receiving party wants the court to hold such a hearing.

Section VII
Costs of Detailed Assessment Proceedings

47.20 Liability for costs of detailed assessment proceedings

(1) The receiving party is entitled to the costs of the detailed assessment proceedings except where –
   (a) the provisions of any Act, any of these Rules or any relevant practice direction provide otherwise; or
   (b) the court makes some other order in relation to all or part of the costs of the detailed assessment proceedings.

(2) Paragraph (1) does not apply where the receiving party has pro bono representation in the detailed assessment proceedings but that party may apply for an order in respect of that representation under section 194(3) of the 2007 Act.

(3) In deciding whether to make some other order, the court must have regard to all the circumstances, including –
   (a) the conduct of all the parties;
   (b) the amount, if any, by which the bill of costs has been reduced; and
   (c) whether it was reasonable for a party to claim the costs of a particular item or to dispute that item.

(4) The provisions of Part 36 apply to the costs of detailed assessment proceedings with the following modifications –
   (a) 'claimant' refers to 'receiving party' and 'defendant' refers to 'paying party';
   (b) 'trial' refers to 'detailed assessment hearing';
   (c) a detailed assessment hearing is 'in progress' from the time when it starts until the bill of costs has been assessed or agreed;
   (d) for rule 36.14(7) substitute 'If such sum is not paid within 14 days of acceptance of the offer, or such other period as has been agreed, the receiving party may apply for a final costs certificate for the unpaid sum.';
   (e) a reference to 'judgment being entered' is to the completion of the detailed assessment, and references to a 'judgment' being advantageous or otherwise are to the outcome of the detailed assessment.

(5) The court will usually summarily assess the costs of detailed assessment proceedings at the conclusion of those proceedings.

(6) Unless the court otherwise orders, interest on the costs of detailed assessment proceedings will run from the date of default, interim or final costs certificate, as the case may be.

(7) For the purposes of rule 36.17, detailed assessment proceedings are to be regarded as an independent claim.

Section VIII
Appeals from Authorised Court Officers in Detailed Assessment Proceedings

47.21 Right to appeal

(1) Any party to detailed assessment proceedings may appeal against a decision of an authorised court officer in those proceedings.

47.22 Court to hear appeal

An appeal against a decision of an authorised court officer lies to a costs judge or a District Judge of the High Court.

47.23 Appeal procedure

(1) The appellant must file an appeal notice within 21 days after the date of the decision against which it is sought to appeal.

(2) On receipt of the appeal notice, the court will –
   (a) serve a copy of the notice on the parties to the detailed assessment proceedings; and
   (b) give notice of the appeal hearing to those parties.

47.24 Powers of the court on appeal

On an appeal from an authorised court officer the court will –
   (a) re-hear the proceedings which gave rise to the decision appealed against; and
   (b) make any order and give any directions as it considers appropriate.

Practice Direction 47 – Procedure for Detailed Assessment of Costs and Default Provisions

CPR PD 47

This Practice Direction supplements CPR Part 47

Time When Assessment May Be Carried Out: Rule 47.1

1.1 [19]For the purposes of rule 47.1, proceedings are concluded when the court has finally determined the matters in issue in the claim, whether or not there is an appeal, or made an award of provisional damages under Part 41.

1.2 The court may order or the parties may agree in writing that, although the proceedings are continuing, they will nevertheless be treated as concluded.

19 CPRPRACTICEDIRECTIONS_CPR Pt 47:Procedure for Detailed Assessment of Costs and Default Provisions (PD47)

1.3 A party who is served with a notice of commencement (see paragraph 5.2 below) may apply to a costs judge or a District Judge to determine whether the party who served it is entitled to commence detailed assessment proceedings. On hearing such an application the orders which the court may make include: an order allowing the detailed assessment proceedings to continue, or an order setting aside the notice of commencement.

1.4 A costs judge or a District Judge may make an order allowing detailed assessment proceedings to be commenced where there is no realistic prospect of the claim continuing.

No Stay of Detailed Assessment Where There is an Appeal: Rule 47.2

2 An application to stay the detailed assessment of costs pending an appeal may be made to the court whose order is being appealed or to the court which will hear the appeal.

Powers of an Authorised Court Officer: Rule 47.3

3.1 The court officers authorised by the Lord Chancellor to assess costs in the Costs Office and the Principal Registry of the Family Division are authorised to deal with claims where the base costs excluding VAT do not exceed £35,000 in the case of senior executive officers, or their equivalent, and £110,000 in the case of principal officers.

3.2 Where the receiving party, paying party and any other party to the detailed assessment proceedings who has served points of dispute are agreed that the assessment should not be made by an authorised court officer, the receiving party should so inform the court when requesting a hearing date. The court will then list the hearing before a costs judge or a District Judge.

3.3 In any other case a party who objects to the assessment being made by an authorised court officer must make an application to the costs judge or District Judge under Part 23 setting out the reasons for the objection.

Venue for Detailed Assessment Proceedings: Rule 47.4

4.1 For the purposes of rule 47.4(1) the 'appropriate office' means –

(a) the district registry or County Court hearing centre in which the case was being dealt with when the judgment or order was made or the event occurred which gave rise to the right to assessment, or to which it has subsequently been transferred;

(b) where a tribunal, person or other body makes an order for the detailed assessment of costs, a County Court hearing centre (subject to paragraph 4.2); or

(c) in all other cases, including Court of Appeal cases, the Costs Office.

4.2

(1) This paragraph applies where the appropriate office is any of the following County Court hearing centres: Barnet, Brentford, Bromley, Central London, Clerkenwell and Shoreditch, Croydon, Edmonton,

Ilford, Kingston, Mayors and City of London, Romford, Uxbridge, Wandsworth and Willesden.

(2) Where this paragraph applies –

(a) the receiving party must file any request for a detailed assessment hearing in the Costs Office and, for all purposes relating to that detailed assessment (other than the issue of default costs certificates and applications to set aside default costs certificates), the Costs Office will be treated as the appropriate office in that case;

(b) default costs certificates should be issued and applications to set aside default costs certificates should be issued and heard in the relevant County Court hearing centre; and

(c) unless an order is made under rule 47.4(2) directing that the Costs Office as part of the High Court shall be the appropriate office, an appeal from any decision made by a costs judge shall lie to the Designated Civil Judge for the London Group of County Court hearing centres or such judge as the Designated Civil Judge shall nominate. The appeal notice and any other relevant papers should be lodged at the Central London Civil Justice Centre.

4.3

(1) A direction under rule 47.4(2) or (3) specifying a particular court, registry or office as the appropriate office may be given on application or on the court's own initiative.

(2) Unless the Costs Office is the appropriate office for the purposes of rule 47.4(1) an order directing that an assessment is to take place at the Costs Office will be made only if it is appropriate to do so having regard to the size of the bill of costs, the difficulty of the issues involved, the likely length of the hearing, the cost to the parties and any other relevant matter.

Commencement of Detailed Assessment Proceedings: Rule 47.6

5.1 In the circumstances provided for in this paragraph, bills of costs for detailed assessment must be in electronic spreadsheet format and compliant with paragraphs 5.A1 to 5.A4 ('electronic bills') while in all other circumstances bills of costs may be electronic bills or may be on paper ('paper bills') and compliant with paragraphs 5.7 to 5.21. Precedents A, B, C and D in the Schedule of Costs Precedents annexed to this Practice Direction are model forms of paper bills of costs for detailed assessment. The circumstances in which bills of costs must be electronic bills of costs are that –

(a) the case is a Part 7 multi-track claim, except –

(i) for cases in which the proceedings are subject to fixed costs or scale costs;

(ii) cases in which the receiving party is unrepresented; or

(iii) where the court has otherwise ordered; and

(b) the bills of costs relate to costs recoverable between the parties for work undertaken after 6 April 2018 ('the Transition Date').

5.A1 A model electronic bill is annexed to this version of this Practice Direction as Precedent S. The online version of this Practice Direction at

http://www.justice.gov.uk/courts/procedure-rules/civil/rules/part-47-procedure-for-detailed-assessment/practice-direction-46-costs-special-cases2

annexes Precedent S in spreadsheet and pdf formats.

5.A2 Electronic bills may be in either Precedent S spreadsheet format online at http://www.justice.gov.uk/courts/procedure-rules/civil or any other spreadsheet format which –

(a) reports and aggregates costs based on the phases, tasks, activities and expenses defined in Schedule 2 to this Practice Direction;
(b) reports summary totals in a form comparable to Precedent S;
(c) allows the user to identify, in chronological order, the detail of all the work undertaken in each phase;
(d) automatically recalculates intermediate and overall summary totals if input data is changed;
(e) contains all calculations and reference formulae in a transparent manner so as to make its full functionality available to the court and all other parties.

5.A3 The provisions of paragraphs 5.7 to 5.21 of this Practice Direction shall apply to electronic bills insofar as they are not inconsistent with the form and content of Precedent S. Where those paragraphs require or recommend division of the bill into parts, electronic bills (unless the format of the bill already provides the requisite information, for example in identifying the costs within each phase) should incorporate a summary in a form comparable to the 'Funding and Parts Table' in Precedent S to provide the information that would otherwise be provided by its division into parts.

5.A4 Where a bill of costs otherwise falls within paragraph 5.1(a) but work was done both before and after the Transition Date, a party may serve and file either a paper bill or an electronic bill in respect of work done before that date and must serve and file an electronic bill in respect of work done after that date.

5.1A Subject to paragraph 5.1B, whenever electronic bills are served or filed at the court –

(a) they must be served or filed in hard copy, in a manageable paper format as shown in the pdf version of Precedent S; and
(b) a copy of the full electronic spreadsheet version must at the same time be provided to the paying party, or as appropriate filed at court, by e-mail or other electronic means.

5.1B Whenever an electronic bill is filed at the Costs Office using Electronic Working (see Practice Direction 51O) –

(a) a copy of the full electronic spreadsheet version and a pdf version must be uploaded; and
(b) the electronic bill must not be filed at court by any other means.

5.2 On commencing detailed assessment proceedings, the receiving party must serve on the paying party and all the other relevant persons the following documents –

(a) a notice of commencement in Form N252;
(b) a copy (or, where paragraph 5.A4 applies, copies) of the bill of costs;
(c) copies of the fee notes of counsel and of any expert in respect of fees claimed in the bill;
(d) written evidence as to any other disbursement which is claimed and which exceeds £500;
(e) a statement giving the name and address for service of any person upon whom the receiving party intends to serve the notice of commencement;
(f) if a costs management order has been made (and if the same information is not already fully provided in an electronic bill), a breakdown of the costs claimed for each phase of the proceedings. Precedent Q in the Schedule of Costs Precedents annexed to this Practice Direction is a model form of breakdown of the costs claimed for each phase of the proceedings.

5.3 The notice of commencement must be completed to show as separate items –

(a) the total amount of the costs claimed in the bill;
(b) the extra sum which will be payable by way of fixed costs and court fees if a default costs certificate is obtained.

5.4 Where the notice of commencement is to be served outside England and Wales the date to be inserted in the notice of commencement for the paying party to send points of dispute is a date (not less than 21 days from the date of service of the notice) which must be calculated by reference to Section IV of Part 6 as if the notice were a claim form and as if the date to be inserted was the date for the filing of a defence.

5.5

(1) For the purposes of rule 47.6(2) a 'relevant person' means –
  (a) any person who has taken part in the proceedings which gave rise to the assessment and who is directly liable under an order for costs made against that person;
  (b) any person who has given to the receiving party notice in writing that that person has a financial interest in the outcome of the assessment and wishes to be a party accordingly;
  (c) any other person whom the court orders to be treated as such.
(2) Where a party is unsure whether a person is or is not a relevant person, that party may apply to the appropriate office for directions.
(3) The court will generally not make an order that the person in respect of whom the application is made will be treated as a relevant person, unless within a specified time that person applies to the court to be joined as a party to the assessment proceedings in accordance with Part 19 (Parties and Group Litigation).

5.6 Where –

(a) a paper bill is capable of being copied electronically; and
(b) before the detailed assessment hearing,

a paying party requests an electronic copy of the bill, the receiving party must supply the paying party with a copy in its native format (for example, in Excel or an equivalent) free of charge not more than 7 days after receipt of the request.

Form and Contents of Bills of Costs – General

5.7 A bill of costs may consist of such of the following sections as may be appropriate –

(1) title page;
(2) background information;
(3) items of costs claimed under the headings specified in paragraph 5.12;
(4) summary showing the total costs claimed on each page of the bill;
(5) schedules of time spent on non-routine attendances; and
(6) the certificates referred to in paragraph 5.21.

If the only dispute between the parties concerns disbursements, the bill of costs shall be limited to items (1) and (2) above, a list of the disbursements in issue and brief written submissions in respect of those disbursements.

5.8 Where it is necessary or convenient to do so, a bill of costs may be divided into two or more parts, each part containing sections (2), (3) and (4) above. Circumstances in which it will be necessary or convenient to divide a bill into parts include the following –

(1) Where the receiving party acted in person during the course of the proceedings (whether or not that party also had a legal representative at that time) the bill must be divided into different parts so as to distinguish between;
  (a) the costs claimed for work done by the legal representative; and
  (b) the costs claimed for work done by the receiving party in person.
(2) Where the receiving party had pro bono representation for part of the proceedings and an order under section 194(3) of the Legal Services Act 2007 has been made, the bill must be divided into different parts so as to distinguish between –
  (a) the sum equivalent to the costs claimed for work done by the legal representative acting free of charge; and
  (b) the costs claimed for work not done by the legal representative acting free of charge.
(3) Where the receiving party was represented by different legal representatives during the course of the proceedings, the bill must be divided into different parts so as to distinguish between the costs payable in respect of each legal representative.
(4) Where the receiving party obtained legal aid or LSC funding or is a person for whom civil legal services (within the meaning of Part 1 of the Legal Aid, Sentencing and Punishment of Offenders Act 2012) were provided under arrangements made for the purposes of that Part of that Act in respect of all or part of the proceedings the bill must be divided into separate parts so as to distinguish between –

(a) costs claimed before legal aid or LSC funding was granted or before civil legal services were provided;

(b) costs claimed after legal aid or LSC funding was granted or after civil legal services were provided; and

(c) any costs claimed after legal aid or LSC funding ceased or after civil legal services ceased to be provided.

(5) Where the bill covers costs payable under an order or orders under which there are different paying parties the bill must be divided into parts so as to deal separately with the costs payable by each paying party.

(6) Where the bill covers costs payable under an order or orders, in respect of which the receiving party wishes to claim interest from different dates, the bill must be divided to enable such interest to be calculated.

(7) Where the case commenced on or after 1 April 2013, the bill covers costs for work done both before and after that date and the costs are to be assessed on the standard basis, the bill must be divided into parts so as to distinguish between costs shown as incurred for work done before 1 April 2013 and costs shown as incurred for work done on or after 1 April 2013.

(8) Where a costs management order has been made, the costs are to be assessed on the standard basis and the receiving party's budget has been agreed by the paying party or approved by the court, the bill must be divided into separate parts so as to distinguish between the costs claimed for each phase of the last approved or agreed budget, and within each such part the bill must distinguish between the costs shown as incurred in the last agreed or approved budget and the costs shown as estimated.

(9) Where a costs management order has been made and the receiving party's budget has been agreed by the paying party or approved by the court, (a) the costs of initially completing Precedent H and (b) the other costs of the budgeting and costs management process must be set out in separate parts.

5.9 Where a party claims costs against another party and also claims costs against the LSC or Lord Chancellor only for work done in the same period, the costs claimed against the LSC or Lord Chancellor only can be claimed either in a separate part of the bill or in additional columns in the same part of the bill. Precedents B and C in the Schedule of Costs Precedents annexed to this Practice Direction show how bills should be drafted when costs are claimed against the LSC only.

Form and Content of Bills of Costs – Title page

5.10 The title page of the bill of costs must set out –

(1) the full title of the proceedings;

(2) the name of the party whose bill it is and a description of the document showing the right to assessment (as to which see paragraph 13.3 of this Practice Direction);

(3) if VAT is included as part of the claim for costs, the VAT number of the legal representative or other person in respect of whom VAT is claimed;

(4) details of all legal aid certificates, LSC certificates, certificates recording the determinations of the Director of Legal Aid Casework and relevant amendment certificates in respect of which claims for costs are included in the bill.

Form and Content of Bills of Costs – Background information

5.11 The background information included in the bill of costs should set out –

(1) a brief description of the proceedings up to the date of the notice of commencement;

(2) a statement of the status of the legal representatives' employee in respect of whom costs are claimed and (if those costs are calculated on the basis of hourly rates) the hourly rates claimed for each such person.

(3) a brief explanation of any agreement or arrangement between the receiving party and his legal representatives, which affects the costs claimed in the bill.

Form and Content of Bills of Costs – Heads of costs

5.12 The bill of costs may consist of items under such of the following heads as may be appropriate –

(1) attendances at court and upon counsel up to the date of the notice of commencement;

(2) attendances on and communications with the receiving party;

(3) attendances on and communications with witnesses including any expert witness;

(4) attendances to inspect any property or place for the purposes of the proceedings;

(5) attendances on and communications with other persons, including offices of public records;

(6) communications with the court and with counsel;

(7) work done on documents:

(8) work done in connection with negotiations with a view to settlement if not already covered in the heads listed above;

(9) attendances on and communications with London and other agents and work done by them;

(10) other work done which was of or incidental to the proceedings and which is not already covered in the heads listed above.

5.13 In respect of each of the heads of costs –

(1) 'communications' means letters out e-mails out and telephone calls;

(2) communications, which are not routine communications, must be set out in chronological order;

(3) routine communications must be set out as a single item at the end of each head;

5.14 Routine communications are letters out, e-mails out and telephone calls which because of their simplicity should not be regarded as letters or e-mails of substance or telephone calls which properly amount to an attendance.

5.15 Each item claimed in the bill of costs must be consecutively numbered.

5.16 In each part of the bill of costs which claims items under head (1) in paragraph 5.12 (attendances at court and upon counsel) a note should be made of –

(1) all relevant events, including events which do not constitute chargeable items;

(2) any orders for costs which the court made (whether or not a claim is made in respect of those costs in this bill of costs).

5.17 The numbered items of costs may be set out on paper divided into columns. Precedents A, B and C in the Schedule of Costs Precedents annexed to this Practice Direction illustrate various model forms of bills of costs.

5.18 In respect of heads (2) to (10) in paragraph 5.12 above, if the number of attendances and communications other than routine communications is twenty or more, the claim for the costs of those items in that section of the bill of costs should be for the total only and should refer to a schedule in which the full record of dates and details is set out. If the bill of costs contains more than one schedule each schedule should be numbered consecutively.

5.19 The bill of costs must not contain any claims in respect of costs or court fees which relate solely to the detailed assessment proceedings other than costs claimed for preparing and checking the bill.

5.20 The summary must show the total profit costs and disbursements claimed separately from the total VAT claimed. Where the bill of costs is divided into parts the summary must also give totals for each part. If each page of the bill gives a page total the summary must also set out the page totals for each page.

5.21 The bill of costs must contain such of the certificates, the texts of which are set out in Precedent F of the Schedule of Costs Precedents annexed to this Practice Direction, as are appropriate.

5.22 The following provisions relate to work done by legal representatives –

(1) Routine letters out, routine e-mails out and routine telephone calls will in general be allowed on a unit basis of 6 minutes each, the charge being calculated by reference to the appropriate hourly rate. The unit charge for letters out and e-mails out will include perusing and considering the routine letters in or e-mails in.

(2) The court may, in its discretion, allow an actual time charge for preparation of electronic communications sent by legal representatives, which properly amount to attendances provided that the time taken has been recorded.

(3) Local travelling expenses incurred by legal representatives will not be allowed. The definition of 'local' is a matter for the discretion of the court. As a matter of guidance, 'local' will, in general, be taken to

mean within a radius of 10 miles from the court dealing with the case at the relevant time. Where travelling and waiting time is claimed, this should be allowed at the rate agreed with the client unless this is more than the hourly rate on the assessment.

(4) The cost of postage, couriers, out-going telephone calls, fax and telex messages will in general not be allowed but the court may exceptionally in its discretion allow such expenses in unusual circumstances or where the cost is unusually heavy.

(5) The cost of making copies of documents will not in general be allowed but the court may exceptionally in its discretion make an allowance for copying in unusual circumstances or where the documents copied are unusually numerous in relation to the nature of the case. Where this discretion is invoked the number of copies made, their purpose and the costs claimed for them must be set out in the bill.

(6) Agency charges as between principal legal representatives and their agents will be dealt with on the principle that such charges, where appropriate, form part of the principal legal representative's charges. Where these charges relate to head (1) in paragraph 5.12 (attendances at court and on counsel) they must be included in their chronological order in that head. In other cases they must be included in head (9) (attendances on London and other agents).

Period for Commencing Detailed Assessment Proceedings: Rule 47.7

6.1 The time for commencing the detailed assessment proceedings may be extended or shortened either by agreement (rule 2.11) or by the court (rule 3.1(2)(a)). Any application is to the appropriate office.

6.2 The detailed assessment proceedings are commenced by service of the documents referred to. Permission to commence assessment proceedings out of time is not required.

Sanction for Delay in Commencing Detailed Assessment Proceedings: Rule 47.8

7 An application for an order under rule 47.8 must be made in writing and be issued in the appropriate office. The application notice must be served at least 7 days before the hearing.

Points of Dispute and Consequences of Not Serving: Rule 47.9

8.1 Time for service of points of dispute may be extended or shortened either by agreement (rule 2.11) or by the court (rule 3.1(2)(a)). Any application is to the appropriate office.

8.2 Points of dispute must be short and to the point. They must follow Precedent G in the Schedule of Costs Precedents annexed to this Practice Direction, so far as practicable. They must:

(a) identify any general points or matters of principle which require decision before the individual items in the bill are addressed; and

(b) identify specific points, stating concisely the nature and grounds of dispute.

Once a point has been made it should not be repeated but the item numbers where the point arises should be inserted in the left hand box as shown in Precedent G.

8.3 The paying party must state in an open letter accompanying the points of dispute what sum, if any, that party offers to pay in settlement of the total costs claimed. The paying party may also make an offer under Part 36.

Procedure Where Costs are Agreed and on Discontinuance: Rule 47.10

9.1 Where the parties have agreed terms as to the issue of a costs certificate (either interim or final) they should apply under rule 40.6 (Consent judgments and orders) for an order that a certificate be issued in the terms set out in the application. Such an application may be dealt with by a court officer, who may issue the certificate.

9.2 Where in the course of proceedings the receiving party claims that the paying party has agreed to pay costs but that the paying party will neither pay those costs nor join in a consent application under paragraph 9.1, the receiving party may apply under Part 23 for a certificate either interim or final to be issued.

9.3 Nothing in rule 47.10 prevents parties who seek a judgment or order by consent from including in the draft a term that a party shall pay to another party a specified sum in respect of costs.

9.4

(1) The receiving party may discontinue the detailed assessment proceedings in accordance with Part 38 (Discontinuance).
(2) Where the receiving party discontinues the detailed assessment proceedings before a detailed assessment hearing has been requested, the paying party may apply to the appropriate office for an order about the costs of the detailed assessment proceedings.
(3) Where a detailed assessment hearing has been requested the receiving party may not discontinue unless the court gives permission.
(4) A bill of costs may be withdrawn by consent whether or not a detailed assessment hearing has been requested.

Default Costs Certificate: Rule 47.11

10.1

(1) A request for the issue of a default costs certificate must be made in Form N254 and must be signed by the receiving party or his legal representative.
(2) The request must be accompanied by a copy of the document giving the right to detailed assessment and must be filed at the appropriate office. (Paragraph 13.3 below identifies the appropriate documents).

10.2 A default costs certificate will be in Form N255.

10.3 Attention is drawn to Rules 40.3 (Drawing up and Filing of Judgments and Orders) and 40.4 (Service of Judgments and Orders) which apply to the preparation and service of a default costs certificate. The receiving party will be treated as having permission to draw up a default costs certificate by virtue of this Practice Direction.

10.4 The issue of a default costs certificate does not prohibit, govern or affect any detailed assessment of the same costs which are payable out of the Community Legal Service Fund or by the Lord Chancellor under Part 1 of the Legal Aid, Sentencing and Punishment of Offenders Act 2012.

10.5 An application for an order staying enforcement of a default costs certificate may be made either –
- (a) to a costs judge or District Judge of the court office which issued the certificate; or
- (b) to the court (if different) which has general jurisdiction to enforce the certificate.

10.6 Proceedings for enforcement of default costs certificates may not be issued in the Costs Office.

Default Costs Certificate: Fixed Costs on the Issue of a Default Costs Certificate

10.7 Unless paragraph 1.2 of Practice Direction 45 (Fixed Costs in Small Claims) applies or unless the court orders otherwise, the fixed costs to be included in a default costs certificate are £80 plus a sum equal to any appropriate court fee payable on the issue of the certificate.

10.8 The fixed costs included in a certificate must not exceed the maximum sum specified for costs and court fee in the notice of commencement.

Setting Aside Default Costs Certificate: Rule 47.12

11.1 A court officer may set aside a default costs certificate at the request of the receiving party under rule 47.12. A costs judge or a District Judge will make any other order or give any directions under this rule.

11.2
- (1) An application for an order under rule 47.12(2) to set aside or vary a default costs certificate must be supported by evidence.
- (2) In deciding whether to set aside or vary a certificate under rule 47.12(2) the matters to which the court must have regard include whether the party seeking the order made the application promptly.
- (3) As a general rule a default costs certificate will be set aside under rule 47.12 only if the applicant shows a good reason for the court to do so and if the applicant files with the application a copy of the bill, a copy of the default costs certificate and a draft of the points of dispute the applicant proposes to serve if the application is granted.

11.3 Attention is drawn to rule 3.1(3) (which enables the court when making an order to make it subject to conditions) and to rule 44.2(8) (which enables the court to order a party whom it has ordered to pay costs to pay an amount on account before the costs are assessed). A costs judge or a District Judge may exercise the power of the court to make an order under rule 44.2(8) although he did not make the order about costs which led to the issue of the default costs certificate.

Optional Reply: Rule 47.13

12.1 A reply served by the receiving party under Rule 47.13 must be limited to points of principle and concessions only. It must not contain general denials, specific denials or standard form responses.

12.2 Whenever practicable, the reply must be set out in the form of Precedent G.

Detailed Assessment Hearing: Rule 47.14

13.1 The time for requesting a detailed assessment hearing is within 3 months of the expiry of the period for commencing detailed assessment proceedings.

13.2 The request for a detailed assessment hearing must be in Form N258. The request must be accompanied by –

(a) a copy of the notice of commencement of detailed assessment proceedings;
(b) a copy of the bill of costs,
(c) the document giving the right to detailed assessment (see paragraph 13.3 below);
(d) a copy of the points of dispute, annotated as necessary in order to show which items have been agreed and their value and to show which items remain in dispute and their value;
(e) as many copies of the points of dispute so annotated as there are persons who have served points of dispute;
(f) a copy of any replies served;
(g) copies of all orders made by the court relating to the costs which are to be assessed;
(h) copies of the fee notes and other written evidence as served on the paying party in accordance with paragraph 5.2 above;
(i) where there is a dispute as to the receiving party's liability to pay costs to the legal representatives who acted for the receiving party, any agreement, letter or other written information provided by the legal representative to the client explaining how the legal representative's charges are to be calculated;
(j) a statement signed by the receiving party or the legal representative giving the name, email address, address for service, reference and telephone number and fax number, if any, of –
    (i) the receiving party;
    (ii) the paying party;
    (iii) any other person who has served points of dispute or who has given notice to the receiving party under paragraph 5.5(1)(b) above;

and giving an estimate of the length of time the detailed assessment hearing will take;

(k) where the application for a detailed assessment hearing is made by a party other than the receiving party, such of the documents set out in this paragraph as are in the possession of that party;

(l) where the court is to assess the costs of an assisted person or LSC funded client or person to whom civil legal aid services (within the meaning of Part 1 of the Legal Aid, Sentencing and Punishment of Offenders Act 2012) are provided under arrangement made for the purposes of that Part of that Act –

  (i) the legal aid certificate, LSC certificate, the certificate recording the determination of the Director of Legal Aid Casework and relevant amendment certificates, any authorities and any certificates of discharge or revocation or withdrawal;

  (ii) a certificate, in Precedent F(3) of the Schedule of Costs Precedents;

  (iii) if that person has a financial interest in the detailed assessment hearing and wishes to attend, the postal address of that person to which the court will send notice of any hearing;

  (iv) if the rates payable out of the LSC fund or by the Lord Chancellor under Part 1 of the Legal Aid, Sentencing and Punishment of Offenders Act 2012 are prescribed rates, a schedule to the bill of costs setting out all the items in the bill which are claimed against other parties calculated at the legal aid prescribed rates with or without any claim for enhancement: (further information as to this schedule is set out in paragraph 17 of this Practice Direction);

  (v) a copy of any default costs certificate in respect of costs claimed in the bill of costs;

(m) if a costs management order has been made, a breakdown of the costs claimed for each phase of the proceedings.

13.3 'The document giving the right to detailed assessment' means such one or more of the following documents as are appropriate to the detailed assessment proceedings –

(a) a copy of the judgment or order of the court or tribunal giving the right to detailed assessment;

(b) a copy of the notice sent by the court under Practice Direction 3B paragraph 1, being notification that a claim has been struck out under rule 3.7 or rule 3.7A1 for non-payment of a fee;

(c) a copy of the notice of acceptance where an offer to settle is accepted under Part 36 (Offers to settle);

(d) a copy of the notice of discontinuance in a case which is discontinued under Part 38 (Discontinuance);

(e) a copy of the award made on an arbitration under any Act or pursuant to an agreement, where no court has made an order for the enforcement of the award;

(f) a copy of the order, award or determination of a statutorily constituted tribunal or body.

13.4 On receipt of the request for a detailed assessment hearing the court will fix a date for the hearing, or, if the costs officer so decides, will give directions or fix a date for a preliminary appointment.

13.5 Unless the court otherwise orders, if the only dispute between the parties concerns disbursements, the hearing shall take place in the absence of the parties on the basis of the documents and the court will issue its decision in writing.

13.6 The court will give at least 14 days' notice of the time and place of the detailed assessment hearing to every person named in the statement referred to in paragraph 13.2(j) above.

13.7 If either party wishes to make an application in the detailed assessment proceedings the provisions of Part 23 apply.

13.8

(1) This paragraph deals with the procedure to be adopted where a date has been given by the court for a detailed assessment hearing and –
   (a) the detailed assessment proceedings are settled; or
   (b) a party to the detailed assessment proceedings wishes to apply to vary the date which the court has fixed; or
   (c) the parties to the detailed assessment proceedings agree about changes they wish to make to any direction given for the management of the detailed assessment proceedings.

(2) If detailed assessment proceedings are settled, the receiving party must give notice of that fact to the court immediately, preferably by fax.

(3) A party who wishes to apply to vary a direction must do so in accordance with Part 23.

(4) If the parties agree about changes they wish to make to any direction given for the management of the detailed assessment proceedings –
   (a) they must apply to the court for an order by consent; and
   (b) they must file a draft of the directions sought and an agreed statement of the reasons why the variation is sought; and
   (c) the court may make an order in the agreed terms or in other terms without a hearing, but it may direct that a hearing is to be listed.

13.10

(1) If a party wishes to vary that party's bill of costs, points of dispute or a reply, an amended or supplementary document must be filed with the court and copies of it must be served on all other relevant parties.

(2) Permission is not required to vary a bill of costs, points of dispute or a reply but the court may disallow the variation or permit it only upon conditions, including conditions as to the payment of any costs caused or wasted by the variation.

13.11 Unless the court directs otherwise the receiving party must file with the court the papers in support of the bill not less than 7 days before the date for the detailed assessment hearing and not more than 14 days before that date.

13.12 The papers to be filed in support of the bill and the order in which they are to be arranged are as follows –

(i) instructions and briefs to counsel arranged in chronological order together with all advices, opinions and drafts received and response to such instructions;

(ii) reports and opinions of medical and other experts;
(iii) any other relevant papers;
(iv) a full set of any relevant statements of case
(v) correspondence, file notes and attendance notes;

13.13 The court may direct the receiving party to produce any document which in the opinion of the court is necessary to enable it to reach its decision. These documents will in the first instance be produced to the court, but the court may ask the receiving party to elect whether to disclose the particular document to the paying party in order to rely on the contents of the document, or whether to decline disclosure and instead rely on other evidence.

13.14 Once the detailed assessment hearing has ended it is the responsibility of the receiving party to remove the papers filed in support of the bill.

Provisional Assessment: Rule 47.15

14.1 The amount of costs referred to in rule 47.15(1) is £75,000.

14.2 The following provisions of Part 47 and this Practice Direction will apply to cases falling within rule 47.15 –
(1) rules 47.1, 47.2, 47.4 to 47.13, 47.14 (except paragraphs (6) and (7)), 47.16, 47.17, 47.20 and 47.21; and
(2) paragraphs 1, 2, 4 to 12, 13 (with the exception of paragraphs 13.4 to 13.7, 13.9, 13.11 and 13.14), 15, and 16, of this Practice Direction.

14.3 In cases falling within rule 47.15, when the receiving party files a request for a detailed assessment hearing, that party must file –
(a) the request in Form N258;
(b) the documents set out at paragraphs 8.3 and 13.2 of this Practice Direction;
(c) an additional copy of any paper bill and a statement of the costs, including a statement of the costs claimed in respect of the detailed assessment drawn on the assumption that there will not be an oral hearing following the provisional assessment;
(d) the offers made (those marked 'without prejudice save as to costs' or made under Part 36 must be contained in a sealed envelope, marked 'Part 36 or similar offers', but not indicating which party or parties have made them);
(e) completed Precedent G (points of dispute and any reply).

14.4
(1) On receipt of the request for detailed assessment and the supporting papers, the court will use its best endeavours to undertake a provisional assessment within 6 weeks. No party will be permitted to attend the provisional assessment.
(2) Once the provisional assessment has been carried out the court will return Precedent G (the points of dispute and any reply) with the court's decisions noted upon it. Within 14 days of receipt of Precedent G the parties must agree the total sum due to the receiving party on

the basis of the court's decisions. If the parties are unable to agree the arithmetic, they must refer the dispute back to the court for a decision on the basis of written submissions.

14.5 When considering whether to depart from the order indicated by rule 47.15(10) the court will take into account the conduct of the parties and any offers made.

14.6 If a party wishes to be heard only as to the order made in respect of the costs of the initial provisional assessment, the court will invite each side to make written submissions and the matter will be finally determined without a hearing. The court will decide what if any order for costs to make in respect of this procedure.

Power to Issue An Interim Certificate: Rule 47.16

15 A party wishing to apply for an interim certificate may do so by making an application in accordance with Part 23.

Final Costs Certificate: Rule 47.17

16.1 At the detailed assessment hearing the court will indicate any disallowance or reduction in the sums claimed in the bill of costs by making an appropriate note on the bill.

16.2 The receiving party must, in order to complete the bill after the detailed assessment hearing make clear the correct figures agreed or allowed in respect of each item and must re-calculate the summary of the bill appropriately.

16.3 The completed bill of costs must be filed with the court no later than 14 days after the detailed assessment hearing.

16.4 At the same time as filing the completed bill of costs, the party whose bill it is must also produce receipted fee notes and receipted accounts in respect of all disbursements except those covered by a certificate in Precedent F(5) in the Schedule of Costs Precedents annexed to this Practice Direction.

16.5 No final costs certificate will be issued until all relevant court fees payable on the assessment of costs have been paid.

16.6 If the receiving party fails to file a completed bill in accordance with rule 47.17 the paying party may make an application under Part 23 seeking an appropriate order under rule 3.1.

16.7 A final costs certificate will show –

(a) the amount of any costs which have been agreed between the parties or which have been allowed on detailed assessment;

(b) where applicable the amount agreed or allowed in respect of VAT on such costs.

This provision is subject to any contrary statutory provision relating to costs payable out of the Community Legal Service Fund or by the Lord

Chancellor under Part 1 of the Legal Aid, Sentencing and Punishment of Offenders Act 2012.

16.8 A final costs certificate will include disbursements in respect of the fees of counsel only if receipted fee notes or accounts in respect of those disbursements have been produced to the court and only to the extent indicated by those receipts.

16.9 Where the certificate relates to costs payable between parties a separate certificate will be issued for each party entitled to costs.

16.10 Form N257 is a model form of interim costs certificate and Form N256 is a model form of final costs certificate.

16.11 An application for an order staying enforcement of an interim costs certificate or final costs certificate may be made either –

(a) to a costs judge or District Judge of the court office which issued the certificate; or

(b) to the court (if different) which has general jurisdiction to enforce the certificate.

16.12 An interim or final costs certificate may be enforced as if it were a judgment for the payment of an amount of money. However, proceedings for the enforcement of interim costs certificates or final costs certificates may not be issued in the Costs Office.

Detailed Assessment Procedure Where Costs are Payable Out of The Community Legal Service Fund or by the Lord Chancellor under Part 1 of the Legal Aid, Sentencing and Punishment of Offenders Act 2012: Rule 47.18

17.1 The time for requesting a detailed assessment under rule 47.18 is within 3 months after the date when the right to detailed assessment arose.

17.2

(1) The request for a detailed assessment of costs must be in Form N258A. The request must be accompanied by –

(a) a copy of the bill of costs;

(b) the document giving the right to detailed assessment (see paragraph 13.3 above);

(c) copies of all orders made by the court relating to the costs which are to be assessed;

(d) copies of any fee notes of counsel and any expert in respect of fees claimed in the bill;

(e) written evidence as to any other disbursement which is claimed and which exceeds £500;

(f) the legal aid certificates, LSC certificates, certificates recording the determinations of the Director of Legal Aid Casework, any relevant amendment certificates, any authorities and any certificates of discharge, revocation or withdrawal and;

(g) a statement signed by the legal representative giving the representative's name, address for service, reference, telephone number, e-mail address and, if the assisted person has a financial interest in the detailed assessment and wishes to attend, giving the postal address of that person, to which the court will send notice of any hearing.

(2) The relevant papers in support of the bill as described in paragraph 13.12 must only be lodged if requested by the costs officer.

17.3 Where the court has provisionally assessed a bill of costs it will send to the legal representative a notice, in Form N253 annexed to this practice direction, of the amount of costs which the court proposes to allow together with the bill itself. The legal representative should, if the provisional assessment is to be accepted, then complete the bill.

17.4 If the solicitor whose bill it is, or any other party wishes to make an application in the detailed assessment proceedings, the provisions of Part 23 applies.

17.5 It is the responsibility of the legal representative to complete the bill by entering in the bill the correct figures allowed in respect of each item, recalculating the summary of the bill appropriately and completing the Community Legal Service assessment certificate (Form EX80A).

Costs Payable by the Legal Services Commission or Lord Chancellor at Prescribed Rates

17.6 Where the costs of an assisted person or LSC funded client or person to whom civil legal services (within the meaning of Part 1 of the Legal Aid, Sentencing and Punishment of Offenders Act 2012) are provided under arrangements made for the purposes of that Part of that Act are payable by another person but costs can be claimed against the LSC or Lord Chancellor at prescribed rates (with or without enhancement), the solicitor of the assisted person or LSC funded client or person to whom civil legal services are provided must file a legal aid/ LSC schedule in accordance with paragraph 13.2(l) above. If on paper (a 'paper schedule') the schedule should follow as closely as possible Precedent E of the Schedule of Costs Precedents annexed to this Practice Direction. If an electronic bill of costs is served on the other person an electronic schedule may, subject to paragraphs 17.7 and 17.8 below, be prepared and filed as if it were an electronic bill.

17.7 The schedule must set out by reference to the item numbers in the bill of costs, all the costs claimed as payable by another person, but the arithmetic in the schedule should claim those items at prescribed rates only (with or without any claim for enhancement).

17.8 Where there has been a change in the prescribed rates during the period covered by the bill of costs, a paper schedule (as opposed to the bill) should be divided into separate parts, so as to deal separately with each change of rate. The paper schedule must also be divided so as to correspond with any divisions in the bill of costs. If the schedule is an electronic schedule, unless the format of the schedule already provides the requisite information it should incorporate a summary in a form comparable to the 'Funding and Parts Table' in Precedent S to provide the information that would otherwise be provided by its division into parts.

17.9 If the bill of costs sets costs claimed against the LSC or Lord Chancellor only, the schedule may be set out in a separate document or, alternatively, may be included in the bill, shown separately from the costs claimed against other parties.

17.10 The detailed assessment of the legal aid/ LSC schedule will take place immediately after the detailed assessment of the bill of costs but on occasions, the court may decide to conduct the detailed assessment of the legal aid/ LSC schedule separately from any detailed assessment of the bill of costs. This will occur, for example, where a default costs certificate is obtained as between the parties but that certificate is not set aside at the time of the detailed assessment of the legal aid costs.

17.11 Where costs have been assessed at prescribed rates it is the responsibility of the legal representative to enter the correct figures allowed in respect of each item and to recalculate the summary of the legal aid/ LSC schedule.

Detailed Assessment Procedure Where Costs are Payable Out of a Fund Other than the Community Legal Service fund or by the Lord Chancellor under Part 1 of the Legal Aid, Sentencing and Punishment of Offenders Act 2012: Rule 47.19

18.1 Rule 47.19 enables the court to direct under rule 47.19(3) that the receiving party must serve a copy of the request for assessment and copies of the documents which accompany it, on any person who has a financial interest in the outcome of the assessment.

18.2 A person has a financial interest in the outcome of the assessment if the assessment will or may affect the amount of money or property to which that person is or may become entitled out of the fund. Where an interest in the fund is itself held by a trustee for the benefit of some other person, that trustee will be treated as the person having such a financial interest unless it is not appropriate to do so. 'Trustee' includes a personal representative, receiver or any other person acting in a fiduciary capacity.

18.3 The request for a detailed assessment of costs out of the fund should be in Form N258B, be accompanied by the documents set out at paragraph 17.2(1) (a) to (e) and the following –

(a) a statement signed by the receiving party giving his name, email address, address for service, reference and telephone number,

(b) a statement of the postal address of any person who has a financial interest in the outcome of the assessment; and

(c) if a person having a financial interest is a child or protected party, a statement to that effect.

18.4 The court will decide, having regard to the amount of the bill, the size of the fund and the number of persons who have a financial interest, which of those persons should be served and may give directions about service and about the hearing. The court may dispense with service on all or some of those persons.

18.5 Where the court makes an order dispensing with service on all such persons it may proceed at once to make a provisional assessment, or, if it decides that a hearing is necessary, give appropriate directions. Before deciding whether a hearing is necessary, the court may require the receiving party to provide further information relating to the bill.

18.6

(1) The court will send the provisionally assessed bill to the receiving party with a notice in Form N253. If the receiving party is legally represented the legal representative should, if the provisional assessment is to be accepted, then complete the bill.

(2) The court will fix a date for a detailed assessment hearing, if the receiving party informs the court within 14 days after receiving the notice in Form N253, that the receiving party wants the court to hold such a hearing.

18.7 The court will give at least 14 days' notice of the time and place of the hearing to the receiving party and to any person who has a financial interest and who has been served with a copy of the request for assessment.

18.8 If any party or any person who has a financial interest wishes to make an application in the detailed assessment proceedings, the provisions of Part 23 (General Rules about Applications for Court Orders) apply.

18.9 If the receiving party is legally represented the legal representative must complete the bill by inserting the correct figures in respect of each item and must recalculate the summary of the bill.

Costs of Detailed Assessment Proceedings – Rule 47.20: Offers to Settle Under Part 36 or Otherwise

19 Where an offer to settle is made, whether under Part 36 or otherwise, it should specify whether or not it is intended to be inclusive of the cost of preparation of the bill, interest and VAT. Unless the offer states otherwise it will be treated as being inclusive of these.

Appeals from Authorised Court Officers in Detailed Assessment Proceedings: Rules 47.22 To 47.25

20.1 This Section relates only to appeals from authorised court officers in detailed assessment proceedings. All other appeals arising out of detailed assessment proceedings (and arising out of summary assessments) are dealt with in accordance with Part 52 and Practice Directions 52A to 52E. The destination of appeals is dealt with in accordance with the Access to Justice Act 1999 (Destination of Appeals) Order 2016.

20.2 In respect of appeals from authorised court officers, there is no requirement to obtain permission, or to seek written reasons.

20.3 The appellant must file a notice which should be in Form N161 (an appellant's notice).

20.4 The appeal will be heard by a costs judge or a District Judge of the High Court, and is a re-hearing.

20.5 The appellant's notice should, if possible, be accompanied by a suitable record of the judgment appealed against. Where reasons given for the decision have been officially recorded by the court an approved transcript of that record should accompany the notice. Where there is no official record the following documents will be acceptable –

(a) the officer's comments written on the bill;

(b) advocates' notes of the reasons agreed by the respondent if possible and approved by the authorised court officer.

When the appellant was unrepresented before the authorised court officer, it is the duty of any advocate for the respondent to make a note of the reasons promptly available, free of charge to the appellant where there is no official record or if the court so directs. Where the appellant was represented before the authorised court officer, it is the duty of the appellant's own former advocate to make a note available. The appellant should submit the note of the reasons to the costs judge or District Judge hearing the appeal.

20.6 Where the appellant is not able to obtain a suitable record of the authorised court officer's decision within the time in which the appellant's notice must be filed, the appellant's notice must still be completed to the best of the appellant's ability. It may however be amended subsequently with the permission of the costs judge or District Judge hearing the appeal.

Forms

Estimate of Costs (Financial Remedy): Form H

Click here to reset form

Estimate of costs (financial remedy)

of

(name of party)

the ☐ Applicant
☐ Respondent

To be completed by the relevant party	
Name of court	Case No.
Name of Applicant	
Name of Respondent	

Estimate of costs relating to a financial remedy application for hearing on: ☐☐/☐☐/☐☐☐☐

Please Note: it is a requirement of the rules to provide full costs information to the court

(Do not include here costs incurred in respect of other aspects of the case, for example, the divorce or civil partnership proceedings, children matters, injunctions, etc.)

Summary of costs estimate

	Prescribed rates for publicly funded services £	Indemnity rate £
Grand Total (Box 7 + Box 14)	0.00	0.00
State what has been paid towards the grand total above.		
Amount of any contributions paid by the funded client towards their publicly funded services.		

Signature of solicitor (or party, if not represented)

Dated ☐☐/☐☐/☐☐☐☐

Name of firm of solicitors

Reference

continued over the page

Form H Estimate of costs (financial remedy) (04.11)

1

Section A:

Costs incurred in the financial remedy proceedings **prior** to issue of Form A

Part 1

	Prescribed rates for publicly funded services £	Indemnity rate £
1. Financial remedy solicitors' costs (including VAT) incurred by any previous solicitors.		
2. Financial remedy solicitors' costs (including VAT) incurred by the current solicitors.		
3. Disbursements (including VAT, if appropriate) incurred by any previous solicitors.		
4. Disbursements (including VAT, if appropriate) incurred by current solicitors.		
5. All counsel's fees (including VAT).		
Sub-Total	0.00	0.00

Part 2

6. Add any private client costs previously incurred (in publicly funded cases only).		
7. **Total of Section A**	**0.00**	**0.00**

Section B:

Costs incurred in the financial remedy proceedings **after** issue of Form A

Part 3

	Prescribed rates for publicly funded services £	Indemnity rate £
8. Financial remedy solicitors' costs (including VAT) incurred by any previous solicitors.		
9. Financial remedy solicitors' costs (including VAT and costs of the current hearing) incurred by the current solicitors.		
10. Disbursements (including VAT, if appropriate) incurred by any previous solicitors.		
11. Disbursements (including VAT, if appropriate) incurred by current solicitors.		
12. All counsel's fees (including VAT).		
Sub-Total	0.00	0.00

Part 4

13. Add any private client costs previously incurred (in publicly funded cases only).		
14. **Total of Section B**	**0.00**	**0.00**

2

Statement of Costs (Financial Remedy): Form H1

Click here to reset form

Statement of costs (financial remedy)

of

(name of party)

the ☐ Applicant

☐ Respondent

To be completed by the relevant party	
Name of court	Case No.
Name of Applicant	
Name of Respondent	

Statement of costs relating to the financial remedy application for hearing on: __/__/____

Please Note: it is a requirement of the rules to provide full costs information to the court

(Do not include here costs incurred in respect of other aspects of the case, for example, the divorce or civil partnership proceedings, children matters, injunctions, etc.)

Description of fee earner:

(a) Name: Status: Hourly rate claimed: £

(b) Name: Status: Hourly rate claimed: £

(c) Name: Status: Hourly rate claimed: £

(d) Name: Status: Hourly rate claimed: £

Summary of costs statement

	Prescribed rates for publicly funded services £	Indemnity rate £
Total Section A (Box 7)	0.00	0.00
Total Section B (Box 14)	0.00	0.00
Total Section C (Box 21)	0.00	0.00
Total Section D (Box 25)	0.00	0.00
Total Section E (Box 26) (if completed)		
Grand Total (A+B+C+D+E)	0.00	0.00
State what has been paid towards the grand total above.		
Amount of any contributions paid by the funded client towards their publicly funded services.		

Signature of solicitor (or party, if not represented)

Dated __/__/____

Name of firm of solicitors

Reference

Form H1 Statement of costs (financial remedy) (04.11)

1

Section A:

Costs incurred in the financial remedy proceedings **prior** to issue of Form A.

Part 1

	Prescribed rates for publicly funded services £	Indemnity rate £
1. Financial remedy solicitors' costs (including VAT) incurred by any previous solicitors.		
2. Financial remedy solicitors' costs (including VAT) incurred by the current solicitors.		
3. Disbursements (including VAT, if appropriate) incurred by any previous solicitors.		
4. Disbursements (including VAT, if appropriate) incurred by current solicitors.		
5. All counsel's fees (including VAT).		
Sub-Total	0.00	0.00

Part 2

6. Add any private client costs previously incurred (in publicly funded cases only).		
7. **Total of Section A**	**0.00**	**0.00**

Section B:

Costs incurred in the financial remedy proceedings **after** issue of Form A up to and including FDR appointment (or, if none, the date of the last Form H).

Part 3

	Prescribed rates for publicly funded services £	Indemnity rate £
8. Financial remedy solicitors' costs (including VAT) incurred by any previous solicitors.		
9. Financial remedy solicitors' costs (including VAT and costs of the current hearing) incurred by the current solicitors.		
10. Disbursements (including VAT, if appropriate) incurred by any previous solicitors.		
11. Disbursements (including VAT, if appropriate) incurred by current solicitors.		
12. All counsel's fees (including VAT).		
Sub-Total	0.00	0.00

Part 4

13. Add any private client costs previously incurred (in publicly funded cases only).		
14. **Total of Section B**	**0.00**	**0.00**

2

Section C:

Costs incurred in the financial remedy proceedings **after** FDR appointment (or, if none, the date of the last Form H) up to the date of this form.

Part 5

	Prescribed rates for publicly funded services £	Indemnity rate £
15. Financial remedy solicitors' costs (including VAT) incurred by any previous solicitors.		
16. Financial remedy solicitors' costs (including VAT) incurred by the current solicitors.		
17. Disbursements (including VAT, if appropriate) incurred by any previous solicitors.		
18. Disbursements (including VAT, if appropriate) incurred by current solicitors.		
19. All counsel's fees (including VAT). (Counsel's fees for final hearing should not be included here, but given in Section D.)		
Sub-Total	0.00	0.00

Part 6

20. Add any private client costs previously incurred (in publicly funded cases only).		
21. **Total of Section C**	**0.00**	**0.00**

Section D:

Estimate of costs expected and incurred in the financial remedy proceedings **after** the date of this form up to the end of the final hearing.

Part 7

	Prescribed rates for publicly funded services £	Indemnity rate £
22. Financial remedy solicitors' costs (including VAT).		
23. Disbursements (including VAT, if appropriate).		
24. All Counsel's fees (including VAT). (All counsel's fees expected to be incurred for final hearing should be included here.)		
25. **Total of Section D**	**0.00**	**0.00**

continued over the page ➪

3

Section E:

Estimate of costs to be incurred in implementing proposed order for the financial remedy.

(Note: Include only those costs which it is known or anticipated will be incurred in giving effect to the order.
If the work to be carried out is only conveyancing, the prescribed rates for public funding services do not apply.)

Part 8	Prescribed rates for publicly funded services £	Indemnity rate £
26. **Total of Section E** **(Total estimated costs of implementing proposed order)**		

4

Statement of Costs (Summary Assessment): Form N260

Print form | Reset form

N260

Statement of Costs (summary assessment)

(CPR PD44 9.5)

In the	
Court	
Case Reference	

Judge/Master

Case Title

[Party]'s

Statement of Costs for the hearing on Date **(interim application/fast track trial)**

Description of fee earners*

(a) *(name) (grade) (hourly rate claimed)*	
(b) *(name) (grade) (hourly rate claimed)*	
(c) *(name) (grade) (hourly rate claimed)*	
(d) *(name) (grade) (hourly rate claimed)*	

Attendances on (party)

Personal attendances				
(a) *(number)*		hours at £		£ 0.00
(b) *(number)*		hours at £		£ 0.00
(c) *(number)*		hours at £		£ 0.00
(d) *(number)*		hours at £		£ 0.00
Letters out/emails				
(a) *(number)*		hours at £		£ 0.00
(b) *(number)*		hours at £		£ 0.00
(c) *(number)*		hours at £		£ 0.00
(d) *(number)*		hours at £		£ 0.00
Telephone				
(a) *(number)*		hours at £		£ 0.00
(b) *(number)*		hours at £		£ 0.00
(c) *(number)*		hours at £		£ 0.00
(d) *(number)*		hours at £		£ 0.00

N260 Statement of Costs (summary assessment) (06.15)

Attendances on opponents (including negotiations):

Personal attendances

(a) *(number)*		hours at £		£ 0.00
(b) *(number)*		hours at £		£ 0.00
(c) *(number)*		hours at £		£ 0.00
(d) *(number)*		hours at £		£ 0.00

Letters out/emails

(a) *(number)*		hours at £		£ 0.00
(b) *(number)*		hours at £		£ 0.00
(c) *(number)*		hours at £		£ 0.00
(d) *(number)*		hours at £		£ 0.00

Telephone

(a) *(number)*		hours at £		£ 0.00
(b) *(number)*		hours at £		£ 0.00
(c) *(number)*		hours at £		£ 0.00
(d) *(number)*		hours at £		£ 0.00

Attendance on others:

Personal attendances

(a) *(number)*		hours at £		£ 0.00
(b) *(number)*		hours at £		£ 0.00
(c) *(number)*		hours at £		£ 0.00
(d) *(number)*		hours at £		£ 0.00

Letters out/emails

(a) *(number)*		hours at £		£ 0.00
(b) *(number)*		hours at £		£ 0.00
(c) *(number)*		hours at £		£ 0.00
(d) *(number)*		hours at £		£ 0.00

Telephone

(a) *(number)*		hours at £		£ 0.00
(b) *(number)*		hours at £		£ 0.00
(c) *(number)*		hours at £		£ 0.00
(d) *(number)*		hours at £		£ 0.00

Site inspections etc.

(a) *(number)*		hours at £		£	0.00
(b) *(number)*		hours at £		£	0.00
(c) *(number)*		hours at £		£	0.00
(d) *(number)*		hours at £		£	0.00

Work done on documents, as set out in schedule: 0.00

Attendance at hearing:

(a) *(number)*		hours at £		£	0.00
(b) *(number)*		hours at £		£	0.00
(c) *(number)*		hours at £		£	0.00
(d) *(number)*		hours at £		£	0.00
(e) Fixed costs				£	

(a) *(number)*		hours travel and waiting time £		£	0.00
(b) *(number)*		hours travel and waiting time £		£	0.00
(c) *(number)*		hours travel and waiting time £		£	0.00
(d) *(number)*		hours travel and waiting time £		£	0.00

Sub Total £ 0.00

(A) Solicitors and Chartered Legal Executives with over eight years post qualification experience including at least eight years litigation experience.

(B) Solicitors and Chartered Legal Executives with over four years post qualification experience including at least four years litigation experience.

(C) Other solicitors and Chartered Legal Executives and fee earners of equivalent experience.

(D) Trainee solicitors, paralegals and other fee earners.

"Chartered Legal Executive" means a Fellow of the Chartered Institute of Legal Executives (CILEx). Those who are not Fellows of CILEx are not entitled to call themselves Chartered Legal Executives and in principle are therefore not entitled to the same hourly rate as a Chartered Legal Executive.

Brought forward £ 0.00

Counsel's fees *(name) (year of call)*

Fee for [advice/conference/documents] £

Fee for hearing £

Other expenses

Court fees £

Others *(give brief description)* £

Total £ 0.00

Amount of VAT claimed

on solicitors and counsel's fees £

on other expenses £

Grand Total £ 0.00

The costs stated above do not exceed the costs which the (party) is liable to pay in respect of the work which this statement covers. Counsel's fees and other expenses have been incurred in the amounts stated above and will be paid to the persons stated.

(party)

Signed

Dated

Name of Partner signing

Name of firm of solicitors

Schedule of work done on documents

Item	Description of work *(one line only)*	(A) hours	(B) hours	(C) hours	(D) hours	Total £
1						
2						
3						
4						
5						
6						
7						
8						
9						
10						
11						
12						
13						
14						
15						
16						
17						
18						
19						
20						
21						
22						
23						
24						
25						
26						
27						
28						
29						
30						
Total						0.00

Print form Reset form

APPENDIX 2

Guideline Solicitors' Fees

SOLICITORS' FEES

The current Guideline Hourly Rates for solicitors' fees are:[1]

Band:	**Fee earner grade A**	**Fee earner grade B**	**Fee earner grade C**	**Fee earner grade D**
London 1	£409	£296	£226	£138
London 2	£317	£242	£196	£126
London 3	£229 – £267	£172 – £229	£165	£121
National 1	£217	£192	£161	£118
National 2 and 3	£201	£177	£146	£111

The rates for London 3, Bands A and B are shown as ranges following the format of Solicitors' guideline hourly rates. These ranges go some way towards reflecting the wide range of work types transacted in these areas.

Fee earner grade:	**Experience:**
A[2]	Solicitors and legal executives[3] with over 8 years' experience.
B	Solicitors and legal executives with over 4 years' experience.
C	Other solicitors or legal executives and fee earners of equivalent experience.
D	Trainee solicitors, paralegals and other fee earners.

1 https://www.gov.uk/guidance/solicitors-guideline-hourly-rates.

2 An hourly rate in excess of the guideline figures may be appropriate for Grade A fee earners in substantial and complex litigation where other factors, including the value of the litigation, the level of complexity, the urgency or importance of the matter as well as any international element would justify a significantly higher rate to reflect higher average costs: https://assets.publishing.service.gov.uk/government/uploads/system/uploads/attachment_data/file/422614/senior-court-costs-summary-assessment-guide.pdf at [43].

3 'Legal executive' was defined as a Fellow of the Institute of Legal Executives: http://webarchive.nationalarchives.gov.uk/20110218200720/http:/www.hmcourts-service.gov.uk/publications/guidance/scco/previous_rates.htm. Now such practitioners are known as Chartered Legal Executives.

London Bands:	
A	City of London: EC1, EC2, EC3, EC4
B	Central London: W1, WC1, WC2, SW1
C	Outer London: All other London post codes

National 1 Band
Aldershot, Farnham, Bournemouth (including Poole)
Birmingham Inner
Bristol
Cambridge City, Harlow
Canterbury, Maidstone, Medway & Tunbridge Wells
Cardiff (Inner)
Chelmsford South, Essex & East Suffolk
Chester
Fareham, Winchester
Hampshire, Dorset, Wiltshire, Isle of Wight
Kingston, Guildford, Reigate, Epsom
Leeds Inner (within a 2 km radius of the City Art Gallery)
Lewes
Liverpool, Birkenhead
Manchester Central
Newcastle – City Centre (within a 2 mile radius of St Nicholas Cathedral)
Norwich City
Nottingham City
Oxford, Thames Valley
Southampton, Portsmouth
Swindon, Basingstoke
Watford

National 2 Band
Bath, Cheltenham and Gloucester, Taunton, Yeovil
Bury
Chelmsford North, Cambridge County, Peterborough, Bury St Edmunds, Norfolk, Lowestoft
Cheshire & North Wales
Coventry, Rugby, Nuneaton, Stratford and Warwick
Exeter, Plymouth
Hull (City)

Leeds Outer, Wakefield & Pontefract
Leigh
Lincoln
Luton, Bedford, St Albans, Hitchin, Hertford
Manchester Outer, Oldham, Bolton, Tameside
Newcastle (other than City Centre)
Nottingham & Derbyshire
Sheffield, Doncaster and South Yorkshire
Southport
St Helens
Stockport, Altrincham, Salford
Swansea, Newport, Cardiff (Outer)
Wigan
Wolverhampton, Walsall, Dudley, Stourbridge
York, Harrogate

National 3 Band
Birmingham Outer
Bradford, Dewsbury, Halifax, Huddersfield, Keighley, Skipton
Cumbria
Devon, Cornwall
Grimsby, Skegness
Hull Outer
Kidderminster
Northampton, Leicester
Preston, Lancaster, Blackpool, Chorley, Accrington, Burnley, Blackburn, Rawtenstall, Nelson
Scarborough, Ripon
Stafford, Stoke, Tamworth
Teesside
Worcester, Hereford, Evesham, Redditch
Shrewsbury, Telford, Ludlow, Oswestry
South & West Wales

APPENDIX 3

Court Fees for Family Proceedings

The table below sets out the court fees payable in relation to family proceedings in the Family Court or High Court:[1]

Issue fees	
Application where no other fee is specified	£245
Application for divorce or nullity of marriage or civil partnership	£550
Application for matrimonial or civil partnership order	£365
Declaration as to marital status, parentage, legitimacy or adoptions effected overseas	£365
Forced marriage protection order	£0
Application for a non-molestation order	£0
Application for an occupation order	£0
Amendment of application for matrimonial or civil partnership order	£95
Answer to application for matrimonial or civil partnership order	£245
Application for an order for assessment of costs	£50
Application for parental order	£215
Proceedings under the Children Act 1989	
Parental responsibility (s 4(1)(c) or (3), 4A(1)(b) or (3))	£215
Parental responsibility (s 4ZA(1)(c) or (6))	£215
Guardians (s 5(1) or 6(7))	£215
Section 8 orders (s 10(1) or (2))	£215
Enforcement orders (s 11J(2))	£215
Compensation for financial loss (s 11O(2))	£215
Change of child's surname, or removal from jurisdiction while residence order in force (s 13(1))	£215
Special guardianship orders (s 14A(3) or (6)(a), 14C(3) or 14D(1))	£215

1 Taken from Form EX50 – Civil and Family Court Fees – High Court and County Court (04.15) and Form EX50A HMCTS: 22 July 2019. Fees related to determination of costs and enforcement are set out at **Chapters 8** and **9** respectively.

Secure accommodation order (s 25 or (Social Services and Well-being (Wales) Act 2014, s 119)	£215
Change of child's surname, or removal from jurisdiction while care order in force (s 33(7))	£215
Contact with child in care (s 34(2), (3), (4) or (9))	£215
Education supervision order (s 36(1))	£215
Variation or discharge etc of care and supervision orders (s 39)	£215
Child assessment order (s 43(1))	£215
Emergency protection orders (ss 44, 45 and 46)	£215
Warrant to assist person exercising powers under emergency protection order (s 48)	£215
Recovery order (s 50)	£215
Cancellation, variation or removal or imposition of condition of registration of child minder or day carer (s 79K)	£215
Warrant to assist person exercising powers to search for children or inspect premises (s 102)	£215
Applications in respect of enforcement orders (para 4(2), 6(2), 7(2) or 9(2) of Sch A1)	£95
Amendment of enforcement order by reason of change of address (para 5(2) of Sch A1)	£95
Financial provision for children (para 1(1) or (4), 2(1) or (5), 5(6), 6(5), (7) or (8), 8(2), 10(2), 11 or 14(1) of Sch 1)	£215
Approval of court for child in care of local authority to live abroad (para 19(1) of Sch 2 or Social Services and Well-being (Wales) Act 2014, s 124(1))	£215
Extension of supervision order (para 6 of Sch 3)	£215
Extension or discharge of education supervision order (para 15(2) or 17(1) of Sch 3)	£215
Paragraph 8(1) of Sch 8 (appeals concerning foster parents)	£215
Application for proceedings under s 31 of the Children Act 1989	£2,055
Hearing for proceedings under s 31 of the Children Act 1989	£0
Adoption and wardship	
Application/permission to apply for adoption	£170
Application for a placement order (under s 22)	£455
Application to the High Court	£170

Proceedings under the Children and Adoption Act 2006	
Application for warning notice to be attached to a contact order	£50
Children Act applications charged within proceedings	
Application (without notice or by consent) unless otherwise listed	£50
Application (under FPR r 7.19) for the court to consider making a decree nisi, conditional order or separation order	£50
Application (on notice) (unless otherwise listed)	£155
Application for a financial order	£255
Appeal	
Filing an appeal notice from a district judge, one or more lay justices, a justices' clerk or an assistant to a justices' clerk	£125
Appeal of any provision of the Children Act 1989, except in relation to appeals for breach of or revocation of an enforcement order	£215
Appeal (Child Support Act 1991, s 20)	£165
Searches – Index of decree absolute or final orders	
Search of the central index of decrees absolute or final orders for any specified period of ten calendar years, or the ten most recent years	£65
Search of the central index of parental responsibility agreements	£45
Search of any specific family court or District Registry index of decrees absolute or final orders for any specified period of ten calendar years, or the ten most recent years	£45
Copy documents	
Copy of a document (10 pages or less)	£10
For each subsequent page	£0.50
Copy of a document in electronic form (for each copy)	£10
Registration of maintenance orders	
Application for a maintenance order to be registered 1950 Act or the Maintenance Orders Act 1958	£50
Financial provision	
Application for an order for financial provision	£215
Service	
Request for service by a bailiff of document subject to exceptions listed in the order	£110

Sale	
Removing goods to a place of deposit	* The reasonable expenses incurred.
Appraisement of goods	* 5p in every £1 (or part of £1) of the appraised value.
Sale of goods (including advertisements, catalogues, sale/commission/delivery of goods)	15p in every £1 (or part of £1) of the amount realised by the sale, or such other sum as the district judge may consider to be justified.
No sale – execution withdrawn, satisfied or stopped	10p in every £1 (or part of £1) or the value of the goods seized, the value to be the appraised value where the goods have been appraised or such other sum as the district judge may consider to be justified. Plus, the two fees in this section marked *
Affidavits	
Taking an affidavit/affirmation/attestation upon honour	£11
For each exhibit referred to and required to be marked	£2

APPENDIX 4

Legal Services Order Precedent

In the Family Court No: [***Case number***]

sitting at [***Court name***]

[The Matrimonial Causes Act 1973] /

[The Civil Partnership Act 2004]

(DELETE AS APPROPRIATE)

The [Marriage] / [Civil Partnership] of [*applicant name*] and [*respondent name*]

After hearing [*name the advocates(s) who appeared*]

After consideration of the documents lodged by the parties

(IN THE CASE OF AN ORDER MADE WITHOUT NOTICE) After reading the statements and hearing the witnesses specified in para [*para number*] of the recitals below

ORDER MADE BY [*NAME OF JUDGE*] ON [*DATE*] SITTING IN [OPEN COURT] / [PRIVATE]

The Parties

1. The applicant is [*applicant name*]

   The respondent is [*respondent name*]

   [The second respondent is [*name*]]

   (SPECIFY IF ANY PARTY ACTS BY A LITIGATION FRIEND)

Recitals

2. **(IN THE CASE OF AN ORDER MADE WITHOUT NOTICE)**
   a. This order was made at a hearing without notice to the respondent. The reason why the order was made without notice to the respondent was [*set out*].
   b. The Judge read the following [affidavits] / [witness statements] / [*set out*] and heard oral testimony from [*name*].

3. **(IN THE CASE OF AN ORDER MADE FOLLOWING THE GIVING OF SHORT INFORMAL NOTICE)**

   This order was made at a hearing without full notice having been given to the respondent. The reason why the order was made without full notice having been given to the respondent was [*set out*].

4. This is a legal services order for an amount of money ("the amount") made pursuant to [s22ZA of the Matrimonial Causes Act 1973] / [para 38A of Schedule 5 to the Civil Partnership Act 2004]. The order was made to enable the applicant to obtain legal services for the purposes of these proceedings. The court was satisfied that without the amount, the applicant would not reasonably be able to obtain appropriate legal services for the purposes of the proceedings.

Agreements

5. **(INSERT ANY AGREEMENTS REACHED BETWEEN THE PARTIES)**

Undertaking to the court

6. The applicant will repay to the respondent such part of the amount if, and to the extent that, the court is of the opinion, when considering costs at the conclusion of the proceedings, that [he] / [she] ought to do so. **(SUCH AN UNDERTAKING OUGHT NORMALLY TO BE REQUIRED)**

IT IS ORDERED (BY CONSENT) THAT:

7. The respondent shall pay as a legal services order the amount of £[*amount*] to [*applicant's legal firm name*], the legal representatives of the applicant, by transfer to their bank at [*bank details*] by payments as set out in the following paragraph.

8. The amount shall be paid as to £[*amount*] by [*date* **(E.G. SEVEN DAYS FROM THE MAKING OF THIS ORDER)**], and the balance by instalments at the rate of £[*amount*] per month commencing on [*date*].

9. **(WHERE APPROPRIATE)** The amount shall be secured as follows. [**(FOR EXAMPLE)** Any unpaid part of the amount shall be a charge on [*property name*] within the terms of the Charging Orders Act 1979; and a final charging order is made accordingly.]

10. **(WHERE APPROPRIATE)** For the purposes of realising the amount the property known as [*family home name*] / [*other property name*] shall be sold and the following directions shall apply in respect of the sale [*set out*].

11 [*Costs*]

Dated [*date*]

(WHERE UNDERTAKINGS HAVE BEEN GIVEN)

Notice pursuant to PD 37A para 2.1

You [*applicant name*] may be sent to prison for contempt of court if you break the promises that have been given to the court

Statements pursuant to PD 37A para 2.2(2)

I understand the undertakings that I have given, and that if I break any of my promises to the court I may be sent to prison for contempt of court

[*applicant name*]

Index

[All references are to paragraph numbers]

D

T

U

V

W

www.ingramcontent.com/pod-product-compliance
Ingram Content Group UK Ltd.
Pitfield, Milton Keynes, MK11 3LW, UK
UKHW051416150926
475561UK00005B/198